AF772307

# Constructing Self-Discovery Learning Spaces Online:

## Scaffolding and Decision Making Technologies

Shalin Hai-Jew
*Kansas State University, USA*

Information Science
REFERENCE

| | |
|---|---|
| Managing Director: | Lindsay Johnston |
| Senior Editorial Director: | Heather Probst |
| Book Production Manager: | Sean Woznicki |
| Development Manager: | Joel Gamon |
| Development Editor: | Michael Killian |
| Acquisitions Editor: | Erika Gallagher |
| Typesetters: | Christopher Shearer |
| Print Coordinator: | Jamie Snavely |
| Cover Design: | Nick Newcomer, Greg Snader |

Published in the United States of America by
Information Science Reference (an imprint of IGI Global)
701 E. Chocolate Avenue
Hershey PA 17033
Tel: 717-533-8845
Fax: 717-533-8661
E-mail: cust@igi-global.com
Web site: http://www.igi-global.com

Copyright © 2012 by IGI Global. All rights reserved. No part of this publication may be reproduced, stored or distributed in any form or by any means, electronic or mechanical, including photocopying, without written permission from the publisher. Product or company names used in this set are for identification purposes only. Inclusion of the names of the products or companies does not indicate a claim of ownership by IGI Global of the trademark or registered trademark.

Library of Congress Cataloging-in-Publication Data

Constructing self-discovery learning spaces online : scaffolding and decision making technologies / Shalin Hai-Jew, editor.
p. cm.
Includes bibliographical references and index.
ISBN 978-1-61350-320-1 (hardcover) -- ISBN 978-1-61350-321-8 (ebook) -- ISBN 978-1-61350-322-5 (print & perpetual access) 1. Self-culture--Computer network resources. 2. Computer-assisted instruction. I. Hai-Jew, Shalin.
LC33.C66 2012
371.39'4--dc23

2011041827

British Cataloguing in Publication Data
A Cataloguing in Publication record for this book is available from the British Library.

All work contributed to this book is new, previously-unpublished material. The views expressed in this book are those of the authors, but not necessarily of the publisher.

# Editorial Advisory Board

Brent A. Anders, *Kansas State University, USA*
Barney Dalgarno, *Charles Sturt University, Australia*
Ramesh C. Sharma, *University of Guyana, Guyana*

# Table of Contents

# Detailed Table of Contents

# Preface

## INTRODUCTION

From its very inception as a public venue, the World Wide Web (WWW) has been a space for intercommunications and the sharing of information. Its connectivity has made the world a virtual Wide Area Network. As this resource has evolved, it has figured more centrally into numerous human endeavors. Foremost is the transfer of learning and knowledge, particularly through spaces that archive, present, and share information.

On a superficial level, the various spaces of the Web have been designed for user awareness and attention, navigation, and usability through savvy user interface designs, information structuring, metadata labeling, personalized recommender systems, and a range of other design features. Search tools have been enhanced for more effective finding along with serendipitous offers. These spaces that are used for self-discovery learning include interactive websites; digital kiosks; open courseware; automated short courses; tutorials; databases; repositories and referatories; digital libraries; knowledge management systems (with informational taxonomies and ontologies); electronic publications; immersive virtual worlds and simulation spaces; collaborative knowledge-building spaces, shared and collegial work spaces; social networking spaces; and intranets and databases on the so-called invisible Web (those less easy to find via existing browsers). Online, there are many closed online discovery spaces. The so-called Deep (or Invisible) Web, which is estimated to be over 500 times the size of the publicly available Web, contains selectively discoverable contents. This level of user interface design has enabled much more intuitive use and has trained generations of users on how to use various sites and to communicate and collaborate effectively through them.

## EMERGENT SELF-LEARNERS

Simultaneous with the popularization of these spaces, individuals have been acquiring skill sets to exploit these spaces for self-learning. Self-discovery learners are those who have high self-motivation and initiative to learn about particular domains of information and to acquire particular skill sets. They are self-driven, and they often self-learn. The concept of designing for self-discovery learners is necessarily learner-centered. This suggests the criticality of understanding who self-discovery learners are and when and how self-discovery learning happens.

Self-discovery learning has existed from infancy, with humans engaging the environment to learn about it. J. Holt long argued for supporting the natural initiative in children to pursue learning and discovery.

Children develop a theory-of-mind which allows them to ascribe intentional states (beliefs, desires, and intentions). They also develop meta-cognition, or the awareness of their own thinking and learning. In the same way, adults will engage in self-discovery learning. There are super self-discovery learners who are able to acquire new learning across a variety of fields with minimal external support. The ability to self-discover is critical for human endeavors given how much knowledge lies unknown and outside the limited reach of formal learning, beyond and in the wild. Self-discovery learning also implies the reality of equifinality—the reality of multiple paths to achieving a particular aim in learning; in other words, there are many possible paths to acquiring a particular skill or knowledge set.

The tasks of self-discovery learners may be informal or formal. They may be ad hoc endeavors or lifelong learning pursuits. The learning may be simple or complex, obvious / defined or non-obvious. They may delve into questions which are closed-ended or those which are ill-structured and open-ended, many without pre-defined or clear answers. They may involve practical problem-solving learning or something as high-minded as self-actualization and personal growth. This learning may involve learning what is already in the world or even surfacing innovative discoveries that were previously unknown or un-observed.

The rationale for guided discovery-learning lies in cognitive load research, which observes that people have limited cognitive load capabilities. When novice learners enter a new learning domain, they use an excessive amount of their cognitive load to orientate themselves and to acquire learning; much of that learning—without guidance—will lead to errant inferential conclusions. The guidance, then, may lighten some of the cognitive load for learners—in order to allow them to apply more of their cognitive resources towards the germane load, which is directly applied to the learning. The guidance, too, may head-off potential negative learning, misconceptions, or incorrect mental models.

Such learners need varying levels of support to form an attraction to a topic; set learning goals (skills acquisition, self-improvement, hobby development, research, or innovations); create a learning strategy; follow-through on their learning; select learning methods and experiences; identify role models and experts; communicate with other co-learners; request appropriate help; assess their own progress, and continue evolving their own goals. Their skills in autodidaxy will vary based on the learner, their environmental affordances for such learning, and motivations (both intrinsic and extrinsic). Their autotelic experiences of flow (per M. Csikszentmihalyi) while engaged in self-learning tasks may motivate many, while others may need external rewards and acknowledgments (to help define the meaningfulness of their work).

In this "use case," individuals or groups (tightly or loosely coupled) co-learn, collaborate, co-create, and build new knowledge and specific identities and ties. Even a cursory look at this challenge reveals the complexities of these challenges. Humans, the very human learning endeavors, and the world are all complex.

## DESIGN FOR GUIDED DISCOVERY

This text proposes a broad design approach to help the Web and Internet further fulfill its potential for human use. This text explores a deeper level of user-focused design—this time for effective self-discovery learning—which is learner-initiated and learner-driven. At one end of the "directed discovery" continuum may be simple and current affordances of the Web—with the fixed clustering of topical information in repositories, the dynamic searches of related topics (albeit with some serendipity for chance learning and branching out), the proper sequencing (and cognitive scaffolding) of learning, and the structuring of knowledge spaces using taxonomies and ontologies. User interface design would continue to enhance site usability, so the site itself will not demand much in the way of cognitive resources. New digital ways of conceptualizing (visualizing) information and new tools for discovery of new information will enhance the potential depth of learning—both in the respective mental modeling and in actual surfacing of new data and patterns. There are online and virtual venues for the sharing of new knowledge. There are supportive designed spaces for human learning communities. At the other extreme end of a theoretical continuum would be even more directive discovery for more complex long-term learning. There could be elite expert-led learning communities with privy access to information and high-functioning analytic tools. There could be highly fixed and intensive learning sequences and opportunities for hands-on practice.

Not only would the building of self-discovery learning spaces and tools online benefit the general act of self-discovery learning, and trained self-discovery learners, but it could potentially build up the self-regulation skills in general learners—for more efficient and effective learning. This approach may enhance the overall learning usability of the WWW and the Internet by making its contents more widely accessible and learnable.

Based on the research literature, self-discovery adult learners begin with a general sense of curiosity, enthusiasm, inquiry, or ambition; the learning itself is understood to be practical, with some application to the individual life, others, and potentially even the larger world. They pursue information and learning purposively, based on intrinsic and extrinsic goals. Such learners may be pursuing authentic (applied) learning goals in some cases and artificial (theoretical or arbitrary) ones in others. Self-discovery learners self-regulate. They are self-reliant and independent, and they maintain their own executive functions. Some would come as amateurs and novices; others may be subject matter experts who want to develop knowledge and skills in unique aspects of a field. On one level, self-discovery learning affects all individuals who take initiative to learn for work, for play, for personal enrichment, and for lifelong learning. Discovery learning also affects those autodidacts who are mature and sophisticated learners who are able to acquire broad domain fields of knowledge and skills by their own initiative.

## POTENTIAL DESIGN EXPLORATIONS

While many in academia support the concept of some level of guided discovery, the actual amount will vary between learners and between those in different learning contexts. Some early design explorations suggest the importance of the following:

- attracting and engaging self-discovery learners to particular fields
- orientating self-discovery learners into particular fields, professional values, and practices through situated (contextualized) learning
- defining the learning context
- enhancing guided discovery and tailored feedback (preferably explanatory vs. merely corrective feedback alone per R. Moreno)
- providing relevant examples, worked examples, and cases
- helping learners surface prior knowledge and to capture and document acquired knowledge and reflect on the learning
- establishing self-learner meta-cognition at every stage of the learning process

- focusing learner goal-setting and planning (and relevant inquiry) and helping them surface and articulate these goals and plans
- supporting learner self-regulation, self-management, and follow-through
- contextualizing and sequencing the learning
- enabling appropriate learner profiling and monitoring for customized support and direction
- providing proper and accurate metadata and labeling of digital learning objects and online learning experiences
- ensuring high-trust distance intercommunications and collaborations
- managing archival and new knowledge
- crediting and rewarding learner innovation (both extrinsically and intrinsically)
- building up self-learner confidence, skills, and sense of self-efficacy in self-learning
- maintaining learner attention and engagement for the long-term

To maintain user attention, discovery learning sites must continue changing; they must remain relevant and offer participant value; they must have a positive Internet profile. Such spaces also need to maintain a high level of human expertise as well as new membership—particularly high-value participants who collaborate effectively in virtual spaces (and do not bring in the disruptive aspects like leadership struggles, dampened communications, social sabotage, or security compromises).

Ideally, self-discovery learning not only leads to enhancements in individuals' and groups' respective lives, but they benefit the larger community through the sharing of new insights, true innovations, and pure discoveries. This assumes that the self-discovery systems must protect innovator intellectual properties or at least be able to definitively define the moment of creation. It also suggests that there must be a system to preserve knowledge and digital creations over time, with all the attendant assumptions of proper metadata labeling, findability, archival, digital accessibility, and potential for re-use. This text begins with a basic premise of the necessarily pro-social nature of teaching and learning, including self-discovery learning.

The goal of *Constructing Self-Discovery Learning Spaces Online: Scaffolding and Decision Making Technologies* is to provide some early thoughts and research in this area. Ultimately, the idea is to make the WWW much more widely usable in a greater variety of ways. This approach aims to enhance efficiencies in human learning by aligning the technologies with human capabilities and objectives.

## CHAPTERS IN THE TEXT

A text is a focused effort to capture the culmination of human expertise on a particular subject matter in a condensed period of time. Efforts at recruiting talented professionals to write started in 2010. The following authors faithfully followed through on their research and writing work. There were some other very promising works; however, they did not make it to press in this endeavor. Ultimately, I am hopeful that those works will eventually see the light of (published) day. While I have worked with some of these authors before on other projects, others were totally new to me. I am grateful for the kind considerations and patience of these authors. I appreciate their sharing with me their discoveries in self-discovery learning and design.

The works in this text cover a broad range of concepts and practices. The chapters are lightly summarized in the following section.

## Section 1: A Foundation for Discovery Learning

To set the context, Brent A. Anders opens this text with Chapter 1: "*Human Motivations and Discovery Learning*." He reviews some of the literature on discovery and self-directed learning, particularly in light of human motivations. He directly explores methods to improve intrinsic and extrinsic human motivations for discovery learning, within a technologically enhanced framework.

Chapter 2: "*Who are Discovery Learners...Online? A Literature Review,*" by Shalin Hai-Jew, offers a look at the parsimonious literature on contemporary self-discovery learners, and what their learning needs may be. Further, this chapter explores who self-discovery learners are *online* and how they behave in those spaces. Given the sparseness of the research data, this work proposes questions of how future researchers may further define self-discovery learners online. Finally, this work offers some suggestions for how those online spaces may be evolved to more closely meet the needs of self-discovery learners.

## Section 2: Discovery Learning Environments and Tools

Authors Sarah D. Kirby and Debra M. Sellers, in Chapter 3: "*The LiveAbility House: A Collaborative Adventure in Discovery Learning,*" describe the efforts of a community-of-practice who are focused on supporting family caregivers. Their case study focuses on The LiveAbility House, a space in Second Life® they've designed as a virtual demonstration home—it embodies universal design principles, which may better enable aging-in-place, even in light of aging, illness, or disability. Their work offers insights on both the uses of the virtual to complement learning in-the-real and ways to harness virtual immersive spaces for deep learning.

Debra C. Burkey-Piecka, Laurie Ruberg, Christopher Ruckman, and Dynae Fullwood's Chapter 4: "*NASATalk as a Discovery Learning Space: Self-Discovery Learning Opportunities*" highlights NASA-*Talk* (www.nasatalk.com), an interactive discovery space of K-16 educators to discuss the self-discovery learning opportunities at the National Aeronautics and Space Administration (NASA) to promote STEM (science, technology, engineering and math) learning.

In Chapter 5: "*Knowledge Spaces for Online Discovery Learning,*" Roger W. McHaney offers a very timely piece on how emerging digital infrastructures have enhanced constructivist learning through virtual environments. He explores knowledge spaces for online discovery learning in a variety of applied contexts: case-based learning, incidental learning, learning by exploring/conversing, learning by reflection, and simulation-based learning. This chapter offers both a solid theoretical grounding and applied uses of extant Web 2.0 and other tools to design online discovery learning.

Nicoletta Adamo-Villani, Kari L. Clase, Robin J. Heyden, and John Wiecha's Chapter 6: "*Web-Based 3D Virtual Learning Environments*" sets the groundwork for the uses of three-dimensional virtual environments for self-discovery learning. They update the research literature on cutting-edge technologies and platforms for the building of virtual environments, and then they introduce two engaging cases of their own: the *Interactive 3D Tour of MSHHD* and *The pilot postgraduate medical education program in Second Life*.

Brent A. Anders, in Chapter 7: "*A Case Study on Using Discovery Learning within a Learning Management System: Axio Learning*™," shows how a learning / course management system is designed to enhance discovery learning using a variety of design tools. This work highlights how the building of a socio-technical space may be enhanced for more effective user acclimation and usage.

## Section 3: Types of Self-Discovery Learning

Ya-Chun Shih's Chapter 8: "*The Meeting Point of Second Life and Web 2.0: Self-Discovery for Writing*" highlights a practical approach to the use of the Second Life® virtual world to support computer-assisted language learning (CALL). The author combines a range of approaches—including blog-writing, exploration of *Second Life*, and effective teaching—to draw out writing from EFL (English as a Foreign Language) graduate students.

In Chapter 9: "*Applied Informal Problem-Solving through Self-Discovery Online: An Approach,*" Shalin Hai-Jew uses a problem-solving framework for the design of self-discovery learning spaces online. She introduces the popular informal problem-solving through information access and crowd-sourcing, but she also highlights the more in-depth informal problem-solving that may be more complex and time-intensive.

## Section 4: Design Strategies for Self-Discovery Learning

If self-discovery learning is about learner empowerment, then one critical feature of that empowerment must be the ability to self-assess the learning. Maria Menendez Blanco, Gerrit C. van der Veer, Laura Benvenuti, and Paul A. Kirschner's Chapter 10: "*Design Guidelines for Self-Assessment Support for Adult Academic Distance Learning*" explores problems that students at the Open University of the Netherlands have in self-assessment and meta-cognition. The authors base their insights on a literature review and student data from their teaching research center—from which they created a conceptual framework. They tested this framework with a questionnaire study and interviews. From this work, they developed guidelines for self-assessment in a distance learning environment.

Kanubhai K. Patel and Sanjay K. Vij introduce their innovative treadmill-style locomotion interface, which they call the "unconstrained walking plane" with a virtual environment, in order to enhance spatial learning. In Chapter 11, "*Unconstrained Walking Plane to Virtual Environment for Non-Visual Spatial Learning,*" these authors explore the phenomenon of non-visual spatial learning using a locomotion interface—to help discovery learners engage the virtual through the physical in new ways—that have implications for accessibility design.

Ramesh C. Sharma and Paul Kawachi, in Chapter 12: "*Engaging Learners in Digital Age through Self-Discovery Learning,*" propose a model that emphasizes the need for providing online learner experiences for self-discovery learning through reflection. Their four-stage model highlights the uses of a variety of technologies to achieve various learning goals. This model also integrates some of the latest technologies in social networking, Web 2.0, and virtual worlds.

Finally, Shalin Hai-Jew posits that self-discovery learning spaces and tools may be used to drive long-term persistence in acquiring complex skills sets. In Chapter 13: "*Addressing the 'Commitment Problem': Driving Long-Term Persistent Focus in Self-Discovery Learning (A Thought Experiment)*" draws on the extant educational research literature and existing technological affordances to carry out a thought experiment about how effectively such spaces may be used to support human persistence in difficult learning. A draft survey is proposed for further learning about long-term informal discovery learning online.

## FUTURE RESEARCH

Next-generation self-discovery learning spaces will necessarily meld human needs along with the affordances and constraints of the new technologies. The potential for important research discoveries in this area is many-fold.

### Theoretical Groundings

More research on pedagogical theories and validated observations about self-discovery learning would enhance the conceptual bases and practices in self-discovery learning space and tool designs. Only a small slice of the current pedagogical research deals with issues of self-regulated, inquiry-based, and discovery-based learning—and the above are not synonymous but highlight different aspects of self-driven learner-based discovery learning (with various levels of guidance, from no guidance to full structured learning). The necessary avoidance of "negative learning" from intuitive self-learning experiences will be critical for the successful deployment of self-discovery learning endeavors.

### Designing to Humans

A number of academic fields (psychology, neuroscience, education, advertising, and marketing and others) have made insightful observations about human perception (for example, sight, hearing, touch, taste, smell, and proprioception); cognition (for example, awareness, attention, short-term and long-term memory); affect (for example, human emotions), and learning. There is already some knowledge about autodidaxy or self-learning. The application of this design research will be critical for the creation of automated as well as human-facilitated self-discovery learning spaces and tools. In this area, it will be important to know more about what works (and what doesn't) for self-discovery learners—at various ages, in various cultures, in various contexts, and with various technologies.

### Federated Learner Identities

As the Web becomes more sentient, with increased uses of personally identifiable information (PII) and more complex tools for tracking and identifying participants, there may well be the creation of federated identities that help employers and employees keep track of their own trainings and formal / informal learning online. These identities would be persistent, and learner preferences, professional interests, and needs may be read by various systems in order to customize learning experiences to different learners' "self-systems" of understanding. There would be need for controlled and designed anonymity for those who want to learn without the trappings of their real-world identities.

### Melding the Real and the Virtual

With the popularization of wireless fidelity (WiFi) connectivity, self-discovery learning extends well into physical spaces—into mobile learning, ambient intelligent ("smart") spaces, augmented reality, and augmented virtuality. The interactive devices that enhance discovery learning may be haptic ones that convey touch information. Or live human movements, body language, and gestures may be the interface, with the popularization of motion-control interfaces. These technological advancements connect the virtual and the real and enable more in-depth explorations of the physical universe with the augmentation of digital information in a location-sensitive way.

## Adaptiveness and Customization

For self-discovery learning to work—whether learners are participating as individuals or as groups—online systems will need to be learning systems that can adapt to changing learner needs (whether the learners themselves may be aware of their respective needs or not). The level of analytical depth of various online systems enables crowd-sourcing to identify optimal learning paths for particular types of learners or those with particular learning profiles, and those may become more popular over time. In the same way that digital intelligent tutors adapt to learner needs, whole systems may be able to reconfigure around unique learner needs. This customization may well extend over lifelong learning, and learners' life spans. Additional adaptiveness would most certainly come from human research and *in vivo* and abductive observations.

## Acculturation to Professional Fields and Understandings

Some self-discovery learning sites help learners acclimate to particular simulated environments (including those which are very hostile to human existence like undersea or deep space environments). They also help learners acculturate into particular fields, such as those that enable individuals to communicate in a foreign language with digital avatars or to role play particular social communications. These spaces may help self-discovery learners acquire a particular habit of mind in terms of information acquisition, learning, analysis, trouble-shooting, problem-solving, decision-making, and innovation.

## Enhanced Virtual Teaming

With the popularization of distance collaborations and connections between people, many types of self-discovery learning involve various "selves." Virtual teams have evolved for different types of apprenticeships with experts. There is shared or evolving leadership; there are cases of dispersed non-defined "leadership." The findings of effective virtual leadership for self-discovery learners will certainly add to the literature.

## Domain Field Specifics

Domain fields will vary in terms of the types of discovery learning designs that will be used and how efficacious these endeavors are. The creation of dedicated spaces for autodidaxy-type learning may not only enhance a field but cross-field acquisition of knowledge.

## Self-Discovery Learners' Self-Management Tools

Different types of learners may find particular self-management tools more effective for their executive functions. The types of tools that may enhance human decision-making about their own learning will also offer value. The unique evaluations of these will provide plenty of promising directions for research.

Certainly, there will be other research directions that have not even been anticipated here. The rising expense of human facilitated learning and the non-scalability of human research and attention will mean that the uses of self-discovery learning will have to suffice for some types of learning. Extant websites, repositories, socio-technical spaces, virtual worlds, and other virtual spaces will benefit from designing for this group of self-motivated self-discovery learners. This book shows that a majority of people use the Internet for informal discovery learning and simple problem-solving. There's much more of human endeavors that may be supported with some adjustments to the site and information and user-interface designs of various Web spaces and Internet-related. This text offers a look at the design of online spaces for self-discovery learners' acquisition of information, knowledge, and skill sets.

It is my hope that you enjoy this text.

Sincerely,

*Shalin Hai-Jew*
*Kansas State University, USA*

# Acknowledgment

The authors are the ones who create a text. The ideas originate with them. Further, they conduct the research and the analyses; they write the actual chapters; they go through a rigorous (sometimes grueling) process of peer evaluation. Theirs is the hard work that results in learning value to others and that inform the practices in the field. For the application of self-discovery learning methods to the design of online sites, these authors are engaging a fresh topic with innovative approaches. First, I would like to acknowledge and thank each of the contributors to this text for their hard-won insights and professional camaraderie.

Plenty of publishing often occurs in a domain field before the possibility of a book arises. In this situation, it was no different. Various professional journals served as incubators of ideas. Their staffs—the editors and reviewers—also offered the support and healthy critique necessary to evolve relevant work. The idea for this text really started in late 2008, with the publication of "Scaffolding Discovery Learning Spaces" in the MERLOT Journal of Online Learning and Teaching (Vol. 4, No. 4). I am deeply grateful to the editors Drs. Edward H. Perry and Michelle Pilati and to the anonymous reviewers who vetted that work and made superb suggestions. That article is available at http://jolt.merlot.org/vol4no4/hai-jew_1208.htm. ("MERLOT" stands for Multimedia Educational Resource for Learning and Online Teaching).

A workplace that is supportive and conducive to learning and research is critical to academic achievements. While this work was created outside the auspices of my workplace, the learning opportunities of my line of work have encouraged my professional growth and pursuit of further learning. For those reasons, I am grateful to the affordances at Kansas State University.

Three highly talented and capable individuals served on the editorial board of this book: Dr. Barney Dalgarno of Charles Sturt University in Australia; Dr. Ramesh C. Sharma at the University of Guyana; and Brent A. Anders, of Kansas State University. All three brought unique insights and skills to the evolution of this text. I am grateful for their contributions.

Thanks to Mike Killian of IGI-Global for supporting the initial phases of manuscript development. Thanks to Chris Wozniak and Hannah Abelbeck for the sprint to the finish. I am also deeply appreciative of the professional people at IGI Global for their consistent and important support throughout this process.

This book, as always, is for R. Max.

*Shalin Hai-Jew*
*Kansas State University, USA*

# Section 1
# A Foundation for Discovery Learning

# Chapter 1
# Human Motivations and Discovery Learning

**Brent A. Anders**
*Kansas State University, USA*

## ABSTRACT

*In identifying ways to facilitate Discovery Learning (sometimes referred to as "self-directed learning") and maximize its educational benefits, it is important to understand the motivating factors behind it. This chapter seeks to identify two different definitions of Discovery Learning (one general, one operational), review some of the general human motivational theories, and offer a better understanding of how to improve motivation for Discovery Learning via both intrinsic and extrinsic modalities, within a technologically enhanced framework.*

## CHAPTER OBJECTIVES

- Define Discovery Learning with regards to motivation; as a pursuit of pure interest and as a part of a larger guided/facilitated pedagogy
- Review the main human motivational theories: Classical Conditioning/ Operant Conditioning, Attribution Theory, Expectancy Theory, Maslow's Hierarchy of Needs and Achievement Motivation: Goal Theory
- Describe how intrinsic motivation can be used to enhanced Discovery Learning
- Describe how extrinsic motivation can be used to enhance Discovery Learning

DOI: 10.4018/978-1-61350-320-1.ch001

## INTRODUCTION

To wonder and seek is a part of all of us and in understanding our underlying motivations for seeking we can harness the full potential of Discovery Learning. In learning about some of the different theories associated with human motivation a clearer picture will emerge as to the subtle workings of successful implementations of content for use by those engaged in Discovery Learning. Although the purpose of this chapter is not to provide a right way or a wrong way to use motivational elements, it can provide possibilities so as to enhance the motivational power manifested within a Discovery Learning student.

Differences and capabilities of both intrinsic and extrinsic motivation will be evaluated as well as described within the framework of online

Copyright © 2012, IGI Global. Copying or distributing in print or electronic forms without written permission of IGI Global is prohibited.

education. By harnessing these two modalities it will become evident that Discovery Learning can and should be enhanced to improve completion, retention and user experience as a whole.

## Discovery Learning Defined

Generally there are two ways to view and therefore define Discovery Learning.

The first definition of Discovery Learning is simply that of a learner exploring and seeking educational opportunities on their own, informally, wherever they might be available (he/she is discovering and in the process learning). An example would be if someone heard the word "pedagogical" for the first time and wanted to learn its full meaning and how to properly use it. The learner in this example would seek the information (look it up via a search engine), on their own, so as to discover and gain understanding (learn the definition and how to use it). This definition is closer to the higher educational term of "autodidaxy," which generally refers to self education/instruction outside of a formal type of educational environment (Candy, 1991).

A second, more formal description, one which for the purposes of this chapter will be the main operational definition, is that "Discovery Learning is an approach to learning that can be facilitated by particular teaching methods and guided learning strategies…through exploring and problem solving, students take on an active role to create, integrate, and generalize knowledge" (Castonova, 2002). The key aspect is that students take on an "active role" in their learning as opposed to passively receiving information such as in a lecture-type of educational environment. There is still facilitation and guiding that occurs but it is not the same as direct (giver to receiver) learning. A specific example of Discovery Learning would be through the use of a WebQuest (developed by Bernie Dodge, 1995). A WebQuest is an educational tool that is comprised of presenting a student learner with a problem (or sets of problems) and giving them minimal direction (framework) so as to allow the students to actively seek out the information and learn/discover while actually doing (finding the answers to the problems). A WebQuest is also enhanced through the use of a scenario or story to aid with making the content more engaging and exciting.

Although the main idea in Discovery Learning is that the student is actively seeking/discovering on their own, much can be done within the guidelines/framework of the educational task as well as the educational interactions and academic online environment. The following review of motivational theories will seek to address how they might be applied within an online Discovery Learning framework.

## Human Motivational Theories Review

### Classical Conditioning and Operant Conditioning

Although Classical Conditioning (physiological response derived from associated stimuli, [Pavlov, 1905]) and Operant Conditioning (the use of consequences: rewards and punishments to directly modify behavior [Skinner, 1953]) aren't necessarily theories of motivation in themselves, they are vital behavioral concepts to realize with regards to possible applications of motivations in Discovery Learning.

As demonstrated by the infamous "Little Albert" experiment, Classical Conditioning can be applied to humans so as to enact an emotional as well as physiological response (Watson & Rayner, 1920). By manipulating stimuli within the student's online learning environment, various positive associations can be made. One pedagogical component could be to present very interesting, fun, and/or exciting material towards the beginning of a module/instructional set, so as to have the student create a positive association with the online learning environment and/or discovery learning as a whole. Positive associations through conditioning can be utilized in various other ways so as to help students to want to learn and feel positive about the process. In essence this is quickly approaching the marketing of a subject matter or experience so as to elicit positive associations. In this way even when some material is being presented that isn't as interesting/fun/exciting, the association will have already been made and the overall experience will remain positive.

The Operant Conditioning technique is more in line with what the majorities of people are used to: rewards and punishment. This can be used as a powerful motivational tool if applied appropriately. To begin with, an understanding of rewards and punishment is needed: positive reinforcement, negative reinforcement, positive punishment, and negative punishment (see Table 1).

Although the Operant Conditioning technique has been shown effective with regards to academic motivation, it is not without it detractions. Controlled administration of both rewards and punishment done in the proper way is vital for effective, long lasting outcomes.

Throughout this chapter multiple theories will be reviewed with a final direct comparison of intrinsic versus extrinsic motivational factors. Additionally various examples of how these theories and factors can be applied to online discovery learning will be described.

## Attribution Theory

This motivational theory deals with higher order (cognitive) processing in that the student learner attempts to explain a situational failure or success dealing with one's self or in others through the use of attributions (Heider, 1958). These attributions are organized as being either within one's self (internal) or outside of one's self (external). Attributions are further organized as either being within one's control or not within one's control (uncontrollable). These organizations then yield one of four attributions: ability, luck, effort and task difficulty (see Table 2).

This theory was further refined by describing attributions as the result of locus of control, stability of the situation and the perceived controllability of the event/situation (Weiner, 1996).

The locus of control deals directly with how a student learner perceives their ability to manipulate the situation and the outcome, equaling control. The stability of the situation has to do with the repeatability of the situation, that is an expectancy or anticipation of future results. The perceived controllability is how the student views the situation or event with regards to the power to influence or manage the outcome. Another important contribution of Dr. Weiner deals with the recognition of emotion in attribution, "... causal ascriptions influence emotions, and that emotional reactions play a role in motivated behavior" (Weiner, 1996). Two sets of emotions are generated within a user; emotions related to attainment or nonattainment of the goal as well as an emotional response as to the reason(s) why: *attribution dependent emotions.*

The key component of this motivational theory when applied to online learning and more specifically to Discovery Learning, is that measures should be taken to directly assist the student

*Table 1. Reinforcements and punishments*

| | |
|---|---|
| **Positive Reinforcement:** | Purposeful presentation of extrinsic award/rewards (consequence, stimuli) such as a tangible item, praise, approval, and/or special treatment when wanted behavior is observed - strengthens behavior |
| **Negative Reinforcement:** | Purposeful removal of aversive (negative) stimulus when wanted behavior is observed (escaping negative stimuli) - strengthens behavior |
| **Positive Punishment:** | Purposeful administering of unpleasant stimuli when unwanted behavior is observed - reduces behavior |
| **Negative Punishment:** | Purposeful removal of pleasant stimuli when unwanted behavior is observed - reduces behavior |

*Table 2. Attribution theory*

| Attribution Theory | Internal (within one's self) | External (outside of one's self) |
|---|---|---|
| **Not Within One's Control** (Uncontrollable) | Ability | Luck |
| **Within One's Control** | Effort | Task Difficulty |

learner in establishing a self-attribution resulting in "Effort" as the reason for the outcomes of educational situations. In using the table above, this would have resulted by the learner viewing educational situations as an internal result fully within one's own control equaling the effort applied as the attribution. Weiner's own research and literature review stated, "…persistence in the face of failure is enhanced when attributions for failure are changed from low ability to lack of effort (Weiner, 1996)." The challenge is to change the learner's attributional thought of "I'm just not any good at this," (low ability at difficult task) to that of "With a little more effort I know I can succeed," (Huitt, 2001).

Comments and directions within online learning should utilize text so as to stress the importance of effort in final knowledge mastery as well as grade accomplishment. Poor grades or educational outcomes should include improvement actionable directions so as to mitigate attributional dependent emotions. Creating mechanisms that would allow students to demonstrate effort to the instructor as well as to the student themselves could be integrated. Examples of this could be: additional optional assignments dealing with a problematic subject matter, or extra instructional modules that would allow for additional study (also referred to as "just in time learning").

## Expectancy Theory

This theory, which originates from a psychological analysis of behavior in organizations and management, views motivation as the multiplicative result of three specific factors: Expectancy, Instrumentality and Valance (Vroom, 1964). Expectancy is an individuals' perception or general belief (probability) in one's actions (effort) resulting in the desired outcome. As an example: "If I study harder (effort) I will get an A on my next test. Instrumentality functions as a belief that if one's desired outcome is achieved, the overall reward will be maximized. As an example: "If I get an A on my next test, then I will get an A in the class." In a slightly different example, it could be viewed as "I see that someone was recognized with having the best answer in a message board. I will work hard to have the best answer because I want to be recognized (maximized reward). The final variable of Valance is the actual perceived value (importance) of the final maximized reward.

Mathematically this value would be expressed in the following equation and Figure 1.

Motivation = Expectancy x Instrumentality x Valance

Since this is a mathematical formula it becomes evident that a low value in any of the variables (Expectancy, Instrumentality, Valance) will result in lower overall motivation. To maximize the motivation of a student, mechanisms would need to be in place so that the learner could always see and understand that their effort would indeed result in increased success (Expectancy).

Stressing the importance of effort through message boards, chats and assignment feedback would help with regards to Expectancy. Students need to be told directly how each achievement within the course/program helps them in their overall success (Instrumentality). Although students have a general understanding of the importance of doing well in a given class, they should be directly told and reminded of just how important and valuable it truly is. Answering the "why" will have great benefits in increasing the Valance variable. Many of these aspects can be

*Figure 1. Expectancy theory*

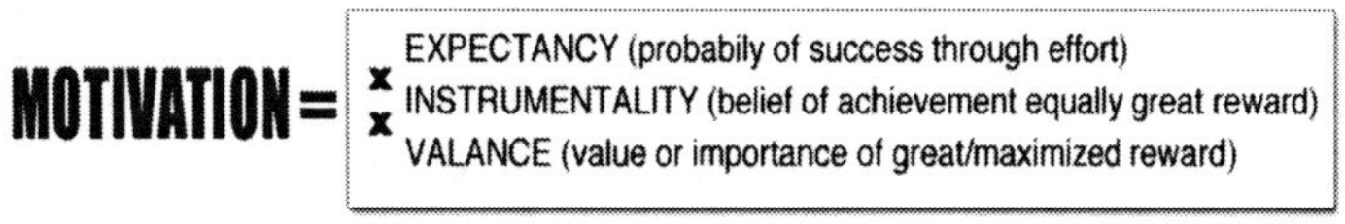


addressed through general policies within class rules, rubrics, or syllabi information, but additional reminders throughout a course (possibly presented with instructions for each assignment) and direct examples so that students could better visualize success or failure would improve over all understanding and motivation.

## Maslow's Hierarchy of Needs

In general terms, this motivational theory describes how learners must first meet the basic needs of Physiological Needs such as hunger and thirst, Safety Needs such as security of one's self and family, Love Needs such as a longing for affection and belongingness and Esteem Needs such as self-esteem and self-respect before Self-Actualization can occur (this is where higher order learning takes place), (Maslow, 1943) (see Figure 2).

Although a manipulation of the importance of the different hierarchal levels can occur, generally lower needs (conative) must be met before higher-order needs (cognitive) can be concentrated on so as to be achieved.

An understanding of Maslow's Hierarchy of Needs theory of motivation with regards to Discovery Learning is applicable in several ways. The Esteem Needs level is an area of interest that offers a functional opportunity. Maslow further described Esteem Needs as "...the desire for strength, for achievement..." as well as "Satisfaction of the self-esteem need leads to feelings of self-confidence, worth, strength, capability and adequacy..." By taking steps to enhance a learners' "desire for achievement" and "feelings of capability," the educational outcomes will be improved.

Techniques for helping to accomplish this would include: using descriptions and instructions that work to enhance learners' self-esteem in a worthwhile way as opposed to simply being patronizing. Instead of a statement such as:

*"View these examples of what I want you to do. Do your best and I know you can do great job."*

An improved statement would be:

*"Each one of you has already achieved this high level of education and are now fully capable of achieving this assignment. View these excellent examples of what other students, just like you, were able to accomplish. Apply yourself and with good effort, you will excel at this assignment."*

*Figure 2. Maslow's hierarchy of needs*

Notice the change of tone and the focus on "you," as opposed to "I" and the use of words such as: achieved, capable, achieving, just like you, accomplish, effort, excel.

Another functional opportunity resides in addressing the Love and Safety Needs. Online applications such as message boards, chat rooms or other group-work tools, could be enhanced by taking these "needs" into account. To maximize participation and higher order thinking/discussion, learners will need to feel a sense of safety and belonging within the courses' community. Making sure that learners know that the message boards, chat rooms, etc. are safe (generally accomplished through password protection) is only part of the solution. Student interaction guidelines (etiquette) should be fully emphasized so as to provide learners the proper technique for debate and conversation so as to enhance emotional safety and assist in fostering a sense of communal bonding.

*"Your answer to the instructor's question was very stupid. Your ideas on how reality television shows are affecting the moral fiber of the U.S. are inept and completely made up and based purely on your own religious upbringing."*

An improved comment would be:

*"I personally did not agree with your answer to the instructor's question. The ideas you presented dealing with how reality television shows are affecting the moral fiber of the U.S. seem to only be your own religious/moral opinions. On what facts do you specifically base these ideas? "*

Notice how the first comment is very confrontational with negative words such as "stupid" and "*inept.*" Also notice that the first comment is overly direct by starting out with "Your answer" as opposed to "I personally." The overall feeling and tone of the second presentation is much lighter, less negative and much more academic. This would occur through established guidelines of how posts/comments are to be presented (netiquette): being positive, address the content not the student, asking for clarification, not being accusational, etc.

Additional components such as professional type pictures of learners and informational profile pages listing educational backgrounds, goals, location, etc. would greatly aid in personalizing the academic online community and allow for more realistic discussion/interaction so as to improve learners sense of satisfying the Love/Safety Need.

A final functional opportunity with regards to Maslow's Hierarchy of Needs and Discovery Learning deals with the final level: Self-Actualization (true final level later subcategorized as "Self-Transcendence," meaning moving beyond ego and wanting more to help others), (Maslow, 1971). In Self-Actualization the learner is constantly seeking more and wanting to improve. If this type of learner stops trying to improve "...a new discontent and restlessness..." will rise within him or her for "What a man can be, he must be," (Maslow, 1943). Although one might presume that a Self-Actualize learner would be an ideal student and go through any and all courseware available so as gain new knowledge and continue to improve oneself, it is not that simple. Self-Actualization is not the same as realization. Take for example the fact that I want to gain an expert understanding of online higher education. So I am Self-Actualized with regards to that subject matter, but I would not necessarily fully realize how a presented courseware or educational opportunity would help me to achieve that. With this understanding it is vital to constantly explain and demonstrate how the course/educational information being presented is important and necessary for the learner so as to achieve near and long-term goals. An explanation of why the information must be learned at the micro level so as to understand the bigger picture at the macro level greatly assists learners in being motivated to continue and proceed so as to gain greater understanding.

As a personal example I remember being discouraged while working on my undergraduate degree and taking Psychology 101. I found the class of 200 students extremely boring and difficult to follow. I ended up not listening to the professor and instead just studying the book. It was very unpleasant and I thought about changing from Psychology to another major. I talked to my guidance councilor and he simply said "A lot of people don't like that class, but it will be over soon and then you will be ready to learn the more interesting things in depth." I thought about what he said and gravitated to the "you will be ready to learn the more interesting things," portion of his comment. That small little explanation motivated me to finish that course and stay in that major.

In a similar manner, explanations as to why and how the courseware/educational content is relative, useful and important to the learner are powerful enhancers in motivating learners to go through the courseware and apply themselves. As a military instructor I am obligated to conduct risk assessments on every class that I conduct so as to mitigate risk to prevent injuries and accidents. Additionally I use this risk assessment tool so as to inform student what the risks and consequence are if they do not learn the material. Not only are short term goals addressed such as "you could fail this course," but longer term goals are also discussed such as "you could cause others to be hurt through negligence, you could fail as a leader by not having the necessary knowledge when the situation arises, your success is important in that you represent the United States of America in every action that you take." Addressing the importance and consequences can go a long way to priming students to deeply learn the information for long-term retention.

## Achievement Motivation: Goal Theory

This motivation theory emphasis a cognitive basis of students' behavior and attributes their motivation and success to the types and combinations of goals that they might have (Ames, 1992; Urdan & Maehr, 1995). Goals are broken down into three distinct categories: mastery goals, performance goals and social goals. Mastery goals are viewed as the best type of goals in that they are intrinsically rooted, include a belief that effort equals success, and are described as "individuals are focused on mastering and understanding content and demonstrating a willingness to engage in the process of learning" (Ames, 1992). Performance goals are described as a focus on one's own feelings of self-worth and a desire to do "better than others, by surpassing normative-based standards, or by achieving success with little effort," with "public recognition" (Ames, 1992). Social goals are described as levels of desire for academic success with regard to others and/or relationships (Urdan & Maehr, 1995). The majority of the educational research has focused on mastery and performance goals resulting in recommendations to focus on enabling and fostering mastery goals. "...research evidence suggests that it is a mastery goal orientation that promotes a motivational pattern likely to promote long-term and high-quality involvement in learning," (Ames, 1992)

With regards to Discovery Learning an application of fostering mastery goals would be on focusing on the effects and results of effort. Keying in when a student improves and using effort attributions within presented feedback. Offering additional assignments (opportunities to learn) to allow students to put forth more effort to enhance their educational understanding could also be utilized. Additionally focusing more on effort as opposed to ability when describing grade results or assignments would aid students in the self-attribution property of mastery goals.

## INTRINSIC VS. EXTRINSIC MOTIVATION TO ENHANCE DISCOVERY LEARNING

The various different motivational theories described have shown that there are many ways to enhance motivation via both intrinsic (internal satisfaction in completion of the work/task in and of itself) and extrinsic (external or outside rewards for completion) means. Either modality can be effective although a large volume of research indicates that extrinsic only techniques will not work in the long term and can be summarized by "When the goodies stop, people go right back to acting the way they did before the program began (Kohn, 1993)." Extrinsic motivation can still be a very effective tool in the short term and coupled with the long-term effects of intrinsic motivation, a lot can be done to enhance Discovery Learning. It is important to also note that the inclusion of extrinsic motivators will most likely not work properly if a zero-sum scoring system is used (Covington and Mueller, 2001). Meaning that if one student does well then other students must do badly due to limited points available, similarly only limited rewards (extrinsic) are available. The goal should always be to aid students in caring for learning in that the attainment of knowledge is its own reward, but various students are at different levels of understanding or progress with regards to learning and psyche in general.

Below is a listing of additional extrinsic and intrinsic applications that could be applied within an online educational environment for Discovery Learning purposes.

### Extrinsic Applications

- **Known Placement:** This application would be accomplished via an auto calculation derived from an online grade book within a learning management system. The value here would be that the student could see how they rank compared to the other students within their class/course. The extrinsic motivation would be to attain the rank of #1 or as close to it as possible. The actual implementation of this type of application could be handled in various ways. Instead of a specific ranking the actual number displayed could be "top 10%," "top 25%,"top 50%," or something along those line. Another technique would be a special marking indicating that the student is currently earning an "A" in the class. These marking could be private (only seen on individual student's screen), or seen on all students' screen through other applications such as chat room and message boards. The power of this application would be in giving the student a placement identity that can be improved upon which would server as the extrinsic reward.
- **Class Hall of Fame:** This idea would involve creating a section within a course that would be reserved for students' projects/assignments that were rated as being exceptionally great. This could then be used as examples for future students to strive for. The power of this application would be in the prestige and honor (extrinsic reward) given to a student who is able to complete an assignment/project so excellently.
- **Certificate of Completion:** In this application, being able to attain a physical document that can be framed and displayed would serve as an extrinsic reward to aid in full completing the course.
- **Additional Duty:** Although this might at first seem counter intuitive, it would actually serve as a great extrinsic reward for many students. Being asked by an instructor to assist in answering questions within a chat room, message board, etc., would again be a large prestige and honor in that a professor would only ask for such assistance from a highly skilled/intelligent student.

- **Progression Indication:** This application would once again require integration with a learning management system. As a student completes each module or section, the system would update a progress indicator showing the student how much he or she had completed or how much of the course was left. The extrinsic reward would come in seeing the progress indicator change and getting closer and closer to accomplishing the task of the overall course (see Figure 3).
- **Letter Grade:** Although already used my most instructors, adding detail when a grade is given can enhance the very extrinsic motivator of a "letter grade," even more. On a personal note, I remember one online professor I had who stated, "If you get a grade of B or lower I will only tell you what you did wrong. If you get an A, I'll tell you what all you did right." It was a very interesting psychological ploy, but I worked so hard to always get "A's" in that I very much wanted to be told what I did right as opposed to what I did wrong. I talked to other students in that class and they all felt the same way. The extrinsic reward of positive feedback can be very effective.
- **Special Response/Feedback:** In a similar manner to the description given for the proposed letter grade application, I once had another online professor who stated, "A lot of your assignments will be through the message board. I'll be asking questions and grading your responses. I won't comment publically on anyone's responses unless they are exceptionally good." That little bit of competition or withholding of appreciation (Love Need) was all it took. Many of us students in the class worked very diligently to answer as directly, intellectually and completely as possible so as to attain the coveted "actual public response" from the instructor. Although this was a very effective application it could also be handled in another way. The professor could respond via text to every student but then only by video for the exceptionally good responses.

## Intrinsic Applications

- **Detailed Explanations of Why:** For many students, gaining a comprehension of why a certain class/course/assignment is important is the greatest motivation of all. By knowing how the information to be learned will benefit them the near and far future, the student will be stimulated to work hard to successfully complete the class/course/assignment.
- **Plan of Action:** Although this application comes from a commonly used military form (DA Form 4856), it has great applicability to assist with online intrinsic motivation. The plan of action is designed so as to show soldiers what "actions" or steps they need to take so as to improve or accomplish a desired result. An online application of this would be to provide students with a specific Plan of Action showing

*Figure 3. Progression indication*

them how each assignment or class works to enable the student to accomplish subsequent assignments or classes. This would intrinsically motivate the student in that they would realize the importance or need of learning the current material.

- **Games and Simulation:** The use of games and simulations are listed here as possible intrinsic motivational tools in that if they are crafted and designed well enough, the learner will enjoy going through them simply for the pleasure of the experience. This then causes internal motivation to improve (beat the game). French researchers Guillaume Denis and Pierre Jouvelot talk of "Intrinsic motivation as a balance between challenges and skills," with regards to educational games (Guillaume and Jouvelot, 2005).
- **Curiosity/Stimulating Content:** This application of intrinsic motivation goes along similar lanes as that listed for Games and Simulations. The curiosity and stimulation of the content will peak interest so that students will want learn so as to satisfy the intrinsic curiosity.
- **Exemplar Videos:** In an effort to enhance students' feeling of self motivation, exemplar videos of graduated students now fully employed and succeeding in their area of study would serve to show students what their successful action will lead to. They could physically see what success in the given class would eventually result in be motivated to employ added effort to embody what they had seen.
- **e-Portfolio:** Although possibly viewed a extrinsic in that it is a physical display of accomplishments, it could also be viewed as assisting in intrinsic motivation. Students could understand that they have done a lot and are capable of doing even more. They could see and remember a hard class or assignment that they were able to complete and know that they can conquer another difficult class as well. Various prepackaged e-Portfolio systems already exist and many learning management system have e-portfolio systems already integrated. The item to be addressed by the instructor would be proper usage and view of the system with regards to intrinsic motivation.
- **e-Journals:** An additional application (possibly associated with e-Portfolio) would be the use of an online journaling system. This educational journal would be kept by the student with entries for each project/assignment and/or class answering specific questions dealing with effort, relevancy, future applicability, importance, and other aspects so as to enhance intrinsic motivation and self attribution.
- **WebQuest:** The use of this type of Discovery Learning assignment (as described in the Discovery Learning Defined section of this document) would function as a powerful intrinsic application. Through this assignment the intrinsic rewards would come in the excitement and interest in both the journey of the WebQuest and in the final accomplishment of the WebQuest. The levels of the intrinsic rewards would come in how the assignment is implemented and the quality of the assignment itself.

## CONCLUSION

There are many different theories associated with motivation and learning applicable to Discovery Learning. By learning about each one a better understanding of the complexities behind the motivating factors of student learners starts to emerge. There are many areas where motivation can be enhanced and manipulated to improve Discovery Learning results, retention and the overall experience. The presented suggestions and examples are all possibilities for teacher, instructors and professors to analyze and experiment with so as to see how they might be used within various subject matters and environments. This informational chapter is a starting point with regards to understanding the motivational theories and that motivation itself within an online environment (for either on-campus or distance education/learning) is a powerful tool that can and should be considered. The extrinsic and intrinsic applications listed are idea-starting points meant to show you that there are many possibilities and opportunities. The important take away of this chapter is to realize that the environment, direction, instruction and implementation of a course/ assignment are all areas where motivation can be influenced.

## REFERENCES

Ames, C. (1992). Classroom goals, structures, and student motivation. *Journal of Educational Psychology, 84*(3), 261-271. Retrieved September 30, 2010, from http://www.unco.edu/cebs/psychology/kevinpugh/motivation_project/resources/ames92.pdf.

Candy, P. C. (1991). *Self-direction for lifelong learning*. San Francisco, CA: Jossey-Bass Publishers.

Castronova, J. (2002). *Discovery learning for the 21st century: What is it and how does it compare to traditional learning in effectiveness in the 21st century?* Retrieved September 10, 2010, from http://teach.valdosta.edu/are/Litreviews/vol1no1/castronova_litr.pdf.

Covington, M., & Mueller, K. (2001). Intrinsic versus extrinsic motivation: An approach/avoidance reformulation. *Educational Psychology Review, 13*(2). Retrieved September 20, 2010, from http://www.unco.edu/cebs/psychology/kevinpugh/motivation_project/resources/covington_mueller01.pdf.

Denis, G., & Jouvelot, P. (2005). *Motivation driven educational game design: Applying best practices to music education.* Retrieved September 28, 2010, from http://citeseerx.ist.psu.edu/viewdoc/download?doi=10.1.1.59.7687&rep=rep1&type=pdf.

Heider, F. (1958). *The psychology of interpersonal relations*. New York, NY: John Wiley & Sons. doi:10.1037/10628-000

Huitt, W. (2001). Motivation to learn: An overview. *Educational Psychology Interactive*. Valdosta, GA: Valdosta State University. Retrieved July 25, 2010, from http://www.edpsycinteractive.org/col/motivation/motivate.html.

Kohn, A. (1993). Rewards versus learning: A response to Paul Chance. *Phi Delta Kappan, 74*, 783–787. Retrieved September 25, 2010, from http://www.li.suu.edu/Library/Circulation/Ellington/eled3200meRewardsVersusLearning-Fall02.pdf.

Maslow, A. (1943). A theory of human motivation. *Psychological Review, 50*, 370-396. Retrieved September 15, 2010 from http://citeseerx.ist.psu.edu/viewdoc/download?doi=10.1.1.152.465&rep=rep1&type=pdf.

Maslow, A. (1971). *The farther reaches of human nature*. New York, NY: The Viking Press.

Pavlov, I. (1927). *Physiological activity of the cerebral cortex – Lecture II.* Retrieved August 2, 2010, from http://psychclassics.yorku.ca/Pavlov/.

Skinner, B. (1953). *Science and human behavior*. Pearson Education, Inc. Retrieved August 5, 2010 from http://www.terapia-conductual-cognitiva.cl/archivos/descargas/B%20F%20Skinner%20-%20Science%20And%20Human%20Behavior.pdf.

Urdan, T., & Maehr, M. (1995). Beyond a two-goal theory of motivation and achievement: A case for social goals. *Review of Educational Research, 65*(3), 213-243. Retrieved September 30, 2010, from http://www.jstor.org/stable/pdfplus/1170683.pdf.

Vroom, V. (1964). *Work and motivation.* New York, NY: Jon Wiley & Sons.

Watson, J., & Rayner, R. (1920). Conditioned emotional reactions. *Journal of Experimental Psychology, 3*(1), 1–14. Retrieved July 30, 2010. doi:10.1037/h0069608

Weiner, B. (1996). Attribution, emotion, and action. In R. Sorrentino & E. Higgins (Eds.), *Handbook of motivation and cognition, volume 3: The interpersonal context* (pp. 281-311). Western Ontario, Canada: The Guilford Press.

## KEY TERMS AND DEFINITIONS

**Achievement Motivation:** Goal Theory: Emphasis a cognitive basis of a person's behavior and attributes their motivation and success to the types and combinations of goals that they might have (mastery goals, performance goals and social goals).

**Attribution Theory:** A higher order process where a person attempts to explain a failure/success through attributions: Ability, Luck, Effort, and Difficulty.

**Classical Conditioning:** The production of a physiological response that is derived from an associated stimulus.

**Discovery Learning:** A pedagogical approach to learning in which the student is actively seeking/discovering on their own with only minimal guidance/facilitation.

**Expectancy Theory:** View of motivation as the result of multiplying Expectancy (probability of success through effort) x Instrumentality (belief of achievement equaling reward) x Valance (value/importance of maximized reward).

**Maslow's Hierarchy of Needs:** Describes how learners must first meet basic needs (Physiological Needs such as hunger, Safety Needs such as security of one's self, Love Needs such as a longing for affection and Esteem Needs such as self-esteem) before Self-Actualization can occur.

**Motivation:** The reason or purpose through intrinsic and extrinsic means for action to occur.

**Operant Conditioning:** The utilization of actual consequences such as rewards and punishments to directly modify a person's behavior.

**WebQuest:** A Discovery Learning implementation technique in which a student is presented with a problem and given minimal direction so as to allow the student to actively seek out the information and learn/discover while actually doing (finding the answers to the problems).

# Chapter 2
# Who are Self-Discovery Learners...Online? A Literature Review

**Shalin Hai-Jew**
*Kansas State University, USA*

## ABSTRACT

*Self-discovery learning may be understood in multiple ways—as a state of expertise and learning maturity; as an attitude and approach to self-directed learning; as a perceptive and learning stance to the world; as a minor everyday skill for informal information-seeking, and even as an inherent part of the self-discovery learner. It is this last conceptualization that is addressed in this chapter, which explores who self-discovery learners are and what their learning needs may be. Self-discovery learning may be a human character trait. Further, this chapter explores who self-discovery learners are online and how they behave in those spaces. Given the sparseness of the research data, this work proposes questions of how future researchers may further define self-discovery learners online. Finally, this work offers some suggestions for how those online spaces may be evolved to more closely meet the needs of self-discovery learners.*

## INTRODUCTION

Self-discovery learning may be understood in multiple ways. It is a state of expertise and learning maturity, a point at which a learner can move forward and develop his or her mastery on his or her own. Self-discovery learning may be conceptualized as a general practice—often for informal types of learning—that may bridge learning for work and personal interests. The self-discovery adult learner may be understood

DOI: 10.4018/978-1-61350-320-1.ch002

It is important to study who self-discovery learners are in order to better meet their needs through design—namely to lower the inefficiencies and barriers to self-discovery learning, to head-off the misconceptions that come with unguided discovery learning, and to enhance self-discovery learning skill sets.

The research literature—in self-regulated learning, inquiry-based learning, autodidaxy, self-learning, independent learning, lifelong learning, autonomic learning, and discovery learning—offer some basic highlights of who self-discovery adult learners are.

Copyright © 2012, IGI Global. Copying or distributing in print or electronic forms without written permission of IGI Global is prohibited.

## REVIEW OF THE LITERATURE

The pure self-discovery learning environment is the world, foremost. Self-discovery learners, by definition, can learn anywhere; using their imaginations and intuition, they can sense-make and engage the environment for information and learning. The world then includes the natural, social, and human-made aspects. One of the foremost aspects of the current learning world would involve online spaces of the Web and the Internet. The pure self-discovery environment may lack any sort of designed learning structure, so self-discovery learners will need to create their own learning opportunities, structures (mental and situational), relationships, and conclusions.

Self-discovery learning may be conceptualized as originating with learner-centered constructs (Malone, 2008), foremost, constructivism—or the idea that learning occurs foremost inside learners, who engage in sense-making. Oehlmann describes the importance of five main phases: evidence collection; awareness of consistencies between the learner's mental model and what is observed; utilization (perspective change), explanation, and elaboration of the new perspective in a new theory (2002, pp. 7-8). In this conceptualization, the self-discovery learner aligns his or her internal knowledge with the external and observed realities in the world.

Social constructivism suggests that people work together to co-construct knowledge whether they interact directly or only peripherally through each other's created digital artifacts (articles, videos, podcasts, and other objects). The sense of a learning community is a critical one for the acquisition of many skill sets. Co-learners may be a source of encouragement and new knowledge; they may provide social camaraderie.

Adult self-discovery learners are understood to be learning outliers in a learner population bell-curve. They are active, self-motivated, and self-driven (Wang & Li, 2007, p. 259); they have an internal locus of control (and do not feel like they're failures are based on external factors) and are intrinsically motivated. They tend to evaluate their own performance and self-correct (DuBois & Staley, 1997).

In alignment with the body of adult learning literature, such self-discovery learners select topics that have relevance to themselves and which may be practically applied to their work and / or personal lives. Some learning pursuits have direct effects on their respective self- (personal) and public identities (social and profession-related). Said another way, learning is part of self-creation: "Learning is becoming" (Ranson, Martin, Nixon, & McKeown, 1996, p. 14).

The educational research literature focuses on three main aspects of self-discovery learners: (1) their self-motivation and drive; (2) their self-regulatory (executive) skill set; and (3) their mixed self-discovery learning outcomes.

### Self-Motivation and Drive

The signature characteristic of self-discovery learners is their self-motivation and drive; they are powered by their own initiative, and they are able to engage the world as a learning space in order to acquire knowledge and skills. In their learning, self-discovery learners are often unsupervised and autonomous. In general, they have to decide their own learning opportunities and their own pacing. They have low dependency needs (Hai-Jew, 2008). They may opt-in occasionally for help-seeking, but often, they use limited guidance or direction. Adult learners tend to become more self-directed in their learning as they mature (Knowles, 1970, 1980, as cited in Merriam & Caffarella, 1999, p. 289). Self-discovery learning has been aligned with a greater sense of learner personal responsibility and ownership of the learning, which is said to lead to improved "acquisition, retention, and transfer of knowledge" and more significant learning, and ultimately, mastery (Malone, 2008, p. 533). Contemporary self-discovery adult learners are "power users" of online spaces.

Self-discovery learners may be motivated by a varying basket of incentives. Intrinsic motivations for self-edification may come from any level of Maslow's hierarchy of needs: physiological, safety, love/belonging, self-esteem, and self-actualization. People learn to meet physical needs; to secure employment; to maintain meaning relationships with others; to build their sense of achievement, and to promote their own creativity and moral senses—with further progress on the upper levels of the hierarchy as the basic human needs are met. Intrinsic motivations may include curiosity; the sense of "flow" that comes from learning and self-actualization; and identity development. Extrinsic rewards and motivations may include public recognition and credit, material and financial rewards, and job promotion.

## Self-Regulatory Skill Set

Educational researchers have explored what skills comprise the self-discovery skill set. In various models, self-regulation of learning is characterized as a cyclical process, which involves four main steps: "(1) goal setting, (2) monitoring process and strategies, (3) feedback and (4) self-evaluation" (Steffens, 2006, p. 354). In other words, in the experiential flow of life, self-discovery learners need to set learning objectives for themselves—from a variety of rich ways to learn. They need to monitor how they are doing over time (through meta-cognition) and make changes to their strategies and tactics to be more effective and efficient. They need to solicit relevant feedback from the environment and others. Feedback (whether internal or external) has been labeled an "inherent catalyst" which promotes learning (Butler & Winne, 1995, p. 246).

Self-discovery learners need to evaluate their progress in their learning. It is understood that self-discovery learners make decisions based on their assessments of the situation. They have to engage their volitional (choice) strategies in order to protect the self-discovery learning against competing interests (DuBois & Staley, 1997). Emotional resilience and the control of learning anxieties are important for continuing focus even in the face of challenges. Further, self-discovery learners have to be able to identify opportunities and risks in their environments and to capitalize on these so-called "chance discovery(ies)" (Oehlmann, 2002, p. 4).

They have to self-manage but also coordinate their learning with others, given the wide dispersal of knowledge bases and skill sets and the rarity of "self-made" expertise without the influence of others. In another model, self-regulatory learning processes include "planning, knowledge activation, metacognitive monitoring and regulation, strategy deployment, and reflection" (Azevedo, 2007, p. 57). The level of abstraction in these conceptualizations highlights a core feature of self-discovery learning—the idea of its applicability in a variety of situations and through various phases of lifespan learning.

In another conceptualization, self-discovery learning is essentially trial-and-error learning. In this concept, learners form hypotheses of the world and then test those hypotheses with the realities. They have to notice counter examples and accept them as "meaningful and acceptable," and these examples have to lead to correct understandings (Horiguchi & Hirashima, 2001, p. 470). Self-discovery learners have to inductively, deductively, and inferentially analyze a large set of data—and avoid ignoring anomalous data; they have to self-correct their internal mental concepts and not fall into self-deceptions, illusions, or metamers. They need to form explanations that align with the facts (Horiguchi & Hirashima, 2001, p. 470).

The limits to the learning, conceptually, are those limits in the environment and in the conceptualization, initiative, and resources of the self-discovery learners. The power of self-discovery learning is that it may be applied to various knowledge domains; it is not only limited to a local learning situation. While there may potentially be varying levels of efficacy in these various domains, the tools of learning may transfer to enable deep learning in a number of contexts.

## Mixed Self-Discovery Learning Outcomes

For all its appeal as a relatively low-cost solution for some types of learning, self-discovery learning faces plenty of challenges. Some researchers have found poorer learning outcomes, with learners carrying a greater cognitive load and sometimes not arriving at the correct learning. Without the benefit of an expert guide, self-discovery learners have to often "sense-make" on their own, and novice mental models tend to misalign with expert conceptual models. Without the necessary mental schema to understand particular learning domains, learners will incur greater cognitive load costs to acquire new information (Ngu, Mit, Shahbodin, & Tuovinen, 2009). Such learners have changing needs over time, possibly needing to rely on some learning scaffolding for a period before being able to progress on their own. Simulations, which can evoke a learning context, are designed for self-discovery learning but tend to be relatively less transparent than expository instruction; because of this, they have sometimes resulted in knowledge gains that were "disappointing and/or unclear" without sufficient instructional support (Swaak & De Jong, 2000, p. 217) or sufficient declarative information (p. 223).

## Design: Guided Discovery

The rationale for limited guided discovery stems from plenty of educational research on human factors (the study of human capabilities from multi-disciplinary fields)—and the limits of human cognition and brain processing. Unstructured self-discovery is too cognitively inefficient and expensive without some degree of temporal scaffolding. Guided instruction works best (Merrill, 2007). That guidance may involve the integration of any number of instructional strategies in online spaces.

Some types of scaffolds involve information: verbal or textual instructions; explanations; examples; learning sequences; learner feedback; the tactical activation of certain types of information or mental states; the surfacing of learner epistemological beliefs of a certain field. Researchers have found that more complex understandings and expectation setting for the learning will lead to deeper explorations of the learning domains and higher learning outcomes (Pieschl, Stahl, & Bromme, 2008). Some scaffolds help learners pay attention to what is relevant in their learning and helps them surface and articulate their discoveries (Horiguchi & Hirashima, 2001). Other scaffolds enhance learner reflection—by encouraging note-taking, doodling, writing, and talking aloud as methods of reflection, exploration, self-generation of knowledge, and self-documentation of the learning. Open writing to a potential Web audience has been shown to enhance self-regulated learning (Baggetun & Wasson, 2006).

This self-documentation by learners may help them interpret the underlying patterns in order to surface broad generalizations of a particular domain (Williams & Lombrozo, 2010). Other tools enhance the ability to self-regulate time and to organize digital learning resources. Yet others enable learners to connect with co-learners and experts in order to learn and innovate together around knowledge construction (Saab, van Joolingen, & van Hout-Wolters, 2005).

If M. David Merrill's assertions are true that there are first principles of instruction, then guided discovery learning may actually benefit from having the structures of task-centered learning that is based on real-world tasks. His model suggests that the relevant cognitive structures have to be activated for the learner. The learners need to experience a demonstration of the skills to be learned in alignment with the content being acquired. And the learners need opportunities to apply the new skills with appropriate "intrinsic or corrective feedback" (Merrill, 2007, p. 269).

## The Affordances of the WWW and Internet for Self-Discovery Learning

The building of guided self-discovery learning has become much easier given the affordances of the World Wide Web (WWW) and the Internet, and the integration of cognitive research with multimedia building techniques (Clark & Mayer, 2008). Learning may be better designed to be complementary to human capabilities and skill sets. There are numerous tools that may be used as "ego extenders" to enhance the reach of human skills. Learning may be packaged into simulations that may be scalable to a much larger audience than a few learners—at relatively minimal marginal cost (after the initial build).

Further, virtual communities have sprung up around shared interests, knowledge-sharing, and knowledge-building, for rich interdependencies in a distributed cognition environment (Boland, Tenkasi, & Te'eni, 1994). Computer conferencing—and other rich technologies—offer more distributed ways to connect and learn (Bures, Abrami, & Amundsen, 2000).

Knowledge bases may be accessed by a variety of stakeholders, and these same users may create contents to share in a dynamic way (dePaula & Fischer, 2005). The knowledge itself is not only textual but of a rich multimedia variety. Various instantiations of software—wikis, blogs, learning management systems, repositories—have enabled work collaborations around knowledge. In the same way that self-efficacy is necessary for risk-taking in learning, researchers suggest that Internet self-efficacy is a critical skill set for self-learning (Joo, Bong, & Choi, 2000).

Online virtual spaces offer users plenty of access and control, which also aligns with the learner-based decision-making and determinacy. Transparent choice-making enhances the quality of the decisions made by learners, and it lowers the cost of following various learning paths.

## Guided Online Self-Discovery

The general research suggests that some structure is desirable for self-discovery learners, but the question is how much structure and what kind. Broadly speaking, some common frameworks for structuring the various instantiations of self-discovery learning include the following: narrations and storytelling, problem-based learning, project-based learning, case-based learning, simple problem-solving, and others. Simulations and games are understood to provide opportunities for experientially implicit learning: here, learners sample the environment, form hypotheses of how things work, and then strive to reconcile anomalies by understanding the underlying rules (Saab & Joolingen, 2005). Piece-meal apprenticeship work hones the skills of discovery-learners, project-to-project.

The "assistance dilemma" suggests a need to balance how much guided discovery support is given. Excessive support results in demotivated learners who become more passive; too little support results in learner frustrations and demotivations from emotional overload (Borek, McLaren, Karabinos, & Yaron, 2009, p. 391). Feedback may be immediate or delayed; adjustable levels of support may be set to offered tailored responses. Borek, et al. (2009) suggest that support may be withheld unless learners are far off track.

Given the range of self-discovery learners from various cultural contexts, it may be helpful to tailor some types of contents to align with those backgrounds. There are differences of self-regulation strategies between learners from different cultural contexts (Purdie & Hattie, 1996).

The scaffolding for discovery learning has to be encapsulated (or partially or fully hidden for simplicity) so it is not intrusive, but it has to be sufficiently attention-getting so as to be used for opt-in help-seeking. The research suggests that there is a theoretical appropriate level of assistance for the most efficient self-discovery learning.

The educational research on self-discovery adult learners is peripheral and incomplete. Often, it is merely descriptive and domain context-sensitive. Understanding who self-discovery learners are will require more information on a number of tracks.

## EXTANT QUESTIONS

Table 1, "Discovering Aspects of Self-Discovery Adult Learners," summarizes some foundational questions about self-discovery learners that have not yet been addressed in the educational literature. While these questions are phrased in a general way, these may be applied to the specific discovery learners targeted by a certain resource or site.

Table 1 capture some issues that may enhance the understanding of who self-discovery learners are, and especially who they are online. Having a stronger baseline understanding of self-discovery learners and their needs may open the way for more sophisticated designs to meet their needs.

### Research Methods

The move to online spaces enables a rich variety of ways to learn about self-discovery learners. This section will propose a few methods.

First, a variety of websites can aggregate back-end trace data from their users. They can track both mass behaviors, and they can track individual users. How may this be useful? With the identifying information removed, an organization may be able to track how a user joins an online community and interacts with it over time to acquire self-discovery learning. Some tools may allow the tracking of individuals through the WWW and Internet to understand how they tap various resources for particular learning.

Second, individual learners themselves may conduct heuristical self-studies and ruminate over their own self-discovery learning. They may maintain electronic diaries and records of their learning. They may highlight critical challenges and core decision points.

Third, online surveys may be used to capture people's experiences acquiring self-discovery learning skill sets and other relevant topics.

### Analyzing the Self-Discovery Learners for a Specific Site

It may be more effective to learn who self-discovery learners are for a particular domain...or even more specifically for a site. The self-discovery learners for the site below are university students who are adjusting to university life and dealing with some challenging stressors, and who may be technologically savvy but may not have the same social supports as when they were in their hometowns prior to attending university. The studies that have gone into who the discovery learners are for this site are beyond the purview of this paper, but a full analysis of the "virtual community" enabled by this site is forthcoming (Hai-Jew, 2011) (in press).

Focusing on specific and targeted users of a site offers sufficient delimiting of the audience for more specific information-gathering and analysis. Figure 1, "Tools for the Self-Discovery Learners at the University Life Café," showcases proximate support for discovery learning built into the features of the site.

The above site was built from scratch in 2008, and plenty of academic research went into its design. The use of information about self-discovery learners is a critical part of the consideration for the building of a site to meet particular aims. In the above circumstance, the focus was on promoting the emotional resilience of college students against suicide.

*Table 1. Discovering aspects of self-discovery adult learners*

| Aspect(s) of Self-Discovery Adult Learners | Some Extant Questions |
|---|---|
| Who | • Who are self-discovery learners?<br>• Who do they socialize with virtually in their learning? Which of these relationships are most conducive to their learning, and why?<br>• What is the sense of self-identity of self-discovery learners? Are there patterns to this self-identity?<br>• What life experiences have helped create self-discovery adult learners? What life experiences dissuade self-discovery learners, and why?<br>• Are there particular personality types that tend towards self-discovery learning? Are there particular personality attributes that are common in self-discovery learners? Why? Why not?<br>• Are there gender effects in terms of self-discovery learning? If so, what? And if so, why? |
| What | • What are the most important types of knowledge and skills for self-discovery learners to acquire in their various stages of learning?<br>• What sorts of opt-in help-seeking may be important for self-discovery learners? When is help-seeking most prevalent? When is it least prevalent?<br>• What are some triggers to help learners know when they should engage in help-seeking?<br>• What online resources are the most helpful for self-discovery learners, and why?<br>• What technologies and tools are the most accessible and user-friendly to self-discovery learners, and why?<br>• What kinds of examples are helpful for self-discovery learners, and why? What kinds of counter-examples are helpful for self-discovery learners, and why?<br>• What kinds of explanations and feedback are most helpful for self-discovery learners, and why? Which are least helpful, and why?<br>• Are there types of explanations and feedback that lead to negative learning? If so, why?<br>• What self-regulation skill sets do self-discovery learners have? Where may they improve? And then how may they improve? Are there tools for self-discovery learner self-awareness?<br>• What types of executive functions are most critical to self-discovery learners? Decision-making in topic selection? The setting of learning goals? The design of the learning path? The discipline and follow-through? The assessment of self-learning? The ability to continue and persist even in the face of setbacks and difficulties? The social interactions? The ability to recruit allies?<br>• Are there cultural differences between self-discovery adult learners from different backgrounds? If so, what are the differences, and how may those differences be designed to for more effective learning? |
| When | • What are the various stages of learning for self-discovery learners? Are these necessarily linear / non-linear or recursive or purely chronological? Why?<br>• At what point do self-discovery learners realize that they have achieved a learning goal? Does that achievement lead to more learning, or does it lead to less motivation for learning?<br>• When should particular types of resources and help support be offered to self-discovery learners in a learning sequence? When shouldn't resources be offered, and why?<br>• What are some methods for encapsulating opt-in help and other scaffolding for learning? What are some nuanced ways to design such support?<br>• Based on different tasks, what sorts of learning should happen when? What learning sequences are most effective?<br>• Are there certain developmental windows when self-discovery adult learners need to develop certain skill sets or awarenesses?<br>• Is there a life cycle of creativity for self-discovery adult learners?<br>• Is there a moment at which self-discovery adult learners peak in their learning (In the context of a life cycle? In the context of acquiring a certain skill set)? If so, when? If so, why? |
| Where | • Where will self-discovery learners go to seek relevant information, proper online experiences, suitable virtual camaraderie, and relevant live expertise (if relevant)?<br>• Where can self-discovery learners go to identify effective co-learners? |
| Why | • Why do self-discovery learners pursue particular types of information? Skill sets?<br>• What motivates self-discovery learners? Why are they motivated? |

*continued on following page*

*Table 1. Continued*

| Aspect(s) of Self-Discovery Adult Learners | Some Extant Questions |
|---|---|
| How | • How do self-discovery learners discover a field that they want to explore? How are they inspired to pursue certain types of learning?<br>• How do they get started acclimating to a new domain field? What is most effective at the early stages?<br>• How can learners maintain a sense of their own metacognition or awareness of their own learning?<br>• How can learners record and capture what is relevant to their own learning?<br>• How can self-discovery learners get past Meno's Paradox—or knowing when they should pay attention to new learning about which they have no background? In other words, how do they know what is relevant?<br>• How do self-learners find out what their own learning preferences are?<br>• How do self-learners know how to set goals for their own learning that are reasonable and possible given their contexts?<br>• How do self-discovery learners know that they have mistakes in their own mental models as compared to experts' conceptual models?<br>• How will self-discovery learners continue to evolve their skill sets from novice to expert levels of skill sets?<br>• How transferable are self-discovery learning skills across different learning domains?<br>• How do self-discovery learners maintain a deep sense of motivation over time? |

*Figure 1. Tools for the self-discovery learners at the University Life Café*

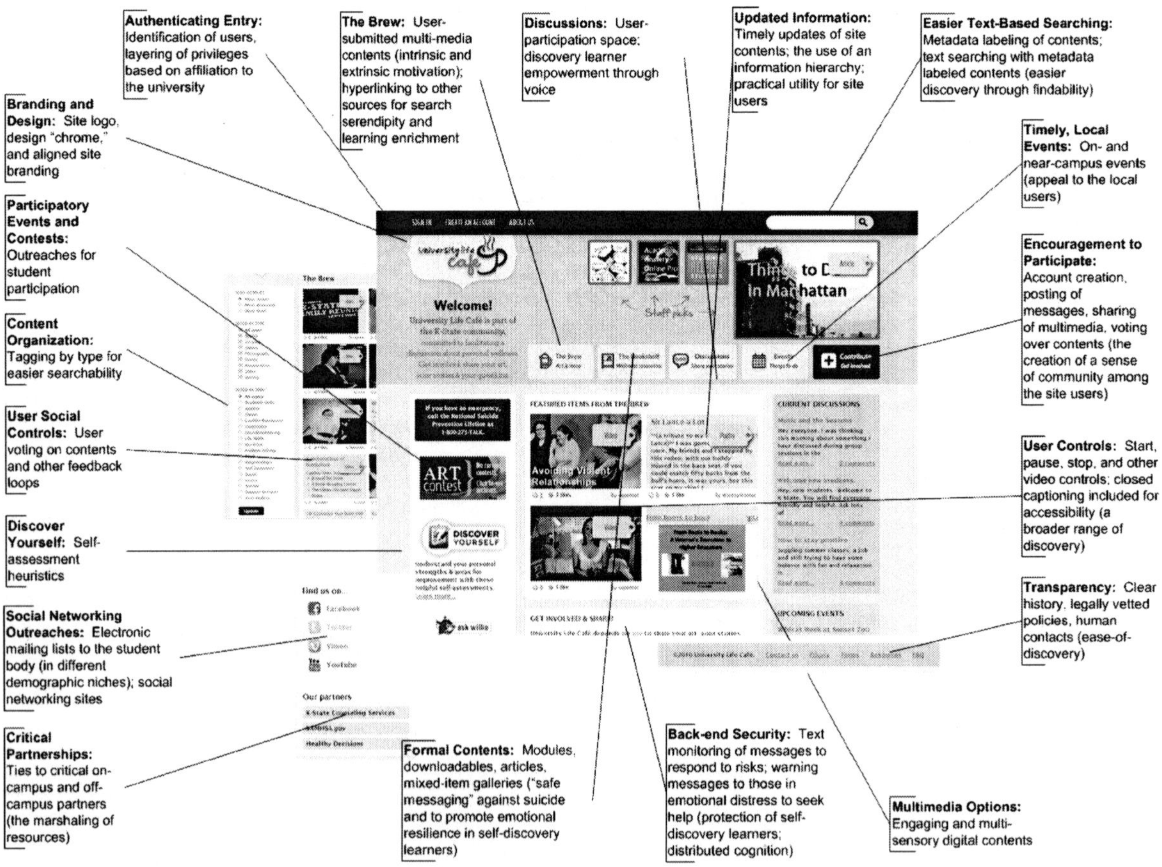

Even if a site is extant, given the ability to componentized different parts, specific tools may be created to enhance the experiences of self-discovery learners.

## FUTURE CONSIDERATIONS

Ideally, academics and others will conduct further research into self-discovery learning and ways that online spaces may be harnessed for richer self-learning. The severe limits of formal higher education structures to meet the needs of the world's burgeoning population are well known, and harnessing the affordances of the WWW and Internet may be a critical tool in ensuring wider learning and improved quality of lives everywhere. Human potential is a terrible thing to waste.

Knowing who self-discovery learners are will certainly not be a simple endeavor. Conceptualizations of who these learners are will also evolve and change with the different learners coming online.

## CONCLUSION

This chapter provides an overview of the educational literature on self-discovery learning in three general facets: (1) their self-motivation and drive; (2) their self-regulatory (executive) skill set; and (3) their mixed self-discovery learning outcomes. It offers a view of many gaps in knowledge which may be addressed through various WWW and Internet and information and communication technology (ICT) affordances and general research approaches. Finally, this chapter offers a very succinct look at some features designed for self-discovery learners in a particular website at a university. This example serves as a small embodiment of the abstract concepts of striving to understand self-discovery learners.

## ACKNOWLEDGMENT

This is for Harold and Amy, who encouraged exploration and risk-taking. Thank you.

## REFERENCES

Azevedo, R. (2007). Understanding the complex nature of self-regulatory processes in learning with computer-based learning environments: An introduction. *Metacognition and Learning, 2*, 57–65. doi:10.1007/s11409-007-9018-5

Baggetun, R., & Wasson, B. (2006). Self-regulated learning and open writing. *European Journal of Education, 41*(3/4), 453–472. doi:10.1111/j.1465-3435.2006.00276.x

Boland, R. J., Tenkasi, R. V., & Te'eni, D. (1994). Designing information technology to support distributed cognition. *Organization Science, 5*(3), 456–475. doi:10.1287/orsc.5.3.456

Borek, A., McLaren, B. M., Karabinos, M., & Yaron, D. (2009). How much assistance is helpful to students in discovery learning? In U. Cress, V. Dimitrova, & M. Specht (Eds.), *The Proceedings of EC-TEL 2009, LNCS 5794*, (pp. 391–404). Berlin, Germany: Springer-Verlag.

Bures, E. M., Abrami, P. C., & Amundsen, C. (2000). Student motivation to learn via computer conferencing. *Research in Higher Education, 41*(5), 593–621. doi:10.1023/A:1007071415363

Butler, D. L., & Winne, P. H. (1995). Feedback and self-regulated learning: A theoretical synthesis. *Review of Educational Research, 65*(3), 245–281.

Clark, R. C., & Mayer, R. E. (2008). *E-learning and the science of instruction: Proven guidelines for consumers and designers of multimedia learning*. San Francisco, CA: Pfeiffer.

dePaula, R., & Rischer, G. (2005). *Knowledge management: Why learning from the past is not enough!* (pp.21 – 53). Retrieved February 13, 2010, from http://l3d.cs.colorado.edu/~gerhard/papers/km-final-2005.pdf.

DuBois, N. F., & Staley, R. K. (1997). A self-regulated learning approach to teaching educational psychology. *Educational Psychology Review, 9*(2), 171–197. doi:10.1023/A:1024792529797

Hai-Jew, S. (2008). Scaffolding discovery learning spaces. *MERLOT Journal of Online Learning and Teaching, 4*(4), 533–548. Retrieved Febrary 14, 2010, at http://jolt.merlot.org/vol4no4/hai-jew_1208.pdf/.

Hai-Jew, S. (2011). (Forthcoming). Creating an emotionally resilient virtual student community at K-State. *The University Life Café*.

Horiguchi, T., & Hirashima, T. (2001). The role of counterexamples in discovery learning environment: Awareness of the chance for learning. In the *Proceedings of JSAI 2001 Workshops, LNAI 2253* (pp. 468–474). Berlin, Germany: Springer-Verlag.

Joo, Y.-J., Bong, M., & Choi, H.-J. (2000). Self-efficacy for self-regulated learning, academic self-efficacy, and Internet self-efficacy in Web-based instruction. *Educational Technology Research and Development, 48*(2), 5–17. doi:10.1007/BF02313398

Malone, D. M. (2008). Inquiry-based early childhood teacher preparation: The personal learning plan method. *Early Childhood Education Journal, 35*, 531–542. .doi:10.1007/s10643-008-0237-4

Merriam, S. B., & Caffarella, R. S. (1999). *Learning in adulthood: A comprehensive guide* (2nd ed., p. 289). San Francisco, CA: Jossey Bass Publishers.

Merrill, M. D. (2008). Why basic principles of instruction must be present in the learning landscape, whatever form it takes, for learning to be effective, efficient, and engaging. In J. Visser & M. Visser-Valfrey (Eds.), *Learners in a changing learning landscape* (pp. 267–275). Springer Science + Business Media B.V.

Ngu, B. H., Mit, E., Shahbodin, F., & Tuovinen, J. (2009). Chemistry problem solving instruction: A comparison of three computer-based formats for learning from hierarchical network problem representations. *Instructional Science, 37*, 21–24. doi:10.1007/s11251-008-9072-7

Oehlmann, R. (2002). Metacognitive and computational aspects of chance discovery. *New Generation Computing, 21*(2003), 3–12. Ohmaha, Ltd., Springer-Verlag.

Pieschl, S., Stahl, E., & Bromme, R. (2008). Epistemological beliefs and self-regulated learning with hypertext. *Metacognition Learning, 3,* 17–37. Springer Science + Business Media, LLC. DOI 10.1007/s11409-007-9008-7

Purdie, N., & Hattie, J. (1996). Cultural differences in the use of strategies for self-regulated learning. *American Educational Research Journal, 33*(4), 845–871.

Ranson, S., Martin, J., Nixon, J., & McKeown, P. (1996). Towards a theory of learning. *British Journal of Educational Studies, 44*(1), 9–26. doi:10.1080/00071005.1996.9974055

Saab, N., & van Joolingen, W. (2005). Supporting collaborative discovery learning by presenting a tool. In the *Proceedings of the Computer Support for Collaborative Learning* (CSCL) (pp. 541–546). International Society of the Learning Sciences.

Saab, N., van Joolingen, W. R., & van Hout-Wolters, B. H. A. M. (2005). Communication in collaborative discovery learning. *The British Journal of Educational Psychology*, *75*, 603–621. doi:10.1348/000709905X42905

Steffens, K. (2006). Self-regulated learning in technology-enhanced learning environments: Lessons of a European peer review. *European Journal of Education*, *41*(3/4), 353–379. doi:10.1111/j.1465-3435.2006.00271.x

Swaak, J., & De Jong, T. (2000). Learner vs. system control in using online support for simulation-based discovery learning. *Learning Environments Research*, *4*, 217–241. doi:10.1023/A:1014434804876

Wang, J., & Li, F.-Z. (2007). Autonomic learning model and algorithm based on DFL. *2007 IEEE International Conference on Granular Computing*, (pp. 259–264). IEEE.

Williams, J. J., & Lombrozo, T. (2010). The role of explanation in discovery and generalization: Evidence from category learning. *Cognitive Science*, *34*, 776–806. doi:10.1111/j.1551-6709.2010.01113.x

## KEY TERMS AND DEFINITIONS

**Authentic:** Real-world, based on reality; non-theoretical but applied.

**Autonomy:** Independence, self-sufficiency, self-regulation.

**Cognition:** Perception and thinking, the state of knowing or being aware.

**Constructivism:** The concept of the importance of a learner actively creating meaning in order to achieve learning.

**Deep Transfer:** The ability to apply learning and skills from one situation to another context.

**Explicit:** Clearly defined or expressed.

**Goal:** A defined aim or objective.

**Implicit:** Suggested or implied, not clearly stated or expressed.

**Instantiation:** The manifestation or express instance of a particular website or software tool.

**Introspection:** Self-awareness.

**Rote Memorization:** The use of repeated exposure to particular ideas to memorize learning.

**Scaffold:** A temporary learning structure.

**Schema:** A conceptualization, a mental model, an underlying pattern.

**Self Discovery Learning:** Learner-initiated and learner-driven acquisition of knowledge and skills.

**Sensemaking:** The phenomena of a person striving to understand new or unfamiliar information or a new context; the reconciling of contradictory elements in a circumstance in order to surface information.

**Situated Cognition:** The phenomenon of learning within a certain applied real-world context; the combination of knowing and doing simultaneously.

**Socio-Technical Space:** An interactive space that brings together people through mediating technologies.

**Temporal:** Based in time, temporary.

**Volition:** Willpower and intention.

**Worked Example:** A story problem or case that is "solved" by professionals for the learners to serve as an example to learn from.

# Section 2
# Discovery Learning Environments and Tools

# Chapter 3
# The LiveAbility House: A Collaborative Adventure in Discovery Learning

**Sarah D. Kirby**
*North Carolina State University, USA*

**Debra M. Sellers**
*Kansas State University, USA*

## ABSTRACT

*This chapter follows efforts of an online community of practice whose mission is to make individual educational experiences for family caregivers widely available. The case study illustrates the collaborative learning and creative processes of the community of practice as it worked to construct and transform informal educational content into engaging, interactive, and immersive educational tools for its intended audience. As part of its efforts, the CoP created The LiveAbility House, a virtual demonstration home, constructed in Second Life®. This virtual home is designed to teach individuals about real life universal design principles and assistive technology devices that may increase their ability to remain living at home despite physical or cognitive challenges they may encounter due to aging, illness, or disability. In addition to the creation of a virtual learning experience, the chapter also addresses plans to then take that experience out of the virtual world and apply and demonstrate learning principles in a real world setting.*

## INTRODUCTION

In this chapter, we detail the development of a specific project, The LiveAbility House (TLH), constructed within the virtual world of Second Life®. The LiveAbility House is a virtual home, built to educate individuals about universal design principles and assistive technology devices. Specifically, the goal of TLH is to raise public awareness of design features and assistive technology that can make it possible to remain in a home with physical or cognitive challenges due to aging, illness, or disability.

DOI: 10.4018/978-1-61350-320-1.ch003

Copyright © 2012, IGI Global. Copying or distributing in print or electronic forms without written permission of IGI Global is prohibited.

This project was formulated and implemented within the structure of a national community of practice with a mission to create informal educational materials for family caregivers. We discuss the importance of the community of practice as a foundation for the project, the partnerships that were formed as a result of the community's work over several years, the expansion of the community into immersive learning environments, and the current status of the project. We will emphasize the challenges that we faced as subject-matter experts exploring the use of an innovative technological platform for informal education. Finally, we discuss the limitations and projected next steps for the project.

## BACKGROUND: LAYING THE FOUNDATION

In order to fully understand the developmental process that took place in developing TLH, we will discuss the context of our work. A holistic, historic, and long-range view of our mission is necessary, we believe, to understand TLH as a progression of innovative educational outreach that has existed for 100 years. The land-grant university and Cooperative Extension systems and the eXtension initiative and corresponding communities of practice provided the foundation for the project's inception; the setting was crucial for its development.

### The Land-Grant University and Cooperative Extension Systems

Land-grant universities were established by the Morrill Act (1862), which provided funds from the sale of public lands to establish colleges concentrating in agricultural and mechanical arts for the "liberal and practical education of the industrial classes on the several pursuits and professions in life." In 1890 a second Morrill Act established sixteen land-grant universities to address the needs of the African-American population, again with a focus on agriculture and mechanical arts. These institutions are often referred to as historically-black colleges and universities.

The Cooperative Extension System (CES) was initially established through the Smith-Lever Act of 1914 and extends the educational mission of land-grant universities to include informal education, outreach, and engagement. CES utilizes the research of academicians at the land-grant university to develop, implement, and evaluate evidence-based educational programs to help citizens improve the quality of their lives.

### The Cooperative Extension System and Adult Learners

Early on, Cooperative Extension targeted the education of adult learners through concrete, hands-on learning application. The Smith-Lever Act specifically mentions the development of practical applications of research knowledge and the provision of instruction and applied demonstrations of existing or improved practices or technologies in agriculture (National Institute of Food and Agriculture [NIFA], 2010a). The Extension Workers' Creed (Lloyd, 1922) is reflective of a philosophy that centers the acquisition of knowledge and application with the learner. The Creed begins with the following statements:

*I Believe in people and their hopes, their aspirations, and their faith; in their right to make their own plans and arrive at their own decisions; in their ability and power to enlarge their lives and plan for the happiness of those they love.*

*I Believe that education, of which Extension is an essential part, is basic in stimulating individual initiative, self-determination, and leadership; that these are the keys to democracy and that people when given facts they understand, will act not only in their self-interest, but also in the interest of society.*

Encouraging adult learning principles therefore has a long history within Cooperative Extension and forms the bedrock of Cooperative Extension educational programming today. Dialogue and discussion about adult learning theory and application is often found within The Journal of Extension, which "expands and updates the research and knowledge base for U.S. Extension professionals and other outreach educators to improve their effectiveness....(it) also serves as a forum for emerging and contemporary issues affecting U.S. Cooperative Extension education (n.d.)." A search conducted in the summer of 2010 in The Journal of Extension for "Knowles," (Malcolm Knowles, widely thought of as the father of adult education theory) resulted in 49 citations; "adult learning" garnered more than 110. Recent examples within the journal include discussions about transformative education (Franz, Garst, Baughman, Smith, & Peters, 2009) and dialogue education (Driscoll, 2009). "As the largest adult education institution in America, Cooperative Extension should ground organizational operations in adult education theory" (Franz, 2007).

## The Cooperative Extension System Network

CES is truly a nationwide system for the dissemination of education, as each state and U.S. territory has a Cooperative Extension office at its land-grant university and a network of regional as well as local offices (NIFA, 2010b). This network is supported by a variety of partnerships, including the United States Department of Agriculture (USDA), part of the executive branch of the Federal Government, and county governments. USDA supports CES through the National Institute of Food and Agriculture (NIFA), formerly known as the Cooperative State Research, Education, and Extension Service (CSREES), and provides federal funding to the system. NIFA's mission is "to advance knowledge for agriculture, the environment, human health and well-being, and communities by supporting research, education, and extension programs in the Land-Grant University System and other partner organizations" (2009).

As part of this mission, NIFA offers programs within the discipline of Family Science. These programs work to strengthen families and improve the quality of life of individuals through national collaborations. An outcome of these programs includes an increase in understanding of the overall well-being of families in American society (NIFA, Family Science, 2010). Through program leadership, NIFA helps the system identify and address current issues and problems on a national level.

These issues and problems have changed since 1914. Initially, Cooperative Extension was important for rural areas and focused on issues in agriculture and home economics. Traditionally, Cooperative Extension relied on face-to-face teaching, field visits, and postal mailings to communicate with clients and to reach its clientele with important educational information. Now, issues within urban and suburban communities must be addressed, and they often represent different needs. In addition, the digital age has changed communication and education. Cooperative Extension, with its 100-year history of providing services, is a well-established national dissemination system for research and evidence-based, non-formal education that is relevant for today's families. However, the Cooperative Extension System (CES) is aware of the need to engage traditional and emerging clients in non-traditional ways. One strategy recently implemented consists of the creation of the eXtension initiative.

## eXtension and Communities of Practice

One national initiative of the Cooperative Extension System is eXtension. It "provides objective and research and evidence-based information and learning opportunities that help people improve their lives" (eXtension, 2010) and is reflective of the CES's historical mission. Meeting the need for credible, accurate real-time learning that is relevant and effective for traditional and non-traditional clients, eXtension is innovative and has created a national presence for the system. The web site for eXtension, http://www.extension.org, is designed as an educational environment that is both interactive and customer-centered (eXtension, 2008). Informational articles, in-depth learning lessons, podcasts, frequently asked questions, decision-making tools, and the opportunity to "ask an expert" an individual question are all methods used to provide educational content to a clientele that may be unaware of Cooperative Extension offices in their states or counties.

The initiative works through partnerships among the land-grant universities and collaborative relationships among their educators. These partnerships and relationships are formalized by eXtension through a community of practice (CoP) structure. Communities of practice are "groups of people who share a concern or a passion for something they do and learn how to do it better as they interact regularly" (Wenger, 2006). Communities of practice also "collaborate over an extended period of time, sharing ideas and strategies, determine solutions, and build innovations" (Learning Theories, 2008). With eXtension support, faculty from many different land-grant universities come together to address critical issues within this community of practice structure.

Collaboration as a strategy for content development is receiving more attention as a viable method of completing needed work within the Cooperative Extension System. Two National Program Leaders within the National Institute of Food and Agriculture advocated for the importance of partnerships (Gerrior & Crocoll, 2008):

*Partnerships between state and community agencies, as well as with private partners, facilitate coordination and expansion of nutrition, health, and housing information and supportive services...the need for these services and for education, and outreach at the state, regional, and community level will continue to grow as the vast Baby Boomer generation ages over the coming decades.*

There are other reasons to establish partnerships to help ensure successful educational programs. While audiences are growing, they are also becoming more diverse, and resources continue to shrink or disappear. Partnerships between Cooperative Extension and other service and state agencies are a possible strategy for leveraging resources (Boone, Sleichter, Miller, & Breiner, 2007).

Faculty members from across the nation join a CoP for various reasons. For some, it is a voluntary activity with perceived benefits of increased collaboration, extension of resources, an opportunity to engage in critical and creative thinking, and an ability to reach a larger audience of citizens for programmatic efforts (eXtension, 2010). Others join because of an interest or need to address a specific topic. Some of the current subjects addressed through eXtension include agrosecurity and floods, home energy, beef cattle, science, imported fire ants, and family caregiving.

## The Family Caregiving Community of Practice

The Family Caregiving Community of Practice (FC/CoP) was formed in 2006 and was created in order to provide a national "one-stop shop" for educational resources created by the Cooperative Extension System. Prior to the development of the FC/CoP, faculty members working in different states could, and did, duplicate each other's programmatic endeavors. The FC/CoP drew faculty members from a variety of disciplines including health, gerontology, family economics, and housing, all of whom shared a common interest in helping family caregivers. Their varied background and expertise brought richness and multi-faceted perspectives to the community: "having others who share your overall view of the domain and yet bring their individual perspectives on any given problem creates a social learning system that goes beyond the sum of its parts" (Wenger, McDermott & Snyder, 2002, p. 34).

Over time, the community began to emerge as a "... group of people who interact, learn together, build relationships, and in the process develop a sense of belonging and mutual commitment (Wenger, McDermott & Snyder, 2002, p. 34). Members worked together to create the overall vision for the CoP, develop educational resources related to their own expertise and provide peer review for other members. Through this process, members often discovered complementary and crossover areas that encouraged natural collaborations (chronic health and dietary concerns; employed family caregivers and family finances). Although we were faculty members from two separate institutions, North Carolina State University and Kansas State University, and two distinctive disciplines, housing and adult development and aging, we discovered a natural collaboration in the area of universal design and assistive technology.

This possible pairing of our subject matter areas encouraged us to consider the integration of key concepts that could significantly impact the lives of family caregivers and individuals who were aging or living with a disability. We explored the possibility of working together in a partnership positioned within the FC/CoP that would allow us to pool resources and efforts to reach the intended audience (Sellers, Crocker, Nichols, Kirby, & Brintnall-Peterson, 2009).

## INTEGRATING SUBJECT MATTER CONTENT

### Family Caregiving

One of the important concepts for the partnership to be successful was to integrate the disciplines represented by both faculty members within the context of family caregiving. The number of older persons with disabilities living in the community has increased in the past two decades (Redfoot & Houser, 2010), and the provision of assistance to older adults to promote their ability to function safely and independently in their homes is a public health issue (Gitlin, Earland, Piersol, & Shaw, 2010). The caregiving population is estimated at 65.7 million people (National Alliance on Caregiving and AARP, 2009), and represents a natural audience for education regarding the creation of living environments that assist caregivers in providing care, and that help care receivers maintain independence. There is a need to promote the usefulness of these types of adaptations (Cooke, Yearns, & Martin, 2005).

Most caregivers are female and are, on average, 48 years old. Care recipients are also largely female, with an average age of 61 (National Alliance on Caregiving and AARP, 2009). One of the main issues faced by these care partners is chronic disease, which is more prevalent as a person ages (Agency for Healthcare Research and Quality, 2002), and is detrimental to an individual's ability to live independently within her own home and community (Tilly, 2010). Common diagnoses for care recipients include Alzheimer's disease, mental/emotional illness, cancer, heart disease, and stroke, and related physical and cognitive limitations often result in a need for caregivers to assist with bathing, feeding, housework, meal preparation and dressing (National Alliance on Caregiving and AARP, 2009).

Other issues are contextual to the home: more than half (55 percent) of care receivers live in their own homes, while twenty-four percent live in the homes of their caregivers (National Alliance on Caregiving & AARP, 2009). However, "most homes were not designed and built for the needs of aging residents or caregiving" (MetLife Mature Market Institute, 2010).

## Universal Design and Home Modifications

Home modifications are those retrofits or changes made to a home that help reduce hazards and provide support for independence (National Resource Center on Supportive Housing and Home Modifications, 2003). Universal design is "the design of all products and environments to be as usable as possible by as many people as possible regardless of age, ability, or situation" (Universal Design Education, 2009). Universal design features include roll-in showers, wider doorways, appliances with front mounted controls, and lever handled door hardware that helps individuals master their environment by supporting and enhancing physical and mental abilities. The home environment can not only provide safety and support for those receiving care, but can also help support and protect the strengths and abilities of those providing care (Olsen, Ehrenkrantz, & Hutchings, 1993). Modifying a home to include universal design features can assist greatly with caregiving. Home modifications may aid healthy outcomes by reducing risks of home injuries, increasing the home's accessibility, and maintaining independence for the home's residents (Oswald & Wahl, 2004).

## Assistive Technology

Assistive technology may bring to mind images of complicated computer systems. There are many definitions of assistive technology, but here we will use the phrase as "a generic or umbrella term that covers technologies, equipment, devices, apparatus, services, systems, processes and environmental modifications used by disabled and/or elderly people to overcome the social, infrastructural and other barriers to independence, full participation in society and carrying out activities safely and easily" (Hersh & Johnson, 2008). Examples of assistive technology include low-cost, low-tech items such as a cane used to aid in mobility or high-cost, high-tech items such as adapted vans. Providing education on this topic is an emerging need as the use of assistive technology appears to be increasing in recent years (Freedman, Agree, Martin, & Cornman, 2005; Houser, Gibson, & Redfoot, 2010) and caregivers may be an instrumental force for assistive technology use, although more research to establish this link is needed (Pressler & Ferraro, 2010).

## The Integration of Family Caregiving, Universal Design, and Assistive Technology

As our first entry into this partnership, we initially operated as a pair to create educational resources that would complement each other's work within the areas of universal design and assistive technology. Utilizing resources provided by the eXtension community of practice, we wrote articles and questions and linked to each other's content. As the work progressed, we began to discuss if and how our complementary disciplines could be more fully integrated and explored whether we could create educational resources together that would not be possible as individuals within our own states. We discussed this concept with other community of practice members and were encouraged by the feedback we received. One of the possibilities presented to us was the use of Second Life®.

## Investigating an Immersive Learning Environment as a Strategy for Integrated Content Development

Faculty members find opportunities through eXtension to engage in new and innovative ways of thinking and creating content, and are encouraged to try innovative outreach methods to audiences as well. Social media was promoted by eXtension as a way to connect with traditional and non-traditional audiences (eXtension, 2009). Examples introduced to community of practice members included Facebook, Twitter, YouTube, and Flickr. In addition, eXtension started to experiment with the possible use of virtual worlds as an educational method. The first eXtension island in Second Life® (SL) was purchased on May 4, 2007 (K. Gamble, personal communication September 20, 2010). Neither of us were familiar with social media, and we had little understanding of its capabilities, reach, or meaning.

We were first fully introduced to Second Life® in February 2008. Second Life® is a free, Internet-based virtual world, but it is not a game. Global users, called residents, interact with each other in a variety of different environments. Some residents choose to build their own environments and items, while others simply visit established places and events. Residents independently choose where to go within the virtual world and also choose what to experience; the choices are extensive, and include social activities such as parties, recreational pursuits such as golfing, educational opportunities, such as attending lectures, and a myriad of other possible activities. Search functions, similar to those on the web, provide SL residents with the opportunity of finding social, recreational, and educational places and events of interest to explore.

Immediately, we viewed SL as a viable strategy for packaging our content in a truly integrated, and innovative, manner. The concept of a virtual home was a natural development in our thinking as our content areas pose specific challenges for adult learners. Effective education for adults includes opportunities to visualize concepts and manipulate products to see how they work. To this end, demonstration homes have been used by a number of universities to display universal design construction, energy efficient building design, and other related principles (Beitz, Brewer & Kirby, 1993; Deitz, Mulford & Case, 2009; LSU Ag Center, 2010; Utah State University, 2010). Many individuals with disabilities are not familiar with assistive technology as a means of providing possible support, and education to raise awareness is needed (Kaye, Yeager, & Reed, 2008). In Kansas, an educational program complemented by an assistive technology device kit has been effective for demonstrating assistive technology and its benefits (Sellers, 2010) and a universal design gadget kit has been used in Iowa (Yearns, 2004). However, demonstration homes and item kits are restricted by their geographical location, limited distribution, need for financial support, and at times, a lack of local expertise.

The idea of The LiveAbility House was grounded in our belief that we could create an environment that would simulate these real-life efforts, as Second Life® is a place "that immerse(s) the participant in a setting that includes sound and visual cues, rich textures and realistic perspective" (Johnson & Levine, 2009, pg. 1). Others have found that SL environments can be used to demonstrate real life principles in similar content areas in a virtual world (Beard, Wilson, Morra, & Keelan, 2009; Boulos, Hetherington, & Wheeler, 2007), and that they are able to "provide a bridge for users that enable them to envision real-life possibilities" (Toth-Cohen & Gallagher, 2009, p. 11).

As well, other sites within SL provide education with similar subject matter. One such example is Health Info Island, from the National Library of Medicine's Special Information Services. This island houses a medical library and a consumer health library (Greater Midwest Region of the National Network/National Library of Medicine, 2010). Other relevant organizations with a presence in SL include The American Cancer Society and the Centers for Disease Control and Prevention (American Cancer Society, 2009; Centers for Disease Control, n.d.). The Centers for Disease Control writes that "Using social media tools has become an effective way to expand reach, foster engagement, and increase access to credible, science-based health messages" (Centers for Disease Control, 2010, p. 1).

Older adults do utilize Internet based resources for information on aging. Those using websites also indicated that they use other social media sites including Facebook, Twitter and YouTube, (Brossoie, Roberto, Willis-Walton, Reynolds, 2010). In addition, SL provides opportunities to reach our targeted population. Virtual Ability Island was built for SL residents with disabilities and utilizes Knowles' theory of adult education in the framework for its development (Zielke, Roome, & Krueger, 2009). Older adults have shown the ability to navigate in virtual worlds (Foreman, Stanton-Fraser, Wilson, Duffy, & Parnell, 2005). Caregiver support also exists in SL (personal communication, C. Perryman, February 19, 2009).

The LiveAbility House project crystallized after discussion with eXtension administrators and staffers regarding the feasibility of this idea from a technical perspective. We decided to pursue TLH within Second Life® as a project that would allow us to:

- Participate in the continuing transformation of Cooperative Extension;
- Provide leadership for other faculty within Cooperative Extension interested in exploring the use of technology for educational programming efforts;
- Leverage the resources found within eXtension and the FC/CoP;
- Support the content development efforts of the FC/CoP
- Establish new partnerships for the FC/CoP;
- Integrate two complementary fields into one shared educational resource;
- Modify, eliminate and add elements with minimal effort and little to no cost;
- Apply adult learning principles in a new, innovative medium;
- Develop, implement, and evaluate a unique educational opportunity for a global audience that would not be possible individually or in a real life setting.

## CONSTRUCTING THE LIVEABILITY HOUSE

### Expanding the Community of Practice to Include Members with Knowledge of Content Delivery through Immersive Worlds

As faculty members, we were subject matter specialists with expertise in housing, gerontology, and adult development, but had no workable knowledge of Second Life® or the use of innovative and emerging technologies for educational dissemination. Although we were enthused by the possibilities and eager to explore the use of a pioneering technological platform for informal education, we were well aware that we were likely to fail as we lacked technical competency and needed to develop skills in this area (Sobrero, 2008). We needed experts in technology to support and engage us, as well as assist with the necessary tasks we needed to complete in order to build TLH (Riel & Polin, 2004). The structure of the FC/CoP, housed as it was within the eXtension initiative, allowed us to explore and develop partnerships that answered this need.

We assembled a team of individuals who joined the project voluntarily because of their own interests. These additional partners included an administrator from eXtension; a staff member from eXtension; and two staff members from Kansas State University Agricultural Experiment Station and Cooperative Extension Service. All of the new members had extensive expertise in SL. The eXtension administrator answered questions regarding financial and other resources at our disposal for the developmental process. He also managed our project as one aspect of the entire eXtension initiative within SL. The eXtension project coordinator supervised the actual endeavor within the SL environment. She queried us as subject-matter experts, and we shared our knowledge and expertise in universal design and assistive technology. She then translated this knowledge into a workable plan within the SL environment. She recruited several volunteers who joined the project as builders. Staff members from Kansas State University Agricultural Experiment Station and Cooperative Extension Service participated in the planning discussions, provided important perspectives about the inner workings of SL, helped with building the project, and provided individual instruction. This instruction was crucial to developing a level of comfort with immersive worlds that enabled the project to move forward.

## Developing Comfort with Immersive Worlds as a Method of Educational Delivery

Johnson and Levine (2009) use Maslow's Hierarchy of Needs (1943) to discuss the learning behaviors of new members in virtual worlds, and we believe that our experiences with instruction and learning reflect this pattern. Maslow's Hierarchy includes five levels of needs. In order for the individual to move to higher levels, the lower levels must first be met. Maslow's five levels, beginning with the lowest, are: physiological, safety and security, love/belonging, self-esteem, and self actualization. Although physiological needs aren't truly evident within SL (beyond clothing and styling of the avatar), there is a need for safety (level 2) that most new residents desire. According to the researchers, safety involves being watchful for possible dangers or situations that should be avoided and warding off potential embarrassments that may arise as a result of being new. Inexperienced residents want to feel safe in their interactions with other individuals.

Early instruction centered on understanding the language of this new world; only then could we take on the next step of visiting SL. Our new community of practice members embraced the daunting task of helping us navigate our way through the world of avatars, islands, landmarks, builds, and sims. The opportunity to visit with a mentor was invaluable, and provided us with the opportunity to begin to comprehend the vast potential for the development of the project. Just within the eXtension site, there were a number of exhibits that we were able to tour, including a virtual state fair. Within our real-life world context, the exhibits were relevant to us.

We were able to pursue this exploration with a "safety net" that prevented us from becoming overly frustrated, placed in a situation where we could be ridiculed by others, and abandoning SL. This is not to say that we did not experience a steep learning curve. Just understanding the commands and attaining the skills necessary to operate our avatars took concentrated time and effort. We needed to design our avatars, including the configuration of a body shape, selection of facial features, and the attachment of hair, jewelry, and clothing. While it seemed to us that this should be a simple and fun task, we did have quite a few mishaps. One of us spent an entire training session without hair due to an accidental detachment and inability to relocate the item in the inventory folder. Fortunately, this incident and other similar types occurred under the safe and watchful eye of our experienced members and we were able to make mistakes and learn new skills with a minimum of embarrassment. The importance of this safety net should not be underestimated in terms of the foundation it supplied for the successful progression of the overall project.

The next two levels are love/belonging and self-esteem. According to Johnson and Levine (2009), these stages reflect the desire of the new resident to seek out friends, while the fourth level may be found through an increase in interaction and exploration in the virtual world. In virtual worlds, learning often happens through experiences and interactions within a social network of friends. At first, we had little interest in interacting with other avatars as we were overwhelmed with learning basic navigational skills. One of us actively avoided interactions by ignoring communications or logging out of SL whenever approached or when another avatar was present. As our skill level increased, we found that we wanted to learn to communicate and engage others.

In our case, we relied heavily on our technical experts to help us develop skills used to communicate within the SL world. Our guides helped us learn and practice communication through chat, with an eventual move to audio interactions. As we toured SL over time with them, we were able to draw upon their expertise, ask questions, and were often introduced to their friends, contacts, groups, and preferred locations and events. From these, we were able to begin to develop our own social network and began to feel more competent in our ability to navigate this new world.

Finally, Johnson and Levine note that eventually the learner becomes more capable and that the learner no longer thinks of him/herself as being new to the virtual world. At this stage the individual moves from "competent" to "expert." As one example, we encountered an issue where another individual appeared to use our intellectual property and we were forced to investigate and resolve possible violation of the DMCA (Digital Millennium Copyright Act) law. This was an unexpected and interesting situation for us and required us to explore not only the copyright foundation involved in virtual worlds, but also how to solve potential conflicts in this new technology. Johnson and Levine write that only at this expert level can one begin to "visualize learning applications that are truly reflective of the potential of the space" (p. 5). Although we do not profess to have achieved self-actualization as represented by this level, we do believe that because of the expansion of the community of practice, our comfort level has significantly increased and we feel with further learning we can fully embrace the potential of this current project.

## Original Vision

As we developed comfort in-world, we were very much aware that this was a new endeavor for us, and for Cooperative Extension. We recognized that our thought processes and decisions were likely to change. In order to capture the developmental course in real-time, one of our first acts was to establish a blog in order to track our progress (http://extensionfamilycaregivingslp.blogspot.com).

Through this blog, we have a historical record of the project as it evolved, and TLH has changed significantly over time. However, even as the project matured, the original goal of raising public awareness of universal design features and assistive technology that can make it possible to remain in the home with physical or cognitive challenges due to aging, illness, or disability has remained constant.

Our original vision was focused on designing a model template home that featured universal design and assistive technology as an illustration of what could be created within SL. Our next planned step was to hold a design competition for builders. The goal of this contest was to collect different homes that featured universal design as demonstrated in the template model. As contest sponsors, we would provide guidelines to the builders to help them incorporate essential features, but builders would have creative freedom in the overall design of their home. We would review all entries and then place the homes on eXtension's Morrill Island. Residents of Second Life® would be invited to visit all of the contest homes and vote for their favorite. We also planned to invite experts in universal design to critique the homes and to select the home with the best design. Both the resident and expert choices would be considered and a winner would be determined. The winner and runner-up would receive a monetary award for their efforts.

After the winning home had been chosen, our plan was to then overlay assistive technology into the contest houses. Each house would highlight different assistive technology items, dependent upon the needs of particular populations: the needs of individuals with traumatic brain injury, as an example, are generally different from those who have rheumatoid arthritis. We would create a neighborhood of houses that would represent some possible choices for people with differing diagnoses or disabilities.

### Changes in the Vision

As the project progressed, we found ourselves revisiting time and time again the original concept of the contest. The members of our community of practice that had experience in SL created a template home that far exceeded expectations, and the idea of the contest came into question. Eventually we decided to sideline the contest in order to more fully explore what could be done with the product that had been developed. Significant time, talent, and resources were invested in the creation of the model home and the product was truly impressive. We knew that there was potential to use the already created product, which we named The LiveAbility House, that reached beyond our initial vision of using it only as an example or model upon which others would improve.

Once we decided to employ The LiveAbility House as the definitive product, we finalized the universal design features and assistive technology devices that we wanted to showcase. During the developmental process, we also generated ideas for additions and improvements to the home. In the hopes that we could share our space with professors, event sponsors, and caregivers we added a meeting space for classes, conferences, and support groups. We supplemented the exterior space surrounding the home with an accessible garden in order to demonstrate the need for accessible spaces outside of the home as well as inside. The inclusion of a resident service dog built upon the concept of independence and demonstrates the variety of options available to provide support and assistance for people with disabilities. The project has undergone many variations from the concept stage, and the process of development has served as a lesson in flexibility, creativity, and imagination.

## ENGAGED LEARNING AND PROJECT BOUNDARIES: THE LIVEABILITY HOUSE TODAY

Currently, The LiveAbility House exists and is open to the public on Morrill Island in Second Life®. The LiveAbility House lends itself to various types of learning including self-guided opportunities and synchronous learning experiences. The home is used for individual independent touring by SL residents or is available for group tours that are conducted by members of the Family Caregiving Community of Practice.

### Foundational Aspects for Learning

In demonstrating real life concepts or physical objects in a virtual world, one goal is to correctly portray the concept or item as closely to the real-world counterpart as possible. The purpose of TLH project is for individuals to understand universal design concepts and assistive technologies demonstrated in a virtual world and apply those to real world situations. An obstacle for the project was determining the best way to portray essential concepts, ideas, designs, and items in TLH that were recognizable and applicable in a real world setting. In the case of housing design, scale and proportion are an important concern. With assistive technology devices, items need to be accurately represented to illustrate both form and function. In order to address these issues and to aid in learners' understanding, the virtual representation of the design feature or assistive device was created, and then was supplemented by a real-world photograph of that feature or device. In addition, audio narration and written text were created.

*Figure 1. Entrance to the LiveAbility house*

*Figure 2. Example of kiosks placed throughout the LiveAbility house*

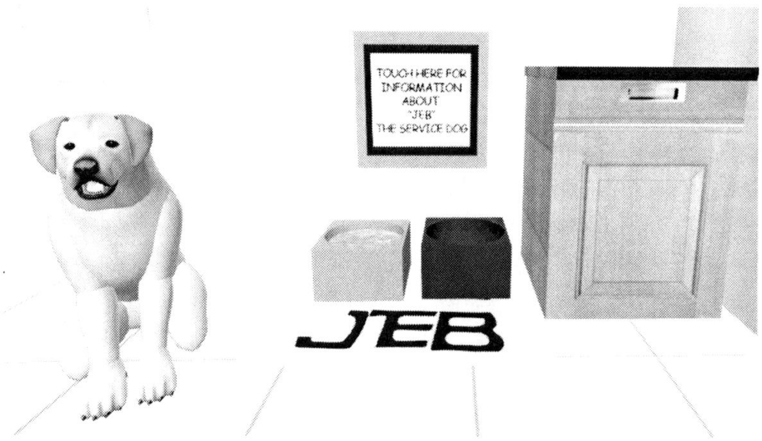


## Self-Guided Learning

A visitor to TLH is able to interact with the home itself: "the core element to any virtual world is the ability for the visitor to interact with the environment" (Johnson & Levine, 2009). When a visitor arrives on Morrill Island, he is able to identify TLH by its exterior signage (Figure 1).

As a visitor views the home from the street, he finds a kiosk that encourages him to "touch for an on-line narration about the project." Information about TLH including the goal and suggested use of the project is provided in text and audio form. As with many accessible homes, TLH has a ramp leading to the front entrance where two additional kiosks provide further information in the form of audio narrations and text (what is universal design; what is assistive technology). Upon entering the home, the visitor encounters other informational kiosks placed in various rooms throughout the home. These kiosks provide supplementary information about family caregiving, universal design, and service dogs (Figure 2).

The main educational aspect of TLH is the actual demonstration of universal design features

*Figure 3. Use of dots to identify universal design features*

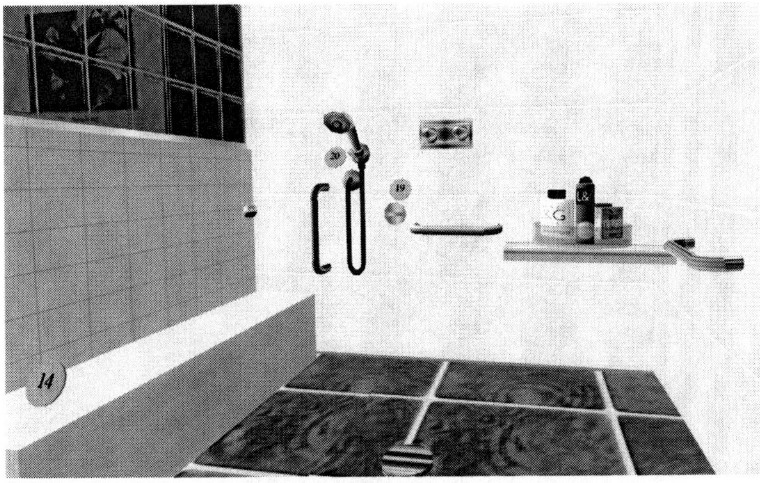


*Figure 4. Example of a learning object in the LiveAbility house*

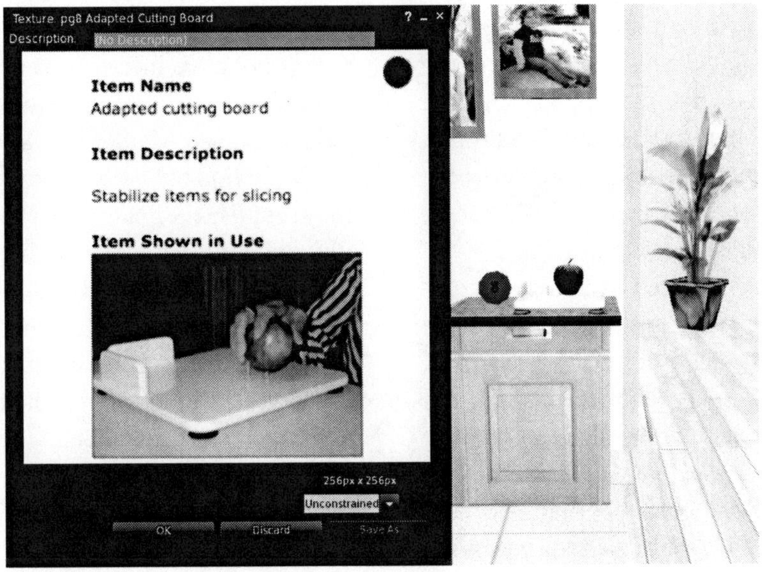


and assistive technology devices. Universal design features are numbered with orange dots, while assistive technology features are identified by purple dots (Figure 3). As the visitor clicks on the desired feature or device, the name, description, and real-world photograph are provided to the learner with text and audio (Figure 4). In all, a visitor may encounter more than 50 universal design and assistive technology features in the home. Examples of universal design features included in TLH are widened doorways, accessible appliances, a curbless shower, and an adjustable hand-held shower hose. Assistive technology examples included within TLH are a long-handled toilet bowl brush, an adapted cutting board, and a standing card holder.

Throughout this exploration, the visitor is in control of his own learning within TLH environ-

*Figure 5. Group learning tour in the LiveAbility house*

ment. If he is interested only in universal design features, then clicking only on the orange dots will provide this individualized instruction; the same is true for assistive technology. Or, if a visitor is interested only in adapting a bathroom, then immersing himself in this particular room and learning the specific requirements for accessibility is an individual option.

As SL is limited in reach to its users, community of practice members developed additional learning options for non-users. As one example, the blog is public, and may be found on eXtension and university web sites. We developed a learning lesson that introduces students to Second Life®, TLH project, and educational opportunities found within TLH. We provide instructions on becoming a Second Life® resident, and have links to additional resources. Also housed within the learning lesson are links to several machinimas featuring TLH, which are animated videos created within the Second Life® environment. These video tools can be useful in illustrating concepts to audiences that are not familiar with immersive worlds. They effectively demonstrate the content of the project as well as the potential for Second Life® as an educational tool.

## Synchronous Learning

Educators have increased the use of immersive virtual worlds (IVW) as options for instruction. Middleton and Mather (2008) write, "The value and attraction of IVWs to education is in the ease they promise the general education user for creating simulations in an immersive, abstracted space, offering students the opportunity to synchronously encounter authentic experiences involving other people, objects, and environments" (p. 207). Synchronous learning occurs when an instructor and a group of students interact together at the same time. Synchronous learning provides opportunities for engagement with—and learning from—others that self-exploration does not. One of the initial reasons for including the meeting space on the grounds was to encourage professors and teachers to visit and explore TLH with their students and then to discuss their experience. What we had not envisioned was that we could give tours of TLH to interested groups. This method of instruction was suggested to us when we were approached about participating in an all-day conference on health care and disabilities sponsored by the NonProfit Commons in Second Life®. As part of the day's conference activities, we provided two tours for attendees (Figure 5).

We began the tour in the presentation area, where the participants received a welcome and overview of Cooperative Extension and eXtension family caregiving. We walked to the house entrance, where we shared some of the history of the house and our vision for the project, how it began, and what we hoped to achieve. We then encouraged participants to tour the house, and we engaged the visitors in discussion and responded to their questions about design and technology features. This activity represented our first entrée into engaging a live audience with TLH apart from other community of practice members. From this effort, we received requests to provide tours for other conferences, and there was much discussion about possible collaborations in the future.

As a result of these first tours and as part of our presence in Second Life®, we are now available to provide guided tours of TLH. Individuals interested in this type of learning activity contact us to schedule an in-world presentation. While we may tailor content to the specific audience, the focus of the tour is the history and development of TLH, the answering of questions from participants about the concepts illustrated in the home, a demonstration of the various devices and features in the home, and open discussion and dialog with the visitors.

## Evaluation of The LiveAbility House

Dialogue and informal feedback has been an important conduit for the development of The LiveAbility House throughout its history. However, an important component to any educational endeavor is formal evaluation to ascertain the impact of the effort. This is helpful in determining what the learner gained from the experience, and also in establishing if any revisions should be made to the existing curriculum in order to maximize the learning event. Further, "learners should be directly involved in developing, implementing, and evaluating learning experiences to encourage critical reflection between teachers and learners and the learning environment" (Franz, 2007, Putting Theory into Practice section, bullet 7). Evaluating the impact of a project in a virtual environment is complex and challenging. For example, Woods (2010) used a complex evaluation scheme involving a chat-based survey that required code access and the teleporting of avatars to other locations in order to measure the impact of an immersive learning experience in SL. The LiveAbility House includes two different methods of collecting impact data, both of which were approved by the Institutional Review Board at Kansas State University.

The first method of data collection utilizes a common communication strategy within SL, called a notecard. We created a short evaluation form, and a kiosk located outside TLH at the mailbox invites visitors to take one of our notecards and answer three questions (Figure 6). A second kiosk, located inside TLH in the living room, provides residents with a link to a web-based survey. This survey is more in-depth, and also includes demographic questions.

Although current analytics indicate approximately 1650 visitors since TLH was developed (L. Phillips, personal communication, July 16, 2010), survey completions, both short and long, have been meager. Gathering survey information from the home's visitors has been difficult and we are exploring ways to increase feedback results. Currently, we are investigating ways of embedding evaluation or assessment into the actual touring experience as: "using paper and pencil, in the form of standardized tests, is not an effective way to evaluate a virtual learning experience. As VR [virtual reality] is a dynamic learning tool, evaluation should be tightly coupled with the actual learning process" (Roussos, Johnson, Moher, Leigh, Vasilakis, & Barnes, 1999, pg. 254).

*Figure 6. Notecard evaluation in the LiveAbility house*

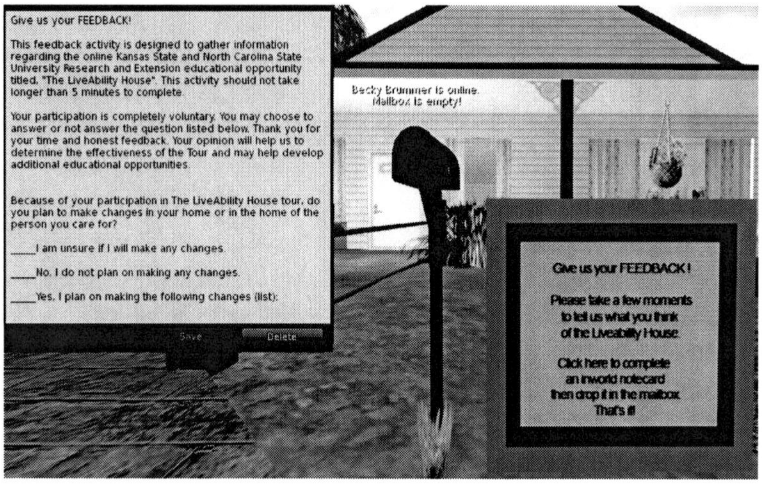


## FUTURE DIRECTIONS FOR THE PROJECT

### Capturing the Essence of The LiveAbility House Outside of the Second Life® Environment

A considerable limitation of The LiveAbility House is its location within the Second Life® environment, an ironic situation, as one of the reasons for creating TLH in SL was to eliminate the geographical restraints found within the real world. We recognize, however, that those who do not choose to engage in this virtual world, those who have limited access to technology, and even those who have difficulty adapting to and navigating a virtual 3-D world cannot benefit from its development. Others have questioned whether virtual world projects serve only those individuals that have the luxury of time to investigate the technology of virtual worlds and if projects limited to virtual worlds reduces the size of the population that can be reached with information (Toth-Cohen & Gallagher, 2009).

Although our presence in SL has enabled us to access a non-traditional audience for Cooperative Extension educational programs, we are unable to use this resource in a broader way within our states. The reasons for this situation are varied, are tied to the historical mission and organizational structure of Cooperative Extension, and are reflective of others' experiences related to computer hardware requirements, technical failures, and the complexity of navigating the SL environment (Siribaddana, 2010).

As educators we create resources and related training for Extension agents in our states. Agents then share these educational opportunities with their constituents in their home counties. As discussed previously, this grassroots approach to informal education was designed approximately 100 years ago. When faced with a new technology such as Second Life®, the infrastructure of the system can become an obstacle. The computer hardware available to Extension agents is varied, as county partners often have different views regarding field needs as well as varying levels of resources available. The use of SL requires a specific level of computer compatibility including the memory, operating system, processor, screen resolution, and graphics (Linden Research, Inc. 2010). Too, technical failure within Second Life® is very real and may result in an inability to access the SL grid. This inability may result in high levels of frustration for the user and abandonment of efforts may occur.

In North Carolina and Kansas, as well as across the country, the availability of high-speed internet connectivity and permitted access to specific sites including Facebook, Twitter, and Second Life® is not consistent across counties. There are county governments that do not allow access to certain sites, as they are viewed as social media, and not as an educational dissemination method. These sites are considered as inappropriate for staff to access during work hours.

As we are well aware, navigating Second Life® requires a commitment of time. Becoming comfortable with the use of an avatar, interacting with other residents, identifying landmarks, and moving through the virtual world requires practice and a willingness to learn new technology. Extension agents and the clients they serve may have limited time to devote to this medium and limited access to technical assistance available to help them traverse this new technology.

We were unwilling, however, to concede that we could not bridge the in-world content with a real-world application that would benefit Extension agents and those they serve. Through discussion with members of the CoP, eXtension collaborators, and other Extension faculty and staff about some of these issues, we decided to explore ways to create educational opportunities that would be useful for those outside of Second Life® (The LiveAbility House-Outside; TLHO).

One of our first steps was to engage Cooperative Extension agents and educators in North Carolina and Kansas in a discussion about the possible uses of The LiveAbility House. Each of us invited Cooperative Extension staff to participate in a webinar where we outlined the project and provided a tour of TLH. We then asked questions and facilitated a free-flowing discussion that encouraged brainstorming. After these discussions, we came together and compared the major themes generated by each group. It became evident that agents viewed TLH as extremely relevant in terms of the current conflicts and needs of wounded warriors in their communities. Young men and women are currently returning from war with significant disabilities and injuries, including amputations and traumatic brain injuries (Hoge, McGurk, Thomas, Cox, Engle & Castro, 2008; Gleicher, Lindenberg & Sumter, 2008; U.S. Congressional Research Service, 2009). These individuals have a very real need for timely information that can assist them in creating home environments and discovering technology that supports their ability levels and increases or maintains independence (Homes for Our Troops, 2009; Gleicher, Lindenberg & Sumter, 2008).

As we further explored the idea of targeting The LiveAbility House-Outside to meet the educational needs of wounded warriors and their families, we began to consider developing characters that lived within TLH. We could use these characters in different scenes to illustrate key concepts through narrative storytelling. Narrative is a tool that facilitates knowledge construction as it organizes information in a way that is memorable (Pachler & Daly, 2009). We began to explore the idea of integrating characters within the SL environment, and specifically, within TLH. We could create interactions and stories among these characters. Digital storytelling consists of "short vignettes that combine the art of telling stories with multimedia objects including images, audio, and video" (Rossiter & Garcia, 2010, p. 37). We decided that we could use our characters in real-life situations in order to teach caregiving concepts. The creation of digital stories in this way would introduce our subject-matter content and would capture the attention of learners (Robin, 2008).

However, as was necessary throughout this project, we required continued flexibility as we developed TLHO. We wanted to address the needs of wounded warriors, but we also wanted to remain relevant for our more traditional audience, consisting of older adults and their caregivers. The

*Figure 7. Sage and Katie, digital narrative characters*

development of a set of two pairs of characters allowed us to achieve both objectives.

This concept was once again, outside of our technical abilities. As with the creation of TLH, it was necessary to add expertise to our team. Our community of practice expanded to include an instructional designer, drama therapy student, radio producer, electronic media coordinator, and community actors.

We embarked on a pilot project to assess proof of concept for our idea. In conjunction with the instructional designer and drama therapy student, we created several characters and scenarios (Figure 7). Sage was an older adult caregiver; Bill was her husband, and had suffered a stroke; Derek was a veteran of the current conflict and had a traumatic brain injury; Katie was Derek's wife. We developed a script that showcased the four characters interacting with each other. The initial situation that we created focused on the physical and emotional issues of caregiving.

To create the digital narrative, we used The LiveAbility House as the setting for the interactions. We created our characters of Sage, Bill, Katie, and Derek as avatars within TLH, and community of practice members positioned them to mirror the interactions occurring within the script. We then took pictures of these interactions. With the help of the radio producer, community actors recorded the script. The pictures and audio were provided to the electronic media coordinator for creation of the digital narrative.

Through the use of this digital storytelling, we facilitate knowledge gain as learners engage with the characters (Rossiter & Garcia, 2010). They hear Sage discuss various topics related to caregiving with Katie. Together, Sage and Katie explore issues such as the importance of a caregiver's physical health and changes that may occur in spousal relationships due to the caregiving role. These initial digital narratives may be viewed at http://www.aging.ksu.edu/DesktopDefault.aspx?tabid=187.

This project continues to evolve; if the pilot is successful, we plan for future modules to include scenes where Bill and Derek talk about the frustrations of living with a disability and strategies that help them successfully adapt, with an emphasis on universal design features and assistive technology devices. We envision that the four characters will move through The LiveAbility House demonstrating its features and highlighting the items that help support care and independence. Ultimately, as a result of taking TLH out of SL and creating these four characters, we hope our audience will identify with the individuals in the story, and visualize using the assistive technology and universal design features to modify their own homes. In addition, we envision the opportunity to proactively address emerging issues as they arise, similar to an educational soap opera.

## CONCLUSION

The LiveAbility House is a virtual home, housed within Second Life® and built to educate family caregivers about universal design principles and assistive technology devices that can help support caregiving. This project is the result of a partnership formed within the eXtension Family Caregiving Community of Practice, where faculty and professionals within land-grant universities came together virtually to share and use research-based knowledge to address the real life critical issues facing family caregivers. The LiveAbility House serves as one example of a virtual immersive learning environment that teaches applicable concepts and principles for the real world.

In terms of a project team, we have exceeded our original expectations for the project. Like-minded yet diverse Family Caregiving Community of Practice members created a strong foundation and creative environment, which nurtured and strengthened the initial vision of the project. The Community of Practice provided a structure that created the synergy among members that was needed to develop The LiveAbility House project, and this structure was essential for the initial and ongoing development of the project. We were able to broaden our community of practice to include team members with technical expertise in virtual worlds and expand our perspectives regarding the possibilities for educational use. These experts helped us translate our nebulous vision into the concrete, instructional opportunity that is represented by The LiveAbility House. It was the efforts and support of the members that moved it to actual completion. We have been able to positively impact the development of the Family Caregiving CoP, contributing to a strong collaborative partnership model.

As a working dyad of subject-matter experts within this model, we shared one essential element, an eagerness to communicate our educational content to new audiences through nontraditional and creative methods. As content specialists, we understood the concepts we wanted to demonstrate using virtual world technology but we lacked basic knowledge regarding its use. It was this desire that motivated us to overcome fears related to technology use and to conquer the many obstacles that faced us due to our inexperience and lack of knowledge. Eventually, we came to realize that the project actualization was not dependent upon us becoming technologically savvy. We did need to become technologically familiar, and the inclusion of others with the needed expertise allowed us to learn from them and experiment under their watchful eye. This was an important aspect of the project's process and eventual ability to produce learning opportunities.

As Extension specialists, The LiveAbility House represents an educational opportunity that is completed, usable, and open to a global audience via Second Life®. We are able to share our subject matter with other educators and content developers. Presentations occurring in-world and in real life demonstrate the potential of similar possibilities to others.

Most importantly, we are able to use this demonstration home to share our subject matter with clients, some of whom may have a very real need for caregiving assistance. Residents of SL are visiting TLH, exploring its contents, and investigating its features. Tours have been conducted for those interested in learning more about family caregiving, universal design, and assistive technology. Although our evaluation of the project has been limited, we have some indication that TLH is providing information and assistance to those who have caregiving needs.

One last aspect of our success may be found within the potential of the project for future educational opportunities. From the earliest establishment of the project, the vision has remained constant, but the methods have been adapted, changed, abandoned, and recreated. We are mindful that with every new Community of Practice member added, skill learned, or innovative technology mastered, the options for using The LiveAbility House as a tool to educate caregivers and care recipients expand and provide additional promise. We are currently in the midst of developing The LiveAbility House-Outside, which will extend the reach of our project to field agents and the citizens that they serve. We look forward to these as yet unknown in-world and real-world opportunities and will continue to explore ways to create quality learning experiences for individuals with functional challenges and their caregivers.

## ACKNOWLEDGMENT

The authors wish to acknowledge the LuAnn Phillips, eXtension; Larry Havenstein, Kansas State University; Larry Jackson, Kansas State University; Kevin Gamble, North Carolina State University; Dmitre Raposo; eXtension and the members of the Family Caregiving Community of Practice for their expertise, guidance and collaboration as we developed The LiveAbility House. Their invaluable and determined assistance helped make this project a reality.

## REFERENCES

Agency for Healthcare Research and Quality. (2002, April). Preventing disability in the elderly with chronic disease. *Research in Action, 3*. AHRQ Publication No. 02-0O18. Retrieved October 13, 2010, from http://www.ahrq.gov/research/elderdis.htm.

American Cancer Society. (2007). *The society in Second Life*. Retrieved October 8, 2010, from http://www.cancer.org/InYourArea/HighPlainsHawaiiPacific/AreaHighlights/the-society-in-second-life.

Beard, L., Wilson, K., Morra, D., & Keelan, J. (2009). A survey of health-related activities on second life. *Journal of Medical Internet Research, 11*, 2. doi:10.2196/jmir.1192

Beitz, B., Brewer, G., & Kirby, S. (1993). Educating consumers about universal design. *Journal of Extension, 31*(1) Article 1IAW5. Retrieved from http://www.joe.org/joe/1993spring/iw5.php.

Boone, K. M., Sleichter, L., Miller, R., & Breiner, S. (2007). Perceptions and preferences of extension programming and sources among extension users and non-users: 10 Kansas counties. *Journal of Extension, 45*(6), Article 6RIB1. Retrieved from http://www.joe.org/joe/2007december/rb1.php.

Boulos, M. N. K., Hetherington, L., & Wheeler, S. (2007). Second life: An overview of the potential of 3-D virtual worlds in medical and health education. *Health Information and Libraries Journal, 24*, 233–245. doi:10.1111/j.1471-1842.2007.00733.x

Brossoie, N., Roberto, K. A., Willis-Walton, S., & Reynolds, S. (2010). *Report on baby boomers and older adults: Information and service needs*. Blacksburg, VA: Virginia Polytechnic Institute and State University, Center for Gerontology.

Centers for Disease Control and Prevention. (2010). *The health communicator's social media toolkit.* Retrieved October 18, 2010, from www.cdc.gov/healthcommunication/.

Centers for Disease Control and Prevention. (n.d.) *Virtual worlds*. Retrieved October 2, 2010, from http://www.cdc.gov/SocialMedia/Tools/VirtualWorlds.html.

Cooke, C. C., Yearns, M. H., & Martin, P. (2005). Aging in place: Home modifications among rural and urban elderly. *Housing and Society, 32*(1), 85–105.

Deitz, M. E., Mulford, J., & Case, K. (2009). The Utah house: An effective educational tool and catalyst for behavior change? *Building and Environment, 44*, 1707–1713. doi:10.1016/j.buildenv.2008.11.007

Driscoll, D. M. (2009). The death of the professor: Dialogue education's learning focus. *Journal of Extension, 47*(5), Article 5TOT2. Retrieved from http://www.joe.org/joe/2009october/tt2.php.

eXtension. (2008). *Community of practice handbook*. Retrieved September 12, 2010, from http://about.extension.org/wiki/Handbook_Introduction.

eXtension. (2009). *Return on investment annual report*. Retrieved September 8, 2010, from http://about.extension.org/mediawiki/files/7/7f/EXtension_annual_report_09.pdf.

eXtension. (2010). *About*. Retrieved September 8, 2010, from http://www.extension.org/main/about.

Foreman, N., Stanton-Fraser, D., Wilson, P. N., Duffy, H., & Parnell, R. (2005). Transfer of spatial knowledge to a two-level shopping mall in older people, following virtual exploration. *Environment and Behavior, 37*, 275–292. doi:10.1177/0013916504269649

Franz, N. (2007). Adult education theories: Informing cooperative extension's transformation. *Journal of Extension, 45*(1), Article 1FEA1. Retrieved from http://www.joe.org/joe/2007february/a1.php.

Franz, N., Garst, B. A., Baughman, S., Smith, C., & Peters, B. (2009). Catalyzing transformation: Conditions in extension educational environments that promote change. *Journal of Extension, 47*(4), Article 4RIB1. Retrieved from http://www.joe.org/joe/2009august/rb1.php.

Freedman, V. A., Agree, E. M., Martin, L. G., & Cornman, J. C. (2005). Trends in the use of assistive technology and personal care for late-life disability, 1992-2001. *The Gerontologist, 46*(1), 124–127.

Gerrior, S. A., & Crocoll, C. C. (2008). USDA CSREES' role in broadening support for an aging nation. *Journal of Extension, 46*(1), Article 1COM2. Retrieved from http://www.joe.org/joe/2008february/comm2.php.

Gitlin, L. N., Earland, T. V., Piersol, C. V., & Shaw, G. (2010). Enhancing quality of life in functionally vulnerable older adults: From randomized trial to standard care. *Generations (San Francisco, Calif.), 34*(1), 84–87.

Gleicher, H., Lindenberg, D., & Sumter, S. (2008). *Troops and family care fund feasibility study*. Retrieved September 27, 2010, from www.montgomerycountymd.gov/.

Greater Midwest Region of the National Network/National Library of Medicine. (2010). *Health and medicine in Second Life*. Retrieved October 8, 2010, from http://healthinfoisland.blogspot.com/.

Hersh, M. A., & Johnson, M. A. (2008). On modeling assistive technology systems-Part I: Modeling framework. *Technology and Disability, 20*, 193–215.

Hoge, C. W., McGurk, D., Thomas, J. L., Cox, A. L., Engle, C. C., & Castro, C. A. (2008). Mild traumatic brain injury in U.S. soldiers returning from Iraq. *The New England Journal of Medicine, 358*, 453–463. doi:10.1056/NEJMoa072972

Homes for Our Troops. (2009). *Homes for our Troops 2009 annual report*. Retrieved September 27, 2010, from http://www.homesforourtroops.org/.

Houser, A., Gibson, M. J., & Redfoot, D. L. (2010, September). *Trends in family caregiving and paid home care for older people with disabilities in the community: Data from the National Long-Term Care Survey*. Washington, DC: AARP Public Policy Institute. Retrieved October 13, 2010, from http://assets.aarp.org/rgcenter/ppi/ltc/2010-09-caregiving.pdf.

Johnson, L. F., & Levine, A. H. (2009). *Virtual worlds inherently immersive, highly social learning spaces*. Retrieved September 16, 2010, from http://Immersive_Learning-Johnson_and_Levine.pdf.

Journal, E. Inc. (n.d.). *Welcome to the Journal of Extension*. Retrieved September 1, 2010, from http://www.joe.org/index.php.

Kaye, H. S., Yeager, P., & Reed, M. (2008). Disparities in usage of assistive technology among people with disabilities. *Assistive Technology, 20*(4), 194–203. doi:10.1080/10400435.2008.10131946

Linden Research, Inc. (2010). *System requirements*. Retrieved October 5, 2010, from http://secondlife.com/support/system-requirements/.

Lloyd, W. A. (1922). *Extension workers creed*. Retrieved September 22, 2010, from http://espnational.com/index.php?option=com_content&view=article&id=71:extension-professionals-creed&catid=59&Itemid=57.

LSU Ag Center. (2010). *La House*. Retrieved September 28, 2010 from http://www.lsuagcenter.com/en/family_home/home/la_house/.

Maslow, A. H. (1943). A theory of human maturation. *Psychological Review, 50*, 370–396. doi:10.1037/h0054346

MetLife Mature Market Institute. (2010, September). *The MetLife report on aging in place 2.0: Rethinking solutions to the home care challenge*. Retrieved on September 22, 2010, from http://www.metlife.com/assets/cao/mmi/publications/studies/2010/mmi-aging-place.pdf.

Middleton, J., & Mather, R. (2008). Machinima interventions: Innovative approaches to immersive virtual world curriculum integration. *Research in Learning Technology, 16*(3), 207–220. doi:10.1080/09687760802526723

National Alliance for Caregiving & AARP. (2009). *Caregiving in the US*. Retrieved September 26, 2010, from www.caregiving.org/data/Caregiving_in_the_US_2009_full_report.pdf.

National Institute of Food and Agriculture. (2009). *About us*. Retrieved September 22, 2010, from http://www.csrees.usda.gov/about/background.html.

National Institute of Food and Agriculture. Family Science. (2010). *Family & consumer sciences*. Retrieved September 22, 2010, from http://www.csrees.usda.gov/familyscience.cfm.

National Institute of Food and Agriculture. (2010a). *About us*. Retrieved September 8, 2010, from http://www.csrees.usda.gov/qlinks/extension.html.

National Institute of Food and Agriculture. (2010b). *About us*. Retrieved September 22, 2010, from http://www.csrees.usda.gov/Extension/.

National Resource Center on Supportive Housing and Home Modifications. (2003). *Home modification resource guide* (4th ed.). Los Angeles, CA: University of Southern California Andrus Gerontology Center.

Olsen, R. V., Ehrenkrantz, E., & Hutchings, B. (1993). *Homes that help: Advice from caregivers for creating a supportive home*. Newark, NJ: New Jersey Institute of Technology.

Oswald, F., & Wahl, H. (2004). Housing and health in later years. *Reviews on Environmental Health, 19*(3-4), 223–252.

Pachler, N., & Daly, C. (2009). Narrative and learning with Web 2.0 technologies: Towards a research agenda. *Journal of Computer Assisted Learning, 25*, 6–18. doi:10.1111/j.1365-2729.2008.00303.x

Pressler, K. A., & Ferraro, K. F. (2010). Assistive device use as a dynamic acquisition process in later life. *The Gerontologist, 50*(3), 371–381. doi:10.1093/geront/gnp170

Redfoot, D. L., & Houser, A. (2010, September). *More older people with disabilities living in the community: Trends from the National Long-Term Care Survey, 1984–2004*. Washington, DC: AARP Public Policy Institute. Retrieved October 13, 2010, from http://assets.aarp.org/rgcenter/ppi/ltc/2010-08-disability.pdf.

Riel, M., & Polin, L. (2004). Learning communities: Common ground and critical differences in designing technical support. In Barab, S. A., Kling, R., & Gray, J. (Eds.), *Designing for virtual communities in the service of learning* (pp. 15–52). Cambridge, MA: Cambridge University Press.

Robin, B. R. (2008). Digital storytelling: A powerful technology tool for the 21st century classroom. *Theory into Practice, 47*, 220–228. doi:10.1080/00405840802153916

Rossiter, M., & Garcia, P. A. (2010). Digital storytelling: A new player on the narrative field. *New Directions for Adult and Continuing Education, 126*, 37–48. doi:10.1002/ace.370

Roussos, M., Johnson, A., Moher, T., Leigh, J., Vasilakis, C., & Barnes, C. (1999). Learning and building together in an immersive virtual world. *Presence (Cambridge, Mass.), 8*(3), 247–263. doi:10.1162/105474699566215

Sellers, D. (2010, June). *Impact report for fashion an easier lifestyle with assistive technology (AT)*. Retrieved September 8, 2010, from http://www.aging.ksu.edu/DesktopDefault.aspx?tabid=86.

Sellers, D., Crocker, A., Nichols, A., Kirby, S., & Brintnall-Peterson, M. (2009). Creating the eXtension family caregiving community of practice. *Journal of Extension, 47*(5), Article 5FEA1. Retrieved from http://www.joe.org/joe/2009october/a1.php.

Siribaddana, P. (2010). *Limitations in using Second Life for adult learning*. Retrieved September 27, 2010, from http://www.helium.com/items/1928727-limitations-in-using-second-life-for-adult-learning.

Sobrero, P. M. (2008). Essential components for successful virtual learning communities. *Journal of Extension, 46*(4), Article 4FEA1. Retrieved from http://www.joe.org/joe/2008august/a1.php.

The Morrill Act, 7 U.S.C. Sec.304. (1862).

Theories, L. (2008). *Communities of practice (Lave and Wenger)*. Retrieved July 28, 2010, from http://www.learning-theories.com/communities-of-practice-lave-and-wenger.html.

Tilly, J. (2010). The Administration on Aging's experiences with health, prevention, and wellness. *Generations (San Francisco, Calif.), 34*(1), 20–25.

Toth-Cohen, S., & Gallagher, T. (2009). Development and evaluation of health and wellness exhibits at the Jefferson Occupational Therapy Education Center in Second Life. *Journal of Virtual Worlds Research, 2*(2), 3–13.

Universal Design Education. (2009). *Learning universal design*. Retrieved September 13, 2010, from http://www.udeducation.org/learn.html.

U.S. Congressional Research Service. (2009). *United States military casualty statistics: Operation Iraqi freedom and Operation Enduing Freedom* (7-5700; March 25, 2009), Congressional Research Digital Collection. Retrieved on September 27, 2010, from www.fas.org/sgp/crs/natsec/RS22452.pdf.

Utah State University. (2010). *Utah house*. Retrieved September 27, 2010 from http://theutahhouse.org/.

Wenger, E. (2006). *Communities of practice: A brief introduction*. Retrieved August 5, 2010, from http://www.ewenger.com/theory/.

Wenger, E., McDermott, R. A., & Snyder, W. M. (2002). *Cultivating communities of practice: A guide to managing knowledge*. Boston, MA: Harvard Business School Press.

Woods, K. (2010). Engaging emerging populations of adults with interactive activities in a 3D virtual learning environment. *Journal of Extension, 48*(5), Article 5FEA3. Retrieved from http://www.joe.org/joe/2010october/a3.php.

Yearns, M. H. (2004). *Universal design for better living*. Iowa State University, University Extension. Retrieved October 13, 2010, from http://www.extension.iastate.edu/UniversalDesign/Resources/

Zielke, M. A., Roome, T. C., & Krueger, A. B. (2009). A composite adult learning model for virtual world residents with disabilities: A case study of the Virtual Ability Second Life® Island. *Journal of Virtual Worlds Research, 2*(1), 3–21.

## KEY TERMS AND DEFINITIONS

**Assistive Technology:** Devices, equipment, and tools that support, enhance, or enable individual ability in order to perform activities of daily living.

**Cooperative Extension:** An informal education, outreach and engagement system focused on the practical application of research knowledge and comprised of land-grant universities.

**Digital Narrative:** Short, digital vignettes that use the products developed in Second Life to illustrate educational principles through storytelling.

**eXtension:** An initiative of the Cooperative Extension System that provides real-time educational opportunities for clientele across the nation and globe.

**Family Caregiving Community of Practice:** A virtual network of land-grant university faculty, educators, and staff, with subject-matter expertise in family caregiving who work together to create educational resources to assist this population.

**The LiveAbility House:** A demonstration home built in Second Life® that illustrates the integration of universal design features and assistive technology devices to enable people to live at home despite physical or mental challenges caused by aging, illness, or disability.

**The LiveAbility House Outside:** Educational opportunities that use the product developed within Second Life in a manner that does not require access to the Second Life platform.

**Second Life®:** An on-line virtual reality world.

**Universal Design:** Design of products and living environments that can be used by all individuals regardless of age, gender, ability or change in ability.

# Chapter 4
# NASA*Talk* as a Discovery Learning Space:
## Self-Discovery Learning Opportunities[1]

**Debra C. Burkey Piecka**
*Wheeling Jesuit University, USA*

**Laurie Ruberg**
*Wheeling Jesuit University, USA*

**Christopher Ruckman**
*Wheeling Jesuit University, USA*

**Dynae Fullwood**
*NASA Johnson Space Center, USA*

## ABSTRACT

*The NASATalk online collaborative (www.nasatalk.com) gives educators a virtual place to talk about the many opportunities available from the National Aeronautics and Space Administration (NASA). NASATalk participants include K-16 educators, NASA-affiliated educators' support staff, and others interested in advancing STEM (science, technology, engineering and math) education. This chapter examines the self-discovery learning opportunities afforded by NASATalk for a three-day professional development workshop from the perspectives of the NASATalk team members, two NASA Aerospace Education Services Project specialists, and the workshop participants. For the conference, NASATalk hosted a public collaborative named the NASA STEM Educators Workshop as well as several blogs. The analysis discusses how various needs are met for orientation and entry, learner decision making, individuated learning, intercommunications and collaboration, and original discovery in the NASATalk content collaborative. A professional virtual community emerges where educators gathered onsite to receive instruction, but they turned to NASATalk to share their ideas and experiences by posting articles, blogs, comments, multimedia, links, and other educational resources.*

DOI: 10.4018/978-1-61350-320-1.ch004

Copyright © 2012, IGI Global. Copying or distributing in print or electronic forms without written permission of IGI Global is prohibited.

## INTRODUCTION

This chapter describes a model of the NASA*Talk* online content collaborative. NASA*Talk* is a Web 2.0 site where educators can come to share ideas, suggestions, success stories, and even frustrations about using National Aeronautics and Space Administration (NASA) resources to enhance science, technology, engineering, and mathematics (STEM) teaching and learning. While NASA provides hundreds of educational outreach resources related to aeronautics and flight, ecosystems, forces and motion, life sciences, engineering design, the solar system, the Moon, and weather and climate, these resources can be difficult to locate and often need some adaptation to fit the needs of the educator.

## NASA*TALK* BACKGROUND AND MILESTONES

The NASA*Talk* online collaborative (www.nasa-talk.com) gives educators a virtual place to talk about the many opportunities available from the space agency. As a collaborative, the site invites teachers, parents, or informal educators such as Scout or 4-H leaders, and NASA-affiliated educators to participate, whether communicating with other educators, reading blogs from fellow teachers and educational researchers, or even creating their own blog. The vibrant site thrives through the contributions of its participants.

As a content collaborative, NASA*Talk* serves as a forum for discussions about educator experiences using NASA educational resources. The open source Joomla-based website provides a professional virtual community of practice for educators using and/or inquiring about NASA educational resources for their K-16 STEM educational settings. NASA*Talk* participants include K-16 educators, NASA-affiliated educators' support staff, STEM content experts, and others interested in advancing STEM education.

NASA*Talk* is designed and managed by the NASA-sponsored Classroom of the Future at the Center for Educational Technologies (CET) at Wheeling Jesuit University in Wheeling, WV. The idea for NASA*Talk* grew out of a 2006 Classroom of the Future™ educational technologies study that profiled effective use of new tools to support STEM learning, with primary focus on NASA science and technology innovators (Ruberg, Calinger, & Howard, 2009). As a result of the guidelines for best practice that resulted from the study, NASA wanted to test a web-based collaborative where educators could discuss how they use NASA resources in their classroom along with what works and what doesn't. Development for the virtual community, originally called the EdTech Collaborative, began in 2007. The EdTech Collaborative site debuted in 2008.

In October 2009 the Classroom of the Future changed the EdTech Collaborative site name and Joomla-based presentation to NASA*Talk* to make its focus clearer to the target audience. The NASA*Talk* name more clearly implies the intent of the virtual community—a place to discuss educational resources related to NASA STEM materials. NASA*Talk* goals align with its Classroom of the Future project proposal.

### NASA*Talk* System

Joomla is a free content management system that serves as the core software backbone of NASA*Talk*. It is written in PHP and utilizes MySql for data management. Websites created with Joomla have a good amount of flexibility. The source code is open and may be modified by developers to fit their specific needs.

Presently, the NASA*Talk* website is running Joomla Core version 1.5.20 along with Mighty Extensions, a third party advanced management system to manage users, content, subscriptions, etc. Plugins for the site include the NASA and NASA Earth Observatory Images of the Day and Tweetboard. NASA*Talk* also has a development server.

## THE EVOLVING IDENTITY OF NASA*TALK*

NASA*Talk* focuses on providing professional communications that differ from other social networking sites, such as Facebook and MySpace. Perhaps the term "procial networking"[2] or a combination of professional networking opportunities in a social virtual community can assist in distinguishing what NASA*Talk* aims to accomplish—providing an online forum that makes it easy for STEM and NASA educators to hear from and respond to their community's needs, ideas, and feedback. When conveying the site's intention to educators, the team often uses the Laurie Ruberg-created byline, "Let's Talk NASA*Talk,*" to set an inviting tone for the learning space.

The migration from EdTech Collaborative to NASA*Talk* was more than just a name change. The transformation also indicated a rethinking of our target audience. As a virtual professional development community, NASA*Talk*'s target audience is made up of teachers interested in integrating NASA resources into their curriculum and STEM educators looking for new materials.

The transition also involved a complete rebuild of the interface. NASA*Talk* removed clip art images from its pages and instead moved to using the plentiful and spectacular images captured by NASA. Figures 1 and 2 show snapshots of the changes from the EdTech Collaborative to NASA*Talk* site design.

*Figure 1. Front page image of the EdTech Collaborative site design*

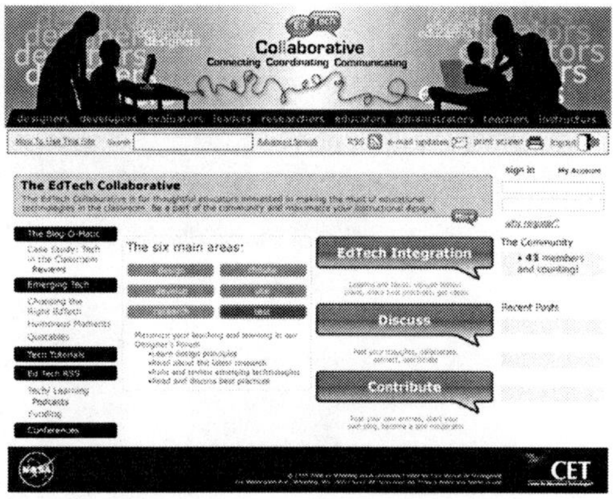


*Figure 2. Front page image of the NASATalk site design*

## NASA*TALK* FEATURES AND NAVIGATION

This section provides a comprehensive review of the organization of the NASA*Talk* website. Later in the Self-discovery Learning Opportunities Afforded by NASA*Talk* section, discussion will point to the NASA*Talk* features that encourage and promote self-discovery learning. This chapter defines self-discovery online learning opportunities as environments that promote independence and purposefulness for the user in addition to high levels of engagement with multimedia. Online discovery learning spaces provide active learning experiences that support autonomy, learner directedness, and creativity (Hai-Jew, 2008a, 2008b).

First, it is important to understand how to navigate the NASA*Talk* site. Begin with a review of the NASA*Talk* front page, shown in Figure 3.

The top of NASA*Talk* web pages (Figure 3) shows three vertical bars. The NASA Group Quick Launch Bar sits at the very top. Table 1 shows the menu buttons of the NASA-related groups, their acronym meanings, and a description. These menu buttons take users directly to a page for articles

*Figure 3. NASATalk front page screenshot showing layout of top banners, login, logos, NASA Earth Observatory and NASA Image of the Day, front page article, recent blogs, mission patches, and STELLAR Awards*

posted by that group. The NASA and NASA*Talk* logos appear on the second bar stretching to an image of the International Space Station. The dialogue bubbles in the NASA*Talk* logo signify the importance of discussing and collaborating about NASA products on the site. The banner underneath the logos houses the main navigation bar for most site visitors and users. These menu buttons highlight current topics relevant to NASA and STEM education. Table 2 explains each topic button on the lower bar.

After the three banner rows the NASA*Talk* site divides into three columns. The center column shows an attractive astronomy image above another version of the NASA*Talk* logo that reads, "We hope that NASA*Talk* (formerly called the EdTech Collaborative) inspires you to explore NASA resources for STEM education. Share your ideas and post your comments." The "Read More" link that follows goes to the NASA*Talk* blog. Underneath, the front page article summarizes and links new events and blogs with short descriptions and images. The last part of the center column lists recent front page articles by title, all of which are hyperlinked.

Atop the left column is the NASA Earth Observatory Image of the Day, and atop the right is the NASA Image of the Day. These splendid images change daily and offer users an opportunity to comment about them.

Continuing in the left column, the login area requests a username and password. Users are not required to register on the site, but some content is not visible unless they are logged in. We encourage users to create a login. All private NASA*Talk* areas, such as blogs and collaboratives, require

*Table 1. NASATalk front page groups featured on the top banner. The shaded rows indicate NASA affiliated groups that have a positive working relationship with NASATalk.*

| Acronym | NASA-related Organization | Description |
|---|---|---|
| AESP | Aerospace Education Services Project | AESP specialists are experienced educators who are broadly knowledgeable about NASA's missions, programs, and educational resources. They deliver teacher professional development and in-class programming in subjects relevant to NASA's missions. |
| AREE | Airborne Research Experiences for Educators | In the AREE project educators participate in airborne research by collecting in-flight sensor data of air, land and sea during flights aboard NASA aircraft. |
| DLN | Digital Learning Network | DLN offers videoconferencing or webcasting at no charge, providing interactive educational experiences to students and educators from kindergarten to university levels across the nation and around the world. |
| ENDEAVOR STC | ENDEAVOR Science Teacher Certificate | ENDEAVOR STC is a specialized science teaching certificate program. |
| NASA NEAT | Network of Educator Astronaut Teachers | The NEAT program identifies K-12 educators who are superior candidates for educator astronaut selection. NEAT members serve as advocates for NASA and promote NASA education efforts. |
| INSPIRE | Interdisciplinary National Science Program Incorporating Research and Education Experience | INSPIRE is a multitier year-round program designed for grades 9-12 students interested in STEM education and careers. |
| NES | NASA Explorer Schools | The NES project provides students in grades 4-12 with inquiry-based experiences directly related to the work of NASA scientists and engineers. |
| ePDN | Electronic Professional Development | NASA ePDN provides modular-based courses for use in NASA programs and by STEM teachers across the nation. The courses promote use of educational technology tools while emphasizing best practices that incorporate inquiry learning, case-based scenarios, and data analysis. |

*Table 2. NASATalk third banner showing NASA and STEM topics*

| NASA*Talk* Menu Buttons in the Third Banner | Description |
|---|---|
| Home | Takes users to the NASA*Talk* front page. |
| NASA Connections | Features categories of selected NASA educational programs and products with an emphasis on or innovative use of educational technologies. |
| TechTopics | Highlights promising educational technologies, tools, websites, resources, software, and hardware arranged by the ISTE National Educational Technology Standards for Students. |
| Blogs | Takes users to public individual, group, and event blogs. |
| Collaboratives | Public and private virtual spaces for groups that share common interests. Collaboratives include an introductory description about the purpose of the group, group announcements, group articles/ topics for discussion, group weblinks, and group files. Collaboratives often feature a blog. |
| TechTalk | Focuses on technical aspects of educational technology. For example, discussions cover topics such as open source software application and administration, software security, software updating, compatibility, application capabilities vs. design needs, user friendliness, and application development. |
| Cool NASA Careers | Features information about NASA career paths, job descriptions, student research and intern positions, and related STEM employment issues. |

users to login to view information. The STELLAR Awards image below the login area links users with details about this initiative. STELLAR Awards recognize educators for exemplary strategies of integrating NASA resources into their teaching. The lower left column shows one of multiple NASA images that rotate every time the page is refreshed. Underneath this picture is a count of users on the site.

The right column shows the titles of the five most recent blogs. Users may select the title to view the blog. Under the blog titles is a NASA Mission Patch module that shows different images and links to a blog about the mission patch history.

## EXAMINATION OF NASA*TALK* SELF-DISCOVERY CASE STUDY

### Methodology

A growing component of professional development evaluation involves the inclusion of online services for knowledge creation, support, interaction, and expanded content. This analysis provides an overview of how NASA*Talk* aligns with a normative model for virtual discovery learning spaces (Hai-Jew, 2008b). The analysis discusses how various needs are met for orientation and entry, learner decision-making, individuated learning, intercommunications and collaboration, and original discovery in the NASA*Talk* content collaborative. Table 3 provides a summary of the pedagogical and design considerations that promote self-discovery opportunities within the NASA*Talk* virtual learning discovery space.

To illustrate how NASA*Talk* provides self-discovery learning opportunities for educators wanting to locate and tailor NASA educational resources for their learning environments, the chapter examines a single case study surrounding the three-day, Second Annual NASA STEM Educators Workshop held in Charlotte, NC, in February 2010. Two NASA Aerospace Education Services Project (AESP) specialists coordinated the event, which featured a keynote address by a NASA STS-129 astronaut, 39 professional development STEM sessions delivered in both face-to-face and distance formats, an Internet café, and attendance by 300 regional K-12 teachers. The 2010 conference built on the success of the AESP specialists' 2009 NASA STEM Educators Confer-

*Table 3. Summary of a normative model for virtual discovery learning spaces (Hai-Jew, 2008a)*

| Phases of a Normative Model for Virtual Discovery Learning Spaces (Hai-Jew, 2008a) | Pedagogical and Design Considerations That Promote Self-discovery Opportunities Within a Normative Model for Virtual Discovery Learning Spaces (Hai-Jew, 2008a). |
|---|---|
| Entry | • Orientation<br>• Learner differentiation and channeling<br>• Informational decision supports<br>• Site reputation as an end destination |
| Virtual Discovery Learning Experience | • Information quality and timeliness<br>• Scaffolding for novices and experts<br>• Opportunities for practice<br>• Options for localized applied learning, design for innovation<br>• Learning feedback loop, opt-in instructional supports<br>• Curricular builds for learner mental models<br>• Incentives for learner focus, persistence, and self-discipline |
| Community in Discovery Learning | • Humanizing of the space<br>• Collaboration affordances<br>• Attraction and retention of quality participants<br>• Encouragement of learner self-enthusiasm<br>• Encouragement of learner self-efficacy |
| Exit | • Enhancement of discovery learning strategies<br>• Encouragement of future learning, building of learner decision-making<br>• Building of learning conceptualization models<br>• Documentation of the learning for professional and personal uses<br>• Outlinks and partnerships<br>• Archival and sharing of participant discoveries<br>• Portability of contents between technological systems |

ence. However, the 2009 event was smaller in attendance, subjects covered, and length. To assist in the increased scope of the conference, the AESP specialists employed NASA*Talk* as a tool for event management, content delivery, workshop assessment, participant reflection, and follow-up. NASA*Talk* hosted a public collaborative named the NASA STEM Educators Workshop as well as several blogs. The case study examines self-discovery learning from three vantage points: the NASA*Talk* Team (the CET authors), two AESP specialists, and the workshop participants. Specifically, this case study represented an intrinsic case study (Stake, 2000) whose purpose was to examine how NASA*Talk* facilitated and supported the community of learners at the professional development workshop.

The analysis employed a qualitative approach to examine data collected from multiple sources: personal correspondence; field notes from planning meetings, teleconferences, and the workshops; blogs and their multimedia content; comments to blogs and their multimedia content; and a collaborative group website to identify how NASA*Talk* afforded self-discovery learning opportunities. The data was analyzed using open coding techniques (Miles & Huberman, 1994) with the support of the Microsoft Excel spreadsheet software. The overall goal of the analysis was to examine the multiple forms of data to find emerging patterns of self-discovery learning in the correspondence, notes, dialogue, postings, and comments of the participants. During open coding the researchers sought to discover, name, and categorize the phenomena according to their properties and dimensions (Strauss & Corbin, 1998).

## The NASA*Talk* Team Self-Discovery

The STEM education conference occurred shortly after NASA*Talk* took steps to refine its focus and practices. Based on discussions with its NASA funder and analysis of usage patterns, the site changed its name and presentation to be more obviously centered on educator use of NASA products, resources, and opportunities and less about generalized educational technology trends and standards. Plans for the transition from the EdTech Collaborative to the NASA*Talk* site began months before the actual cutover. Hosting the conference was a vital component of the strategic plan for the migration as it provided a forum for hundreds of new users to become familiar with and to register on the NASA*Talk* website. Months before the workshop, NASA AESP specialists E. Dynae Fullwood and Jonathan Pane worked with the NASA*Talk* team to design and test a collaborative that would meet the needs of the participants and the presenters. Pseudonyms are used for all individuals besides the authors. This planning was a partnership in itself, a self-discovery awakening, as the two organizations worked to understand what a mutually beneficial online environment would look like. Issues in the development of the collaborative focused on four key objectives:

- Enable user collaborations.
- Deliver content in a highly personalized, secure, and in-context manner.
- Provide user-friendly interfaces to NASA content.
- Make the content readily available

During the months leading up to the conference, NASA*Talk* team members teleconferenced and e-mailed with the AESP specialists to design the collaborative, using existing Joomla-based resources. One of the greatest learning moments for Chris Ruckman, the NASA*Talk* programming specialist, was surprise at how well a small group of people can discuss a problem or need for new features and create a solution that can be implemented (most often) using existing resources.

Introducing a new spin on an existing resource, the team faced the task of creating a collaborative where conference attendees could share files, announcements, and weblinks in addition to having open, online discussions about the 39 workshop sessions. The idea of how to accomplish this organization did not strike immediately, but through team discussions and some trial and error, Ruckman recommended nesting 39 blogs, one for each conference meeting, inside the main conference blog (Figure 4). The default method for listing blogs moves the one with the most recent comments to the top of the list. However, this could be confusing to workshop participants seeking information about a particular session. So, blogs needed to be listed in numerical order. Through trial and error Debbie Piecka, one of the NASA*Talk* administrators, discovered how to enter the blog information to keep them in the correct order. The blogs were created in descending order from 39 to 1 using a period after the number and no spaces for the title. Piecka entered the blog information for each workshop, including a title and description matching the AESPs list in addition to an image for visual recognition and appeal (Figure 5).

The NASA STEM Educators Workshop collaborative featured a link to the blogs at the bottom of the first section through a link called Conference Presentations (Figure 4). Users could toggle between the collaborative website and the blog site (Figure 5) by using this link.

The screenshot of a workshop session blog (Figure 6) highlights several other features of blogs used by participants and presenters. Participants used the star voting system to rate their workshop experiences, and they took advantage of the comments capability as well. Presenters often upload their slideshows, weblinks, and handouts in the comments section. Both presenters and participants used comments for follow-up, to ask and answer questions, and to post resources and images.

*Figure 4. Screenshot of the NASA STEM educators conference collaborative*

*Figure 5. Screenshot of some conference blogs/workshops*

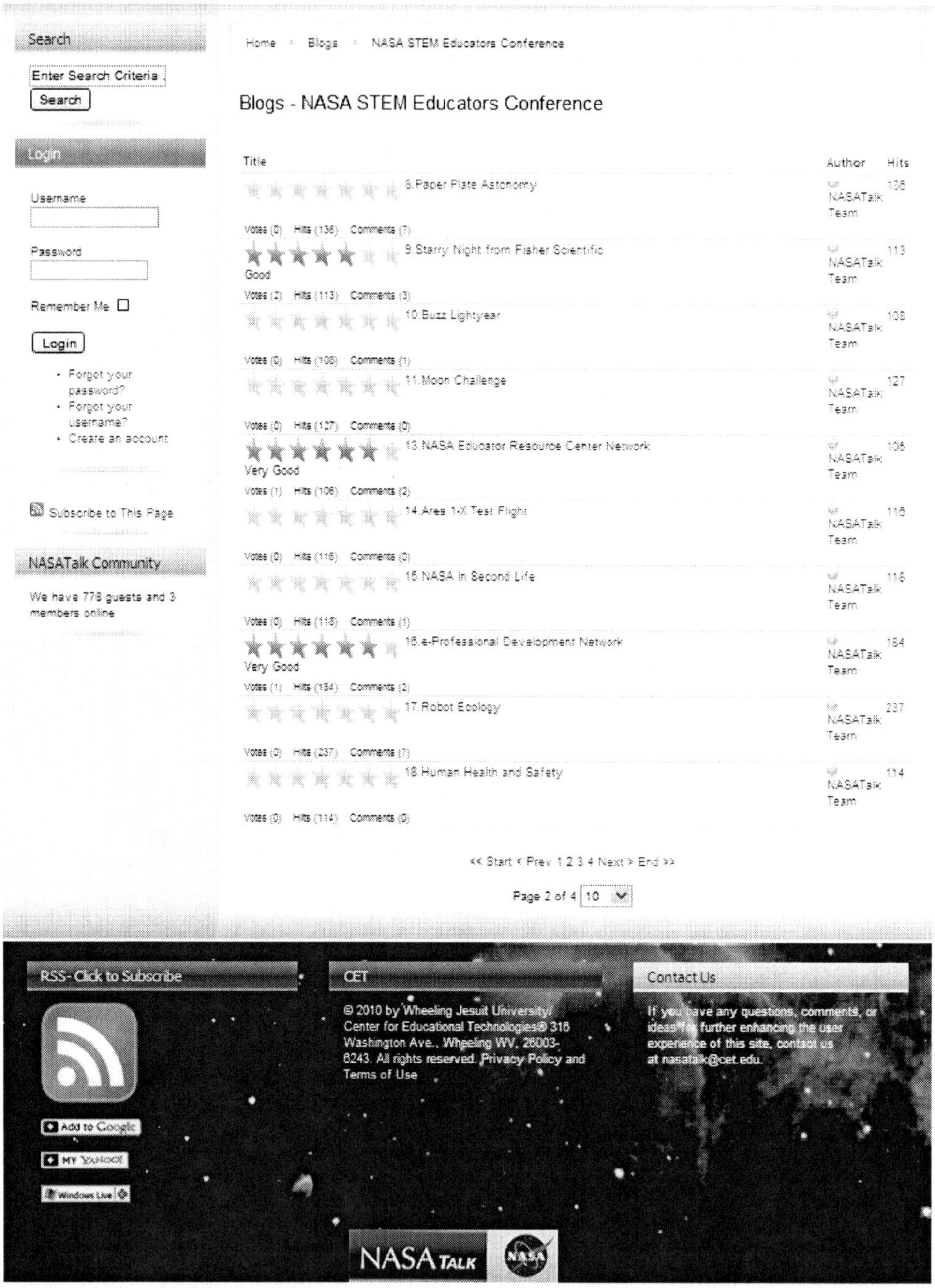


The NASA*Talk* Team and the AESPs communicated regularly by phone and e-mail during the last few days before the conference. NASA*Talk* focused on supporting the AESPs, who in turn were introducing their presenters and participants to the NASA*Talk* learning space. This latter point is covered in the next section. Several last minute requests by the AESPs forced the team to prioritize the requests in order to meet the workshop's deadline. AESP Fullwood notified the team about

*Figure 6. Screenshot of Blog 12.Robots in Education*

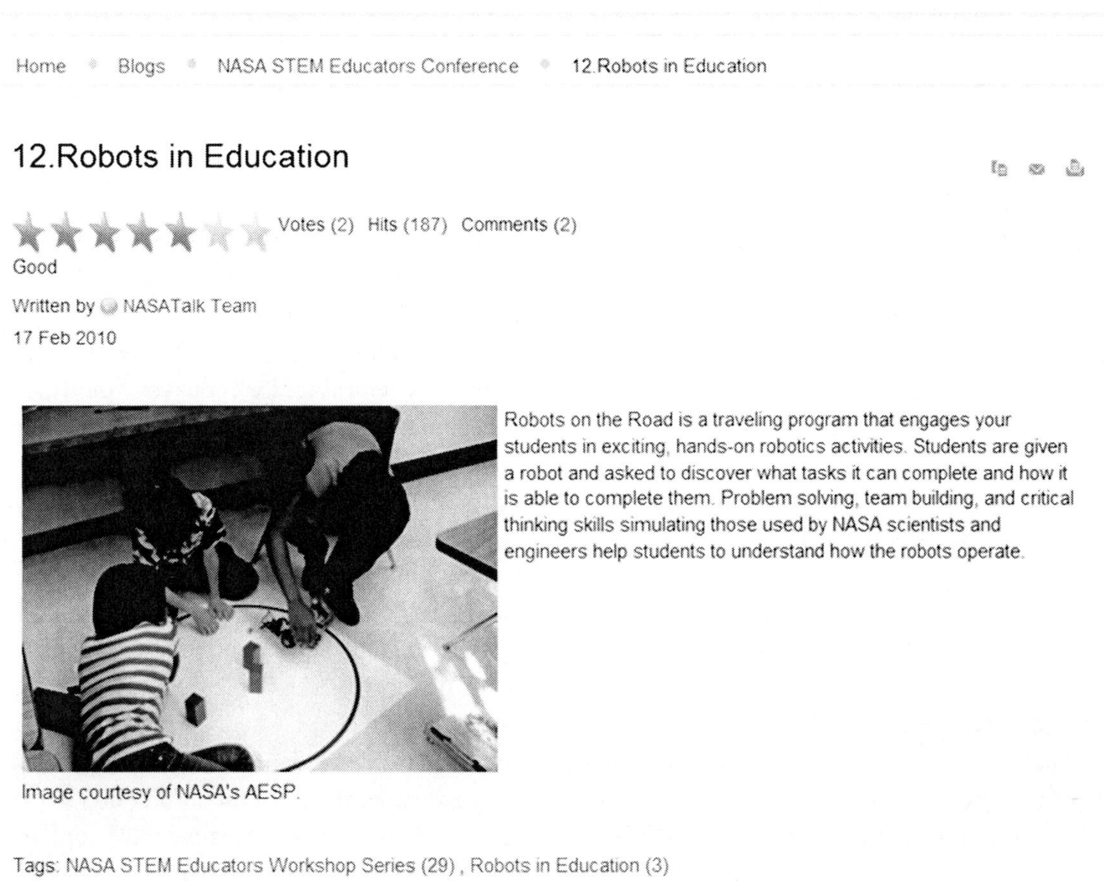
Home • Blogs • NASA STEM Educators Conference • 12.Robots in Education

12.Robots in Education

Votes (2) Hits (187) Comments (2)

Good

Written by NASATalk Team

17 Feb 2010

Robots on the Road is a traveling program that engages your students in exciting, hands-on robotics activities. Students are given a robot and asked to discover what tasks it can complete and how it is able to complete them. Problem solving, team building, and critical thinking skills simulating those used by NASA scientists and engineers help students to understand how the robots operate.

Image courtesy of NASA's AESP.

Tags: NASA STEM Educators Workshop Series (29) , Robots in Education (3)

a need to keep track of participant comments for assessment and door prize purposes. Default notification of these comments went to the NASA*Talk* team e-mail address but not to Fullwood. Ruckman investigated ways that Joomla could alert a moderator about new blog or collaborative comments. Within the comments feature for blogs, there is an e-mail notification field that permits the addition of alternate e-mail addresses. After adding Fullwood's e-mail to the field, the NASA*Talk* team tested the notification system and resolved the problem of sending e-mail alerts to collaborative and blog moderators.

Sometimes, the team learned about problems by "reading through the lines." Less than a week before the conference, Piecka inquired with AESP Pane about his experiences with populating the blogs. (Fullwood and Pane also presented at the conference and needed to add content to the blogs.). Pane replied, "The only issue I am having is remembering to use compatible file formats." For Piecka this signaled a problem. While blogs and collaborative groups provided generous acceptance of upload formats, the comments editor was much more restricted. Pane formatted all of his work in PDF files to accommodate this limitation. Ruckman immediately changed the types of acceptable attachment formats for comments so that participants had liberal options for attaching files to their comments.

Security is an important concern for Joomla websites, especially when assigning user privileges. As the team created user privileges, it quickly became apparent that Fullwood and Pane required user levels that permitted them to publish content on the website. As the team collaborated with the AESPs, the AESPs received new authorship user levels that enabled them to post and edit their content without going into the administrative side of the site.

Setting up a virtual community framework for a large conference represented a new challenge for the NASA*Talk* Team, one that was replicated many times. The team's discovery learning saw a great following. There are now at least four similar setups for collaborative groups with an associated blog, and more and more it seems not only to be a trending occurrence, but more of a question: "Why wouldn't my collaborative group have a blog associated with it? (or vice versa)." Having blogs within blogs has also led to another "aha" moment. While there are quite a few publicly accessible blogs and collaborative groups on NASA*Talk*, there also are some that remain private to only a particular group.

Branching the main blog and collaborative group categories into public and private areas is an idea that did not really seem necessary when the NASA*Talk* site was designed, but as the number of both categories have grown, the need to separate them has been steadily increasing; in fact, separating them may be the next design modification for the site. Groups seeking a collaborative or blog complete the NASA*Talk* author form that provides the team with information about meeting the specific needs of each organization.

Part of the self-discovery process for the team was recognizing which NASA-affiliated groups reacted positively to forming partnerships. The shaded rows of Table 1 indicate the NASA-affiliated groups that had positive intercommunication and collaboration with NASA*Talk*. The team realized that developing a personal relationship and networking with the NASA groups was integral to the success of joint online collaborations.

## AESP Specialists' Self-Discovery

As the conference organizers, the AESP specialists worked with the NASA*Talk* team, conference steering committee, presenters, participants, technology support staff, and NASA education staff. When Ruberg, lead administrator of NASA*Talk*, began discussions with Fullwood about supporting the NASA STEM Educators Workshop, Fullwood recognized many potential benefits in creating a virtual learning environment for the conference. Immediate returns for the endeavor would include dissemination about workshop happenings in these areas: registration, workshop availability, equipment notes such as bringing headphones, lunch arrangements, directions, and a place for general dialogue about the conference.

Having coordinated the event in 2009, Fullwood envisioned the complexities of taking a one-day, face-to-face conference and growing it to a three-day event. She also needed to receive approval from the conference steering committee to work with NASA*Talk*. Fullwood began to identify more benefits as plans for the conference developed. She looked at NASA*Talk* as a tool for distributing information as well as for evaluation and assessment.

In January 2010 Fullwood copied Ruberg on an e-mail she sent to the conference steering committee seeking its opinion about working with NASA*Talk*. She advised members that a NASA project had learned about the conference and was interested in setting up an online community for pre and post discussions. In her note Fullwood described the online community as "something between a message board and Facebook" (Fullwood, personal communication, January 5, 2010). She noted that it would be collaborative in nature and that teachers could create discussions about topics such as good hotel rates, sessions that they were not able to attend but wanted to know more about, and curriculum resources. She added the online community could also be used to post announcements, get feedback, and upload presentations and web links. Fullwood also shared that it would be easy to notify the teachers by e-mail about the online community because their registration data included their e-mail addresses. She advised the committee that she had approached her superiors and that they were onboard with the idea and that she sought their input about forming a partnership with NASA*Talk*.

Fullwood received affirmation from the steering committee shortly after sending the note, and the NASA*Talk* team moved forward to design and identify ways that NASA*Talk* could support the conference.

Ruberg directed these questions to Fullwood in order set up their collaborative group:

1. What do you want to call the collaborative?
2. How do you want to introduce the collaborative? (Short paragraph to introduce the collaborative in the group announcements area of the collaborative web page.)
3. Is the group going to be an open (public) or private (closed to all but members) collaborative? (NASA*Talk* recommended the collaborative be public to make it easier for the conference audience.)

After receiving approval from the conference steering committee and answers to the collaborative questions, the NASA*Talk* team moved forward to create the NASA STEM Educators Workshop collaborative. When users visited the collaborative web page, they were greeted with the following description and a related conference image:

- 2nd Annual NASA STEM Educators Workshop Series. Anyone in the education community is invited to collaborate on the experience of the 2nd Annual NASA STEM Educators Workshop Series. It is a place where everyone can stay connected before, during, and after the event.
- It is a place where teachers can create discussions about topics from good hotel rates to their most memorable workshop experience. We encourage teachers to show off how they are using the resources they learned of in the classroom in this forum.
- It is a place where presenters and facilitators can make presentations, web links, handouts, and other resources available to others. Use this forum for pre-gathering readings and post-gathering updates.
- It is a place where feedback and announcements can be posted. Use this forum for constructive and substantive dialogues about the betterment of delivery of STEM education to our nation's youth. (NASA*Talk*, 2010).

The AESP specialists immediately began to promote NASA*Talk* as the online "go to" place for the conference. Participants received e-mails advising them to check NASA*Talk* for updates. The specialists also posted information about how and why to join the NASA*Talk* collaborative. Their communications identified NASA*Talk* as an online discovery learning space with the following advantages:

1. As a hub to stay connected before, during, and after the event.
2. As a place to showcase how educators are using resources, such as those from the 2009 conference.
3. As a discussion forum for a wide range of topics, such as hotels and NASA STEM resources.
4. As a repository (uploading and downloading) for content, including presentations, web links, handouts, and updates.
5. As a place for feedback, announcements, and constructive and substantive dialogues.

As participants began to register on the NASA*Talk* site, the team worked to create each of the 39 workshop sessions as individual blogs. The AESP specialists were the first presenters to populate the blogs. Meantime, they also added content to the collaborative: information about registration, hotels, the keynote speaker, and more. Fullwood quickly alerted the team that she needed to keep track of new comments for assessment and incentive purposes. Fullwood viewed NASA*Talk* as much more than a just an electronic bulletin board. She identified multiple benefits for its use. She foresaw NASA*Talk* as a vehicle to disseminate conference information about registration, availability, headphones, lunch, directions, and general dialogue. Fullwood used the hit counter to identify popular sessions and the comments counters to learn about the number of comments submitted. Fullwood viewed NASA*Talk* as a transparent tool to track conference progress. Participants learned to use the rating feature, submitted comments during visits to the Internet café, and talked about ways they would use the resources in their own classrooms. One of the benefits Fullwood identified surprised the team. During the 2009 conference Fullwood burned CD-ROMs with the session materials. NASA*Talk* removed this burden and made users accountable for downloading the session materials they wanted.

Throughout the conference, the AESP specialists guided the teachers to use NASA*Talk*. They promoted the site to the teachers and touted its 24 x 7 accessibility, ease of use, potential for building a community of practitioners, and the importance of sharing with others.

The specialists provided a window to the team about how they perceived their NASA*Talk* experience. They reported that teachers were confident and comfortable using the site and that NASA*Talk* might even make it easier for teachers to give feedback, especially when some might have been disinclined to provide input in the past.

## NASA STEM Education Workshop Participants and Presenters' Self-Discovery

NASA*Talk* provided a discovery learning space for the NASA STEM Educators Workshop participants. During the conference participants visited the Internet café and posted their comments about the sessions. Some rated the presentations using the star voting feature. Others examined the presentation materials posted for sessions that they were unable to attend, or they left suggestions for improvement. Presenters supported one another and used the comments section to leave copies of their instructional materials and often provided hyperlinks for further study.

Teachers used NASA*Talk* to selectively comment about sessions, clarify their inquiries, or ask for help. The AESP specialists monitored the blog comments while the NASA*Talk* team remained on the sidelines to escalate resolutions to login problems or navigation issues.

Many participants left comments about personal discovery moments at the conference. The quotes in this section reveal participants' reflections, observations, and personal discovery learning opportunities.

Belinda remarked about her experiences in the Mapping the Moon with WALL-E session: "I had a great time in your presentation. I think one of the aha moments was when folks realized the graph was upside down." (2010, Feb. 23).

At the Robot Ecology presentation, Phoebe Wood shared her thoughts about this practical workshop: "This was the best presentation thus far. Being able to make the items to utilize will make more sense for the children to see the end result and have more invested in the outcome." (2010, Feb. 24).

Dana Smith expressed similar thoughts about the Robot Ecology session:

*"I really enjoyed this workshop and could see many practical applications: Newton's laws, team building, simple machines, problem solving. I loved that it used simple, inexpensive materials and that everyone could be successful. This was one of my favorite workshops so far." (2010b, Feb. 25).*

There were numerous examples of presenters adding their presentations as comments to their blogs. Other resources, such as lesson plans, links for extended study, and YouTube links, were also common blog comments and attachments. Here, the presenter of NASA eClips: NASA Launchpad noted where participants could find additional information about NASA eClips:

*"Thanks to all who attended the workshop. Here is the link for our hot list: http://www.kn.att.com/wired/fil/pages/listnasaresbj.html*

*"If you have any questions, please don't hesitate to contact me! My e-mail address is: [presenter's email address]." (Downing, 2010, Feb. 25).*

For Paper Plate Astronomy, Pane posted the objectives, standards, and multiple handouts for follow-up after the session. He used the collaborative as a content repository for lesson materials, including some multimedia files:

*"It's almost time! Soon we will be together in the Paper Plate Astronomy session, and you will be learning new ways to use common materials like paper plates to engage your students in learning about the sun-Earth-moon relationship, motion in the sky, moon phases, etc. I am attaching the PPT presentation as a.pdf file for you to download and use as you see fit. I certainly hope you enjoy the session and the rest of the NASA STEM conference, and for those of you not attending the session, feel free to take any of the materials you see attached and e-mail Fullwood or myself anytime with any questions you may have about these activities."*

*Objectives:*

*To identify patterns, recognize relationships, and draw conclusions about the Earth-sun system by interpreting a variety of representations/models (e.g., diagrams, sundials, distance of sun above horizon) of the sun's apparent movement in the sky. Changes in movement of objects in the sky have patterns that can be observed, described, and modeled. The sun appears to move across the sky in the same way every day, but the sun's apparent path changes slowly over seasons. Data collected can be used to identify patterns, recognize relationships, and draw conclusions about the Earth and sun system.*

*Standards:*

*NSES: Science as Inquiry*

*Earth and Space Science*

** Objects in the sky*

** Changes in Earth and sky (Pane, 2010, Feb. 19)*

Fullwood posted similar comments. Here is an excerpt from the Buzz Lightyear presentation:

*"To get to the Buzz Lightyear activities, visit NASA Kids' Club [hyperlinked]. Watch Buzz Aldrin talk to Buzz Lightyear about his training for a NASA mission at YouTube—Buzz Lightyear trains for NASA mission [hyperlinked]." (Fullwood, 2010, Feb. 25).*

Fullwood's follow-up comments to the NASA Educator Resource Center Network blog provided a robust set of links about robotics and the STS-

131 mission. STS-131 launched on April 5, 2010, a little more than a month after the conference.

*Shuttle Mission STS-131—During STS-131 Mission Specialist Dorothy Metcalf-Lindenburger, Educator Astronaut, will use the shuttle arm to inspect the space shuttle for any damage that may have occurred during launch or while in space. Other members of the STS-131 crew will use the space station's Canadarm2 to move equipment from the shuttle's payload bay to the station. http://www.nasa.gov/mission_pages/shuttle/shuttlemissions/sts131/index.html*

*Hear the message from the Educator Astronaut at the NASA Education Robotics website.*

*NASA Education Robotics website—Innovation, creativity, problem solving—the world of robotics at NASA is all of these things. Spend some time on this site to see if robotics might be in your future. http://www.nasa.gov/audience/foreducators/robotics/home/index.html*

*ROVER—Robotic Online Virtual Exploration Rover—Test your programming skills and move the robot around the obstacles with this interactive, web-based, and educational simulator. http://www.nasa.gov/audience/foreducators/robotics/home/ROVER.html*

*STS-131 Robotics Kit—The STS-131 Robotics Kit we showcased during the conference can be attained from the Central Operation of Resources for Educators (CORE). CORE is a worldwide distribution center for NASA's educational multimedia materials. Educators may purchase exciting materials for a minimal charge. http://education.nasa.gov/edprograms/core/home/index.html*

*See also the PowerPoint presentation created for this session attached. (Fullwood, 2010, Mar. 1).*

Some comments praised the presenters. A NASA administrator who attended Rocket Science commented, "Well thought out and polished presentation. This is a great introduction to the science of rocketry and the DLN program." (NASA administrator, 2010c). At the STEM Resources from Discovery Education presentation, the same administrator noted, "The range of resources is astounding." (NASA administrator, 2010a). Comments like this make others curious about checking out the resources.

Some participants responded to blogs with recommendations and constructive criticism. For the Starry Night session Smith inquired, "Could we have met in the media lab? It would have been better if we could have heard the presentation and then played with the software ourselves. I would have loved to have given it a try!" (2010a, Feb. 25).

After the Space Mysteries session Samantha Bird made an interesting observation about implementing the NASA materials in a high school classroom: "This session was really interesting. Even with high school I know there would have to be more directives for the students since they don't read and follow directions on their own." (2010, Feb. 25). Comments like this are ripe for educators to share ideas about best practices for implementing the NASA resources.

Some participants offered words of encouragement. A NASA administrator offered these supportive words: "The activities presented here are intriguing. I think the presentation will shape up with more practice." (2010b, Feb. 25).

In this example co-presenters began a dialogue in the comments. Pane presented Paper Plate Astronomy with assistance from another teacher on the conference steering committee, Kevin Janta, who encouraged Pane with these words:

*"I enjoyed working together at the STEM workshop in Charlotte. I will encourage my teachers in CMS who attended the sessions to be active*

*participants in this online forum. That is a hard task based on similar projects I've been trying to do that involved online exchange of good ideas. But it's certainly worth having a go!" (2010, Feb. 26).*

Pane responded, "Thanks, Kevin!" (2010, Feb. 26).

Participants responded to Fullwood and Pane's request to blog about their experiences at the conference. The AESPs scaffolded participants' online commenting through practice exercises. Educators received paper comment cards. First, teachers recorded their comments on the cards. When the teachers visited the Internet café, the computers opened to a NASA*Talk* home page. Teachers then navigated to the blogs to add their comments electronically.

One member of the conference steering committee was very enthusiastic about using the NASA*Talk* collaborative for the conference. Janta investigated the conference blog pages and descriptions on NASA*Talk* and exclaimed:

*"Wow! This is awesome! I like how mostly all the information about the workshop is in one place! That's convenient!*

*"I also like how presenters can upload presentations.... and I assume participants will be able to download. My teachers will love that feature!*

*"I am excited about helping to make all of this happen, and I look forward to welcoming everyone to Charlotte later this month." (2010, Feb. 7).*

As the three-day workshop ended, the best evidence of the teachers' self-discovery experiences came in the form of their comments. Several teachers offered concrete ideas about when and how they were going to implement the resources gained at the workshop in their own classrooms. The following teacher comments speak to their immediate plans to integrate conference resources into their own classes.

*"It has been a great 2 days...looking forward to our final sessions! I am using Buzz Lightyear on Monday with 5th grade to study physical science. Thanks again, Mary Blueman." (Blueman, 2010, Feb. 25).*

*"I loved the Lunar Robot Ecology. Please steer me to other similar activities that require easily available materials and yet provide such a huge impact on students' creativity and imagination. Benjamin Ward." (Ward, 2010a, Feb. 27).*

*"Maria was awesome! She spent extra time with me during lunches and between sessions to get me up to speed on the moon's geology. Thank you all for your dedication to help us in the classroom. Benjamin." (Ward, 2010b, Feb. 27).*

## SELF-DISCOVERY LEARNING OPPORTUNITIES AFFORDED BY NASA*TALK*

NASA*Talk* combines many technologies to offer users the chance to independently maneuver around the site. In the NASA STEM Educators Workshop case study the NASA*Talk* team guided AESP specialists Fullwood and Pane through the collaborative and blog interfaces. Setting up example pages provided the AESPs with ideas about how their presenters and teacher participants could use the platform. In early February 2010 before creating the workshop session blogs, the NASA*Talk* team created a chronological list of the STEM workshops and hyperlinked them to the online description of the sessions. These "test" pages allowed the AESP specialists to visualize how their users could use the same pages and empowered the specialists to discuss NASA-*Talk*'s strengths and advantages. The specialists opened doors for the NASA*Talk* team as they became knowledgeable proponents for the virtual professional development community. The name change to NASA*Talk* also contributed to the site's reputation as an end destination (Hai-Jew, 2008b).

The NASA*Talk* team along with other Classroom of the Future groups presented to the Charlotte-based workshop via videoconferencing. Ruberg's *Introduction to NASATalk* presentation showcased examples of discovery learning opportunities afforded by NASA*Talk*. Today, this same slideshow remains an integral tool for introducing new users to the site. Two other blog articles, *Let's Talk NASATalk* and *What is NASATalk?*, provide additional information about the site's goals and objectives. The team also added a short video tutorial to guide users through the main areas of the site.

The NASA*Talk* team and Fullwood and Pane took advantage of an opportune moment to demonstrate how NASA*Talk* meets the needs for virtual professional development. The conference gave AESP specialists, presenters, and teacher participants the chance to practice using the online collaborative. This was especially true in the Internet café area of the conference where teachers could go to check e-mail and comment on the NASA*Talk* site. According to Fullwood, teachers are unaccustomed to having access during professional development courses, so they viewed the Internet café as a real bonus. During a debriefing meeting with the team, Fullwood recounted that NASA*Talk* was the "go to" place for follow-up. Teachers' conversations reflected knowledge about going to NASA*Talk* for resources and comments. The NASA*Talk* team enjoyed hearing about this ingenuity in supporting the teachers' experiences.

Fullwood also built incentives for the teachers to use the site; each time a teacher made a comment on the NASA*Talk* site, their name went into a drawing for a door prize. Other incentives on the site include the STELLAR Awards. They recognize educators for strategic and exemplary uses of NASA resources in their teaching. In fact, the team gave a virtual slideshow presentation about the STELLAR Awards at the conference. And a conference attendee won the next round of STELLAR Awards for his submission that centered on resources acquired at the NASA STEM Educators Workshop.

The case study descriptions included in the chapter illustrate the emergence of a community of practice (CoP) surrounding the conference. A community of practice provides an environment that connects people and encourages them to share ideas and experiences (Dale, 2010). At the conference educators gathered onsite to receive instruction, but they turned to NASA*Talk* to share their ideas and experiences through posting articles, blogs, comments, multimedia, links, and other educational resources. The collaborative and blog sections show numerous, thoughtful comments that were encouraged throughout their professional development event.

Lave and Wenger (1991) define a CoP across three dimensions: what it is about, how it functions, and what capability it produces. In NASA*Talk* the CoP is a joint enterprise comprised of STEM content experts, K-16 educators, Classroom of the Future and NASA support staff, and other members interested in using NASA STEM resources in education. The NASA*Talk* CoP binds members together as a virtual networking repository for the discussion of using NASA STEM resources to create awareness and to educate students and teachers about the many ways to use NASA materials in the classroom. NASA*Talk* produces a shared repertoire of communal resources (lesson plans, web links, vocabulary, best practice methods, multimedia, and events) that members develop over time.

In addition to being a CoP (Dale, 2010; Lave & Wenger, 1991), NASA*Talk* is also recognized as a professional virtual community. As its name implies, in a professional virtual community the community concept is extended to a virtual form identified by the following characteristics: 1) the community is built upon a computer-mediated space, or cyberspace; 2) activities are enabled by Information and Communications Technology

(ICT); 3) virtual community topics or contents are driven by the participants; 4) community relationships evolve through interactions among members; and 5) a professional virtual community accrues people who share common interests and collaborate to achieve common goals (Lin, Lin, & Huang, 2008). Bieber et al. (2002) define a professional virtual community as being comprised of researchers, practitioners, students, teachers, and organizations who participate to better understand its domain and improve their own professional understanding. Likewise, Bieber et al. noted that both members and nonmembers participate in the professional virtual community.

As the NASA STEM Education Workshop drew to a close, participants were encouraged to continue to visit NASA*Talk* and network with one another. They left behind documentation about their learning in the form of new articles, comments to blogs, lesson plan ideas, pictures, movies, photos, web links, and contacts. Several of the teacher participants shared ideas about how they were going to implement their new learning. Knowledge acquisition and learning are greatly facilitated by interaction and collaboration with others (Lave & Wenger, 1991; Vygotsky, 1986; Wenger, 1996). A CoP's knowledge resides in its "documents, discussions, decisions, conceptual models, formal educational modules, processes, and the awareness by members of other members' expertise" (Rice et al., 1999, as cited in Bieber et al., 2002, p. 2). NASA*Talk* blends attributes of online discovery learning spaces (i.e., websites and the Internet, repositories, virtual communities of practice, and collaborative design spaces) into a single learning environment for advancing STEM learning (Hai-Jew, 2008b).

This chapter is a stepping off point for further investigation of the kinds of metrics necessary for evaluating virtual professional development communities. Register on the NASA*Talk* online collaborative (www.nasatalk.com) and comment about self-discovery learning opportunities.

## CONCLUSION

The NASA*Talk* online collaborative provides K-16 educators, NASA-affiliated support staff, and others interested in furthering STEM education with a virtual forum for discussing NASA educational resources and their integration into existing curriculum. NASA provides hundreds of educational outreach resources aligned to aeronautics and flight, ecosystems, forces and motion, life sciences, engineering design, the solar system, the Moon, and weather and climate. However, locating and adapting these resources to fit educators' needs can be difficult. NASA*Talk*'s online discovery environment supports the process of discussing what works and best practices for implementing NASA resources by providing an asynchronous, multimedia online resource that supplements face-to-face communications and formal evaluation survey procedures.

As the selected participants' excerpts (pages 12-16) show, having NASA*Talk* available in the conference Internet café area provided a way to document, archive, and publicize comments that typically are shared only verbally or are hidden in end-of-event privacy-protected evaluations surveys. This use of NASA*Talk* stimulated the kind of buzz that is typically associated with Facebook and Twitter social media tools. The quoted excerpts show how the informal ratings of conference sessions and events stimulated participant identity sharing. In future offerings of this workshop where a social and/or content collaborative is used, it would be worthwhile to track participant workshop attendance and participation in sessions as well as the impact of the virtual community sharing on both presenter and participant expectations.

The chapter describes NASA*Talk* self-discovery learning affordances in the context of a single case study surrounding a three-day, NASA STEM professional workshop in Charlotte, NC. Two NASA AESPs organized the event and used NASA*Talk* as a tool for event management, content delivery, workshop assessment, reflection, and follow-up. The case study examines self-discovery learning from three perspectives: NASA*Talk* team, two AESP specialists, and the workshop participants.

Data collected from personal correspondence, field notes, blogs and their multimedia, comments to blogs and their content, and other NASA*Talk* website content were coded to find emerging patterns of self-discovery learning. The NASA*Talk* team identified how to organize the conference blogs, one for each session, to provide opportunities for commenting, resource posting, and workshop assessment. The team also realized that forging personal relationships and networking with NASA groups was integral to the success of joint online collaborations. The AESP specialists recognized several immediate benefits surrounding the event collaboration: dissemination about workshop logistics and availability; session assessment capabilities for rating and commenting; a place where presentations, web links, handouts, and other resources are available to others; and promotion of a community of STEM educator practitioners.

While the NASA*Talk* team and AESP specialists identified self-discovery learning opportunities through their partnership, the participants and presenters really appreciated and took advantage of the discovery affordances offered in the virtual space. Educators used NASA*Talk* to selectively comment about sessions, clarify their inquiries, or ask for help. They frequented the Internet café to talk about the workshops, search the NASA*Talk* website, and correspond with other conference participants.

NASA*Talk* brings together many Web 2.0 technologies to offer users the chance to independently maneuver around the site and locate content relative to their individual needs. The case study describes the emergence of a community of practice surrounding a professional development STEM conference where content experts, teachers, AESPs, and the NASA*Talk* team extended and constructed new knowledge. Conference participants, or the community of practice, facilitated one another's knowledge acquisition and learning through interaction and collaboration (Lave & Wenger, 1991; Vygotsky, 1986; Wenger, 1996).

## REFERENCES

Bieber, M., Im, I., Rice, R., Goldman-Segall, R., Paul, R., Stohr, E., et al. (2002). Toward knowledge sharing and learning in virtual professional communities. In R. H. Sprague (Ed.), *Proceedings of the 35th Annual Hawaii International Conference on System Sciences* (vol. 8, pp. 2843-2852). Los Alamitos, CA: IEEE Computer Society.Bird, S. (2010, Feb. 25). *RE: 28.space mysteries*. Retrieved from http://www.nasatalk.com/blog/article/bylines/99-nasa-stem-educators-conference/627-28.html.Blueman, M. (2010, Feb. 25). *RE: 2nd Annual NASA STEM Educators Workshop Series*. Retrieved from www.nasatalk.com.

Cortez, B. (2010, Feb. 23). *RE: 3.mapping the moon with WALL-E*. Retrieved from http://www.nasatalk.com/index.php?option=com_resource&controller=article&article=723&category_id=99&Itemid=147.

Dale, S. (2010, May). *Cultivating knowledge through communities of practice*. Paper presented at the Congreso Internacional EDO 2010.

Downing, E. (2010, Feb. 25). *RE: 6.NASA eClips: NASA Launchpad*. Retrieved from http://www.nasatalk.com/blog/article/bylines/99-nasa-stem-educators-conference/720-6-nasa-eclips-nasa-launchpad.html.

Fullwood, D. E. (2010, Feb. 25.). *RE: 10.Buzz Lightyear*. Retrieved from http://www.nasatalk.com/index.php?option=com_resource&controller=article&article=716&category_id=99&Itemid=147.

Fullwood, D. E. (2010, Mar. 1). *RE: 13.NASA Educator Resource Center Network*. Retrieved from http://www.nasatalk.com/index.php?option=com_resource&controller=article&article=711&category_id=99&Itemid=147.

Hai-Jew, S. (2008a). Designing discovery learning spaces. In S. Hai-Jew (Ed.), Scaffolding discovery learning spaces. *Journal of Online Learning and Teaching, 4*(4), 533-548. Retrieved from http://jolt.merlot.org/vol4no4/Self%20Discovery%20Learning%20Spaces.ppt.

Hai-Jew, S. (2008b). Scaffolding discovery learning spaces. *Journal of Online Learning and Teaching, 4*(4), 533–548. Retrieved from http://jolt.merlot.org/vol4no4/hai-jew_1208.htm.

Janta, K. (2010, Feb. 7). *RE: RE: 2nd Annual NASA STEM Educators Workshop Series*. Retrieved from http://www.nasatalk.com/index.php?option=com_resource&controller=article&article=578&category_id=2&Itemid=0.

Janta, K. (2010, Feb. 26). *RE: 8.paper plate Astronomy*. Retrieved from http://www.nasatalk.com/index.php?option=com_resource&controller=article&article=718&category_id=99&Itemid=147.

Lave, J., & Wenger, E. (1991). *Situated learning: Legitimate peripheral participation (learning in doing: Social, cognitive and computational perspectives)*. Cambridge, UK: Cambridge University Press.

Lin, F., Lin, S., & Huang, T. (2008). Knowledge sharing and creation in a teachers' professional virtual community. *Computers & Education, 50*(3), 742–756. doi:10.1016/j.compedu.2006.07.009

Miles, M. B., & Huberman, A. M. (1994). *Qualitative data analysis: An expanded sourcebook*. Thousand Oaks, CA: Sage.

NASA. *Talk*. (2010). *2nd Annual NASA STEM Educators Workshop Series*. Retrieved from http://www.nasatalk.com/collaboratives/nasa-stem-educators-workshop.html.

NASA administrator. (2010a, Feb. 25). *RE: 1.STEM resources from discovery education*. Retrieved from http://www.nasatalk.com/index.php?option=com_resource&controller=article&article=725&category_id=99&Itemid=147.

NASA administrator. (2010b, Feb. 25). *RE: 4.seeing the moon*. Retrieved from http://www.nasatalk.com/blog/article/bylines/99-nasa-stem-educators-conference/722-4-seeing-the-moon.html.

NASA administrator. (2010c, Feb. 25). *RE: 7.rocket science*. Retrieved from http://www.nasatalk.com/blog/article/bylines/99-nasa-stem-educators-conference/719-7-rocket-science.html.

Pane, J. (2010, Feb. 19). *RE: 8.paper plate Astronomy*. Retrieved from http://www.nasatalk.com/index.php?option=com_resource&controller=article&article=718&category_id=99&Itemid=147.

Pane, J. (2010, Feb. 26). *RE: 8.paper plate Astronomy*. Retrieved from http://www.nasatalk.com/index.php?option=com_resource&controller=article&article=718&category_id=99&Itemid=147.

Ruberg, L., Calinger, M., & Howard, B. (2009). Evaluating educational technologies: Historical milestones. In Tomei, L. A. (Ed.), *Designing instruction for the traditional, adult, and distance learner: A new engine for technology-based teaching* (pp. 285–297). Hershey, PA: IGI Global.

Smith, D. (2010a, Feb. 25). *9.starry night from Fisher Scientific*. Retrieved from http://www.nasatalk.com/index.php?option=com_resource&controller=article&article=717&category_id=99&Itemid=147.

Smith, D. (2010b, Feb. 25). *RE: 17.robot ecology*. Retrieved from http://www.nasatalk.com/index.php?option=com_resource&controller=article&article=707&category_id=99&Itemid=147.

Stake, R. E. (2000). Case studies. In Denzin, N. K., & Lincoln, Y. S. (Eds.), *Handbook of qualitative research* (2nd ed., pp. 435–454). Thousand Oaks, CA: Sage.

Strauss, A., & Corbin, J. (1998). *Basics of qualitative research* (2nd ed.). Thousand Oaks, CA: Sage.

Vygotsky, L. S. (1986). *Thought and language: The development of higher psychological processes* (Kozulin, A., Ed.). Cambridge, MA: MIT Press.

Ward, B. (2010a, Feb. 27). *RE: 2nd Annual NASA STEM Educators Workshop Series*. Retrieved from www.nasatalk.com.

Ward, B. (2010b, Feb. 27). *RE: 2nd Annual NASA STEM Educators Workshop Series*. Retrieved from www.nasatalk.com.

Wenger, E. (1996). Communities of practice: The social fabric of the learning organization. *The Healthcare Forum Journal*, *39*(4), 20–26.

Wood, P. (2010, Feb. 24). *RE: 17.robot ecology*. Retrieved from http://www.nasatalk.com/index.php?option=com_resource&controller=article&article=707&category_id=99&Itemid=147.

## KEY TERMS AND DEFINITIONS

**Community of Practice:** A community of practice provides an environment that connects people and encourages them to share ideas and experiences (Dale, 2010). In NASA*Talk* the community of practice is a joint enterprise comprised of STEM content experts, K-16 educators, Classroom of the Future and NASA support staff, and other members interested in using NASA STEM resources in education. The NASA*Talk* community of practice binds members together as a virtual networking repository for the discussion of using NASA STEM resources to create awareness and to educate students and teachers about the many ways to use NASA materials in the classroom. NASA*Talk* produces a shared repertoire of communal resources (lesson plans, web links, vocabulary, best practice methods, multimedia, and events) that members develop over time.

**NASA*Talk*:** An online collaborative that focuses on providing professional communications that differ from other social networking sites, such as Facebook and MySpace. Perhaps the term procial networking or a combination of professional networking opportunities in a social virtual community can assist in distinguishing what NASA*Talk* aims to accomplish—providing an online forum that makes it easy for STEM and NASA educators to hear from and respond to their community's needs, ideas, and feedback.

**Online Discovery Learning Spaces:** Online environments that provide active learning experiences that support autonomy, learner directedness, and creativity (Hai-Jew, 2008a, 2008b).

**Professional Virtual Community:** In a professional virtual community the community concept is extended to a virtual form identified by the following characteristics: 1) the community is built upon a computer-mediated space, or cyberspace; 2) activities are enabled by information and communications technology (ICT); 3) virtual community topics or contents are driven by the participants; 4) community relationships evolve through interactions among members; and 5) a professional virtual community accrues people who share common interests and collaborate to achieve common goals (Lin, Lin, & Huang, 2008).

**Self-Discovery Online Learning Opportunities:** Online environments that promote independence and purposefulness for the user in addition to high levels of engagement with multimedia.

## ENDNOTES

[1] This study was supported by U.S. Federal Grant NNX08AJ71A.

[2] Procial networking term first used on NASA*Talk* by NASA program manager.

# Chapter 5
# Knowledge Spaces for Online Discovery Learning

**Roger W. McHaney**
*Kansas State University, USA*

## ABSTRACT

*Constructivist learning environments have been enhanced with emerging digital infrastructures, particularly those based on Internet and Web 2.0 technologies. In this chapter, the impact of these technologies on a constructivist-rooted pedagogy known as discovery learning is discussed in detail. Specifically, the use of knowledge spaces for online discovery learning is explored within the context of case-based learning, incidental learning, learning by exploring/conversing, learning by reflection, and simulation-based learning. This chapter first provides a theoretical rationale for enhancing these approaches and then describes several low cost and free tools that can be used in each of the five areas. Technology implementation and practitioner-oriented examples are provided for each with a particular emphasis on Web 2.0 applications in higher education venues.*

## INTRODUCTION

Emerging digital infrastructures, particularly those based on Internet and Web 2.0 technologies, have enabled significant advancements in constructivist learning environments. Students and teachers are finding numerous low cost and free tools suited to the construction of meaningful digital artifacts embodying the idea that reality is manifest in human thought. According to constructivist views, each new concept is mediated by previous constructions of reality. Human cognitive development, therefore, is a continually adaptive process of assimilation, accommodation, and correction (Piaget, 1972). Additionally, a social element can be added to constructivism suggesting socialization plays an important role in human cognitive development. This dialectical learning process shapes technology which in turn influences human interaction and enhances understanding (Bijker, 1995). In other words, humans change in response to their use of technology, and technology changes in response to human use (Lemke, 1993). A mutually beneficial ecosystem results in which knowledge is developed, shared, and enhanced. The conjoined processes of teaching and learning are integral elements in this construction (Ryder, 2009).

DOI: 10.4018/978-1-61350-320-1.ch005

Copyright © 2012, IGI Global. Copying or distributing in print or electronic forms without written permission of IGI Global is prohibited.

Whereas learning theory is a belief that knowledge is assimilated according to particular mechanisms, pedagogy refers to strategies of instruction and teaching methods useful in implementation of learning, generally approached from the perspective of the teacher. Often this means developing a style of instruction to support student learning. Learning theories do not offer descriptions of teaching nor do they provide instructional approaches for classroom use. Instead they are philosophical approaches that enable and facilitate learning. Practical use of learning theories can be manifest through pedagogies. Several of which are consistent with constructivist learning theory. Among these constructivist-rooted pedagogical approaches are team learning, service learning, experiential learning, and discovery learning.

This chapter specifically explores the constructivist-rooted pedagogy, discovery learning, when applied to knowledge spaces. First, overviews of constructivism and discovery learning concepts are provided. Next, examples of how knowledge spaces enhance discovery learning are explored in five topical areas often associated with this pedagogy. Among these areas are: case-based learning, incidental learning, learning by exploring/conversing, learning by reflection and simulation-based learning. In addition, the first topical area, case-based learning, is used to illustrate a number of Web 2.0 tools that enable wide-scale and inexpensive deployment of knowledge spaces in the emerging and increasingly digital learning environments found in institutions of higher education. Other tools and techniques are described in the remaining four topical areas. Finally, the concepts presented in this chapter are discussed and summarized.

## CONSTRUCTIVISM CONCEPTS

The conceptual foundations of constructivism were influenced heavily by elements many theorists believed were missing from other learning theories. For instance, prior to constructivism, behaviorism, rooted in work by Pavlov, Skinner, and others suggested learning could be measured by behavioral change. Behaviorists viewed learning as a concept which could not be measured directly. Therefore, they believed a surrogate, instantiated as *behavioral change,* had to be measured instead. They posited that behavioral change was shaped by (1) the environment, (2) how close in time two events occur, and (3) reinforcement (either positive or negative). Behaviorists suggested that if a process influences behavior in a meaningful, long term way, then it was reasonable to assume learning had occurred.

The concept of behaviorism spawned a number of pedagogies. For instance, the idea of testing and giving grades is a form of behavioral reinforcement. Exam scores are viewed as measurable surrogates for learning. Instructivism (or direct instruction) is a common representation of behaviorism in education (Kim & Axelrod, 2005). Instructivist learning theory suggests knowledge exists outside the learner and is taught to the student by a teacher. Instructivism and other forms of behaviorism are generally teacher-centered. The student passively receives information from an authority.

Learning theory became the subject of numerous studies and several scholars suggested behaviorism did not adequately explain the process of learning. Among them, Bode (1929), believed behaviorism oversimplified learning. His ideas centered on cognitive changes internal to the individual and relied less on overt behavior (Bode, 1929). His research resulted in a learning theory called cognitivism. Bode's ideas drew on his era's understanding of the brain in the following ways: (1) the brain comprises an active memory system that organizes and processes information, and (2) learning is influenced by prior knowledge. Bode believed learning was far more than behavioral change and had a brain-level physical component. Cognitivists suggest that short term information stored in the brain was transferred into long term memory when learning took place. Cognitivism, therefore, suggested learning occurred at the individual level.

Constructivism was pioneered by in the early 1930's (Bartlett, 1932). Early constructivists believed cognitivism lacked several important practical elements and reframed learning theory by suggesting (Fosnot, 2005):

1. learning is a building process where the learner actively constructs new ideas and conceptual understandings based on prior knowledge and current experiences.
2. learning largely takes place while learners reflect on their experiences.
3. learning is a personal experience that enables an individual to apply knowledge in the real world.
4. learning is the journey, not the outcome

In other words, "[w]hat someone knows is grounded in perception of the physical and social experiences which are comprehended by the mind (Jonassen, 1991)." Various manifestations of constructivism exist. Included are active learning, service learning, self-directed learning, experiential learning, reflective practices, discovery learning, and knowledge building. All of these variants promote exploration within an appropriate framework. This means the constructivist teacher facilitates learning by providing infrastructure for knowledge building. The actual learning becomes the student's responsibility.

A criticism of constructivism relates to these concepts: if each learner constructs his/her reality and interprets it based on personal experience, then how as a society, can everyone communicate and coexist? A concept called social constructivism emerged to explain.

## Social Constructivism

Social constructivism extends constructivism by recognizing the importance of other actors, society, and culture in the process of learning. It primarily focuses on an individual's learning that takes place during group interactions. However, social constructivism recognizes common platforms for understanding can emerge and enable communication on agreed-upon concepts (Vygotsky, 1978). Reality then emerges through social negotiation.

As a result, social constructivists believe social interaction and communication result in commonly constructed knowledge. Talking, communicating, and engaging in shared activities result in learning. Therefore, social constructivist learning is the process of skilled societal members facilitating knowledge transfer to others (Driver, Asoko, Leach, Mortimer, & Scott, 1994).

## Constructivist Teaching

The Internet and Web 2.0 technologies have provided the potential for significant advancements in constructivist learning environments. Pedagogies consistent with constructivist thought are much easier to implement in this emerging world and readily capture the imagination of students, many of which already use a wide array of technologies in their daily lives (Pew Research Center, 2010). Many successful pedagogies use emerging digital infrastructures to transform students from passive learners into active participants. These concepts promote the idea that learning through the construction of online artifacts and engagement of unique, individual experiences is possible in a growing number of ways. Constructivist teachers are able to creatively facilitate students who learn through exploration, discovery, and artifact creation in the emerging digital world. Since many students have a base of technical knowledge, they are comfortable and eager to participate in learning this way.

Knowledge spaces are a primary feature in the emerging digital environment. The term *knowledge space* has several meanings. In the field of mathematical psychology, a *knowledge space* is a combinatorial structure describing all possible states of a human learner's knowledge in a particular domain (Doignon & Falmagne, 1999). A knowledge space can be created through first modeling the entire domain as a set of all potential, relevant concepts. A subset containing known (or knowable) concepts is extracted and this becomes the knowledge space.

Pierre Lévy in *Collective Intelligence* (1997) describes a practical view of knowledge space. He uses the term *collective intelligence* to describe the power of diffuse collaboration and the use of technology to collectively create knowledge. Knowledge space then becomes the virtual implementation of social learning in various cyberspace representations such as wikis and other social media (Lévy, 1997). This chapter operationalizes Lévy's sense of knowledge space in discovery learning.

## DISCOVERY LEARNING

Discovery learning is a successfully applied pedagogy. This constructivist method of inquiry-based instruction characterized by three important attributes (Bicknell-Holmes & Hoffman, 2000): (1) students engage in exploration and problem solving to create, integrate, and distill knowledge; (2) students learn and progress at their own pace, driven by their own interests; and, (3) existing knowledge forms the basis for constructing new knowledge (Gijlers & Jong, 2005). These three attributes often are manifest effectively in social environments where students interact with peers, have access to peer knowledge, build upon existing knowledge (scaffolding), explore new surroundings, and experience various objects (digital and otherwise).

Not all critics agree that discovery learning is a sound pedagogical approach. Among elementary school aged subjects, empirical study (Klahr & Nigam, 2004) and research (Kirschner, Sweller, & Clark, 2006); (Rittle-Johnson, 2006) suggest discovery learning may be problematic and less effective than instructor-led education. These findings, however, are disputed by empirical research citing a long term perspective is required to truly determine whether Instructivism results in better knowledge acquisition than discovery learning approaches (Dean & Kuhn, 2007).

A variety of possible architectures are possible in the implementation of discovery learning. Among these are (Shank & Cleary, 1994):

1. case-based learning
2. incidental learning
3. learning by exploring/conversing
4. learning by reflection
5. simulation-based learning

While originally envisioned in traditional environments, all five of these architectures can be implemented within emerging digital environments. The next sections of this chapter explore potential implementations in each category and provide suggested tools for implementation of related digital discovery learning and examples of use in learning. A particular focus on online knowledge spaces (as defined by Lévy, 1997) will be highlighted in each section.

## CASE-BASED LEARNING

Case-based learning uses stories or vignettes that provide students with details about complex situations. Often, cases are based on real-world examples and require decisions to arrive at particular outcomes. Sometimes, a case will be investigated by several student groups. The groups' decisions will be compared and the consequences of their proposed actions will be discussed. In cases based on real-world situations, historic outcomes also can be incorporated into knowledge creation. Case-based learning is frequently used in business, medical, law, and veterinarian schools. Teachers facilitate the cases attempting to create 'teachable moments' where the students arrive at deeper understanding. Most of the learning, however, is the student's responsibility and requires learners to explore, build new knowledge based on existing experiences, and reflect on decisions that lead to consequences.

Case-based learning requires several items for implementation. Foremost, it requires a vignette. Additionally, a forum is needed for interaction, structuring a solution, and feedback. Finally, if the case is based on a real-world incident, the instructor can provide resources that indicate the actions taken and the resulting consequences.

## Vignettes

The use of vignettes and stories promote learning for a variety of reasons. For instance, students can identify with a vignette's connection to the real world. Often, empathetic responses are generated bringing the character 'to life' in the students' minds. Additionally, stories may be viewed as entertaining and engaging (Neuhauser, 1993). Cases often deal with human experiences which provide a sense of reality. Discussions of the vignette make the learning compatible with social constructivism as envisioned by Vygotsky (1978). Stories can make dull information memorable because the learner becomes involved with the actions and intentions of the characters. Since a story can't provide all details, individual student experiences from the past provide the unspoken details together with deeper meanings in the story. Stories are likely to provide more than information and encourage transformation (Jackson, 1995). Stories of achievement can function as motivation, enlightenment, and inspiration.

A variety of online resources and knowledge spaces can be used to for case-based learning. For example, blogs can provide knowledge space for developing and sharing cases. The instructor can use the blog as a central location to post a vignette and then use the blog's discussion threads for feedback and comments from the case participants. A knowledge space related to the case will emerge. Not only is the information posted and discussion displayed, an instructor can determine the contributions of each student and determine if a particular learner might require additional guidance or facilitation in their exploration.

A classroom blog can be developed by the teacher as a starting point for the case to be displayed. Once established, this digital space can be used by the learners to build a relevant knowledge base. This space will belong to the entire class to foster communication and collaboration. Although the classroom blog contains common contributions, the teacher can subtly guide the conversation and move learning in an appropriate direction by revealing additional sources or by introducing new resources. The information generated by a group or class can be removed at the conclusion of the learning exercise or it can be preserved and used as a starting point for future student discussions in subsequent semesters.

Following the posting of a case, teachers may elect to provide prompting entries to stimulate discussion. Blogs may enable shy students to participate more comfortably in class. Blogs also permit learners to post links to images, audio files and videos. In general, students will learn from their peers and create a collective knowledge space that gives a sense of cohesion to individual projects.

### Blogger

Blogger is an example of a blog website where case studies can be developed and stored. Blogger is a free service launched in 1999 by Pyra Labs as one of the first Web sites to successfully promote blog publishing. It helped standardize and popularize the format used by most blogs today (Blood, 2004). In 2003, Blogger was purchased by Google and integrated with Picasa to enable photo posting. Additional features have been added since that time including multimedia support, RSS feed capability, and various widgets to perform tasks that enrich blog entries (Blogger, 2010). Blogger can be found at http://www.blogger.com (see Figure 1).

## Open Educational Resources

Cases can also be obtained from existing knowledge spaces such as open educational resources, online magazines and journals, forums, existing discussions and so forth. An example comes from an organization called the OpenCourseWare Consortium or OCW. OCW promotes the exchange and publication of free and open high quality digital educational materials (Johnstone, 2005). Currently, the consortium has memberships from over 200 higher education institutions and organizations. A knowledge space such as OCW provides a repository for digital case material and allows learners to interact in ways that can enhance their educational experiences. OCW has several goals including (Open Courseware Consortium, 2008):

- extend the reach and impact of open courseware by encouraging the adoption and adaptation of open educational materials around the world;
- foster the development of additional open courseware projects;
- ensure the long-term sustainability of open courseware projects by identifying ways to improve effectiveness and reduce costs.

OCW's courseware is free to anyone wishing to use it, however in order to contribute material, a university must commit to publishing material from at least 10 courses. This ensures only committed universities are contributing and it helps provide a measure of quality control. The OCW website is illustrated in Figure 2.

## Connexions

Another environment for sharing collaboratively developed content on the Web is Connexions (Connexions, 2010). Like OCW, Connexions is not dedicated to case material. It does provide a venue for teachers and educators to share case studies in a collaborative way (Rice University, 2010). It was started by Richard G. Baraniuk, an engineering professor at Rice University with a $6 million grant from the William and Flora Hewlett Foundation. The idea behind Connexions is based on the music industry with its *rip, burn and mash* mindset. Rather than material being locked into textbooks, Baraniuk envisions textbook publishing becoming a changing and growing ecosystem and not a profit-producing pipeline (Cohen, 2008).

*Figure 1. Blogger website*

*Figure 2. OCW website*

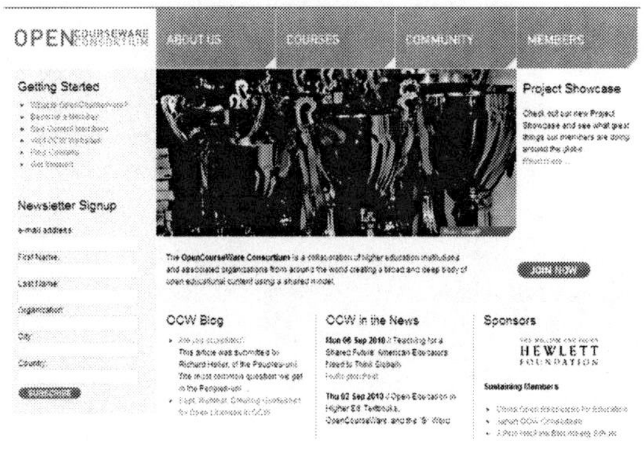

Connexions utilizes the idea of a *Content Commons* where educational material can be contributed and shared by anyone ranging from kindergarten teachers to distinguished professors at top universities. This material is stored in modules that form collections, courses, or books depending on the authors' paradigms and needs. Case studies can be stored as modules or compilations based on topic. All material on the site is free under the Creative Commons "attribution" license (Connexions, 2008). Connexions promotes the following approach to education, learning, and knowledge (adapted from the Connexions Website, see Figure 3).

- **Modular and Non-Linear Content:** Most textbooks are a mass of information in linear format. However, human brains are not linear. People learn by linking new concepts with familiar ones. Connexions mimics this by breaking down content into smaller chunks, called modules, that can be linked together and arranged in different ways.
- **Sharing:** When people share their knowledge, they can select from the best ideas to create the most effective learning materials.
- **Technological:** Content is stored in XML to ensures it works on multiple computer platforms.

*Figure 3. Connexions website: http://cnx.org/*

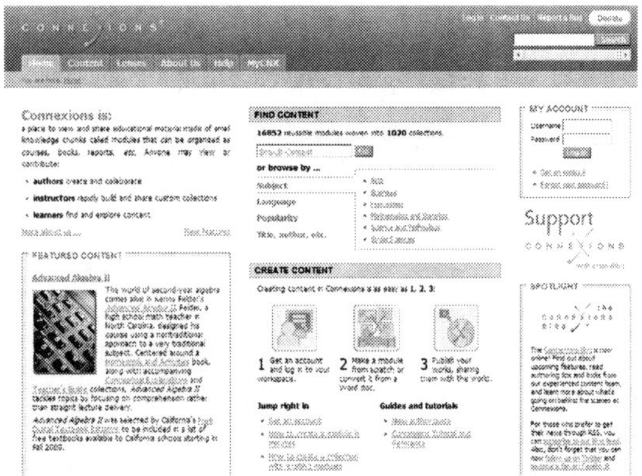


- **Legal:** Creative Commons open-content licenses make it easy for authors to share their work, allowing others to use and reuse it legally, while still getting recognition and attribution for their efforts.
- **Educational:** Authors are encouraged to write each module to stand on its own. This is done so others can adapt material for use in different courses and contexts.
- **Collaboration:** Just as knowledge is interconnected, people don't live in a vacuum. Connexions promotes communication between content creators and provides various means of collaboration. Collaboration helps knowledge grow more quickly, advancing the possibilities for new ideas from which all can benefit.

## Scribd

A popular social publishing and online knowledge space website is Scribd.com. Scribd houses a number of case studies suitable for classroom use that can be accessed for prices ranging from free to several dollars. It also provides access to a wide range of online books and textbooks. Scribd offers analytics describing the frequency and pattern in which documents are downloaded and read (Locke, 2010). Scribd views itself as the *YouTube of the written word* and reports that more than 60 million people visit its website each month to share original books, digital documents, and articles (see Figure 4).

## Stories2Learn

Another example of a Web 2.0 enabled social publishing site, relevant to case study development and sharing, is Stories2Learn.com (S2L). The founder, Ray Jimenez, welcomes "trainers, teachers, eLearning designers and developers, leaders, designers, subject matter experts (SMEs) and everyone in all types of organizations to share stories and collaborate to refine and fine tune

*Figure 4. Scribd.com houses many case studies*

stories. The ultimate goal is to build a site where everyone can share their stories and borrow stories to use in their learning activities." S2L is a social website that encourages the collaborative development of story creation and sharing to promote learning (Stories2Learn, 2010). See Figure 5.

## Forums

The constructivist approach suggests *learning is* a building process. From this perspective, students actively construct new ideas and create conceptual understanding based on prior knowledge and current experiences. A case-based approach to online discovery learning requires that students interact through digital tools that enable social interaction, discussion, idea formulation, and decision-making. Some students may also elect to use online forum tools to aid in reflection activities.

*Figure 5. Stories2Learn website*

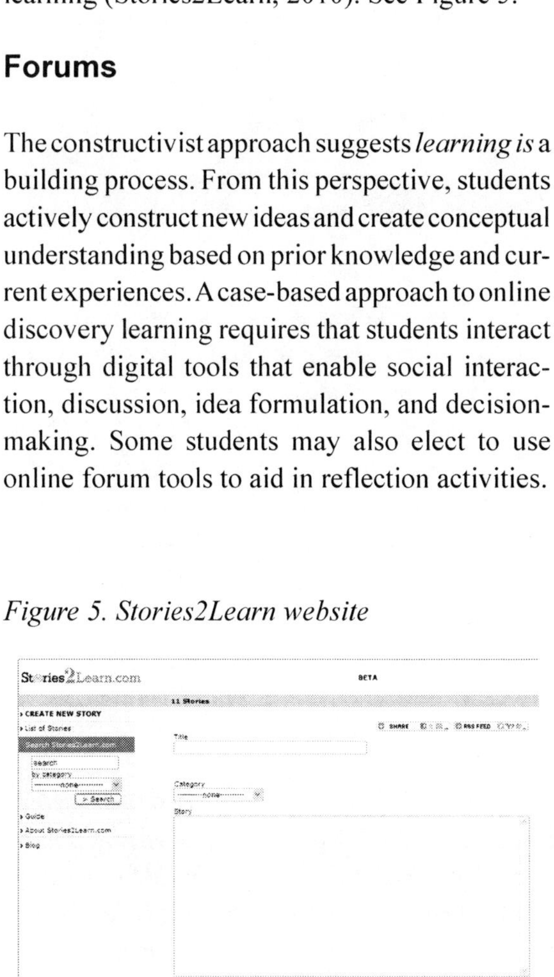


A number of tools can facilitate social interaction for learning within this context. For instance, we already discussed how blogs provide space for feedback. Other tools also can be used to construct online knowledge spaces. For instance, threaded discussion board technology, which preceded the advent of the World Wide Web, can be used in this way. Many free and low cost tools exist online for the creation of these forums. One example is Google Groups (See Figure 6). A Google group is initiated by a user. Once created, the 'owner' can manage email mailing lists, and engage in communication and collaboration with members. The resulting threaded discussions are maintained on Google's servers (Whitney, 2010).

Other commercially hosted forum tools are plentiful. One example, FastTalk is a threaded discussion group program intended to facilitate and manage traditional forums (Web Transitions, 2010). As a hosted application, it requires very little administration (FastTalk, 2010). Other examples can be found as parts of Websites. For instance, computing.net maintains an iPhone forum on its web site: http://www.computing.net/forum/iphone/1.html.

In addition to hosted offerings such as Google groups, forums can be installed and administered through a user's web server using tools such as Drupal's free forum module or, perhaps the best known bulletin board software, phpBB (See Figure 7).

PhpBB is free, scalable software intended to support large, multi-category boards for corporate websites (Douglass, Little, & Smith, 2005). PhpBB offers an extensive administration panel to permit customization of intricate features without the need to edit code directly (phpBB, 2010).

Web 2.0 technology has enabled threaded discussion software to move beyond text messages to richer forms of media such as voice and video forums. Among these, VoiceThread and Grapevinetalk stand out. VoiceThread allows groups to construct and post a multimedia slide show relevant to an ongoing discussion. Images,

*Figure 6. Google groups website*

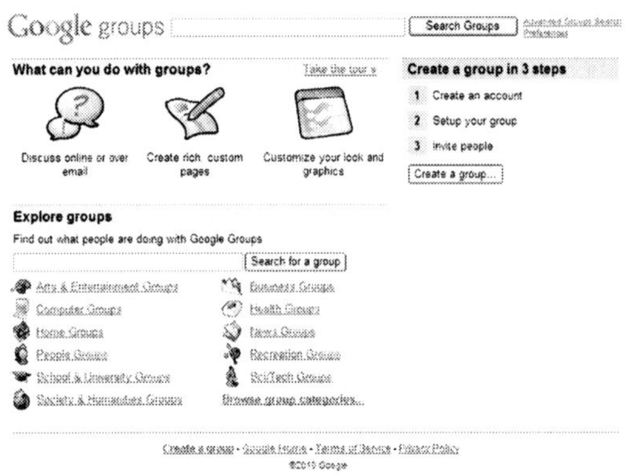


*Figure 7. phpBB website for bulletin board software*

documents, voice, and video elements can all be included. Learners can navigate the slides and leave comments in five different ways--- voice with a microphone, voice with a mobile phone or smart device, text, audio file recorded on a computer, or video with a webcam. The comments form a group conversation (VoiceThread, 2010). This tool can facilitate group discussions, decision-making, and documentation (Weir, 2008). Similarly, Grapevine Talk permits the posting of audio material and enables an asynchronous conversation to emerge (Grapevine Talk, 2010). Figures 8 and 9 show VoiceThread and Grapevine Talk.

### Real World Outcomes

Discussing real-world outcomes and implications are often a concluding activity in case-based learning. The results of real-world cases can either be provided by teachers or located by students through

*Figure 8. VoiceThread website*

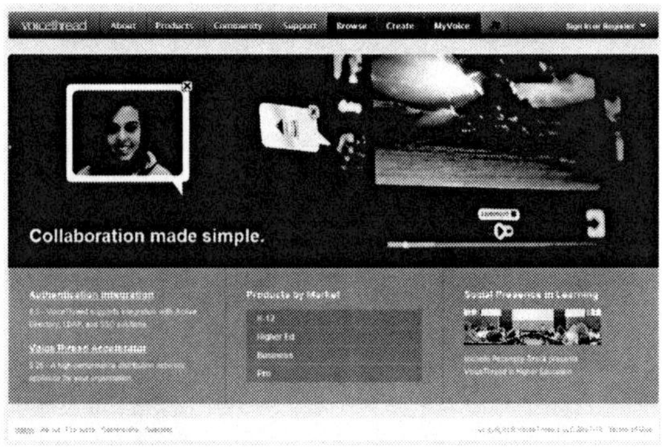


*Figure 9. Grapevine talk website*

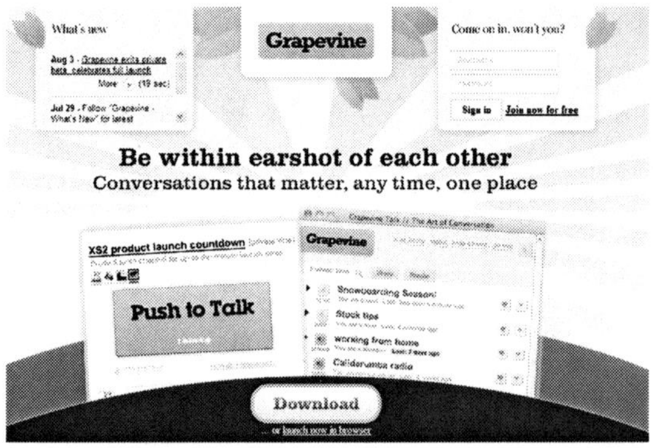


exploration. Online news searches, magazine articles, library databases and other venues can provide the raw material for this phase. Access to this material can be provided through a blog or by sharing the digital location where information might be found. A closing discussion can be implemented as an online knowledge space using forum technology as discussed in the preceding section.

## INCIDENTAL LEARNING

The term *incidental learning* is used in discovery learning to represent peripheral knowledge gained by students (Shank & Cleary, 1994) as they engage in other learning activities. This form of acquiring knowledge has a way of sneaking up on students and they might not realize they are learning until later. This makes incidental learning powerful and natural. Incidental learning may occur in a number of different ways (Kerka, 2000):

1. When working
2. When using computers
3. Through observation, repetition, social interaction, and problem solving
4. From implicit meanings in classroom or workplace policies
5. When socially interacting with colleagues or experts
6. From mistakes, assumptions, beliefs, and attributions
7. From adapting to situations

Many of these categories match other forms of discovery learning since incidental learning involves the unexpected knowledge acquired during other activities or discussions. Incidental learning in often associated with games (Castronova, 2002) and although, it is incidental, teachers can direct activities in a way that increases students' likelihoods of encountering this knowledge. To move incidental learning into online self-discovery learning spaces, students can be directed to activities that require interacting in virtual worlds (metaverses) or engaging in MMORPGs (Massively multiplayer online role-playing games).

## Metaverses[1]

These are perhaps one of the most riveting online knowledge spaces available to learners. Virtual worlds are entered through a user's computer. The student interfaces with that world and its virtual inhabitants through visual images on the screen and various voice, text, and keystroke commands. Like real worlds, metaverses have limitations and "natural laws" that govern the actions of its inhabitants.

Metaverses can be used for learning in several, very different ways. Students can essentially be asked to replicate their real world educational experiences online. In other words, a "normal" class can be held with lectures, discussions, exams, labs, and projects. While this provides a good starting point, classes can be extended to utilize the features of a virtual world not available to a traditional classroom. For instance, students can take a field trip where they fly together over ancient Rome or swim through an ocean.

Innovative classes take a different form and move closer to the idea of an online discovery learning space. By expanding learning into a 3-D environment that can be simultaneously synchronous and asynchronous, students suddenly find themselves acquiring enormous amounts of incidental knowledge. Much of this information comes from unexpected experiences that students encounter while interacting in the virtual world. In the same way that a study abroad trip introduces students to countless undocumented customs, small unexpected experiences, annoyances, pleasures, and other unplanned learning moments, experience in online worlds can provide learning with respect to topics outside the class syllabus such as understanding the environment; developing communication capabilities; being able to navigate the world; understanding commerce in the virtual world; technology options; identity choices; social interaction; online tools; content management and digital property ownership issues; currency exchange; team work; skills for exploring and acquiring new knowledge; and the ability to use construction tools and techniques (Calongne, 2008).

Incidental learning can be facilitated by a teacher that asks their class to enter and interact within the context of a virtual world. For instance, a teacher might ask students to complete a class project within a virtual world such as Second Life or Active Worlds. While the eventual content of the project might be similar to a term paper or other traditional artifact, the construction, delivery, and presentation methods will be very different. In order to complete the project, students will need to become acclimated to the environment. This process generally will result in incidental learning.

A basic approach that helps students adapt to a virtual world[2] can take the following form (Calongne, 2008):

1. The experience can begin with a basic orientation. Since a variety of islands, educational centers, virtual buildings, museums, cities, and other interesting places already exist and are publically accessible, providing a quick glimpse of the possibilities helps motivate students for their entry and use. Some students may find the environment overwhelming and providing a quick overview may help eliminate these fears.
2. Students will need to create accounts and find ways to get online. Incidental learning with respect to technology, communications, network speeds, and other areas will be acquired.
3. Students need to create avatars, establish an identity and learn how to move about in the world. In virtual worlds like Second Life, students can customize their avatar and experience various levels of social acceptance based on how they look and their level of sophistication. They should be allowed to spend time exploring the possibilities and mastering basic movement and navigation skills. This activity is important because it enables students to personalize their online experience. Without feeling connected to their world, students will be less likely to understand and experience the benefits of using this environment and will experience less incidental learning.
4. Students should spend time exploring public virtual sites. At first, they may feel clumsy and lacking sophistication. This will change as they experience other avatars that interact with them in a variety of ways. Incidental learning related to acceptable social behaviors and others' perceptions of their avatar will occur.
5. Other aspects of a cyberworld need to be learned. For instance, taking snapshots of surroundings, being able to view avatars' current appearance and understanding how to view the landscape from above, in a 360-degree motion, or in other ways.
6. After exploring the environment, students are ready for a project that will move them into the domain of interest.

Since virtual world learning can be fun, students are likely to engage in incidental learning. Class settings can be varied. Communication methods can include voice, text, animated movement and demonstration. There is no need to be constrained in a chair during the exercise or a need to look a certain way. Various physical handicaps are mitigated and contribution styles and types can take a variety of forms. Also, online tools for creativity exist and can be used in virtual worlds, giving students options for constructing artifacts to enhance their learning.

## Online Game Worlds

Online game worlds are a subset of virtual worlds and metaverses that are currently experiencing a great deal of popularity and have become a booming industry. Online games worlds generally focus on a particular theme (often fantasy-related) and involve using an avatar to achieve tasks and progress through interactive and dynamic storylines influenced by actions, decisions, and peers. Generally, this progression is competitive and involves winning contests or beating foes.

Nearly all sizable virtual game worlds are commercial since a large programming staff is required to keep the games fresh and innovative. Most game worlds are classified as MMORPGs (Massively multiplayer online role-playing games) and accommodate tens of thousands of simultaneous users. MMORPGS continue to change and evolve even when a player's character is not being used. Example MMORPGs include *World of Warcraft* and *Guild Wars*.

### World of Warcraft

World of Warcraft, or WoW, is by Blizzard Entertainment, is the leading MMORPG with more than 11.5 active, million paid monthly subscribers (Cavalli, 2008). Users in WoW develop skills that help succeed in quests. Successful quests provide connections to other players, new skills, access to new territory and adventures. Quests promote group learning, team work and group decision making dynamics (World of Warcraft, 2010). See Figure 10.

Like any virtual world, online game worlds and MMORPGs are intended to be fun experiences. This makes these ideal venues for incidental learning and for acquiring new knowledge while engaging in a variety of activities.

*Figure 10. Virtual Avatars (Photo courtesy of John E. Lester)*

## LEARNING BY EXPLORING / CONVERSING

Discovery learning by exploring and conversing is very much like the Socratic method of questioning, answering, and questioning more. Students are provided with a starting point or mystery together with a venue for assembling clues, findings, evidence, and new questions. This can be a formal question and answer exploration involving multiple people or it can be more of a research project approach where information is assembled and vetted, then presented as an artifact.

Online knowledge space is ideal for this activity using many of the tools mentioned in earlier sections of this chapter. For instance, blogs can be used for individual efforts. Wikis make ideal online spaces for collective efforts of team members whether they are separated by time and space or working in close proximity. Web 2.0 tools such as VoiceThread and Grapevine Talk can provide methods to collect information and facilitate asynchronous discussions. Other spaces including online discussion sites such as Topix.com and ExperienceProject.com give students a voice and place to learn through conversation.

### ELATEwiki

ELATEwiki, the Electronic Learning and Teaching Exchange (ELATEWiki, 2009), is an online venue intended to facilitate the creation and documentation of innovative teaching approaches (McHaney, 2009). This online space is primarily used for that purpose but has also served as online knowledge space for discovery learning. This has been manifested in the form of students projects documenting various technologies used in innovative teaching.

Students use the wiki as a central point to collect information, organize their findings, and create knowledge artifacts. As an example, students explored a Web 2.0 technology called TubeRadio.FM

*Figure 11. TubeRadio.FM on ELATEwiki*

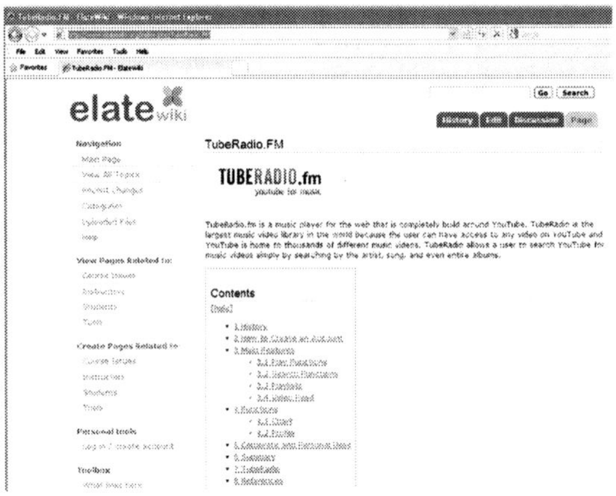


that collects various radio stations being broadcast over the internet (ElateWiki, 2010). See Figure 11.

The initial phase of the project involved a group of students collecting information about the topic and using the wiki as a location to assemble their findings. Figure 12 shows the revision history of the page and how students in the group interacted within the online space provided by the wiki.

*Figure 12. Revision history for TubeRadio.FM on ELATEwiki*

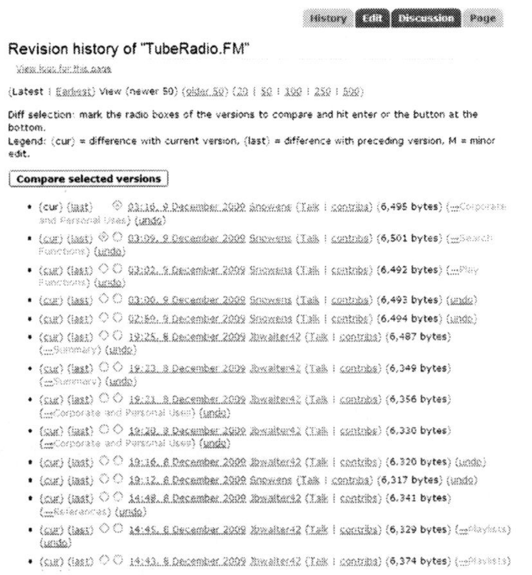


*Figure 13. Website interface embedded in ELATEwiki*

Students added images, embedded information videos, and a live interface to the Website. Figures 13 and 14 provide examples of the material assembled by the students.

A venue like ELATEwiki provides an interface to the real world so students can get comments and feedback from a variety of people including their instructor, peers, and interested people from outside the class. The wiki provides a *talk page* where discussions about the material can be held without disrupting the page that might be seen by anyone in the outside world.

## LEARNING BY REFLECTION

Learning by reflection is often considered a primary manifestation of discovery learning. A basic premise of this approach is the application of interrogation that seeks to link current experiences to prior ones to form a more complex and interrelated mental model of the situation. This interrogative approach should attempt to find commonalities, relationships, differences, and unique elements that extend beyond the superficial. Reflection particularly is suitable when applied to complex

*Figure 14. Embedded video in ELATEwiki*

situations that can be improved or better understood through mentally testing interpretations and alternatives. Traditionally, activities associated with reflection have included journaling, group discussions, and guided inquiries. Research also has shown that social interaction may enhance reflective activities and result in higher quality results that are inclusive of more information than an individual might generate (Smith & Hatton, 1993). Further, Bandura suggests environments that promote this interaction may result in greater levels of reflection (Bandura, 1977). For this reason, computer mediated environments could have an impact on the results of reflection.

Hatton & Smith (1993) provide four elements crucial to reflection that help perform an interrogation in a systematic and logical way:

1. **Description:** Describing events without worrying about reasons
2. **Descriptive reflection:** Ascribing reasons to the events based on prior personal experience and opinion
3. **Dialogic reflection:** Reviewing reasons and attempting to develop alternatives based on personal experience and opinion. This may involve the use of social interaction.
4. **Critical reflection:** Revisiting reflection to consider external context for reasons and modify conclusions.

Each of these areas can be implemented effectively using online discovery space.

## Description

A primary activity in reflection is to describe events as they occur to ensure a complete memory of the situation is preserved. It is important that a sense of timing and sequence also is maintained. A variety of online tools can be used for this activity. Reflection experts and practitioners may recommend using blogging software. It is online, accessible from a variety of locations and on convenient platforms, often includes calendaring, and is automatically preserved. Blogs are generally public websites but can be made private via various settings. As mentioned in a prior section of this chapter, a variety of blogging tools are available. In addition to the ones discussed, WordPress is often mentioned as "a clear favorite thanks to its ease of use, ability to keep entries completely private, and a [low cost] price tag (Fitzpatrick, 2009)." See Figure 15.

Another online tool available for journaling is LiveJournal.com. LiveJournal is a virtual com-

*Figure 15. WordPress.com website*

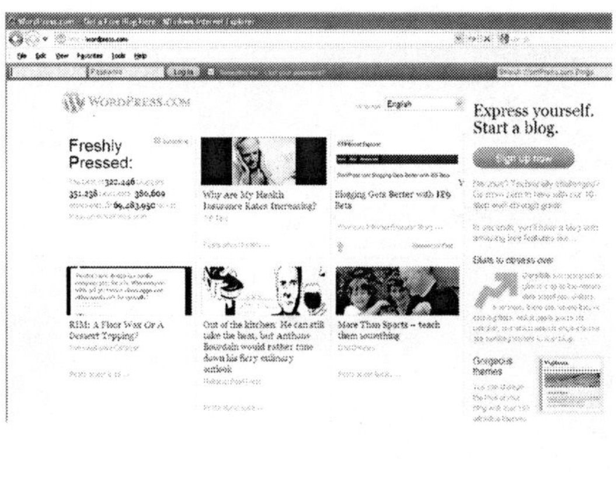

munity that permits various levels of interaction and provides tools that create online entries in the form of blog, journal or diary (LiveJournal, 2010). LiveJournal is similar to WordPress but adds features generally only found with social networks (Fruhlinger, 2010). In addition, LiveJournal allows "voice posts" for users with paid accounts. This streamlines descriptive reflection and provides capability to create an audio record of events as they occur (See Figure 16).

Evernote is another popular application for creating an online descriptive journal. Evernote provides features for taking notes and capturing a variety of digital information including handwritten material (using touch screens and tablet PCs), clippings from Web pages, and optical character recognition from web pages and printed documents (EverNote, 2010). Evernote also provides a mobile interface that permits entries to be created on cell phones and other portable smart devices with Internet connections. It supports Android, Windows, and Mac operating systems. Images can be captured and integrated into the entries and geolocation tags can be added to the notes if appropriate hardware is used (Van Grove, 2010). Evernote also integrates with Twitter and permits remote notes to be added to a journal through tweets (See Figure 17).

*Figure 16. LiveJournal provides journaling space online*

*Figure 17. EverNote allows online notes to be developed*

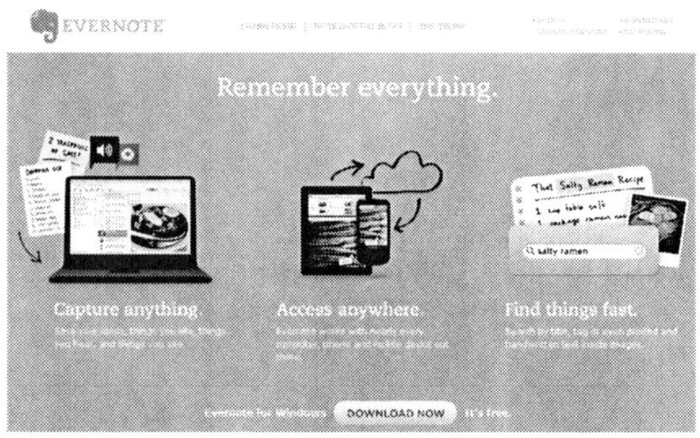


## Descriptive Reflection

Descriptive reflection takes the information captured with journaling or other descriptive techniques for further analysis. The idea is to take personal experience and opinion and begin to organize and make sense of what was collected.

All the blogging and journaling software examples mentioned allow the user to edit entries, add details, tag entries and reorganize notes to begin the process. Newly emerging tools also exist to help with the process of transforming descriptive information into a personal knowledgebase. One example is FreeMind, available on sourceforge. Freemind is a mind-mapping application specifically designed to permit essays, journal entries, ideas, and writings to be refactored (FreeMind, 2010). It uses the idea of a personal knowledgebase to manage, prioritize, and direct people as they think through their experiences (Kazmierski, 2010)

Other examples of software that facilitate descriptive reflection include Mindomo (Mindomo, 2010). This software permits the visual organization of collected information and permits reflection that reorganizes ideas and notes in an online knowledge space (Koznov & Pliskin, 2009). See Figure 18.

*Figure 18. Mindomo provides visual online knowledge space*

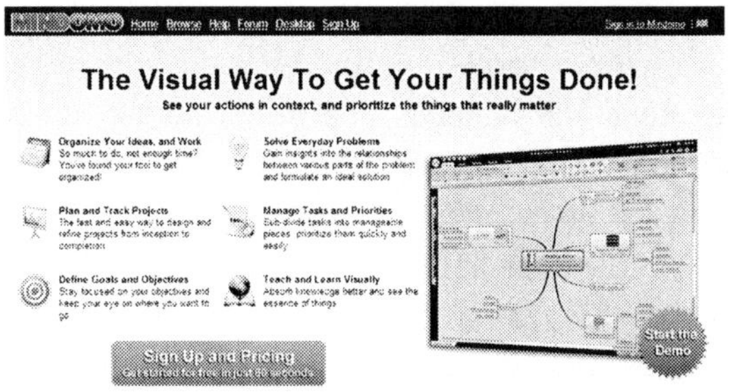


## Dialogic Reflection

This form of reflective practice involves reviewing reasons behind the events and decisions organized and categorized during descriptive reflection. The exercise of dialogic reflection involves determining if alternative outcomes are feasible. In other words, dialogic reflection seeks to ensure no reasonable possibilities have been overlooked. The starting point for this exercise is to develop alternatives based on personal experience and opinion. It may, however be extended through social interaction on blogs or journals.

Most online knowledge space, such as blogs, journals, and mind-mapping tools provide features for sharing and exchanging information. Most blogs provide discussion forum features where questions can be posted and opinions collected. Journal applications have various levels of sharing where the content can be selectively provided to particular peers or can be more widely shared with the public. In either case, feedback and a variety of opinions can be used to ensure reflections are not incomplete or missing key elements.

Social networking tools such as Facebook, Ning or LinkedIn can be used to share information and opinions. Grapevine Talk and Voicethread can be used for developing voice and text forums. Overall, Web 2.0 seeks to leverage social interaction and this makes a wide variety of tools worth investigating.

## Critical Reflection

Critical reflection revisits the reflection process to consider how external context impacts decisions and events that have occurred. Critical reflection may result in modified conclusions. This aspect of reflection requires continuing use of tools selected for initial reflection (such as blogs, online journals, social networks, or specialty tools). Feedback provided by peers is considered in the context of external information. This information may be acquired from online sources using database searches, news searches, and other relevant information gathering tools.

Critical reflection can be complex and might require seeking information from sources that are not known initially. New tools that work well in online discovery learning are beginning to emerge. These tools support the creation of a quest that draws on individual experiences and conversations to generate a connection point linking text, websites, multi-media files, blogs, wikis, and other resources. This central point or node allows critical reflection to consider a wide range of possibilities.

Experience Project is a Web 2.0 site developed to facilitate quest development. It helps develop an informal learning network which allows the user to learn from others through posting experiences and commenting on them (Neviarouskaya, Prendinger, & Ishizuka, 2010). Experiences are collections of information categorized into areas defined by the users. Communicating and discussing experiences represents an informal aspect to everyday learning. Experience Project is a place for mini-blogging, conversation, discussion, opinions and recommendations from peers rather than experts. Members create a learning network based on the Website's toolset and their personal contacts (Experience Project, 2010). See Figure 19.

Overall, learning through reflection can be facilitated and even enhanced within an online knowledge space. First, information can be re-

*Figure 19. Experience project for personal learning*

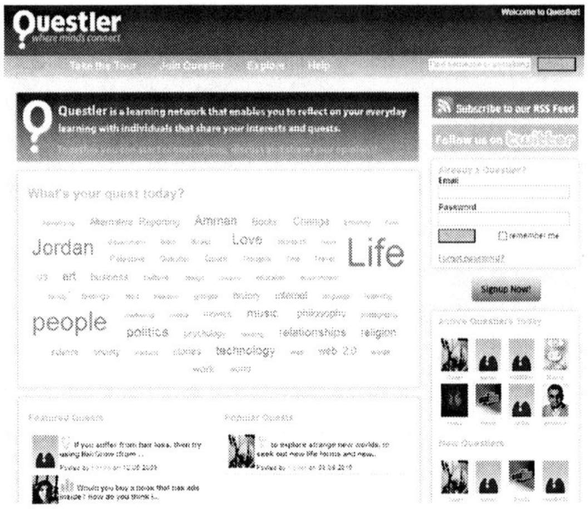


corded from anywhere at anytime (provided an Internet connection exists through a standard or mobile interface). Second, organizing and categorizing collected information can be accomplished with the tools available online. Third, social aspects of reflection and the resulting synergy can be improved in an online knowledge space by removing the constraints of time and geography. And fourth, external information can be acquired more easily and decisions vetted with richer resources.

## SIMULATION BASED LEARNING

Simulation based learning can be implemented effectively in the context of online knowledge spaces (Harper, Squires, & McDougall, 2000). Essentially, simulation based learning involves role-playing. A learner selects and pursues an experience that resembles a real world situation. The simulations in online knowledge space differ subtly from online game experiences or the experience of visiting online worlds. In a simulation situation, the environment often is manipulated by an instructor to guide the discovery process.

Simulations in this context can be defined as learning experiences that emulate the real world by reproducing selected functions of the world within the context of defined learning objectives that generally includes a narrative or storytelling element (Aldrich, 2009).

A variety of online knowledge spaces can be used as the context for a simulation. For instance, 3-D worlds such as Second Life can become the environment for the simulation's implementation. Beyond that, the video game industry has increased learner expectations and created market demand for simulation based learning (SBL) using platforms like Nintendo's Wii, Sony's PlayStation 3, and Microsoft's Xbox 360.

Simulations can take many forms and formats (Grune-Yanoff & Weirich, 2010). They can be text-based, computer program-based, graphically oriented, or exist in a 3-D environment. In spite of these differences, the goal remains providing a learner with an experience that resembles what might happen in the real world. If created properly, simulations can be detailed with sufficient reality to ensure students obtain hands on experience and learn real skills.

Simulations offer a number of advantages (McHaney, 2009). First, simulations are scalable. A real world system can be simulated in all detail if needed or a subset of a system can be simulated to provide knowledge in a particular area. Simulations that focus on a particular area are more affordable and can be delivered to multiple participants at a given time.

Second, simulations are flexible. Since they are recreations of reality, various configurations, including ones that can't be created in the real world, can be experienced by learners. In the real world, some situations are too rare to experience, too expensive to create, too dangerous, or impossible to stage.

Third, simulations are generally portable. On-line knowledge spaces can be accessed from a variety of locations, at convenient times by multiple learners. This means instructors can facilitate the learning experience from a distance and that multiple learners can interact in the same discover space simultaneously.

A variety of tools exist for implementing simulations in online knowledge space. As mentioned earlier, 3-D virtual worlds such as Second Life or Active Worlds can be used as a platform for simulation implementation. For instance, Swiss-Projects.ch reports the development of a Second Life simulation that enables learners to experience ways a kitchen fire starts, spreads, and can be controlled. According to the web site, "[T]he visitor experiences with his avatar in an almost real, three-dimensional environment, how a fire can develop, originated from an overheated fryer, and how it should be fought (Swiss-Projects, 2010)." Figure 20 illustrates.

In this simulation, the learner can explore and react in a variety of ways as part of the learning process. Multiple users can visit the site simultaneously and experience the simulation in a social setting.

NexLearn SimWriter is another tool that enables the development of simulations in online knowledge spaces (See Figure 21). SimWriter enables the facilitator to create storylines without needing to be a programmer (Chapman, 2008). The result is a customized, scenario-based social

*Figure 20. Swiss Projects' simulation of kitchen fire in Second Life*

*Figure 21. NexLearn SimWriter software*

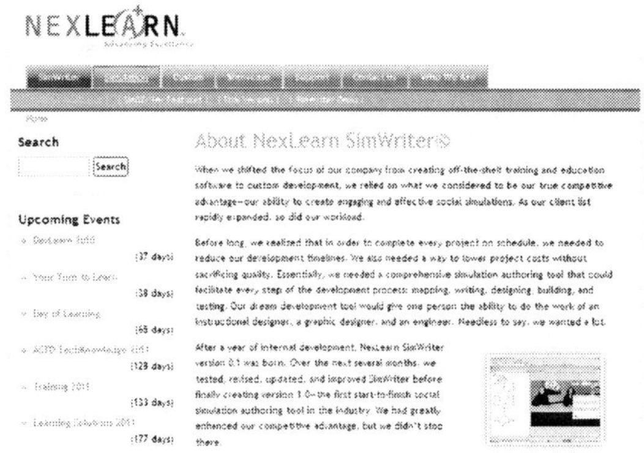


simulation with progressive feedback. The tool offers two simulation modes: text only or enhanced with audio or video elements (NexLearn, 2010).

In a simulation, a learner's experiences are assembled as they respond to questions, make decisions, and experience various stimuli. Online knowledge spaces make excellent venues for computer-based learning environments and advances in technology have resulted in dynamic and interactive visualization capability to add more power and create richer experiences for learners. Simulation-based environments allow learners to become engaged, active learners and provide substance for later reflection and discussions.

## SUMMARY

Knowledge spaces in discovery learning are an important aspect of constructivist learning approaches. With the emergence of the Internet, the World Wide Web, and most recently, Web 2.0 technologies, discovery learning has moved online and has been implemented using modern ideas. As a result, significant new capabilities are available.

Discovery learning empowers students with active, hands-on approaches for learning and enables instructors to shift their focus from teaching content to providing processes and tools for learning. The power of Web 2.0 ensures the availability of social connections and permits access to existing and new knowledge spaces. These new ways of learning motivate students to take ownership of their own educational experiences and enables them to learn at their own pace.

Online knowledge spaces comprise Web 2.0 tools, existing information repositories, and social interaction venues suited to the construction of meaningful digital artifacts. These constructivist-related artifacts are central to discovery learning.

Several architectures for discovery learning were explored in this chapter including case-based learning, incidental learning, learning by exploring/conversing, learning by reflection, and simulation-based learning. These architectures were originally developed in traditional venues but have now been redeployed in the emerging digital environments. Among the key technologies used to create the online knowledge spaces required to implement discovery learning are threaded discussions, blogs, wikis, virtual worlds, games, simulations, social networks, organizational software, note-taking systems, quest web sites, and other venues.

The potential of discovery learning and its use of online knowledge spaces are just beginning and promise to enhance education in the future.

## REFERENCES


Aldrich, C. (2009). *The complete guide to simulations and serious games: How the most valuable content will be created in the age beyond Gutenberg to Google*. Pfeiffer.

Bandura, A. (1977). *Social learning theory*. Englewood Cliffs, NJ: Prentice-Hall.

Bartlett, F. (1932). *Remembering: A study in experimental and social psychology*. Cambridge University Press.

Bicknell-Holmes, T., & Hoffman, P. S. (2000). Elicit, engage, experience, explore: Discovery learning in library instruction. *RSR. Reference Services Review*, *28*(4), 313–322. doi:10.1108/00907320010359632

Bijker, W. (1995). *Of bicycles, Bakelites, and bulbs: Toward a theory of sociotechnical change*. Cambridge, MA: MIT Press.

Blogger. (2010, August). *Blogger home page*. Retrieved September 12, 2010, from http://www.blogger.com.

Blood, R. (2004). How blogging software reshapes the online community. *Communications of the ACM*, *47*(12), 53–55. doi:10.1145/1035134.1035165

Bode, B. (1929). *Conflicting psychologies of learning*. New York, NY: Heath.

Calongne, C. M. (2008). Educational frontiers: Learning in a virtual world. *EDUCAUSE Review*, *43*(5).

Castronova, J. (2002, Fall). *Discovery learning for the 21st century: What is it and how does it compare to traditional learning in effectiveness in the 21st century?* Retrieved September 30, 2010, from http://teach.valdosta.edu/are/Litreviews/vol1no1/castronova_litr.pdf.

Cavalli, E. (2008, December 23). *World of Warcraft hits 11.5 million users*. Retrieved July 4, 2010, from http://www.wired.com/gamelife/2008/12/world-of-warc-1/.

Chapman, B. (2008). Learning technology primer. In Biech, E. (Ed.), *ASTD handbook for workplace learning professionals* (pp. 383–406). Danvers, MA: ASTD Press.

Cohen, N. (2008, September 15). Don't buy that textbook, download it free. *New York Times (NY Edition)*, C3.

Connexions. (2008). *Connexions: About us*. Retrieved October 16, 2008, from http://cnx.org/aboutus/.

Connexions. (2010). *Connexions home page*. Retrieved July 10, 2010, from http://cnx.org/.

Dean, D., & Kuhn, D. (2007). Direct instruction vs. discovery: The long view. *Science Education, 91*(3), 384–397. doi:10.1002/sce.20194

Doignon, J. P., & Falmagne, J. C. (1999). *Knowledge spaces*. Springer-Verlag. doi:10.1007/978-3-642-58625-5

Douglass, R. T., Little, M., & Smith, J. w. (2005). *Building online communities with Drupal, phpBB, and WordPress*. Apress.

Driver, R., Asoko, H., Leach, J., Mortimer, E., & Scott, P. (1994). Constructing scientific knowledge in the classroom. *Educational Researcher, 23*(7), 5–12.

ELATEWiki. (2009, March 28). *E-learning paths*. Retrieved July 10, 2010, from http://www.elatewiki.org/index.php/E-Learning_Paths.

ElateWiki. (2010, September). *TubeRadio.FM*. Retrieved September 30, 2010, from http://www.elatewiki.org/index.php/TubeRadio.FM.

EverNote. (2010, September). *EverNote home page*. Retrieved September 22, 2010, from http://www.evernote.com.

Experience Project. (2010, December 13). *Experience Project home page*. Retrieved December 13, 2010, from http://www.experienceproject.com.

*FastTalk*. (2010, September). Retrieved September 16, 2010, from http://www.webtransitions.com/components-discussion.asp.

Fitzpatrick, J. (2009, May 10). *Five best journaling tools*. Retrieved August 20, 2010, from http://lifehacker.com/5246819/five-best-journaling-tools.

Fosnot, C. T. (2005). *Constructivism: Theory, perspectives, and practice* (2nd ed.). New York, NY: Teachers College Press.

FreeMind. (2010, September). *FreeMind home page*. Retrieved September 11, 2010, from http://freemind.sourceforge.net/wiki/index.php/Main_Page.

Fruhlinger, J. (2010, November 28). *9 technologies that were ahead of their time*. Retrieved December 12, 2010, from http://www.pcworld.com/article/211779/1999_live_journal.html.

Gijlers, H., & Jong, T. d. (2005). The relationship between prior knowledge and students' collaborative discovery learning processes. *Journal of Research in Science Teaching, 42*(3), 264–282. doi:10.1002/tea.20056

Grapevine Talk. (2010, July 28). *GrapevineTalk homepage*. Retrieved July 28, 2010, from http://grapevinetalk.com/index.html.

Grune-Yanoff, T., & Weirich, P. (2010). The philosophy and epistemology of simulation: A review. *Simulation & Gaming, 41*(1), 20–50. doi:10.1177/1046878109353470

Harper, B., Squires, D., & McDougall, A. (2000). Constructivist simulations: A new design paradigm. *Journal of Educational Multimedia and Hypermedia, 9*(2), 115–130.

Hart, J. (2008, July 28). *Jane's pick of the day selected by Jane Hart of the Centre for Learning & Performance Technologies*. Retrieved December 13, 2010, from http://janeknight.typepad.com/pick/2008/07/questler.html.

Jackson, P. (1995). On the place of narrative in teaching. In McEwan, H., & Egan, K. (Eds.), *Narrative in teaching, learning, and research* (pp. 3–23). New York, NY: Teachers College Press.

Johnstone, S. (2005). *Open educational resources serve the world.* Retrieved December 12, 2010, from http://www.educause.edu/apps/eq/eqm05/eqm0533.asp.

Jonassen, D. (1991). Objectivism versus constructivism: Do we need a new philosophical paradigm? *Educational Technology Research and Development, 39*, 5–14. doi:10.1007/BF02296434

Kazmierski, J. (2010, December 2). *May the source be with you.* Retrieved December 12, 2010, from http://www.unogateway.com/may-the-source-be-with-you-1.1817794.

Kerka, S. (2000). Incidental learning. *Trends and Issues Alert No.18*. Retrieved from http://www.eric.ed.gov/PDFS/ED446234.pdf.

Kim, T., & Axelrod, S. (2005). Direct instruction: An educators' guide and a plea for action. *Behavior Analyst Today, 6*(2), 111.

Kirschner, P., Sweller, J., & Clark, R. (2006). Why minimal guidance during instruction does notwork: An analysis of the failure of constructivist discovery, problem-based, experiential, and inquiry-based teaching. *Educational Psychologist, 41*, 75–86. doi:10.1207/s15326985ep4102_1

Klahr, D., & Nigam, M. (2004). The equivalence of learning paths in early science instruction: Effects of direct instruction and discovery learning. *Psychological Science, 15*, 661–667. doi:10.1111/j.0956-7976.2004.00737.x

Koznov, D., & Pliskin, M. (2009). Computer-supported collaborative learning with mind-maps. In *Communications in Computer and Information Science* (*Vol. 17*, pp. 478–489). Springer.

Lemke, J. (1993). Hypermedia and higher education. *Interpersonal Computing and Technology, 1/2*.

Lévy, P. (1997). *L'intelligence collective: Pour une anthropologie du cyberspace*. La Decouverte.

LiveJournal. (2010, September). *LiveJournal home page*. Retrieved September 22, 2010, from http://www.livejournal.com.

Locke, L. (2010, November 24). *Scribd stats: New social dashboard for reading.* Retrieved December 12, 2010, from http://www.pcworld.com/article/211693/scribd_stats_new_social_dashboard_for_reading.html.

McHaney, R. (2009, March). Implementation of ELATEwiki. *EDUCAUSE Quarterly, 32*(4). Retrieved July 10, 2010, from http://www.educause.edu/EDUCAUSE+Quarterly/EDUCAUSEQuarterlyMagazineVolum/ImplementationofELATEwiki/192968.

McHaney, R. (2009). *Understanding computer simulation.* Retrieved May 3, 2010, from http://bookboon.com/us/textbooks/it/understanding.

Mindomo. (2010, September). *Mindomo home page*. Retrieved September 10, 2010, from Mindomo.com: http://www.mindomo.com.

Neuhauser, P. C. (1993). *Corporate legends and lore: The power of storytelling as a management tool*. New York, NY: McGraw-Hill.

Neviarouskaya, A., Prendinger, H., & Ishizuka, M. (2010). Recognition of affect, judgment, and appreciation in text. *23rd International Conference on Computational Linguistics (Coling, ed.)*, (pp. 806-814). Beijing.

NexLearn. (2010, August). *SimWriter*. Retrieved September 21, 2010, from http://www.nexlearn.com/?q=node/1.

Open Courseware Consortium. (2008). *Open Courseware Consortium homepage.* Retrieved October 16, 2008, from http://www.ocwconsortium.org/.

Pew Research Center. (2010). *Millennials protrait of generation next: Confident. Connected. Open to change.* Pew Research Center. phpBB. (2010, September). *phpBB home page*. Retrieved September 20, 2010, from http://www.phpbb.com/.

Piaget, J. (1972). *To understand is to invent.* New York, NY: The Viking Press, Inc.

Questler. (2010). *Questler FAQs*. Retrieved September 23, 2010, from http://questler.com/faqs.

Rice University. (2010, December 1). *FirstScience news*. Retrieved December 12, 2010, from http://www.firstscience.com/home/news/science-business/ieee-signal-processing-society-offers-free-educational-content-via-connexions_96496.html.

Rittle-Johnson, B. (2006). Promoting transfer: Effects of self-explanation and direct instruction. *Child Development, 77*, 1–15. doi:10.1111/j.1467-8624.2006.00852.x

Ryder, M. (2009). The cyborg and the noble savage: Ethics in the war on information poverty. In Luppicini, R., & Adell, R. (Eds.), *Handbook of Research on Technoethics* (pp. 232–249). Hershey, PA: IGI Global.

Shank, R. C., & Cleary, C. (1994). *Engines for education.* Hillsdale, NJ: Lawrence Erlbaum.

Smith, D., & Hatton, N. (1993). Reflection in teacher education: A study in progress. *Education Research and Perspectives. The University of Western Australia, 20*(1), 13–23.

Stories2Learn. (2010, September). *Stories2Learn home page*. Retrieved September 14, 2010, from http://www.stories2learn.com/alllist.php.

Swiss-Projects. (2010, January 1). *Kitchen Fire - Fire simulation in Second Life*. Swiss. Retrieved August 20, 2010, from http://www.swiss-projects.ch/?q=de/node/243.

Van Grove, J. (2010, December 10). *How Evernote turned note taking into a $10 million business.* Retrieved December 12, 2010, from http://mashable.com/2010/12/10/evernote-growth/.

VoiceThread. (2010, July 28). *About VoiceThread.* Retrieved July 28, 2010, from http://voicethread.com/about/.

VoiceThread. (2010, September). *VoiceThread home page*. Retrieved September 3, 2010, from http://www.voicethread.com.

Vygotsky, L. (1978). *Mind and society: The development of higher mental processes*. Cambridge, MA: Harvard University Press.

Web Transitions. (2010). *FastTalk: Easy to use threaded discussion software.* Retrieved December 12, 2010, from http://www.webtransitions.com/components-discussion.asp.

Weir, L. (2008). *VoiceThreads: Extending the classroom with interactive multimedia albums.* Retrieved December 12, 2010, from http://www.edutopia.org/voicethread-interactive-multimedia-albums.

Whitney, L. (2010, December 8). *Google Groups gets a revamp.* Retrieved December 12, 2010, from http://news.cnet.com/8301-1023_3-20025009-93.html.

World of Warcraft. (2010, July 10). *Info.* Retrieved July 10, 2010, from http://www.worldofwarcraft.com/info/basics/guide.html.

## KEY TERMS AND DEFINITIONS

**Blog:** A type of website that permits an individual to post a message intended to be communicated to a mass audience. The audience is usually permitted to provide feedback. Originally blogs were associated with personal journals or reflections but now are often commercial and used in business or education.

**Case-Based Learning:** An instructional design method often used in business or law schools that involves a collaborative, student-centered exploration of a complex, realistic situation that requires in-depth analysis to arrive at a reasonable solution. Most cases do not have a particular "right" answer.

**Constructivism:** A learning theory that views human learning in terms of constructing meaning from a combination of prior experience and the learner's current environment. Constructivists believe learning is an active, often self-directed process.

**ELATEwiki:** Electronic Learning and Teaching Exchange wiki website originally developed and implemented by a team from Kansas State University.

**Incidental Learning:** Indirect or unplanned learning that occurs in conjunction with a planned learning experience structured around a set of objectives.

**Learning Theory:** Various psychological research streams that describe ways that people modify their behaviors as the result of knowledge acquisition or personal experience.

**NexLearn SimWriter:** Simulation software package produced by NexLearn of Wichita, Kansas for the purpose of developing realistic training simulations.

**Pedagogy:** An approach to teaching generally thought to become more effective when implemented consistently with a learning theory.

**Scribd:** A popular social publishing web site that permits users to exchange all types of electronic documents and eBooks either for free or for pay.

**Simulation-Based Learning:** A form of learning that uses simulation to engage the learner and provide a sense of realism in order to better prepare the learner for a real world experience which may have costly or dangerous consequences.

**Social Publishing:** The process of adding collaboration (generally in the Web 2.0 sense) to the publication process either prior to, or following publication so the writer(s) may have open conversations involving the book and its content.

**VoiceThread:** A Web 2.0 application that adds an asynchronous social element to presentation material that may take the form of text, voice, video, or other forms of commentary added by viewers.

## ENDNOTES

1 The term metaverse comes Neal Stephenson's 1992 novel, *Snow Crash*, and his description of virtual 3-D worlds where humans interact in various scenarios with each other and with software-based agents.

2 This example uses Second Life.

# Chapter 6
# Web-Based 3D Virtual Learning Environments

**Nicoletta Adamo-Villani**
*Purdue University, USA*

**Kari L. Clase**
*Purdue University, USA*

**Robin J. Heyden**
*Education Consultant, USA*

**John Wiecha**
*Boston Medical Center, USA*

## ABSTRACT

*This chapter is an overview of web-deliverable three-dimensional (3D) virtual learning environments. In Section 1 (Introduction) we define Virtual Reality (VR) Technology and Virtual Learning Environments; in Section 2 (Virtual Environments and Learning) we discuss literature findings on the benefits of using web-based VEs for self-discovery learning. In Section 3 (Developing online VE: technologies, challenges and solutions) we give an overview of the latest technologies/platforms used to develop online VEs, discuss development and delivery challenges posed by complex, information-rich web-based 3D environments, and describe possible solutions that can be adopted to overcome current limitations. In Section 4 (A review of two projects) we present two 3D web virtual learning environments that were recently developed by the authors: the Interactive 3D Tour of MSHHD and The pilot postgraduate medical education program in Second Life. A summary and conclusive remarks are included in section 5 (Summary and Conclusion).*

## INTRODUCTION

VR is a technology that allows users to explore and manipulate computer-generated, three dimensional, interactive environments in real time. VR is based on the theory that people do not experience reality directly, they receive a series of external stimuli which are interpreted by the brain as reality. "If a computer application can send the same external stimuli that the brain can interpret, then the simulated reality is potentially undistinguishable from reality" (Sherman & Craig 2003).

A web interactive Virtual Environment (VE) is defined as a web-deliverable designed "information space in which the information is explicitly

DOI: 10.4018/978-1-61350-320-1.ch006

Copyright © 2012, IGI Global. Copying or distributing in print or electronic forms without written permission of IGI Global is prohibited.

represented, educational interactions occur, and users are not only active, but actors (i.e., they co-construct the information space)" (Dillenburg 2000). VEs offer three main benefits: (a) representational fidelity; (b) immediacy of control and high level of active user participation; and (c) presence. "(a) Representational fidelity refers to the degree of realism of the rendered 3D objects and the degree of realism provided by temporal changes to these objects. (b) User control and high level of participation refer to the ability to look at objects from different points of view, giving the impression of smooth movement through the environment, and the ability to pick up, examine and modify objects within the virtual world. (c) The feeling of presence, or immersion, occurs as a consequence of realism of representation and high degree of user control." (Dalgarno et al. 2002).

An online virtual world is a particular type of web VE where users can interact with each other. It is defined as "an electronic environment that visually mimics complex physical spaces, where people can interact with each other and with virtual objects, and where people are represented by animated characters" (Bainbridge 2007). The features of virtual worlds include shared space, graphical user interface, immediacy, interactivity, persistence, and community (Lesko & Hollingsworth, 2010; Penfold 2010).

Virtual Environments can be non-immersive (i.e. desktop VEs) or total immersion. Non-immersive virtual environments can be viewed on a PC with a standard monitor; interaction with the virtual world can occur by conventional means such as keyboards, mice, trackballs, and joysticks or may be enhanced by using 3D interaction devices such as a SpaceBall or DataGlove. Non-immersive VR has advantages in that it does not require special hardware; it can be delivered via web, and therefore can reach broad audiences. Immersive VR applications are usually presented on single or multiple screens, or through a stereoscopic head-mounted display unit. The user interacts with the 3D environment with specialized equipment such as a data glove, a wand or a 3D mouse. Sensors on the head unit and/or data glove track the user's movements/gestures and provide feedback that is used to revise the display, thus enabling smooth, real time interactivity.

In this chapter we focus on non-immersive VEs and we discuss learning benefits that have been explored with both single-user web VEs and multi-user, collaborative online virtual worlds.

## VIRTUAL ENVIRONMENTS AND LEARNING

### Discovery Learning

Discovery learning is defined as a "self-directed way of learning in which the planning and monitoring of the learning process are in the hands of the learner" (de Jong, 2005, p. 218). Virtual environments support discovery learning as they are motivating, active experiences controlled by the individual (Coffman & Klinger 2008). Immersion of students within a virtual environment can cultivate "learning by doing" as students use and apply their related prior experiences and further develop them by interacting with the environment (Land 2000). The discovery learning provided by virtual environments also supports the upcoming generation of "digital natives" (Prensky 2001, p.1) which think and learn in interactive, multimedia environments and need options for learning that are collaborative and creative (Loureiro & Bettencourt 2010). Learning is shifting from sets of knowledge transferred between teacher and students towards a more learner-centered approach focused on experience and exploration (De Freitas et al. 2009). Previously, a significant focus of education has been to teach the basics of literacy and mathematics, but now, with the advances of technology, it is becoming necessary to address 21st century workforce skills, such as digital literacy, which will ultimately impact productivity and creativity (Bavelier et al. 2010).

## Pedagogical Benefits of Interactive Virtual Learning Environments

The pedagogical benefits of interactive Virtual Learning Environments have been examined by researchers in the areas of computer graphics, cognitive psychology, visual cognition, and educational psychology. In general, research findings show that Virtual Learning Environments are often more effective than traditional teaching tools (Dalgarno 2004; Shin 2003; Winn 2002). More specifically, learning affordances include: "the facilitation of tasks that lead to enhanced spatial knowledge representation, greater opportunities for experiential learning, increased motivation and engagement, improved contextualization of learning and more effective collaborative learning as compared to tasks made possible by 2-D alternatives" (Dalgarno & Lee 2010, p.10). Technologies, such as VR, can be used to create interactive learning environments where learners can visualize abstract concepts easily and receive feedback to build new knowledge and understanding (Hmelo 1998; Kafail 995; Schwartz 1999; Bransford 1999). VR is also effective in teaching students how to be critical and creative thinkers as it supports learning in a nonlinear fashion (Strangman 2003). VR environments are intrinsically motivating and engaging as they give the users the illusion of being part of the reconstructed world, and allow them to focus entirely on the task at hand. In addition, several studies have shown that VR applications can provide effective tools for learning in both formal and informal settings (Dalgarno & Harper 2004; Winn 2002; Shin 2003).

Reviews have concluded that technology has great potential to enhance young student achievement, but there is a need for additional research (Cognition and Technology Group at Vanderbilt 1996; Dede 1998; President's Committee on Advisors on Science and Technology 1997). Although the availability of technology has increased dramatically and is impacting how children learn, develop and behave, it is still not clear how to best use the technology for desired learning outcomes (Bavelier et al, 2010; Linebarger & Walker, 2005; Owen 2010; Zimmerman 2007). Different behavioral effects have been observed as the media changes in "content, task requirements, and attentional demands" and "some products designed to benefit cognitive development actually hinder it while some products designed purely for entertainment purposes have been shown to lead to long-lasting benefits" (Bavelier et al. 2010, p. 693).

Interactive 3D animations have been shown to increase student interest and make material more appealing (Korakakis et al. 2008). Computer simulations can be an effective approach to improve student learning and may help students develop more accurate conceptions (Jiang 1994; Kangassalo 1994; Zietsman 1986; Brna 1987; Gorsky 1992). Virtual environments can also provide situated learning that is effective in generating useful knowledge for the real world (Dede, 2009). The potential for learning in virtual worlds, especially for providing a real world quality for role- play activities has been noted by other researchers (Broadribb & Carter 2009). Virtual worlds allow students to "go places that cannot be visited, overcome stereotypes, role-play, collaborate in groups, conduct scenario simulations and interact with a global audience" (Lesko & Hollingsworth 2010, p.9).

## Virtual Learning and Creative Collaboration

VEs have been shown to be effective as a scaffolding tool for learners to learn and have been proposed to provide an innovative and stimulating learning environment for students to encourage innovation (Penfold 2010). Specific features of VEs, such as immersion and interaction, have been identified as important for enhancing problem-solving ability and increasing learners' motivation and imagination (Huang et al. 2010). Online Virtual Worlds have a social aspect that is distinct from Virtual Environments as the multiple online users can help provide a sense of community and support learning and collaboration. The real time collaborative web with its "humanization of the virtual space" where humans collaborate and network as avatars in virtual environments with no boundaries has been referred to as Web 3.0 (Loureiro & Bettencourt, 2010, p.3; Hayes, 2006). The social and collaborative tools provided by the current Web environment facilitates independent learning and "enhances information sharing, participative behavior, collaboration and possibly even creativity" (Smith 2009, p.90). An evaluation of a 3D multi-user virtual environment, found a strong correlation between learning and the perception of awareness, presence, and belonging to a learning community (De Lucia 2008). Other strengths associated with virtual worlds include: "the ability for an individual to design and construct unique environments that are available all the time and then share them collaboratively with others; provide virtual training and improve access to places that would be difficult to reach in the real world; make spatial representation useful for hands-on learning; support discovery-based learning through real-time social interaction; and utimately increase interest in learning by providing experiences that encourage creative expression, independent problem solving and collaboration" (Hansen 2008). Given these benefits, educators have been applying technology to many different content domains within education.

## Interactive Virtual Learning Environments and Science Education

Recent studies suggest that learning outcomes valued in science education can be taught through virtual environments. Diverse examples of technology integration into science education include: virtual classrooms integrated with real classrooms at Scripps Research Institute in Florida and California, virtual lab series at the Howard Hughes Biointeractive website, virtual worlds for teaching chemistry concepts such as orbital shapes, and the SciLands continent within the virtual world platform, Second Life (Zagorski 2010; Lang & Kobilnyk 2009). Researchers have shown that integration of web-based technology and real-life scientific material motivates students' creativity and enhances their expression of "sensitivity, fluency, flexibiity, originality, and elaboration of scientific creativities" (Jang 2008, p. 253).

Virtual labs have been used to make authentic research activities more accessible to students, improve their problem solving ability, and encourage their creativity (Loureiro & Bettencourt 2010). It has been suggested that VR also provides highly interactive learning experiences that can help learners acquire knowledge and actively apply their new skills with less cognitive effort (Chittaro 2007; Huang et al. 2010). Quest Atlantis, a 3-D virtual environment for young children, helped students learn "stewardship, respect for others, creativity, computer skills and commitment" in addition to enhancing engagement and learning (Gerstein 2009, p.7). Lifelab (http://www.lifelab.de), an interactive 3D laboratory, promoted the active participation of students in the scientific reasoning process, independent of their prior knowledge and level of motivation (Zumbach et al. 2006). Virtual Cell (http://vcell.ndsu.edu) was shown to significantly improve students' ability to solve authentic problems (McClean 2001). Results of studies from River City, another multiuser virtual environment, showed that students gained substantial knowledge and skills in scientific inquiry through immersive simulation (Dede 2009).

## Pedagogical Models and Theoretical Frameworks for Virtual Learning Environments

As education incorporates newer technologies, new pedagogies and theoretical frameworks are being explored to support the integration of technology with novel approaches for learning. The application of Roger's diffusion of innovation theory has been proposed to address the initial delay of positive outcomes from adoption of new technology. In addition, with the advent of multiple users within the virtual environments and the tools provided by Web 3.0, communication and socialization have a greater impact on the learning process. Virtual learning environments support communication, community and sharing. Siemens connectivism has been applied to address " the formation of 'connections' and how, from these connections, a building of 'networked' learning occurs." (Hansen 2008; Beard 2009; Roger 2003; Siemen 2008).

Different learning frameworks have been proposed to incorporate the unique learning experience from virtual environments. The proposed Six Learnings framework can be used to critically analyze and evaluate virtual worlds. The six learnings include: "learning by exploring, collaborating, being, building, championing and expressing" (Lim 2009). In self-discovery learning the focus is shifted from the teacher to a more learner-centered environment. A four dimensional framework has been proposed as applicable to immersive learning environments which emphasizes the importance of interaction between learner and environment, the pedagogical perspective, the representation including interactivity and immersivity and finally the context and where the learning takes place (De Freitas 2009). Applying the theory of Connectivism could help address the unique learning situations that can occur with multi-user virtual environments. Some of the principles of Connectivism address learning as a process of connecting specialized information sources and nurturing and maintaining connections to facilitate continual learning (Loureiro & Bettencourt 2010). Communal Constructivism has been identified as another pedagogical approach that is appropriate for use in virtual worlds. Recent research found that learners collaboratively constructed knowledge for themselves as a group and for others as "learning artifacts created by one group of learners were fed back into subsequent iterations of the learning task." Interestingly, while communal Constructivist learning within a virtual world can successfully facilitate learning at a group level, this is not necessarily applicable to learning at an individual level (Girvan & Savage, 2009).

Virtual Learning Environments can provide situated learning and collaborative experiences that support a constructivist learning approach (Dickey 2003; Chittaro and Ranon 2007; Coffman & Klinger 2008; Huang et al 2010) and thus several researchers have applied constructivist models for learning to studies with virtual learning environments. A research study exploring the use of a virtual world as a platform for distance learning found that it can support constructivist learning environments for geographically distant learners (Dickey 2003). The social presence provided by the virtual world platform supports social learning and the premise that "learning and understanding is 'socially constructed' through a wide range of activities afforded by a rich social learning space where students can interact with other fellow students, tutors, and the instructional elements in a wide range of social activities (Penfold 2010, p. 10)." In addition, the freedom to choose and use their identity through the use of avatars supports the development of student "self identity" (Penfold 2010, p. 10). Bronack, et al, 2006 proposed a social constructivist framework for learning in a 3-dimensional virtual world that included five assumptions: "learning is participatory (communities of practice), knowledge is social (situated), learning leads development through predictable stages via shared activity with others (engaging with others) and learners develop dispositions relative to the communities in which they practice (attitudes, beliefs, and values)"

There is a need to consider which pedagogical approaches can best leverage the unique characteristics and potential of emerging educational technologies over the traditional classroom teaching model (De Freitas et al. 2010; Girvan & Savage 2009). Advances in technology and the social environments provided by virtual worlds are impacting the design and delivery options for learning and their application to learning has changed perspectives where learning is examined as "an ongoing set of processes mediated via social interactions and experiential learning circumstances within designed virtual and hybrid spaces" (De Freitas et al 2010, p.69). In fact, findings from a recent study which focused on a constructivist approach, pointed towards the strengths of supporting social learning and researchers thus concluded that pedagogical models designed to support more social activities should be considered in future design (De Freitas et al. 2009).

## Benefits and Challenges of Online Virtual Worlds

Although the benefits of virtual environments for learning have been noted by many researchers, there are also challenges that may hinder widespread adoption. Some of the disadvantages associated with the use of virtual environments in education include the time and cost needed to create a virtual learning space. In addition, VR tools may be challenging as they require higher programming skills than traditional 2D tools (Huang et al 2010; Hansen 2008). However, many educators have initially overcome these hurdles by using the popular virtual world platform Second Life.

The use of virtual worlds in higher education is increasing (Dickey 2003; De Freitas & Neumann 2009), and currently, the virtual world platform provided by Second Life is the most mature and popular multiuser virtual world platform that has been used for this purpose (Warburton 2009; Esteves et al. 2010). One of the advantages of Second Life that allows researchers to explore the pedagogical potential of virtual worlds includes the ability to create innovative, 3D simulations in a safe environment where students from diverse geographic locations can work together with others and practice skills (Penfold 2010).

The SL environment includes features that facilitate experiential learning. Researchers found that a project-based approach within this virtual world environment helped students connect theory and practice as their virtual actions had relevance to the real world. The SL environment was noted to stimulate imagination and creativity with its increased sense of personal presence and providing an environment where learners can test hypotheses and actively participate without the risk in the real world (Jarmon, et al, 2008). Others have noted that Second Life also has the potential to encourage creativity as it provides numerous imaginative educational possiblities through its illusion of 3-D spaces allowing users to create and do what could not be done before (Salmon 2009).

A successful virtual environment binds together interactivity, engagement, and learning (Roussou 2004). Second Life has many of these characteristics. Second Life is immersive, simulates the real-world in a safe environment, and facilitates social networks that can support teaching and learning (Loureiro & Bettencourt 2010). Other features of Second Life that have been proposed to facilitate innovations in pedagogy include "extended or rich interactions; visualization and contextualism; exposure to authentic content and culture; individual and collective identity play; immersion in a 3D environment; simulation; community presence; and content production" (Warburton 2009, p.421). Simulations can enhance knowledge retention, imagination and confidence while allowing freedom of expression in a non-threatening environment (Penfold 2010). Current tools provided by SL support the construction of flexible environments and provide a sense of self and presence which can facilitate socialization and collaborative learning (Girvan & Savage 2009). The ability for users to create their own content has been widely adapted by the health care field (Beard et al. 2009).

Many health care related sites have been established in Second Life. The purpose of the sites fall into five major catagories: dissemination of health information, peer-support, professional training, marketing and the promotion of health institutions and products and those focused on virtual and real-world health research (Beard et al. 2009). Virtual environments have also been used for medical education. Medical simulations help students practice skills without risk prior to working with real patients (Danforth et al. 2009). The presence and active participation provided by a virtual world has also been shown to increase satisfaction in distance-based higher education health care (Johnson et al. 2009). Simulations have been used in education to help learners visualize a location and also experience being a part of it. Unfortunately, most simulations are expensive. In contrast, the SL platform makes simulations affordable and thus accessible (Salmon 2009).

Virtual world Second Life with its interactivity and usability improves upon previous platforms and methods used for distance collaboration and communication. Initial findings have been encouraging showing an increase in student interest, participation and amusement (Andreas et al. 2009). An evaluation conducted by De Lucia, 2008, demonstrated that the learning in SL is related to characteristics of a virtual world such as the user perception of belonging to a learning community, in addition to the perception of awareness, presence and communication (De Lucia 2008).

Most assessments of virtual world environments initially focus on the looks instead of functionality (Lesko & Hollingsworth 2010). However many researchers have noted functional challenges as the number of studies applying VW to education have increased. The technical skills needed by the students may require additional training in order for the students to fully realize the educational benefits (Petrakou 2010). In addition, the levels of fidelity and interactivity found in current virtual worlds are not comparable to existing games and previous gaming experience may actually have a negative impact on the learning experience (De Freitas 2009).

The major drawbacks of the SL virtual world platform include: technical, such as hardware and use within the world; identity, as it can be difficult to build social relationships when individuals have freedom to change identity and act without accountability; unique culture; time invested to find and participate in communities; difficult collaborations as there is a need for additional tools to support interactions and conversations between avatars; time as even simple tasks may take longer than anticipated; economic; lack of open standards and interoperability with other virtual world platforms; and scaffolding persistance and social discovery (Warburton 2009). In addition, even though one of the advantages of SL is the potential for global collaboration, it is not available in all languages (Loureiro & Bettencourt 2010). Some have proposed that SL could be strengthened by the integration of current technologies and the support of resources beyond the defined SL space (Livingstone & Kemp 2006; Matei et al 2007)

## DEVELOPING WEB 3D VEs: TECHNOLOGIES, CHALLENGES AND SOLUTIONS

Three open standards can be used to develop Web3D VEs: VRML (Virtual Reality Modeling Language), an open ISO standard (VRML, 1997) which was created in 1995, X3D, eXtensible 3D Graphics (X3D, 2004), proposed as a successor of VRML, and WebGL (WebGL, 2010), released very recently and still under development. In addition to open standards, other commonly used web 3D technologies include Java3D (Java3D, 2010), Unity (Unity, 2010), Flash 3D (Adobe Flash 3D graphics, 2010), Quest 3D (Quest3D, 2010), and more.

*VRML* (Carey and Bell 1997), is a language that "integrates 3D graphics, 2D graphics, text, and multimedia into a coherent model, and combines them with scripting languages and network capabilities " (Chittaro et al. 2007). VRML supports common primitives used in 3D applications, such as light sources, cameras, geometry, animation, material shaders, and texture mapping. 3D objects are described using a hierarchical scene graph structure in which entities are represented as nodes whose properties are stored in fields. This structure facilitates the creation of complex 3D worlds starting from simple objects; in addition, it is possible for the VE programmer to define new nodes (i.e. extend the language). VEs created with VRML can be immersive or non-immersive. In other words, they can be experienced using special hardware such as head-mounted displays and specialized input devices (i.e. wands or data gloves); or can be used with standard input/output devices such as CRT/LCD monitors and mouse and keyboard.

*The EXtensible 3D Graphics (X3D)* for defining interactive Web-based 3D content " ...was recently released as the successor of VRML, and was approved in 2004 as an ISO standard (X3D, 2004). X3D inherits most of the design choices and technical features of VRML and, as a result, it is largely backward-compatible ..."(Chittaro et al., 2007). X3D presents three main improvements over VRML: it supports several of the latest advancements in 3D computer graphics such as programmable shaders and multi-texturing; it enables better data compression and hence, faster downloads; and lastly "... it divides the language into functional areas called components, which can be combined to form different profiles (i.e., subsets of the entire language) that are suited to specific classes of applications or devices (e.g., one could create a specific profile to take into account the limited capabilities of mobile devices)..."(Chittaro et al, 2007).

*WebGL* is a cross-platform, royalty-free web standard for a low-level 3D graphics API based on OpenGL ES 2.0, exposed through the HTML5 Canvas element as Document Object Model interfaces. It is managed by the non-profit technology consortium Khronos Group, and its working group includes Apple, Google, Mozilla, and Opera. WebGL, still under development, brings plug-in-free 3D to the web, and is implemented in the development release of most major browsers including Mozilla Firefox, Google Chrome, Safari. The WebGL is intended to provide a common design for developing high quality immersive virtual experiences on the web.

*Java 3D* is another technology that can be used to develop web based virtual environments. Java 3D is a scene graph-based 3D application programming interface (API) for the Java platform that runs on top of either OpenGL or Direct3D. The Java 3D classes extend the Java language functionality to support geometry construction, manipulation, surface appearance definition, and animation. In addition to supporting standard I/O devices such as mouse, keyboard and monitor, it also provides a number of classes and interfaces to support specialized input devices. Java 3D has been used to develop many web based VEs including applications for architectural design and civil engineering project management.

*Unity, Flash 3D, Quest 3D* represent a sample of commercial virtual environment development tools that support web delivery in addition to standalone. *Unity* has been adopted by companies such as EA, Cartoon Networks, Disney, Warner Bros, and LEGO to develop and deliver their online content. It supports some of the latest real-time computer graphics advancements ranging from geometry batching to occlusion culling which can be used to speed up the downloading process and improve real-time performance. *Flash3D* extends the capabilities of the Adobe Flash multimedia platform ad allows for creation and display of simulated 3D environments using 2D graphics. *Quest 3D* is an integrated development environment (IDE) that allows to create web3D VEs using Visual Programming, hence it is an ideal development platform for artists and users with limited programming expertise; its main drawback is that it is not truly cross-platform as it does not support MacOS and iOs.

Although many options are currently available for development of web3D environments and web 3D technology has improved significantly in the past few years, creating complex, graphically-rich web 3D environments is still a challenging task. Due to diversity of network connections and computer performance, efficient representation of virtual objects is a fundamental factor for web presentations (Zara 2004). Virtual scenes are always a simplification of reality and this is particularly true for 3D web-based VEs, which have to balance between visual quality and rendering/data download speed. In order to overcome the quality/performance trade-off problem, the 3D models need to be carefully prepared for efficient web delivery using a variety of techniques including optimization methods for converting 3D models to web based format, and Level of Detail (LOD). LOD allows for describing a complex 3D model using different representations, from very detailed to extremely simple ones. A presentation system switches among these representations based on the distance between the virtual camera and the rendered object.

In addition to problems of download and rendering speed, a barrier is posed by the fact that VR content cannot be viewed with just a standard browser; a special viewer - either a special-purpose browser or a plug-in – is often needed. Since a universal viewer that can display all VR web content does not exist yet, it is often necessary to download a different plug-in for each different web VEs. Plug-ins can be large and their installation may require a certain degree of technical expertise, thus making web VR content inaccessible to people who have very little computer knowledge. Although WebGL promises to bring plug-in free 3D to the web, the technology is not mature yet.

Another current limitation of web-based VEs is the lack of a standard user interface for navigating 3D worlds and for interacting with 3D objects. Users are often accustomed to Graphical User Interfaces (GUIs) that use point-and-click as the major interaction technique. Moreover, web pages with hyperlinks are also based on the same click-and-go interaction method. On the contrary, a large number of different navigation/interaction paradigms have been suggested and/or implemented by researchers in VEs. According to Bowman et al. (1997) most of these techniques fall into four categories: natural travel metaphors, that is techniques that use physical locomotion or some real/pseudo world metaphor for travel; steering metaphors that involve continuous specification of direction of motion (i.e., gaze-directed, pointing, and physical device techniques); target-based metaphors which require a discrete specification of goal; and manipulation metaphors which involve manual manipulation of viewpoint (i.e., for instance, 'camera in hand'). A user interface for travel and object selection/manipulation in web-based virtual environments is not yet standardized. Even VRML browsers complying with ISO standards differ in a number of control elements and in their arrangement on the screen. This fact can increase difficulties, and therefore skepticism, in web users with limited computer knowledge. In order to overcome the problem of absence of a standard web 3D interface, the User Interface (UI) can be designed as an integral part of the 3D scene. For instance the UI could consist of a HUD (Heads-Up Display) that remains in the same position on the screen while the user navigates through the virtual world (Adamo-Villani et al. 2009).

From the discussion above it is clear that developing graphically-rich web 3D VEs is a challenging, costly and time-consuming process that requires a team of professionals with expertise in many different fields (i.e. programming, 3D graphics, UI design). To overcome the development barrier, companies such as Linden Lab (2010) have developed online virtual world platforms (i.e. Second Life) that include a set of authoring/modeling tools to allow non-expert users to easily create web 3D interactive environments within an existing virtual world. Forterra's OLIVE (Forterra Systems, 2010), The Croquet Consortium (2010),

Sun Microsystem's Project Wonderland (2009), ProtonMedia's Protosphere (2010), and Linden Lab's Second Life are all examples of such virtual world platforms. While these platforms do not support sophisticated 3D graphics, they offer an easy way to build interactive VEs for a variety of applications, including education and training.

Second Life (SL), one of the best known of these virtual world platforms, consists of a flat-earth simulation of roughly 1.8 billion square meters. First launched in 2003, SL is an example of an immersive, three-dimensional (3D) environment that supports a high level of social networking and interaction with information. Visitors can access the virtual world through a free, client program called the SL viewer. They enter the SL virtual world, which residents refer to as "the grid," as an avatar (SL "users" are referred to as "residents"). Once there, they can explore environments, meet and socialize with other residents (using voice and text chat), participate in group and individual activities, and learn from designed experiences. Built into the software is a three-dimensional modeling tool, based around simple geometric shapes, that allows non-expert users to build virtual objects. These objects can be used, in combination with a scripting language, to add functionality.

## A REVIEW OF TWO PROJECTS

In this section we discuss two web-based virtual environments that were recently developed by the authors: the *'Interactive 3D Tour of MSHHD'* and *'The pilot postgraduate medical education program in Second Life.'* Although both projects are examples of web VEs, they differ significantly in many ways. Interactive MSHHD was developed using Quest 3D by a team of artists, historians, architects and programmers, whereas the pilot postgraduate medical program was created in SL by non-expert developers. MSHHD is an example of single-user, graphically-rich VE whose goal was accurate reconstruction of a historic site, hence the quality of the 3D graphics was of great importance. The second project is an example of collaborative, multi-user virtual world whose objective was to evaluate the effectiveness of SL as a tool for continuing medical education. Thus the quality of the graphical representation was not of primary importance, as the emphasis of the project was on the effectiveness of the instructional design and user interaction.

### The Interactive 3D Tour of Muscatatuck State Hospital Historic District (MSHHD)

Virtual MSHHD is a web-based digital heritage application that uses VR as a tool to document and preserve historic sites, and educate the public about them (Adamo-Villani et al. 2010). MSHHD (Columbus, IN), founded in 1920 as the Indiana Farm Colony for Feeble-Minded Youth, includes buildings of historic value built in Deco, Moderne, Industrial, and Twentieth-Century Functional architectural style. The site is currently being transformed into an urban training facility for homeland security and natural disaster training and the plans for converting the area include major modifications to the district and its buildings. In 2006, The Indiana Army National Guard (INARNG) agreed to several mitigation stipulations for the adverse effect it will have on MSHHD. One stipulation was the creation of a photorealistic web-based interactive virtual tour to document and virtually preserve the historic area.

A team of Purdue University students and faculty was charged with the task of developing the tour. The team selected 3D animation and Virtual Reality (VR) as the technologies of choice. VR-based cultural heritage applications have gained popularity in recent years and some examples have been reported in the literature (Hirose 2006; Roussou et al. 1999). Researchers argue that VR application for cultural heritage offer several benefits including an effective way of communicating the scientific results of historical investigations through photorealistic reconstructions of places and people that no longer exist, may not be easily experienced, or are threatened; intuitive visual representation of abstract concepts, systems and theories that would be difficult to communicate with diagrams, textual descriptions and static images; and enhanced viewer's engagement and motivation through high level of interactivity and "immersion." Immersion is defined as "the illusion of being in the projected world….. surrounded by images and sound in a way which makes the participants believe that they are really there" (Roussou 2001).

These reported strengths have motivated the choice of VR and 3D animation as the base technologies for the interactive application. The tour is deliverable on CD-ROM for distribution to schools, and on the web for the general public. In addition, it is designed for display in portable immersive devices for museum exhibits.

## MSHHD Historical Information

The Muscatatuck State Hospital Historic District was originally the Indiana Farm Colony for Feeble-Minded Youth, intended for males suffering from mental illness. Founded in 1920, it was one facility in a system of eight in Indiana's mental health care system in the nineteenth and early twentieth centuries. The original colony covered an area of 1836 acres and included three farmhouses. It was identified as a home, and not a hospital or institution, and inmates earned their keep by working on the farm, and by raising crops and livestock in an effort to make the facility self-sustaining.

By 1933, after much argument and debate, the first female inhabitants were admitted to the colony. Separate quarters were constructed and maintained, and more "female oriented" work was added to the colony curriculum. In 1938 the colony received financial assistance from the Public Works Administration and widespread construction began. Several additions were made to the original facility including an Administration Building, a Medical Center, the Superintendent's Residence, the Power Plant, the School Building, a female dormitory, underground utilities, sewer lines, roads, and ditches. Architect/engineers W. C. McGuire and W. B. Shook of Indianapolis utilized Deco, Moderne, Industrial, and Twentieth-Century Functional architectural styles. These styles were not found in use in other state mental health facilities.

In the 1950s MSHHD shifted its mission from housing the developmentally disabled to developing individual programs to enhance personal development and its name was changed to the Muscatatuck State School and Training Center. Physical changes to the facility were made, including a decrease in acreage and the construction of new buildings to accommodate the shift in mission. By the 1980s, MSHHD encompassed 576 acres and included a summer camp area and a reservoir. Its new philosophy was that people who are developmentally disabled have the same civil and human rights as other citizens, including the right to live in the most normal and least restrictive environment possible.

In 2000, MSHHD was ordered closed due to the loss of Medicaid and other federal funding, the decrease in the number of patients, and rising maintenance costs. The final inhabitants left the facility in 2005. The property was then transferred to the INARNG to develop the MUTC (Muscatatuck Urban Training Center), an urban training facility for the war on terror, homeland security training, and natural disaster training. The plans for converting the site include major modifications to the buildings, designation of drop zones, construction of helicopter landing pads, construction of a 30-acre portable shantytown, 10-acre portable cemetery, and development of a mock port training facility. The conversion of the site into training camp is currently undergoing.

## 3D Content

Sixty-four (64) buildings and six (6) historic features were identified at MUTC. The buildings date between 1924 and circa 1980. Of the 64 buildings, 34 are over 50 years of age and are considered contributing buildings within the MSHHD. In addition, all 6 features (4 tunnels and 2 drainage ditches) and the unique "butterfly" pattern of roads, not seen in any other Indiana mental health facility, are considered contributing elements to the historic district. The virtual tour includes 3D reconstructions of all thirty-four buildings, two tunnels, the road layout, vegetation, and bodies of water. Figure 1 shows an aerial view of the historic site and a photograph of one of the buildings of interest.

To get geometrical information about real 3D objects various techniques and devices could be utilized. Fully automated methods are not available yet and while most automated techniques involve limited user input, they require a substantial amount of interactive work to covert the resulting data into renderable structures (Zara 2004). Therefore, due to the lack of directly applicable automatic reconstruction techniques, the team made the decision to build all 3D models using commercial modeling software (i.e., Autodesk Maya and 3D Studio MAX). To provide accuracy and realism, the 3D objects were developed from maps, architectural blueprints, photographs, drawings, and layout information, and were textured using procedural maps, digitally captured images, light maps, and ambient occlusion maps. Figure 2 shows the 3D reconstruction of the hospital building.

The models were then exported from Autodesk Maya and 3DS MAX to different formats for display on the various delivery platforms, including the WWW. To achieve good visual quality, as well as high speed of response in a real-time web-based environment, the models were optimized in different ways to limit the poly-count. In addition, Level of Detail (LOD) techniques were used extensively in order to lower the client's hardware requirements. The application detects the client's hardware configuration and the amount of detail displayed on models and textures changes dynamically depending on the user's computer system. The terrain was created using a 2D height map. The resolution of this height map changes according to the LOD system. Cube maps were used to generate the sky and atmosphere as well as allow for reflections of 3D geometry on certain surfaces. How often and at what resolution the reflection cube map is rendered changes according to the LOD system.

*Figure 1. From the left: aerial view of MSHHD with clearly identifiable 'butterfly' pattern of roads; façade of school building with Art Deco architectural elements*

*Figure 2. From the left: photo of façade of hospital building; 3D reconstruction of hospital building: façade and back view*

## Application Development

Quest 3D (2010) is the integrated development environment (IDE) that was chosen to develop the web-based interactive VE. The selection of this third party game engine was motivated by several considerations. Quest 3D allows for a relatively short development time, as all of the coding is done using Visual Programming. Because it is a DirectX 9 game engine, it is supported by all DirectX 9 compliant graphics cards and operating systems. Lastly, Quest 3D supports a large number of delivery formats including web, executable, installer and windows screensaver. Although the user is required to download and install a plug-in in order to view the content, the size of the plug-in is relatively small and its installation is straight-forward.

The online virtual tour is a single-user VE and exists within a website that presents historical information about the area (http://idealab.tech.purdue.edu/muscatatuck/). The 3D tour is rendered inside the browser window using a web player plug-in specific to the graphics engine used for development (i.e. Quest 3D). Users are required to download the plug-in and install it on their computer the first time they visit the web 3D tour. The 3D tour loads automatically on subsequent visits to the website. A standard mouse and keyboard setup is used as the default control option; however users may also use a gamepad. The web 3D tour was tested on a variety of computers with different hardware/software configurations. In particular, low-end computers without dedicated graphics cards were used to test real-time performance and the dynamic LOD system. The VE was iteratively developed with continuous feedback from a group of experts in VR, Archaeology, and Instructional Design. In addition, several formative evaluations with users were conducted in order to assess and improve the usability and functionality of the application.

## The User's Experience

Before starting the tour the participant has the option to choose between a "Quick Tour" and a "Detailed Tour." Each tour presents a different level of information about the facility and its history. The "Quick Tour" is a narrated story (with closed captions) aimed at $4^{th}$-5th grade students; the "Detailed Tour" presents in-depth information with references, and gives the user access to digital copies of original text documents and images.

Viewers begin the virtual tour of MSHHD by selecting one of two possible start locations. While all 34 buildings can be explored from the outside, only 6 are 'active' (i.e. they can be entered). Upon approaching or entering a building, information about its history, functions and previous inhabitants can be displayed in a variety of media formats such a text, images and narration. Users navigate the environment with mouse, keyboard, and/or gamepad and have the option to 'walk' through the environment or 'fly' to any location. If the 'walk' option is chosen, a terrain following constraint limits the subjects to only a specific plane. In other words, users can only 'walk' on the paths instead of being able to 'fly' freely through the virtual site. While the user is in 'walk' mode, there are three main actions: move, look, and interact. Moving 'pushes' the camera around the environment, while looking 'rotates' the camera. While in 'fly' mode, the user does not have direct control over the view, but rather controls the camera in order to take certain actions. While in this mode there is only one main action: interact. The user can click on a building and the camera automatically frames the building and displays appropriate information. The user can then take a step back, or interact with a door on the building and the camera will take appropriate actions to show the interior.

The main objective of the interactive VE is to allow the public to explore and experience the historic site as it was before the recent transformations, and learn through text, images and narrated stories, what life was about for the patients and employees of MSHHD. Figure 3 shows 4 screenshots of the web-based interactive tour.

In the following section we describe our second project, a collaborative web-3D multi-user virtual environment developed in Second Life. The purpose of the application was to explore the potential of using a virtual world platform for medical education.

## The Pilot Postgraduate Medical Education Program Delivered in Second Life

While virtual worlds with their 3D landscapes and customizable avatars, seem similar to popular massively multiplayer online games, they do not adhere to the traditional definition of a game. Virtual worlds, like SL, are more focused on socializing, exploring, and building. As a result, there is an active educational community in SL. Over 300 colleges and universities have "builds" in SL where they teach courses and conduct research. A number of organizations (NASA, NOAA, NIH, Jet Propulsion Laboratory, National Public Ra-

*Figure 3. Four screenshots of the web 3D tour. Clockwise from top left: Intro screen with menu selection; main cabin in Camp Holland; dentist's room (hospital interior); aerial view of entire 3D site.*

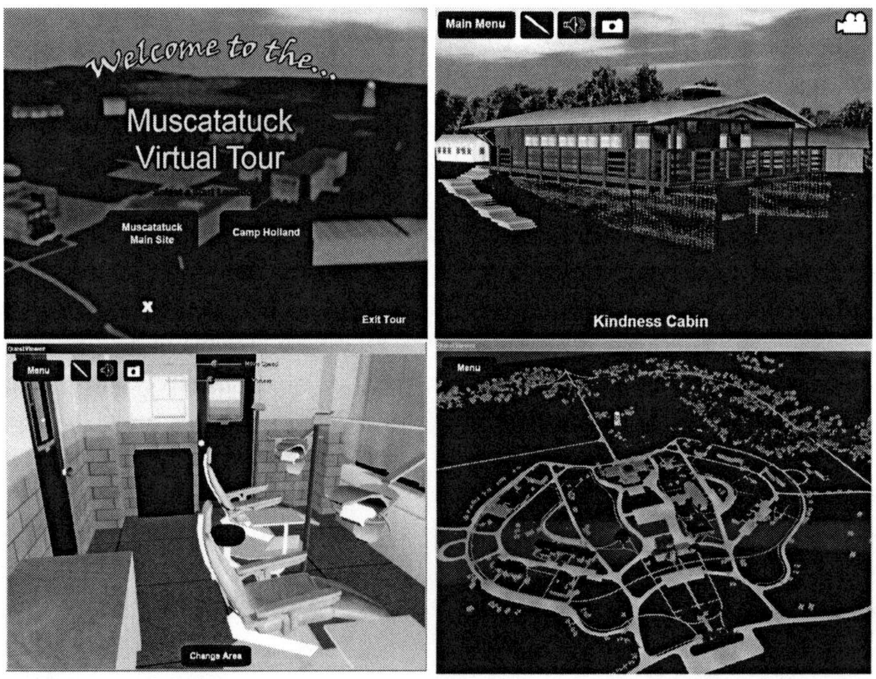

dio), along with a host of government agencies, museums, and educational groups stage regular events, seminars and workshops in world.

Second Life demographics show that 83% of the population is 25 years or older with the users over 44 years of age being the heaviest users on average. There is a close to even gender split among residents (57% male, 43% female) and more than 55% of the SL citizens come from outside the United States. In the month of January 2008, residents spent a total of 28,274,505 hours in world and, on average, 38,000 residents were logged in at any particular moment. As of January 2009, just over 18 million accounts were registered (from over 150 countries), although there are no reliable figures for actual, long-term consistent usage.

Individuals enter SL as avatars that can take any form the user chooses. Avatars are personalized by altering shapes, size, skin, hair, and clothing. They can be enlivened with animations to simulate facial expressions, posture, and gestures.

There are multiple channels for communication in the virtual world. Avatars can communicate by typing through local chat or instant messaging (IM), or by speaking through voice chat. The virtual world is not constrained by real-world physics. This is an important consideration when constructing educational activities. Avatars can fly, float to observe goings-on from any angle, teleport in order to materialize in a different location, fall and recover, and change their visual perspective at will.

Second Life has tremendous potential as a learning environment. The virtual world offers opportunities for student interaction, intense engagement, scripted immersive experiences, simulations, role-playing, and constructivist learning. The anonymity afforded by the avatar appears to lead to less inhibition and greater interaction. In addition, the greater sense of "presence" in a virtual world positively influences group process and cohesiveness, as well as engagement and attention. We decided to use Second Life in our pilot since it is the most widely used virtual world platform and there is no charge to access it.

The problems with using a virtual world like SL for education and training lie mostly in the realm of technical and security issues. The software requires a download and has significant system requirements (processing power, up-to-date video card, and a fast broadband internet connection), the learning curve for navigation and interaction is steep, and the possibilities for technical problems and failures during the actual event are numerous. Many corporate or university firewalls do not allow access to public virtual worlds, like Second Life. For healthcare applications, virtual world events need to be carefully controlled and private. Fortunately, designers can construct a Second Life venue where access is completely controlled and privacy is assured.

## Purpose

The purpose of this project was to explore the potential of using a virtual world platform for medical education through the development of a one-hour, interactive seminar on the topic of insulin therapy for Type 2 Diabetes for post-graduate primary care physicians. With 25.8 million U.S. children and adults suffering from diabetes and rising obesity trends, diabetes care management is a serious concern among primary care physicians. The objectives of this pilot study were to: 1) explore the potential of the virtual world, Second Life, for CME activities; 2) determine possible instructional design approaches for using SL for CME; 3) understand the limitations of SL for CME activities; 4) understand the barriers, solutions, and costs to using SL, including participant and presenter training; 5) measure participant learning outcomes and feedback. The learning objectives for the participating physicians were to: 1) be aware of insulin inertia; 2) learn to use glycemic patterns to choose starting insulin; 3) learn to decide among basal, prandial, and premixed insulins; 4) feel confident titrating insulin. We felt that the prevalence of diabetes and the particular physician learning objectives for proper diabetes care leant themselves particularly well to the virtual world environment.

## Recruitment

Since this was a pilot, the plan was to keep the attendance small. Institutional Review Board approval was obtained from Boston University School of Medicine. Participants were recruited from two family medicine listservs and from prior participants in online CME courses. Given the anticipated time commitment, including training and pre and post surveys, participants were offered an honorarium for completion of all activities. Since this was a pilot and not an accredited CME program, no CME credits were provided. Participants were offered a Second life coaching session if they had no previous SL experience.

Forty-one physicians expressed interest in the program. Ongoing email contact helped to further qualify the candidates, arrange coaching sessions, clarify objectives, confirm hardware/software requirements, and send candidates to the online pre-survey. Over the course of three weeks, the original 41 was pared down to 14. Some had conflicts with the workshop date, some did not have a compatible computer, and still others did not respond to emails.

The 14 participants were all primary care physicians (family medicine specialty), with an average of 16 years in practice, 60% female and 40% male, residing in seven different states (North Carolina, Illinois, California, Massachusetts South Carolina, Conneticut, and Kentucky), along with one observer attending the session logged in from Geneva, Switzerland. One-third reported having previously logged into Second Life and two-thirds described themselves as "daily internet users."

The organizers commissioned Dr. Elliot Sternthal (MD, FACP, Director of Outpatient Diabetes Program, Boston Medical Center) to provide the session content. The instructional emphasis was to understand the options around diabetes patient assessment, insulin administration, and titrating dosage.

## Instructional Design

The organizers worked with Dr. Sternthal to create an instructional design for the hour-long session and build an avatar that resembled him in real life. Dr. Sternthal started with a PowerPoint deck to support a 40-minute, insulin therapy talk. We found that this deck, which would work well for a face-to-face talk, was too long and did not allow opportunities for the interaction and activity afforded by the virtual world. The organizers worked with him to shorten the talk, focus in on the key concepts, add visual elements, increase the interactivity, and leverage the unique capabilities of Second Life. Strategic questions were inserted (answers to be given by the doctors in local chat) in order to surface misconceptions and points of confusion among the participants. We also decided to introduce two mock diabetes patients to the session in order to apply the session content to a real-world scenario. This entailed designing two age-appropriate, overweight avatars. During the actual session, Dr. Sternthal gave a lecture interspersed with active engagement junctures. At those points, Dr. Sternthal asked questions related to his lecture, interviewed the patients, displayed their lab results, and requested input from participant doctors on treatment plans. With these methods we hoped to address the compliance difficulties that physicians face when urging their diabetic patients to adhere to regular medication and dietary regimes.

## Results

### The Event

The event was held on Monday, June 15th, 2009 from 7:00 pm to 8:00 pm (EST). Avatars were asked to arrive 30 minutes early, to get everyone settled and resolve any technical issues. The session officially ended at 8:00 pm but the physicians stayed until 8:30 pm, asking questions and socializing. See Figures 4 and 5 for scenes from the actual event.

### Findings

On a seven-point Likert-type scale measuring confidence, participants' reported confidence increased from pre to post Second Life event with respect to selecting insulin, initiating insulin, and adjusting insulin dosing for patients with Type 2 Diabetes. On test cases, the percent of participants providing a correct insulin initiation plan increased from 60% pre, to 90% post, and correct initiation of mealtime insulin increased from 40% pre to 80% post. All participants agreed that this experience in Second Life was an effective method of medical education, that the virtual world approach to CME was superior to other methods of online CME, and that they would enroll in another such event in Second Life. Only 9% disagreed with the statement that this potential Second Life method of CME is superior to face-to-face CME.

*Figure 4. Avatars assembling just before the event on the Boston University/World Health Organization Second Life location*

*Figure 5. Dr. Elliot Sternthal, diabetes specialist, reviews lab results with diabetic patient, Mariana Hexicola*

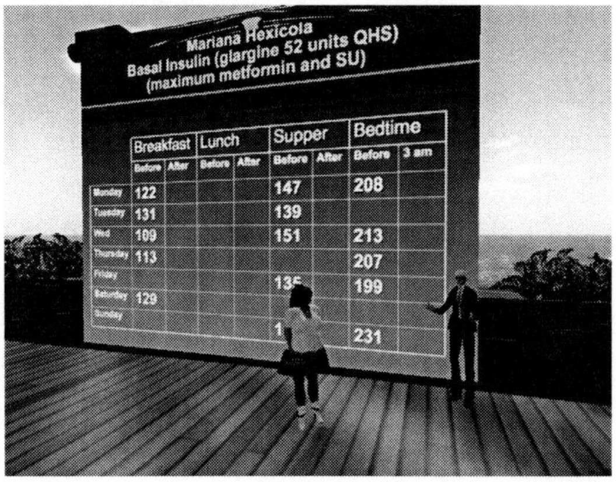


Overall, this pilot was very successful. The participant physicians' responses indicated that this was a positive and engaging experience, which could meet their actual CME needs and better fit their busy schedules. Many of the participants noted the convenience of an online seminar as one of the most important advantages – no travel is required and they can participate from the comfort of their own homes. Since other online methods of instruction also offer this convenience, what justifies the expense of a virtual world course?

This pilot points to at least two important virtual world advantages: the added sense of presence afforded by a representative avatar and the added real-life application provided by mock-patients. Judging by the participant comments, the injected realism of mock patients was effective and added to the seminar's impact.

## Overall Lessons Learned

Since this pilot was primarily designed to develop expertise in designing and running CME and other medical education events programs in the virtual world, it is important to capture key lessons for future programs. They are:

1. An event like this has to be designed in such a way so that it answers the question, "why SL?" before it gets asked. In other words, it is critical to take advantage of the unique affordances of the virtual world to push the experience beyond what could be delivered via a web site or a webinar.
2. With so many opportunities to "go wrong" in a technically complex platform, it is clear that thorough planning is paramount. This event was meticulously planned, rehearsed, and buttressed with contingency plans.
3. The time investment to plan, prepare, and deliver a one-hour event is steep and the learning curve for the doctor-participants is not trivial. From our experience, delivering a CME event in Second Life is much more time consuming that a face-to-face event and certainly more than a webinar event.
4. Virtual world events require a skilled and unflappable speaker. They must be knowledgeable, confident in their expertise, unruffled with the inevitable technical glitches, good humored, in-tune with the students, and able to field questions from the backchat, while still keeping an eye on the content and the timing.
5. There is a certain excitement that comes from just being there, all together, in the virtual world. The physician participants are more forthcoming, brave, involved and present.
6. There is an interesting "protection" effect that comes with the avatar anonymity that promotes disclosure and sharing. Many of the doctors commented on it and you could certainly sense an openness and willingness to venture further from the backchat log.
7. The informal exchange and learning resulting from the backchat suggests less of a top-down, and more of a Socratic approach to learning and instruction, with participants and experts exchanging strategies and ideas more fluidly. What's more, the backchat exchange might result in enhanced professional connections among participants that could extend beyond the boundaries of the single event.
8. While the backchat offers an opportunity for increased interactivity, it can be distracting. Organizers should prepare participants for this and set ground rules about keeping the chat to a professional level.
9. It is important to leverage the more playful aspects of Second Life, without drifting into unprofessional behavior. In this event, the mock-patient avatars' responses, the 15-minute conversational warm-up before the session started, and a social phase (including "serving" champagne) at the end all helped to serve that purpose.

## DISCUSSION

The results of this pilot suggest that virtual worlds offer the potential of a new medical education pedagogy that can enhance learning outcomes beyond those provided by more traditional online or face-to-face post-graduate professional development activities. Strong potential exists for application of these methods at the residency and medical school levels as well.

There are many instructional design possibilities to consider that will further leverage the unique advantages of these innovative technological environments. In future events, we will consider expanding the mock patient element so that physician pairs (or teams) could interview their own mock patients and compare findings. This should enhance learning on the psychosocial aspects of patient care, allowing doctors to interact with other avatars (patients, staff, experts) in a safe, simulated environment and reflect on their learning. The local chat could be used more specifically to boost engagement and information transfer. Simulated physiology models could be created to provide a deeper understanding of the biology behind the disease state. We intend to further investigate the unique potential of Second Life as a learning environment.

The results of this pilot suggest that virtual worlds offer tremendous opportunity to provide a space for constructivist learning at its best and to enhance learning outcomes beyond that provided by traditionally designed CME courses.

## SUMMARY AND CONCLUSION

The chapter is an overview of web 3D virtual learning environments. It includes a general definition of Virtual Reality Technology and Virtual Learning Environments, discusses literature findings on the benefits and challenges of using web-based VEs for self-discovery learning, and presents a review of the latest technologies/platforms used to develop online VEs. In addition, the chapter includes a description of two 3D web virtual learning environments that were recently developed by the authors. The purpose of this chapter is to let the reader develop a general understanding of web 3D virtual environment technologies and trends, and their prospective application in education for the promotion of effective interactive learning experiences.

## REFERENCES

X3D International Standard. (2004). *X3D framework & SAI.* ISO/IEC FDIS (Final Draft International Standard) 19775:200x. Retrieved from http://www.web3d.org/x3d/specifications/ISO-IEC-19775-IS- X3DAbstractSpecification/.

Adamo-Villani, N., & Johnson, E. (2010). Virtual heritage applications: The 3D tour of MSHHD. *Proc. of ICCSIT 2010 - International Conference on Computer Science and Information Technology*, April 28-30, Rome.

Adamo-Villani, N., Johnson, E., & Penrod, T. (2009). Virtual reality on the Web: The 21st Century project. *Proc. of M-ICTE 2009 - V Int. Conf. on Multimedia and Information and Communication Technologies in Education*, 22-24 April, Lisbon, (pp. 622-626).

Adobe. (2010). *Flash 3D graphics.* Retrieved from http://help.adobe.com/en_US/Flash/10.0_UsingFlash/WS3D3F757E-6EEB-4f6b-BC7F-BE8F94D329E1.html.

Andreas, K., Tsiatsos, T., Terzidou, T., & Pomportsis, A. (2010). Fostering collaborative learning in Second Life: Metaphors and affordances. *Computers & Education, 55*(2), 603–615. doi:10.1016/j.compedu.2010.02.021

Bainbridge, W. S. (2007). The scientific research potential of virtual worlds. *Science, 317*(5837), 472. doi:10.1126/science.1146930

Bavelier, Green, and Dye (2010). Children, Wired: For Better and For Worse. Neuron 67, 692-701.

Beard, L. (2009). A survey of health-related activities on second life. *Journal of Medical Internet Research, 11*(2). doi:10.2196/jmir.1192

Bowman, D. A., Koller, D., & Hodges, L. F. (1997). Travel in immersive virtual environments: An evaluation of viewpoint motion control techniques. *Proc. of VRAIS '97 - Virtual Reality Annual International Symposium*, Albuquerque, NM, 1997.

Bransford, J. D., Brown, A. L., & Cocking, R. R. (1999). *How people learn: Brain, mind, experience, and school.* Washington, DC: National Academies Press. Retrieved from http://books.nap.edu/catalog/6160.html.

Brna, P. (1987). Confronting dynamics misconceptions. *Instructional Science*, *16*, 351–379. doi:10.1007/BF00117752

Broadribb, S., & Carter, C. (2009). Using Second Life in human resource development. *British Journal of Educational Technology*, *40*(3), 547–550. doi:10.1111/j.1467-8535.2009.00950.x

Bronack, S. (2006). Learning in the zone: A social constructivist framework for distance education in a 3-dimensional virtual world. *Interactive Learning Environments*, *14*(3), 219–232. doi:10.1080/10494820600909157

Carey, R., & Bell, G. (1997). *The annotated VRML-97 reference manual*. Reading, MA: Addison-Wesley.

Chittaro, L., & Ranon, R. (2007). Web3D technologies in learning, education and training: Motivations, issues, opportunities. *Computers & Education*, *49*, 3–18. doi:10.1016/j.compedu.2005.06.002

Coffman, T., & Klinger, M. B. (2008). Utilizing virtual worlds in education: The implications for practice. *International Journal of Social Sciences*, *2*(1), 29–33.

Cognition and Technology Group at Vanderbilt. (1996). Looking at technology in context: A framework for understanding technology and education research. In Berliner, D. C., & Calfee, R. C. (Eds.), *The handbook of educational psychology* (pp. 807–840). New York, NY: Macmillan.

Dalgarno, B., & Harper, B. (2004). User control and task authenticity for spatial learning in 3D environments. *Australasian Journal of Educational Technology*, *20*(1), 1–17.

Dalgarno, B., Hedberg, J., & Harper, B. (2002). The contribution of 3D environments to conceptual understanding. *Proc. of ASCILITE*, 2002, New Zealand.

Dalgarno, B., & Lee, M. J. W. (2010). What are the learning affordances of 3-D virtual environments? *British Journal of Educational Technology*, *41*(1), 10–32. doi:10.1111/j.1467-8535.2009.01038.x

Danforth, M. P. D. (2009). Development of virtual patient simulations for medical education. *Journal of Virtual Worlds Research*, *2*(2).

De Clerck, N. M. (2010). Children, wired: For better and for worse. *Neuron*, *67*(5), 692–701. doi:10.1016/j.neuron.2010.08.035

De Freitas, S. (2010). Learning as immersive experiences: Using the four-dimensional framework for designing and evaluating immersive learning experiences in a virtual world. *British Journal of Educational Technology*, *41*(1), 69–85. doi:10.1111/j.1467-8535.2009.01024.x

De Freitas, S., & Neumann, T. (2009). The use of exploratory learning for supporting immersive learning in virtual environments. *Computers & Education*, *52*(2), 343–352. doi:10.1016/j.compedu.2008.09.010

De Freitas, S., Rebolledo-Mendez, G., Liarokapis, F., Magoulas, G., & Poulovassilis, A. (2010). Learning as immersive experiences: Using the four-dimensional framework for designing and evaluating immersive learning experiences in a virtual world. *British Journal of Educational Technology*, *41*(1), 69–85. doi:10.1111/j.1467-8535.2009.01024.x

De Jong, T. (2005). The guided discovery principle in multimedia learning. In Mayer, R. E. (Ed.), *The Cambridge handbook of multimedia learning*.

De Lucia, A. (2009). Development and evaluation of a virtual campus on Second Life: The case of SecondDMI. *Computers & Education*, *52*(1), 220–233. doi:10.1016/j.compedu.2008.08.001

Dede, C. (Ed.). (1998). *Introduction. Association for Supervision and Curriculum Development (ASCD) Yearbook: Learning with technology* (pp. v–x). Alexandria, VA: Association for Supervision and Curriculum Development.

Dede, C. (2009). Immersive interfaces for engagement and learning. *Science, 323*(5910), 66. doi:10.1126/science.1167311

Dickey, M. D. (2003). Teaching in 3D: Pedagogical affordances and constraints of 3D virtual worlds for synchronous distance learning. *Distance Education, 24*(1), 105–121. doi:10.1080/01587910303047

Dillenburg, P. (2000). Virtual learning environments. *Proc. of EUN Conference 2000 - Workshop on Virtual Learning Environments.*

Esteves, M. (2010). Improving teaching and learning of computer programming through the use of the Second Life virtual world. *British Journal of Educational Technology, 42*(4).

Forterra Systems. (2010). *Website.* Retrieved from http://www.forterrainc.com/.

Gerstein, J. (2009). Beyond the game: Quest Atlantis as an online learning experience for gifted elementary students. *Journal of Virtual Worlds Research,* 403.

Girvan, C., & Savage, T. (2010). Identifying an appropriate pedagogy for virtual worlds: A communal constructivism case study. *Computers & Education, 55*(1), 342–349. doi:10.1016/j.compedu.2010.01.020

Gorsky, P., & Finegold, M. (1992). Using computer simulations to restructure students' conceptions of force. *Journal of Computers in Mathematics and Science Teaching, 11,* 163–178.

Hansen, M. (2008). Versatile, immersive, creative and dynamic virtual 3-D healthcare learning environments: A review of the literature. *Journal of Medical Internet Research, 10*(3). doi:10.2196/jmir.1051

Hayes, G. (2006). *Virtual worlds, Web 3.0 and portable profiles.* Retrieved February 2, 2008, from http://www.personalizemedia.com/virtual-worlds-web-30-and-portable-profiles.

Hirose, M. (2006). Virtual reality technology and museum exhibit. *The International Journal of Virtual Reality, 5*(2), 31–36.

Hmelo, C., & Williams, S. M. (Eds.). (1998). Special issue: Learning through problem solving. *Journal of the Learning Sciences, 7*(3), 4.

Huang, H. M. (2010). Investigating learners' attitudes toward virtual reality learning environments: Based on a constructivist approach. *Computers & Education, 55*(3). doi:10.1016/j.compedu.2010.05.014

Jang, S. J. (2009). Exploration of secondary students' creativity by integrating web-based technology into an innovative science curriculum. *Computers & Education, 52*(1), 247–255. doi:10.1016/j.compedu.2008.08.002

Jarmon, L. (2009). An ecology of embodied interaction: Pedagogy and homo virtualis. *Journal of Virtual Worlds Research, 2*(1).

Java 3D. (2010). *Home page.* Retrieved from https://java3d.dev.java.net/.

Jiang, Z., & Potter, W. D. (1994). A computer microworld to introduce students to probability. *Journal of Computers in Mathematics and Science Teaching, 13*(2), 197–222.

Johnson, C. M. (2009). Virtual worlds in health care higher education. *Journal of Virtual Worlds Research, 2*(2).

Kafai, Y. B. (1995). *Minds in play: Computer game design as a context for children's learning*. Hillsdale, NJ: Erlbaum.

Kangassalo, M. (1994). Children's independent exploration of a natural phenomenon by using a pictorial computer-based simulation. *Journal of Computing in Childhood Education, 5*(3/4), 285–297.

Korakakis, G., Pavlatou, E. A., & Spyrellis, N. (2009). 3D visualization types in multimedia applications for science learning: A case study for 8th grade students in Greece. *Computers & Education, 52*(2), 390–401. doi:10.1016/j.compedu.2008.09.011

Land, S. M. (2000). Cognitive requirements for learning with open-ended learning environments. *Educational Technology Research and Development, 48*(3), 61–78. doi:10.1007/BF02319858

Lang, A. S., & Kobilnyk, D. (2009). Visualizing atomic orbitals using Second Life. *Journal of Virtual Worlds Research, 2*(1).

Lesko, C. J., & Hollingsworth, Y. (2010). Compounding the results: The integration of virtual worlds with the Semantic Web. *Journal of Virtual Worlds Research, 2*(5).

Lim, K. T. (2009). The six learnings of Second Life™: A framework for designing curricular interventions in-world. *Journal of Virtual Worlds Research, 2*(1).

Linden Lab. (2010). *Home page*. Retrieved from http://lindenlab.com/.

Linebarger, D. L., & Walker, D. (2005). Infants' and toddlers' television viewing and language outcomes. *The American Behavioral Scientist, 48*, 624–645. doi:10.1177/0002764204271505

Livingstone, D., & Kemp, J. (2006). Putting a Second Life "metaverse" skin on learning management systems. *Proc. of the Second Life Education Workshop at the Second Life Community Convention*, (pp. 13-18).

Loureiro, A., & Bettencourt, T. (2010). Building knowledge in the virtual world–Influence of real life relationships. *Journal of Virtual Worlds Research, 2*(5).

Matei, S. A., Miller, C. C., Arns, L., Rauh, N., Hartman, C., & Bruno, R. (2007). Visible past: Learning and discovering in real and virtual space and time. *First Monday, 12*(5).

McClean, P., Bernhardt, S. E., Donald, S., Slator, B., & White, A. (2001). Virtual worlds in large enrollment biology and geology classes significantly improve authentic learning. In J. A. Chambers (Ed.), *Selected Papers from the 12th International Conference on College Teaching and Learning (ICCTL-01)*, (pp. 111-118). Jacksonville, FL: Center for the Advancement of Teaching and Learning, April 17-21.

Owen, A. M., Hampshire, A., Grahn, J. A., Stenton, R., Dajani, S., & Burns, A. S. (2010). Putting brain training to the test. *Nature, 465*, 775–778. doi:10.1038/nature09042

Penfold, P. (2010). A Second Life first year experience. *Journal of Virtual Worlds Research, 2*(5).

Petrakou, A. (2010). Interacting through avatars: Virtual worlds as a context for online education. *Computers & Education, 54*(4), 1020–1027. doi:10.1016/j.compedu.2009.10.007

President's Committee on Advisors on Science and Technology. (1997). *Report to the President on the use of technology to strengthen K-12 education in the United States*. Washington, DC: U.S. Government Printing Office.

Protonmedia Protosphere. (2010). *About Protosphere*. Retrieved from http://protonmedia.com/resourcePage/10/about-protosphere.pdf.

Quest 3D. (2010). *Home page*. Retrieved from http://quest3d.com/.

Rogers, E. M. (2003). *Roger's diffusion of innovations theory*. New York, NY: Free Press.

Roussou, M. (2001). *Immersive interactive virtual reality in the museum*. Intuition Network of Excellence. Retrieved from http://www.intuition-eunetwork.org/documents/papers/Culture%20History/mroussou_TiLE01_paper.pdf.

Roussou, M. (2004). Learning by doing and learning through play: An exploration of interactivity in virtual environments for children. [CIE]. *Computers in Entertainment*, *2*(1), 10. doi:10.1145/973801.973818

Roussou, M., & Efraimoglou, D. (1999). *High-end interactive media in the museum* (pp. 59–62). ACM SIGGRAPH Computer Graphics.

Salmon, G. (2009). The future for (second) life and learning. *British Journal of Educational Technology*, *40*(3), 526–538. doi:10.1111/j.1467-8535.2009.00967.x

Schwartz, D. L., Lin, X., Brophy, S., & Bransford, J. D. (1999). Toward the development of flexible adaptive instructional designs. In Reigelut, C. M. (Ed.), *Instructional design theories and models* (*Vol. II*, pp. 183–213). Hillsdale, NJ: Erlbaum.

Sherman, W. S., & Craig, A. B. (2003). *Understanding virtual reality*. Morgan Kaufmann.

Shin, Y. S. (2003). Virtual experiment environments design for science education. *Proc. of IEEE International Conference on Cyberworlds* (CW03).

Siemens, G. (2008). *Siemens' connectivism theory: Learning as network creation*. Elearnspace. Retrieved from http://www.elearnspace.org/Articles/networks.htm.

Smith, M. S. (2009). Opening education. *Science*, *323*(5910), 89–101. doi:10.1126/science.1168018

Strangman, N., & Hall, T. (2003). *Virtual reality/simulations*. Wakefield, MA: National Center on Accessing the General Curriculum. Retrieved March 2007 from http://www.cast.org/publications/ncac/ncac_vr.html.

Sun Microsystems. (2009). *Project Wonderland*. Retrieved from http://www.sun.com/solutions/landing/industry/education/pdf/ed_project_wonderland.pdf?facet=-1.

The Croquet Consortium. (2010). *Home page*. Retrieved from http://www.opencroquet.org/index.php/Main_Page.

Unity 3D. (2010). *Home page*. Retrieved from http://unity3d.com/.

VRML International Standard. (1997). *VRML-97 functional specification*. International Standard ISO/IEC 14772- 1:1997. Retrieved from http://www.web3d.org/x3d/specifications/vrml/ISO_IEC_14772-All/index.html.

Warburton, S. (2009). Second Life in higher education: Assessing the potential for and the barriers to deploying virtual worlds in learning and teaching. *British Journal of Educational Technology*, *40*(3), 414–426. doi:10.1111/j.1467-8535.2009.00952.x

Web, G. L. (2010). *Kronos Group*. Retrieved from http://www.khronos.org/webgl/.

Winn, W. (2002). Current trends in educational technology research: The study of learning environments. *Educational Psychology Review*, *14*(3), 331–351. doi:10.1023/A:1016068530070

Zagorski, N. (2010). Virtual reality in science education. *ASBMB Today*. September 2010. Retrieved from http://www.asbmb.org/asbmbtoday/asbmbtoday_article.aspx?id=9178.

Zara, J. (2004). Virtual reality and cultural heritage on the Web. *Proc. of the 7th International Conference on Computer Graphics and Artificial Intelligence* (3IA 2004), Limoges, France, 2004, (pp. 101-112).

Zietsman, A. I., & Hewson, P. W. (1986). Effect of instruction using microcomputer simulations and conceptual change strategies on science learning. *Journal of Research in Science Teaching*, *23*, 27–39. doi:10.1002/tea.3660230104

Zimmerman, F. J., Christakis, D. A., & Meltzoff, A. N. (2007). Associations between media viewing and language development in children under age 2 years. *The Journal of Pediatrics*, *151*, 364–368. doi:10.1016/j.jpeds.2007.04.071

Zumbach, J., Schmitt, S., Reimann, P., & Starkloff, P. (2006). Learning life sciences: Design and development of a virtual molecular biology learning lab. *Journal of Computers in Mathematics and Science Teaching*, *25*(3), 281.

## KEY TERMS AND DEFINITIONS

**Computer Assisted Language Learning:** CALL is the acronym for Computer Assisted Language Learning and is defined as (the study of) the use of computers in language learning and teaching. Computer technology in the language learning domain is a promising field in Information and Learning Technology, as well as in Language Instruction.

**Descriptive Writing:** Descriptive writing refers to portraying people, places, or objects vividly. Readers construct the meaning from the content the writer has described, and share in the writer's experiences.

**Multi-User Virtual Environments (MUVEs):** Multi-User Virtual Environments (MUVEs), also known as virtual worlds such as Second Life, refer to online three-dimensional environments created to facilitate multi-user synchronous interaction and immersion through incorporating networks, computer graphics, and sound. Users are embodied as avatars in the shared virtual environments and interact with one another through real-time text and/or voice chat.

**Second Life (SL):** Second Life © is a registered trademark of Linden Research, Inc. Second Life (SL) is a computer-generated three-dimensional multi-user virtual environment (MUVE). Users are called residents and are embodied as avatars who interact with one another through text chat, voice chat, avatar gestures, instant messaging, and notecards in SL. Second Life allows residents to discover a vast virtual world, socialize with others, trade virtual properties, and join events and activities held by various communities.

**Web 2.0:** The term "Web 2.0" originates from "a brainstorming session between O'Reilly and MediaLive International" (O'Reilly, 2005). Web 2.0, including web applications, such as blogs, wikis, video-sharing Web sites, is used to foster collaboration, interaction, communication and information sharing on the World Wide Web.

# Chapter 7
# A Case Study on Using Discovery Learning within a Learning Management System:
## Axio Learning™

**Brent A. Anders**
*Kansas State University, USA*

## ABSTRACT

*To better illustrate how an online learning environment can be used as scaffolding for the purposes of Discovery Learning, the learning management system (LMS) known as Axio Learning was reviewed and evaluated. Axio Learning, developed from the ground up by Kansas State University (student population of about 25,000) since 1997, is a modern, full-featured learning/course management system.*

## INTRODUCTION

The utilization of an LMS such as Axio Learning (known as K-State Online on the Kansas State University campus) is a valuable component in maximizing the uses and success of Discovery Learning. The tools and capabilities within such an LMS will aid Discovery Learning with regards to pacing, sequencing, empowerment of the learner, decision supports, learner community creation, as well as addressing various issues such as learning styles (presentation modes), accessibility, usability, tracking, and anxiety mitigation (Hai-Jew, 2008). Additionally the LMS scaffolding will provide ample tools for use as strategic guidance in enhancing the use of Discovery Learning as an exemplar method of instruction, that is using specific guidance when needed and necessary in order to maximize learning and understanding (Lavine, 2005).

The following shows how different tools found within the Axio Learning LMS can be used to enhance Discovery Learning. Scott Finkeldei, assistant director for the Office of Mediated Education at Kansas State University, was asked to provide technical descriptions of the many tools within the Axio Learning LMS (Finkeldei, 2011). Finkeldei has been directly involved with the development and implementation of this LMS within the Kansas State University learning community

DOI: 10.4018/978-1-61350-320-1.ch007

Copyright © 2012, IGI Global. Copying or distributing in print or electronic forms without written permission of IGI Global is prohibited.

since its inception. He explains that the tools were developed from feedback from both instructors and students and designed to be as easy to use as possible so as to assist in interaction and comprehention of presented material. A major effort was made so that the tools themselves would not be a distracter and could be quickly and easily used so as to minimize any acclimation that would need to accrue within the LMS learning environment/community. Additionally being able to easily use the tools and quickly seeing/understanding the value in them would allow for greater self-efficacy to both student and instructor.

Each of the following tools are described with regards to its general functionality and then possibilities are presented on how it could be used as effective scaffolding for various Discovery Learning pedagogical endeavors.

## LMS TOOLS FOR DISCOVERY LEARNING

Although the Axio Learning LMS has many tools, this document will focus on the tools: Announcements, File Management Tools, Gating Tool, Interactive Tools, Student Grouping, Assessment Suite, Course Statistics and Recent Activity (see Figure 1). Information is presented in this order as a logical student progression through an online Discovery Learning course. These tools have great possibilities for use as scaffolding and guidance manipulators with regards to Discovery Learning.

### Announcements

This tool allows the instructor to post and edit text or audio course announcements. These are displayed on the course homepage, can have publish and expire dates and can be archived to a student-viewable archive. This is used mostly for important course-level communication and announcements. Some instructors use it to announce and describe assignments (see Figure 2).

#### Discovery Learning Usage

Guidance and motivational expressions would be great uses for this type of tool. Personalized messages (text and audio) for the class can go a long way to aid students in real community building in general and Discovery Learning group work specifically. Offering special guiding instructions that are new and current also aid in the motivational aspect of the learning being current and relevant.

*Figure 1. Instructor view of tools interface*

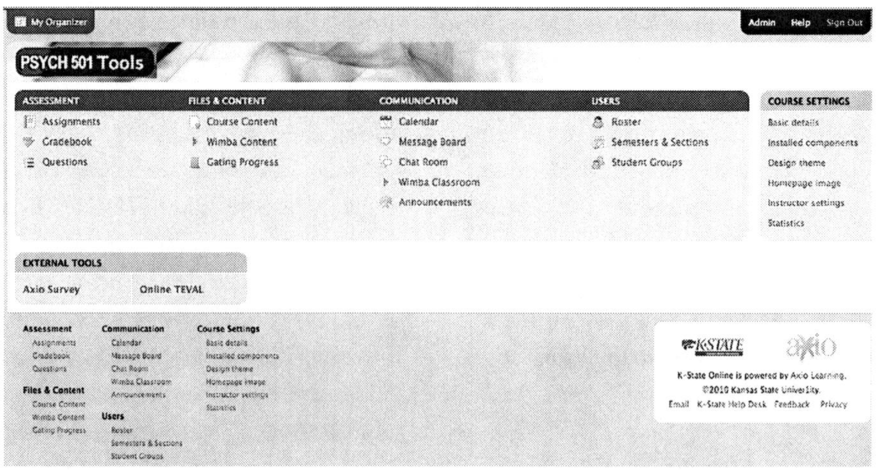

*Figure 2. Instructor announcement interface*

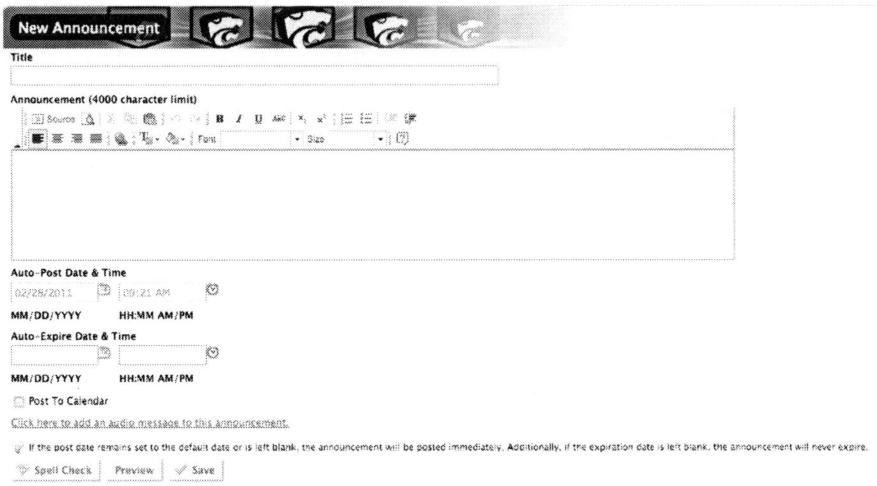


## Discovery Learning Example

A use for this tool could be realized as follows; a professor in a psychology course on consumer psychology decides to use a Webquest (scenario driven challenge/adventure type of assignment) to motivate her students while at the same time utilize Discovery Learning pedagogy. She uses the Announcements Tool to tell her students the following:

*"Three potato chip companies are in the process of suing each other. Each company is claiming to be the best tasting potato chip via a blind taste test. The companies have agreed to arbitration and have decided that they will agree to adhere to the results of third party scientific survey results. They have hired us as consumer psychologists to conduct the testing. The court sanctioned, agreed upon guidelines document is in module three. This is a high profile case so be sure to strictly follow the scientific method and work with the other assigned consumer psychologists in your group."*

In this example the instructor could use the Announcements tool to guide her students as well as to add realism to the assignment. Greater clarification (as well as possibly a grading rubric) would be given in the "court sanctioned, agreed upon guidelines document," but the impact of placing preliminary instructions within the Announcements tool would add to motivation in general as well as specifically to the follow on information that the students would be exposed to within the course.

## File Management Tool

This allows the instructor to upload, create, edit, manage and publish course content and information. Instructors can upload files of any type. The File Management tool is 'file agnostic' meaning it does not care what file type is used by the instructor. As long as it can be uploaded and shared on the web and their students can view it/use it, they can upload and publish it. This allows for instructor freedom for interacting with their students. Mp4 videos can be set to streaming, download or both (this allows for easy use with mobile devices). Large data sets, interactive Flash games, video, Office-type documents, spreadsheets or HTML can all be published and shared with sub folders, page headers, separators and links. RSS feeds of folders to announce newly published files can be enabled to alert users of each new posting (this can be used for podcasting and instant delivery of content).

## Discovery Learning Usage

Through the use of the File Management tool the instructor can utilize many different types of files to address many different situations and/or learning styles. Content could be provided as text as well as via audio, audio/video, games or any combination thereby enhancing usability and accessibility. The content could be within the File Management tool or linked to (but presented within if wanted) via the use of a built in link tool or HTML creation page. The File Management tool provides a framework so as to organize the presentation of information as well as to provide additional areas for student use or "just-in-time-learning" (added resource area for students who need additional topic learning). Since folder organization is easily accomplished via this tool, multiple versions or cognitive levels of the content can be utilized for maximum customization/personalization.

## Discovery Learning Example

Continuing with the previously stated scenario of the consumer psychology class; realism, comprehension, and information attainment could be enhanced even more via the use of multiple file types and content presentation through the File Management tool. The professor in this case could create a video pretending to be the main arbitrator stating the terms of court sanctioned, agreed upon guidelines document. This video would of course have captions (accessibility) available to assist those who have difficulty hearing as well as those who are in a noisy environment or for those that English is a second language. The actual court sanctioned, agreed upon guidelines document could also be made available for text-based learners.

At this point the instructor can choose the amount of guidance to provide the learner so as to throttle the amount of full "discovery" that occurs with the learner.

At one end of the spectrum the professor could choose to provide no further guidance or resources and allow the students to "discover" everything else needed to accomplish the task/assignment. In the middle ground of the spectrum the professor could suggest links to areas on the web where students could gain knowledge of how to properly conduct an empirical blind taste test. At the other end of the spectrum the professor herself could have video examples of how to properly conduct the scientific method procedures as well as past class examples of how it was conducted and presented. The instructor could have different levels of complexity in terms of requirements and examples based off of class type and/or background. Different versions of the course's presentation style and sophistication can easily be accomplished through the use of the File Management tool. Individual access to this content by student already within a course can be managed through the use of a Gating Tool.

## Gating Tool

This is a function within the File Management tool as well as a later described Assessment Suite that allows instructors the ability to control student access to content and assignments by choosing gating criteria. Instructors can create and setup "gates" to certain assignments or content that requires students have previously accessed other data or have successfully completed a previous assignment. This gating step then provides instructors with reports of students' progress through the gates. Professors can reset gates and/or grant exceptions to gates as needed. The gating tool can be used to control the pace of the course or to facilitate different levels of guided/unguided course progression (see Figure 3).

### Discovery Learning Usage

One of the general worries or criticisms of Discovery Learning deals with the possibility of students learning the wrong information or process of accomplishing a task (Mayer, 2004). Through the use of Gating, instructors can ensure that students have been exposed to or display knowledge/mastery of correct knowledge/process in order to proceed to more advanced or different materials. Through various feedback mechanisms, the student and instructor could address situations that might arise preventing students from being able to "open the Gate," if the Gating option is used in more than just an ensure-exposure-tool and actually tied to successfully fulfilling an assignment.

### Discovery Learning Example

Gating could be utilized in the consumer psychology class in that in order to view the "court sanctioned, agreed upon guidelines document," the students would first have to go through a module containing videos on what the scientific method is, links to examples of how to properly conduct a blind taste test, and/or various examples of how to organize and present the data findings. Another technique would be to not provide so much detail and simply present students with a short quiz that they would have to successfully pass (ensuring that they know the proper preliminary information) before they can view the "court sanctioned, agreed upon guidelines document." The instructor would always be able to manipulate the amount of guidance (as well as proper feedback) needed in order to ensure proper learning.

## INTERACTIVE TOOLS

### Chat Room, Message Board, Wimba Classroom

These are three different tools but are all used so as to engage the students in different interactive ways. The Chat Room provides a standard web, text-based chat room for students and instructors to meet in synchronously and discuss in real-time. Instructors can create and schedule more than one chat room to allow multiple discussions to go on or different topics to be discussed and can also leave chat rooms open full time to facilitate student ad-hoc study. Chats are archive and instructors can edit and publish the transcript within the course. The Message Board provides an asynchronous communication method. A threaded message board keeps

*Figure 3. Simplified gating tool explanation*

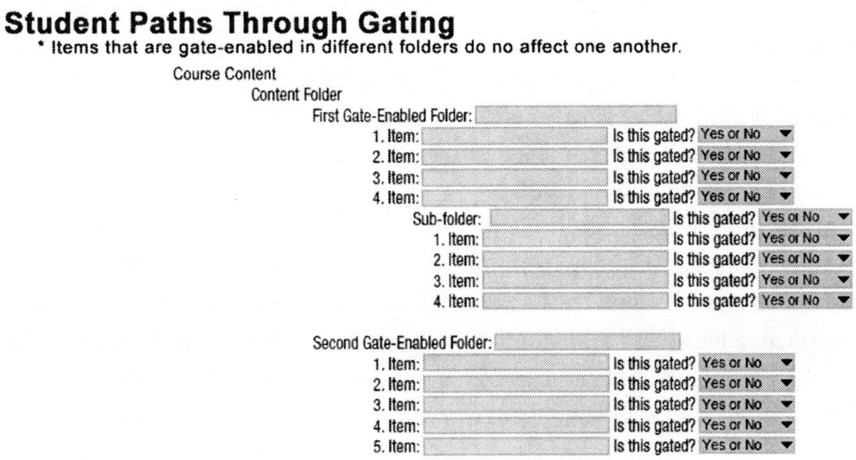

all conversations on context and association with each other as opposed to a forum that is organized by showing messages in the order in which they are received regardless of topic. Instructors can have more than one message board, create thread topics and allow students to also create threads or just reply. Instructors can allow attachments to messages and view stats on usage, popularity of threads and other key reporting factors. The message board can be sorted several different ways and provides 'New Unread' jump-to features and offers searching and clean printing of threads or entire boards. The Wimba Classroom is a 3rd party provided tool integrated with Axio providing live virtual classroom supporting multi-way audio and video chat, application and desktop sharing, content display, group web browsing, polling, and the ability to turn over control to another student or instructor to allow for student presentations, outside expert visits or just lively discussion.

### Discovery Learning Usage

Use of these interactive tools can greatly enhance the success of discover learning in that it can enhance the tele-presence of both the instructor/facilitator as well as the students themselves. In this online learning the LMS itself becomes a "social network" (socio-technical online learning environment) and that combined with the self seeking behavior, community sharing of information, and discussion of meaning of content and content source, is the learning experience (Vesely, et al., 2007) and (Liccaridi, et al., 2007). By providing such tools and areas for students to interact with the instructor and with one another, confidence is increased and resiliency is generally boosted (as well as a sense of self-efficacy) in that students learn from each other as well as from the instructor and see that their own actions and comments effect the class and themselves. The instructor can again choose the level of guidance to provide by stepping in when warranted on message boards and chat rooms when false information is put out or when information is being misinterpreted or poorly understood. General rules and instructions should be made available at the beginning of the course to better aid in general student interactions, netiquette and how to best share information and respond to varying ideas/opinions.

### Discovery Learning Example

The Consumer Psychology course could utilize the interactive tools by creating message boards for students to post relevant sources of information, to discuss which is the best way to properly conduct a blind taste test, to talk about what would be the most professional way to present the findings and why, to ask questions on procedures, etc. The Wimba Classroom tool could be used as a way for the instructor to show via video how she specifically wants the blind taste test to occur or she could simply use it to only talk about the scientific method and let the students discover the best method for the blind taste test. Additionally the instructor could state that students would be using the Wimba interactive tool to present their findings as if they were presenting to the client. One could even require the students to record their blind taste testing session and then show the rest of the class through the Wimba tool and then be ready to answer questions via audio or text chat. Another very powerful usage of the listed interactive tools would be to give instances of them over specifically to individual student groups for the purposes of their own collaborative efforts (see Figure 4).

## Student Grouping

This provides Instructor managed student-to-student workspaces. The groups act like mini courses within the course. They can have a group homepage with announcements and recent activity, file upload and management including version control, a chat room, message board, inter-group email, a Wimba Live Classroom and assignment

*Figure 4. Message board interface*

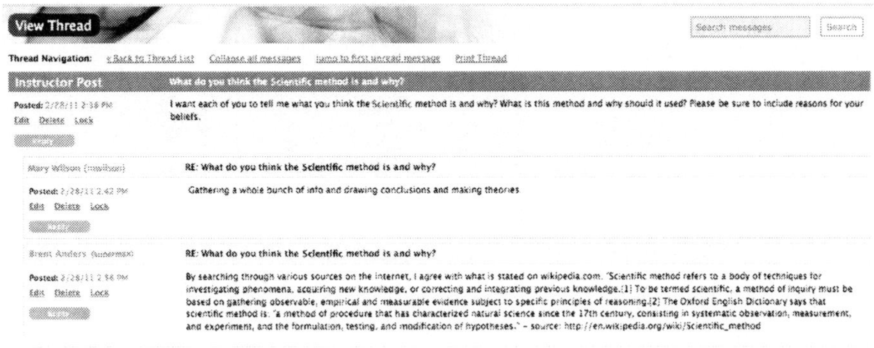


submission tools. Instructors can view logs of all work within the groups, get statistics and usage information and interact with all groups as needed. The groups can be created randomly or by selected groupings, named, themed and customized by the group members and instructors can move people between groups seamlessly whenever needed.

## Discovery Learning Usage

A real supportive online community for learning can be created, and using multiple forms of interaction can help facilitate learning and understanding (Johnson, 2001). By properly instructing students on how to use the interactive tools, instructors can easily facilitate group work (done either synchronously or asynchronously) to enhance the Discovery Learning process.

## Discovery Learning Example

One of the most powerful aspects of Discovery Learning is that it is an aspect of experiential learning (learning by doing). Through the use of these interactive tools the students in the Consumer Psychology class will not just learn data, they will learn the experience of actually "doing" the subject matter. Having to learn to work together better matches the process and procedures in the "real world" as well as being able to clearly split up the work, express concerns dealing with a situation as well as help each other understand the problems and possible solutions. Since each Student Group could be given its own mini-virtual classroom, the students could use their own message boards to answer each other's questions and present preliminary ideas. They could arrange times when they could all meet in the chat room to clarify information and ensure that they were all in agreement on the assignment and how to proceed. They could also then have live Wimba Classroom sessions and videoconference with each other to further discuss or practice how they would conduct the blind taste test as well as present their finding to the rest of the class. The possibilities are only limited by the instructor's and students' imagination or constraints within the pedagogical approach utilized.

In addition to evaluating students via experiential learning, various other assessments can be incorporated within the overall Discovery Learning process (see Figure 5).

## Assessment Suite

This is a very powerful tool set dealing with the creation and usage of multiple types of assignments and grading techniques. Instructors can control the release of the assignments, their expiration, the release of the answer key and scores all independently. They can also release basic stats to students about mean, median, aver-

*Figure 5. Wimba interface*

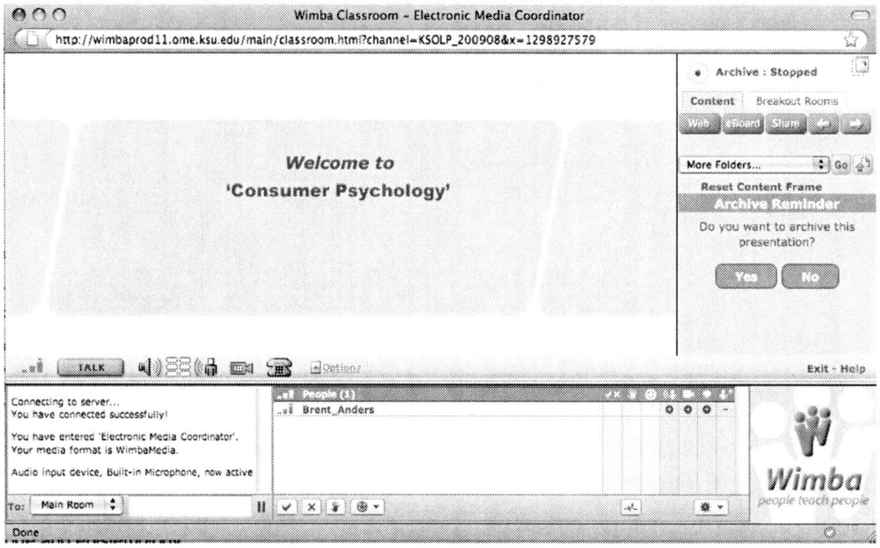


age and distribution of scores. Instructors can put assignments into categories to organize them and add grading rules to those categories to weight a category a certain percentage of the course total, drop lowest scores in a category or round or curve the category. Rules on individual assignments and on the course's online grade book as a whole are also available.

Instructors can allow students to submit comments/feedback at the end of an assignment, can provide feedback per question on the answer key to the student, can send confirmation numbers to students on successful submission to provide tracking and eliminate 'the internet lost my homework' issues and can determine the number of accesses and submissions students receive for each exam.

Instructors have access to a number of reports available per assignment and per student. Statistical Analysis report covers standard stats and distribution of scores. The Scores Analysis report allows the instructor to see each individual's submitted answers and their score and manually manage the score from there. Item Analysis report displays the number and percentage of students that answered correctly. Both the number and the percentage of students within the top and bottom that answered the questions correctly are displayed.

Within the Online assignments there are a variety of question types that can be created by instructor. The Multiple-Choice question type allows the instructor to create a question and allow the student to select an answer or answers from multiple answer options. The True or False question type is similar to the multiple-choice question type but with only the two possible responses of true (positive) or false (negative). Short Answer is a question type where the instructor can define acceptable short answer variations for automatic grading and easily grant exceptions on a mis-grade. Matching questions requires the student to select one specific word/phrase and match it with another specific word/phrase. Numeric is a question type that accepts numeric answers exactly or within a defined range. Finally the Essay question type allows the instructor to collect essay responses online that allows for keyword highlighting, word counts, grading per question as well as per assignment (see Figure 6).

*Figure 6. Assignment/test/quiz question selection list*

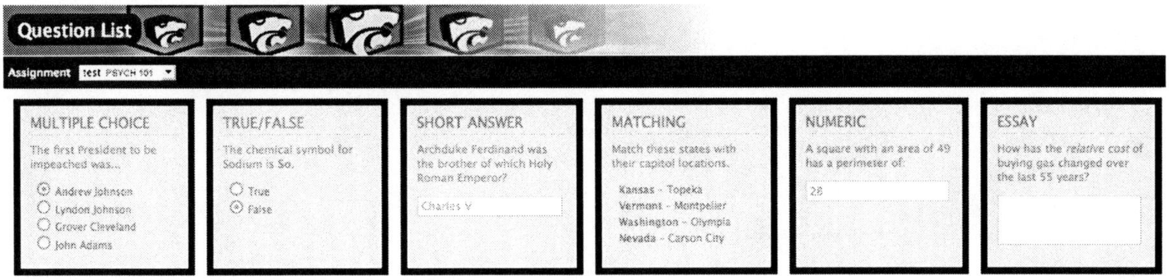


## Discovery Learning Usage

Through the use of many different types of assessment questions, instructors can insure that students are discovering the correct information so as to properly learn the content. Feedback, both to the student as well as from the student can be gleaned so as to monitor understanding as well as to re-evaluate the pedagogy and level of guidance given to students.

## Discovery Learning Example

Through the utilization of various gated quizzes the professor in the Consumer Psychology course could ensure that students understood the material enough to progress to the next assignment or portion of the class. Alternatively, the professor could have students take a procedural type quiz just to check comprehension or gain incite to how/what the student was doing. The professor could ask a True/False questions such as "Do you understand what the Scientific Method is and how to apply it?" This could be followed up by a short answer question such as "Please list the URLs or sources of information you used in order to learn about the Scientific Method." Various other feedback questions could also be used; multiple choice: "please select which of the following online resources you used in order to prepare for conducting the blind taste test: youtube.com, facebook.com, wikipedia.org, pbs.org, lib.k-state.edu (Kansas State University Library website), and/or other" (see Figure 7).

A short answer could then follow that question: "If you selected other as a response, please list those websites." For a more in-depth answer, a short answer question could also be posed such as "Please list why you chose the websites selected as your source of information, also explain how you found this information source. How reliable and valid do you believe that information source to be?"

In addition to experiential learning/project evaluations and assignments/test/quizzes assessments, course statistics of participation and activity can also be used rate students and the course overall.

## Course Statistics and Recent Activity Indicators

Course Statistics provides instructors with specific stats on student usage and progress. It shows real-time graphs and stats of trends in student usage such as most visited time of day and day of week. It shows individual student's file accesses and progress. Recent Activity is a live feed of important course events tailored to students and instructors for quick notification. It is shown to both students and instructors on their Course Organizer, which lists all the courses they

*Figure 7. Question creation preview interface*

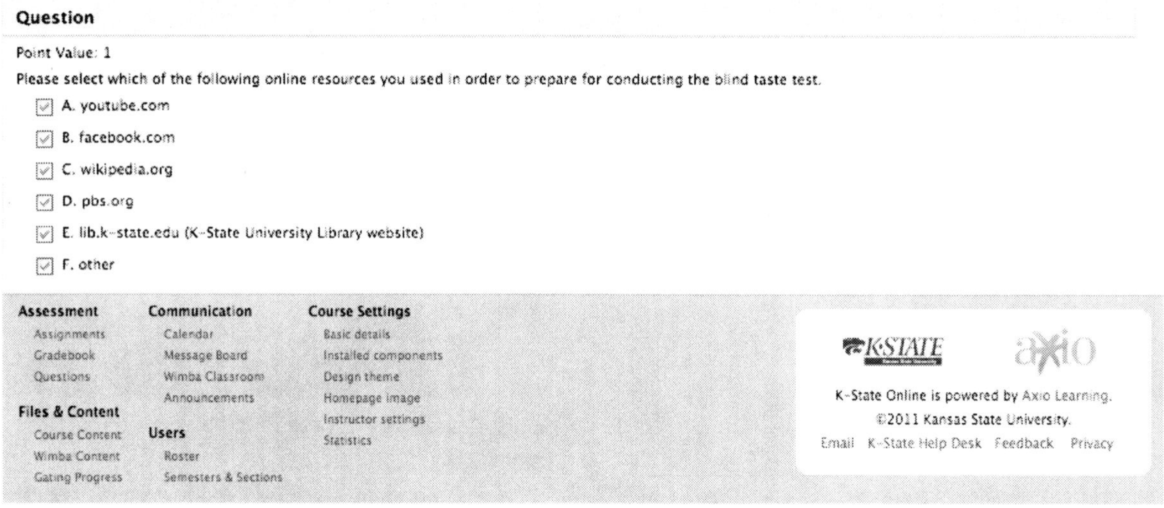


have access to. For each course students can see new files published, grades posted, assignments available and message board activity. Instructors see assignments submitted, course visits, uploads and message board posts.

## Discovery Learning Usage

A key element in a successful online learning environment and experience is proper and adequate instructor/facilitator feedback (Swan, 2002). Through the use of the LMS statistics and activity indicators instructors can monitor student progress and interactions. Based upon the amount or type of activity observed various forms of guidance or interventions can occur so as to provide the right amount and type of feedback at the appropriate time. An instructor who wants to provide very limited feedback so as to encourage more "discovery" can continue to monitor so as to see if a problem arises or the student does not sufficiently progress. At that time the instructor can then choose to modify his level of guidance/feedback so as to maximize the experience and educational outcome. The instructor however needs to set the tone and model/show the type of behavior/interaction that is needed for the given course (Vesely, et al., 2007).

## Discovery Learning Example

Again using the example of the Consumer Psychology class, the instructor could use the Course Statistics and Activity tool to identify students that aren't fully participating in message boards/chat rooms or haven't been able to pass preliminary quizzes set up to ensure all students know the fundamentals of the scientific method. These students could then be given access to additional instructional material or added to student groups with more advanced students that could peer assist the struggling students understand. The instructor could also monitor discussions on the message board and offer feedback when someone provides an exceptionally excellent answer or a very incorrect answer. Statistical and activity reports of the Consumer Psychology course could also be used for part of the grade given to students or used for extra credit for those students actively engaging and enhancing the discussions of the class.

The Consumer Psychology professor could also use a combination of the assessment suit tools and the course statistics and recent activity indicators for the purposes of overall course assessment. Pre, during, and post student evaluations can be accomplished via an online questionnaire which would function as a survey. Various types of formative assessment questions could be integrated throughout the course via the message board, chats, online test and quizzes and other assignments. The LMS framework would allow the professor to apply a multiple of assessment techniques such as evaluating what the students know (at multiple times), what they can do, their user-experience throughout the course, participation impacts, allowing for peer reviewing of other students': actions, comments, and/or work (projects, assignments, presentations, etc.), as well as students' direct perception and ideas about the course, its methods of instruction and the level/type of feedback they received. To enhance the validity and reliability of the information, the professor would use multiple assessment sources and techniques of deriving the information. Additionally since versioning of the entire course is possible, the professor could create a more lecture based version of the course and compare that to the Discovery Learning version so as to directly compare pedagogy assessment results and outcomes (see Figure 8).

## CONCLUSION

Through the use of the many different tools available through an LMS like Axio Learning from Kansas State University, Discovery Learning can be maximized. Both students' and instructors' experiences can be improved through the powerful scaffolding support that the integrated online tools provide. Students can gain a richer, realistic understanding through the presentation of materials in multiple formats as well as through the use of different types of interactive tools and challenging assignments/projects. The ability to work in online groups through the tools listed also greatly enhances the realism that students will face once they reach the ever-changing workplace. Instructors also gain through these scaffolding tools in that it allows them more options with how to present information as well as pacing of student progress. The level, type and amount of

*Figure 8. Course statistics interface*

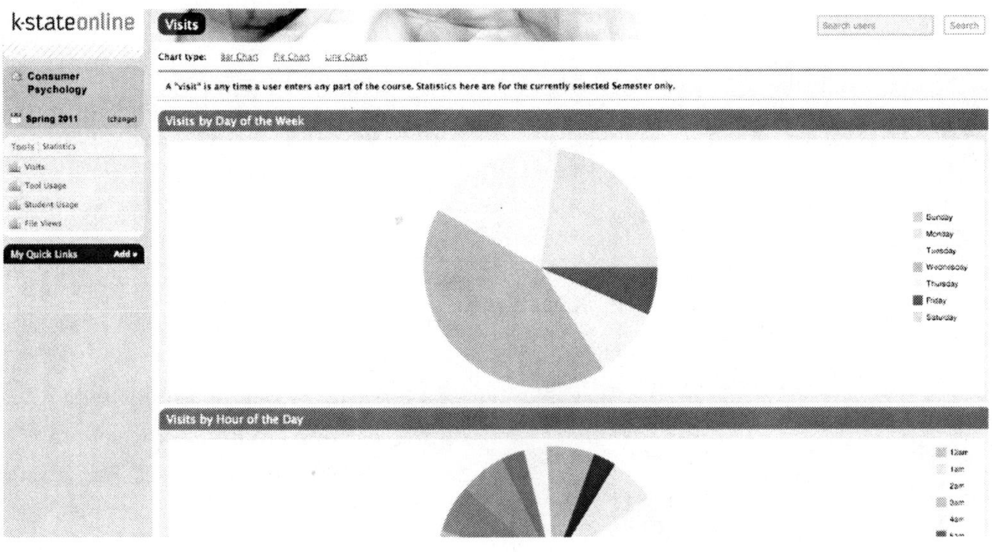

guidance/feedback that the instructor provides are also enhanced via the multiple mechanisms of interaction available. Finally, various assessment tools and enhanced ability to track students progress and view statistics on students performance and participation can be easily viewed and used to assist students as well as evaluate the course design. Using the presented tools available within the LMS, Discovery Learning can be well supported so as to create a long lasting, motivating, educational experience for both the student and the instructor.

## REFERENCES


Finkeldei, S. (2011). *K-State online learning management system: Development, tools and uses*. Kansas State University Axio Learning internal document, January 2011.

Hai-Jew, S. (2008). Scaffolding discovery learning spaces. *MERLOT Journal of Online Learning and Teaching, 4*(4). Retrieved January 3, 2011, from jolt.merlot.org/vol4no4/hai-jew_1208.pdf.

Johnson, C. (2001). A survey of current research on online communities of practice. *Internet and Higher Education, 4*. Retrieved February 26, 2011, from http://citeseerx.ist.psu.edu/viewdoc/download?doi=10.1.1.106.5848&rep=rep1&type=pdf.

Lavine, R. (2005). Guided discovery learning with videotaped case presentation in neurobiology. *Journal of the International Association of Medical Science Educators, 15*(4). Retrieved February 1, 2011, from www.iamse.org/member/article/volume15-1/15-1-4-7.pdf.

Liccardi, I., Ounnas, A., Pau, R., Massey, E., Kinnunen, P., & Lewthwaite, S. … Sarkar, C. (2007). The role of social networks in students learning experiences. *ACM SIGCSE Bulletin, 39*(4). Retrieved February 25, 2011, from http://portal.acm.org/ft_gateway.cfm?id=1345442&type=pdf&CFID=11918280&CFTOKEN=72547543.

Mayer, R. (2004). Should there be a three-strikes rule against pure discovery learning? *American Psychologist, 59*(1), 14–19. Retrieved February 12, 2011, from http://www.katharinenewman.com/Research/Desktop/amp-59-1-14.pdf.

Swan, K. (2002). Building learning communities in online courses: The importance of interaction. *Education, Communication & Information, 2*(1). Retrieved February 28, 2011, from http://coe.nevada.edu/larchambault/CIG%20790/Lit.%20Review/Building%20Online%20Community.pdf.

Vesely, P., Bloom, L., & Sherlock, J. (2007). Key elements of building online community: Comparing faculty and student perceptions. *Journal of Online Learning and Teaching, 3*(3). Retrieved February 28, 2011, from http://jolt.merlot.org/vol3no3/vesely.htm.


## KEY TERMS AND DEFINITIONS

**Autodidaxy:** A pedagogical approach in which the student is actively seeking/discovering on their own with only minimal guidance/facilitation.

**Educational Social Network:** The internet framework used for student instruction and interaction used for Discovery Learning.

**Gating:** The ability to control when a student has access to new content within a learning management system. Accomplished by date/time, requiring a student to first access other content, and/or requiring a student to achieve a certain score on a test/quiz/assignment.

**Interactive Tools:** Online tools that allow for student to student, student to instructor (and vice versa) communications (via text, image, audio, and/or video) through the online learning management system.

**Learning Management System:** An enclosed online learning environment with multiple tools used to create content, instruct, interact and assess.

**WebQuest:** Discovery Learning implementation technique as well as an assignment type that could be used for assessment/evaluation.

# Section 3
# Types of Self-Discovery Learning

# Chapter 8
# The Meeting Point of Second Life® and Web 2.0:
## Self-Discovery for Writing

**Ya-Chun Shih**
*National Dong Hwa University, Taiwan*

## ABSTRACT

*Researchers and practitioners endeavoring to incorporate Second Life® (SL) and Web 2.0 into language classrooms promise greater practical value from computer-assisted language learning (CALL). This chapter provides an innovative approach to blog writing, exploring SL as an immersive experience that stimulates follow-up description, imagination, and writing creativity. Drawing on experiences in 2009 and 2010 in linking SL and Web 2.0 applications to inspire the writing of EFL (English as a Foreign Language) graduate students, this chapter describes the characteristics of descriptive writing and presents the process of learning and writing of these students in cooperation with their peers in order to discover within themselves the motivation to be creative writers.*

## INTRODUCTION

One of the fundamental challenges facing instructors is teaching students how to write naturally and instilling in them the pleasure of writing. This paper proposes a blended learning solution to inspire internal motivation and self-discovery for descriptive writing through the integration of various learning approaches, within a multi-user virtual environment (MUVE) or collaborative virtual environment (CVE), under Web 2.0. This approach emphasizes writing the act of self-discovery, through participation in task-based activities involving blogs, YouTube, Flickr, and 3D MUVEs or CVEs, such as Second Life (SL). The introduction of these technologies enables

DOI: 10.4018/978-1-61350-320-1.ch008

Copyright © 2012, IGI Global. Copying or distributing in print or electronic forms without written permission of IGI Global is prohibited.

students to take the initiative in describing their perceptions to overcome the hurdles associated with natural writing.

This long-term case study collected writing samples from four graduate students, following their discovery of a virtual world, as expressed through the blog entries made describing their experiences. This study employed a variety of data collection strategies to gain insight into the experiences of students with regard to cooperation with peers and self-discovery through virtual learning. The data collection strategies included interviews, observations, and writing samples from student blogs, with their reflections on the discovery of a virtual world. This investigation centered on student writing motivation, attitudes, writing features, and creativity. Observational checklists and rubric analysis of writing samples were used to investigate the progress of students in acquiring writing skills and developing creativity. The current work shares the latest study results using SL and Web 2.0 to practice descriptive writing, addressing the following research questions:

- How will linking Second Life and Web 2.0 develop descriptive writing?
- What are the characteristics of descriptive writing as performed by students?
- What is the linkage effect on the writing attitudes and practices of students?

## Empowering Language Learners with Web 2.0 Technologies and Second Life

Researchers predict that a new generation of language learning will be ushered in on a Web 2.0 platform featuring MUVEs, such as SL. Graham Stanly (2006) indicated that emerging Web 2.0 technology such as Blogs, Wikis, Podcasts, and SL, labeled "Web 3.0" provided a "prototype" for future learning that would serve as an important resource and platform for language learners in the 21st century. Lim (2009) provided a "Six Learnings framework," consisting of "learning by exploring," "learning by collaborating," "learning by being," "learning by building," "learning by championing," and "learning by expressing," for the design of curriculum in a virtual world. Lim (2009, p. 9) claimed that "Learning by expressing," covers sharing and expressing experience gained from virtual world activities through creating and publishing blogs, podcasts and *machinima*. The learning results would be related to the development of students' abilities in the literary criticism and creative writing emphasized by language departments. In-world curriculum, exploration, discussion, interaction, and collaboration followed by "learning by expressing" via Web 2.0 tools could provide students with an effective means to learn a language through methods, such as creative writing.

## Second Life for Language Learning

Second Life (Linden Research, Inc., n.d.) is an avatar-based MUVE or CVE, launched on June 23, 2003 by Linden Lab. Users of SL are referred to as residents who interact with one another through text chat, voice chat, limited avatar body language, instant messaging, and notecards. SL allows residents to explore a vast virtual world, socialize with others, and join events and activities in thematic communities. These communities are categorized according to their emphasis on a variety of special interests, themed attractions, and the trade of virtual property. Simultaneously, SL invokes immersion, (social) interaction, engagement, and (multimodal) communication, which together represent the driving force behind all successful language learning. Hundsberger (2009) indicated, "Foreign language learning is a strong feature within SL due to its interactive and immersive nature. The 3D effect intensifies communication and contributes to social interaction" (p. 5).

Two recent projects, "Talk with Me" and AVALON, funded by the European Commission, are devoted to virtual reality assisted language learning (VRALL) and practices in SL, and a great many researchers and practitioners are already involved in advancing this goal. The aim of "Talk with Me" project (http://www.talk-with-me.eu) is to provide a blended learning experience by connecting SL, Moodle (Modular Object-Oriented Dynamic Learning Environment) and other platforms such as Facebook for the learning of foreign languages, including Czech, Slovak, Hungarian and Slovenian, and "to stimulate a rich multi-directional intercultural dialogue between the participants and the 'outside world'" (Talk with Me Project, n.d., Section: About the Project, ¶2), through activities and social interaction. Participants first view the materials via Moodle, after which they access SL, where they meet others, play, exercise, and travel abroad. The experience concludes with a discussion via Web 2.0 tools.

The AVALON (Access to Virtual and Access Learning Live ONline) project (available at http://avalon-project.ning.com/) is meant to foster "real world language skills" by enabling participants to share their experiences within the language teaching community through announced events or activities in SL and/or sharing their opinions via Web 2.0 tools, such as twitter and blogs. This project encompasses six categories language learning tasks, including "Authentic communication," "Mutual language exchanges," "Exploiting the spatial dimension," "Exploiting SL as a source for learning," "Role playing in SL," and "Exploiting the creative potential of SL" (AVALON Project, n.d., pp. 11-15). For two years prior to December 2010, numerous sessions and virtual workshops related to language learning were held or announced as part of the project.

The Electronic Village Online (EVO) project is hosted by the CALL (Computer-Assisted Language Learning) Interest Section (http://www.call-is.org/info/) of TESOL (Teaching English as Speakers of Other Languages). EVO plans to initiate discussion through online workshops held between mid-January and mid-February, with a focus on issues related to Language Learning & Technology. One of the EVO sessions is VILLAGE (Virtual Language Learning and Group Experience) (http://village.grouply.com/) centered on the issue of "Language Learning and Community Building in SL" and with English teachers brainstorming ideas related to the issue of "language learning in virtual worlds." Using SL, wiki pages, blogs, and forums, participants were advised of weekly events and discussions between January 10, 2011 and February 13, 2011.

Few empirical studies have been conducted on the design or implementation of SL or its effect on language learning. In this section, we review findings from the latest two studies addressing research related to participation and interaction. First, a comparative action research study of two courses on the development of oral proficiency in SL was conducted by Deutschmann, Panichi and Molka-Danielsen in 2009. They investigated the in-world participation of learners through the observation of a conversational floor space occupied by individual participants, including teachers and students, observing and measuring the average duration of turns taken by a particular participant to speak during different sessions in SL and the patterns of turn-taking such as learner-to-learner and instructor-learner. Participants' turn durations and turn-taking patterns were compared, evaluated and interpreted to investigate the impact of various task designs on oral participation. Communicative tools such as e-mail, class blogs, and Skype served as alternatives and/or supportive tools to SL. This study reached two main conclusions related to learner benefits and course design: "Results seem to indicate that meaning focussed task design, which involves authenticity and collaborative elements, has a direct impact on learner participation and engagement," and "our results seem to suggest that technical and social initiations into a complex environment such as SL are important factors that have to be worked into the course design." (Deutschmann, Panichi, & Molka-Danielsen, 2009, Abstract section). This research is currently limited to "task design and one mode of communication, namely oral communication using voice chat" (p. 224), and further efforts will be required to expand the scope of this research. In particular, it is important to identify the means by which multimodal communication occurs in a virtual world incorporating social networking tools, and to determine the impact this environment has on language learning.

Mark Peterson (2010) conducted an exploratory case study into the participation of EFL students and patterns of strategy employed in SL USQ Island, operated by the University of Southern Queensland in Australia. Data was gathered primarily through the analysis of discourse in in-world text chat transcripts, in which interactional and transactional strategy patterns used by seven students were investigated. Peterson (2010) concluded, "Second Life presents a dynamic, motivating and engaging new context for language learners, offering opportunities to participate in beneficial forms of collaborative TL interaction" (p. 291). In addition, the degree of learner-learner interaction and participation; two interactional strategies defined by Peterson as, "politeness" and "keyboard symbols;" and five transactional strategy patterns: "split turns," "time saving devices," "addressivity," "upper case," and "quotation marks" were identified and examined for the frequency with which they occurred in the study.

## WEB 2.0 TECHNOLOGIES AND LANGUAGE LEARNING

Most recent research into computer assisted language learning has focused on the means by which Web 2.0 technologies facilitate language learning and teaching. Current Web 2.0 technologies refer to second generation networks. Tim O'Reilly and ReillyMedia Inc. created the "Web 2.0" (O'Reilly, 2005) term including Web 2.0 applications such as social networking websites, blogs, podcast, wikis, and YouTube. Web 2.0 technologies enhance communication, cooperation among peers, social interaction, and the sharing of information, which are all critical components of language learning. Most recent research into computer assisted language learning has focused on the means by which Web 2.0 technologies facilitate authentic social interaction that takes place between people who participate in online discourse communities such as Twitter and Facebook. Because further research is required in this area, IGI Global in 2009 published the *Handbook of Research on Web 2.0 and Second Language Learning* (Thomas, 2009) to explore second language learning possibilities, such as speech development, communication, and mobile language learning, available through Web 2.0 technologies such as blogging, whiteboards, and podcasts.

Web 2.0 is emerging as an important field of inquiry for its sociocognitive approach to computer-assisted language learning (CALL), suggesting the importance of "meaningful interaction in authentic discourse communities" (Kern & Warschauer, 2000, p. 11), wherein instruction focuses on the use of language "form (including genre, register, and style variation) in contexts of real language use" (p.7). Web 2.0 tools enhance language learning within the sociocognitive framework of CALL, described by Kern and Warschauer. Web 2.0 tools provide authentic, situational context with sociocultural relevance, establishing speech communities in which the acquisition of language skills may be enhanced. Students learn how language is used in its authentic context within specific discourse communities. Discourse-based research uses authentic written and spoken discourse collected via Web 2.0 platforms as a source of data within the context of network-based language teaching and learning.

Many researchers (e.g., Alm, 2006; Campbell, 2003; Godwin-Jones, 2003; Pinkman, 2005; Rosen, & Kato, 2006; Stanley, 2006) are becoming increasingly interested in the role of Web

2.0 in language learning, commonly employing a blended learning approach to increase student participation, interaction and engagement. Alm (2006) used Web 2.0 applications, including MySpace, blogs, wikis, and YouTube, to form a target language community, to enhance intermediate German language learning. A number of studies (Lee, 2010; Franco, 2008; Maranto & Barton, 2010) have reported positive results from the incorporation of Web 2.0 technologies such as social networking tools into various writing exercises.

Blog assisted language learning (BALL) introduces a new trend to the instruction of composition, veering away from the traditional approach in which discrete elements of language are the main focus. Structure and vocabulary no longer have to be taught acontextually. Blog writing, embedded in authentic context and discourse communities, is really an ideal way to inspire students to write more creatively and descriptively. In addition, the BALL approach is not limited to writing, and has been extended to reading and speaking to develop oral communication skills and cultural understanding. Researchers (e.g., Campbell, 2003; Godwin-Jones, 2003, Pinkman, 2005) integrated blogs with English classrooms for academic and practical purposes to facilitate online collaborative language learning. Pinkman (2005) conducted small-scale action research aimed at blog-based EFL teaching in a foreign language classroom at a Japanese university. He regarded blogs as "authentic, interesting, and communicative resources that can serve a variety of purposes in the foreign language classroom. A medium to reflect on material, inquire into issues, and interact with others, blogs provide a rich and easy-to-use environment for both learners and instructors" (p. 21).

Many other applications of Web 2.0 tools such as wikis, twitter, podcast, and video-sharing websites are enjoying immense popularity for their ability to enhance language skills. Rosen and Kato (2006) performed a case study in which wiki was integrated into teaching to develop a learning community, increase cultural understanding, and improve oral proficiency. Twitter, a popular social networking and microblogging tool, is being used for language teaching, although research at this point remains in the embryonic stage. Researchers (e.g., Stanly, 2006; McCarty, 2005; Aguilar, 2007; Kim, 2010) have also developed podcasts for various areas of language learning, particularly listening comprehension (e.g., O'Bryan & Hegelheimer, 2007; Kavaliauskienė, 2008; Sze, 2006), pronunciation (Ducate & Lomicka, 2009; Lord, 2008), and even speaking skills (Sze, 2006).

## Mashup Second Life and Web 2.0 for Language Learning

Currently, language learning and teaching incorporates SL with Web 2.0 tools. Sykes, Oskoz, and Thorne (2008) reviewed research literature and pedagogical reports related to virtual environments, identifying Web 2.0 as having "powerful potential" for second language learning. Recent trends have been observed combining synchronous language learning in virtual worlds with Web 2.0 tools for asynchronous discussion and learning. The "Talk with Me" project and AVALON project, for instance, used both SL and Web 2.0 for (a) synchronous and immersive language learning, multimodal communication, and interaction.

A number of CALL practitioners and researchers (e.g., Vickers, 2007a, 2007b) have investigated this issue empirically, while SimTeach (http://www.simteach.com/) has undertaken the task of informing and supporting educators seeking to integrate MUVEs into their teaching. For instance, SurReal Language Quests (Vickers, 2007a, 2007b) is a pioneer in combining virtual worlds, such as SL and Web 2.0 technologies, blogs, and podcasts of web-based online and real-life teaching approaches for language learning. Vickers (2007b) mentioned in the article *SurReal Quests: Enriched Purposeful Language Learning in Second Life,* with regard to the value of combining social communication and information sharing in distance education and the traditional classroom:

*Second Life tends to add most value to language teaching when it is used in combination with other tools [Web 2.0], be they on- or offline. While the Web offers language learners a wealth of information, Second Life adds a real-time, social and communicative dimension. In doing so, it complements, perhaps even revolutionises, distance teaching for languages. (p. 4)*

The quest entitled "Travel Podcast," (Vickers, 2007a, 2007b) is an example of combined Web 2.0 technologies, including blogs and podcasts. Learners proceed through a process of inquiry as they discover travel destinations via websites, blogs, podcasts, and forums and interview people in SL. Learners engage in different stages of the learning process: planning and research for podcasts, and the final stage of task recording, and uploading a podcast.

However, current empirical findings related to the integration of SL and Web 2.0 for language learning are limited (Shih, 2010). Most studies and projects have highlighted how SL and Web 2.0 are implemented to facilitate language learning, but most of these studies demonstrate an obvious lack of concrete findings. The present study aims to evaluate the influence of a blended environment on the descriptive writing of EFL students.

## Technology-Based Descriptive Writing

Descriptive writing portrays places, people, objects, or things. Readers capture meaning from writing by visualizing what the writer has described. In this manner, they share the writer's experiences through their own imagination and in so doing, shape their own experience. Hollingsworth (1988) referred to descriptive writing as "... giving dimensions, colors, surroundings, origins, placement, and other information to help readers get a mental picture of an object, person, or idea, and how it operates" (as cited in Black, 1993, p. 8). Black (1993) defined descriptive writing as a process of particularizing and clarifying selected notions using precise words and appropriate phrases to describe something vividly, and sharing experiences with the reader (p. 9).

Black (1993) conducted a study using visual and auditory stimuli as prewriting aids for the instruction of descriptive writing in a tenth grade English class. Black used pictures, photos, and slides, with music as stimuli, and then evaluated the progress made by four groups of participants (audio/visual treatment, audio-visual treatment, and the control group) in their descriptive writing essays. The results showed that combining visual and auditory stimuli was effective in improving the descriptive writing of these teenagers.

An ideal language-rich environment is one that encourages students to write and allows peers to collaborate (Corona, Spangenberger, & Venet, 1998, p. 31) Advanced technologies satisfy writing requirements and offer new possibilities for writing activities. Warren, Dondlinger, and Barab (2008), in their literature review, commented that:

*With the visual, audio, and rapid feedback affordances of immersive learning environments, it is possible that they could perform these functions [such as writing instruction] and more, addressing issues such as learner motivation (Dede, Ketelhut, & Ruess, 2006; Tuzun, 2004) and the inclusion of heavily scaffolded activities to supplement the instructor (Barab et al., In Press). (p. 118)*

Innovative technologies have taken writing instruction to a new level, by providing an environment rich in sensory and language input, encouraging collaborative writing and discussion among peers.

An online multi-user virtual environment (MUVE) named Anytown (Warren, Dondlinger, Stein, and Barab, 2009; Warren, Dondlinger, and Barab, 2008) was built within the framework of

Active Worlds, a sub-project of Quest Atlantis (Barab, Thomas, Dodge, Carteaux, and Tuzun, 2005). This environment was developed to assist in the face-to-face instruction of a fourth grader writing class. This case study investigated the differences between traditional writing classrooms (face-to-face) and computer-aided writing classrooms (face-to-face plus 8 hours of descriptive writing practice in Anytown). The learning tasks were designed to prompt descriptive and creative writing in conjunction with critical thinking. The hypothesis related to descriptive writing is as follows:

*The quality of student descriptive writing achievement in the treatment condition should be, at a statistically significant level, greater than the descriptive writing achievement of students who receive instruction in a face-to-face, traditional classroom writing unit that includes the same objectives. (Warren, Dondlinger, & Barab, 2008, p. 121)*

Repeated-measures analysis of variance was used to monitor the difference in outcome between the two groups. The results indicated that the standardized writing achievement scores, including close, proximal, and distal level scores were improved.

In the current study, SL provides a sensory-rich environment for prewriting activities, as well as visual and auditory stimuli to enhance creative thinking in the descriptive writing activities that follow. Students explore ideas in SL discussion groups, whereupon they perform a variety of writing activities using Web 2.0 tools.

## DESIGN AND IMPLEMENTATION

This study approached the development of descriptive writing tasks by blending a variety of learning environments with diverse teaching methodologies. This work focuses on the following: prewriting, discussion, and input within a socio-cultural context; virtual environments, SL; collaborative writing; and self-discovery experiential learning via Web 2.0 applications, including Blogger, YouTube, and Flickr. EFL graduate students performed writing tasks by immersing themselves (as avatars) in sensory- and input-rich environments, such as Winterfest Celebration (see Figure 1 and the following mission description), Lunamaruma, and Titanic through what they experienced in SL and by watching YouTube videos. After SL immersion, participants were asked to post descriptive pieces to a Blogger weblog, featuring spell check, preview, and the addition of links and images. Students were able to present photos or images, such as those taken with the SL Viewer snapshot function, either by adding images to their blog entries or via Flickr. Peers were encouraged to comment on photos, which made this an ideal situation for stimulating discussion and writing. They described the people they met, the places they visited, the voices they heard, the virtual scenes and objects they saw, and the events in which they participated. Topics for creative writing emerged from the experiences gained in SL, in which participants described the details of the sensory data that aroused their imaginations. The following lists (Table 1) seven representative tasks:

### Winterfest (Mission Description)

#### Prewriting Task

- Check out YouTube videos.
- Join a celebration of winter fun at Winterfest Second Life 2009.
- Search for groups to join.
- Explore spectacular scenery in SL.
    - Gathering Place: Dansher in SL
    - Take a snapshot named "Winterfest Fun."
- Share your snapshot via Flickr and Blogger with your instructor and partners.

*Figure 1. Screenshot of a webpage: task description of winterfest celebration*

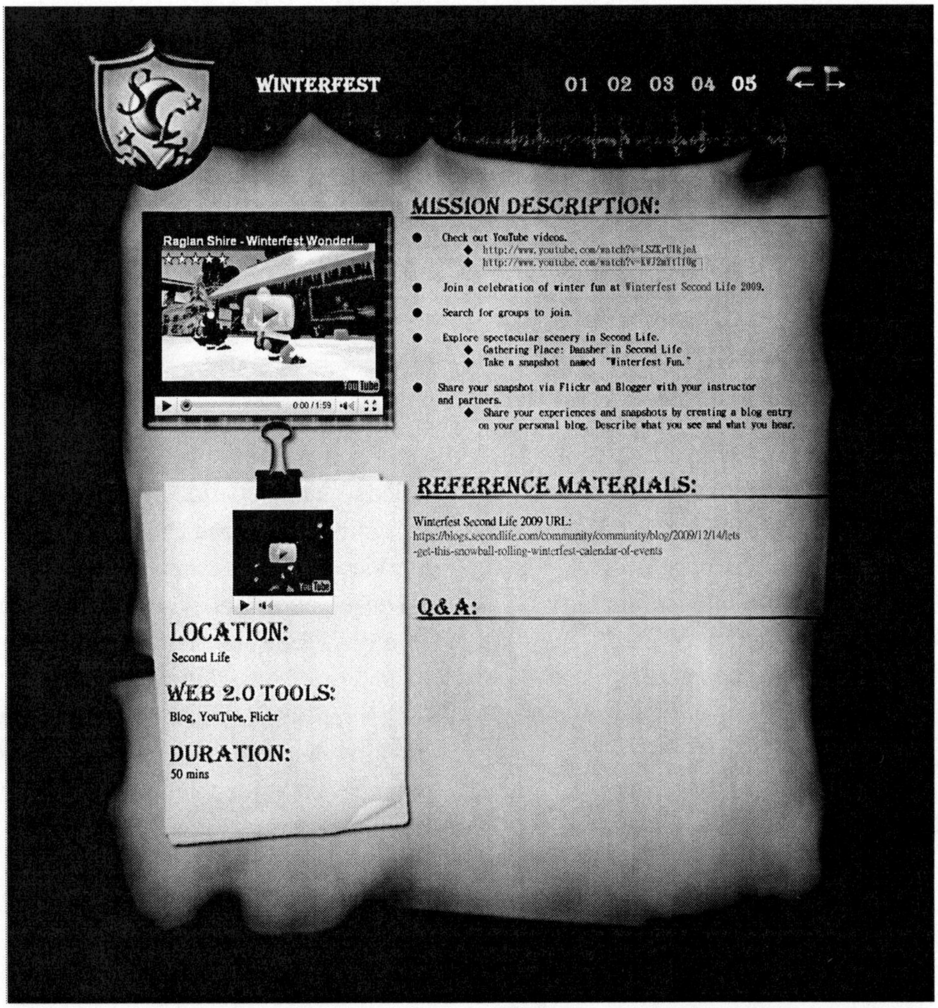


## Writing Task

Share your experiences and snapshots by creating a blog entry on your personal blog. Describe what you see and what you hear (see Figure 2).

*Figure 2. Snapshot taken by the researcher in Dansher in Second Life*

## Lunamaruna (Mission Description)

Mission of the Week – April 26-30, 2010:

1. Explore Lunamaruna in SL. (Prewriting Task) Location: Lennox Hill (42, 171, 3811)

*Table 1. Task list: Selected examples*

| Task Title | Description summary |
|---|---|
| 1. First Experience in SL[1] | Describe your first experience/impressions from SL. |
| 2. The Trip to Banff | Share your experiences of traveling to Banff National Park. |
| 3.Canadian Food | Describe Canadian food and surrounding environment like a cafe. |
| 4. Winterfest[2] | Join a celebration of winter fun at "Second Life Winterfest 2009" and describe what you see and hear. |
| 5. Christmas | Describe what people do when celebrating Christmas in SL. |
| 6. Lunamaruma[3] | Explore Lunamaruna in SL. What impressed you most about your adventure in Lunamaruna? |
| 7. Titanic[4] | Dress up & Walk on the deck of the virtual Titanic. Describe your avatar's appearance and style preferences. |

2. What impressed you most about your adventure in Lunamaruna?
3. Read This Blog! Lunamaruna in EUREKA - The Destination Guide Blog (https://blogs.secondlife.com/community/community/eureka)
4. Try to write a descriptive piece.
5. Edit a blog entry and publish it on your blog.

## DATA COLLECTION AND ANALYSIS

The research project integrated a MUVE in conjunction with Web 2.0 applications to motivate students in their descriptive writing. We implemented a theoretical model by means of small-scale and long-term case studies to identify features of descriptive writing and discover the motivation and attitudes of learners with regard to writing and creativity. This research project has been progressing since September 2009. Four Taiwanese graduate students aged between 23 and 25 majoring in language education were recruited for this study.

Data collection and analysis tools selected for this research consisted of bi-weekly blog entries, observation checklists, interviews, a post study attitudinal survey, and a descriptive writing rubric scale. Participants were provided descriptive writing tasks based on weekly events held in SL. The scale and observation checklists were used to monitor writing progress and record various characteristics of the descriptive writing samples analyzed each week. Students were interviewed after completing the writing tasks, and observations relating to their writing process were recorded. The writing samples of the four graduate students, their reflections of what they discovered in SL, interviews and observations provided data sources and illustrated the learning experiences of the participants. The writing samples revealed writing creativity, engagement and descriptive writing skills.

Descriptive writing portrays people, places, events, and things, and through this process, writers demonstrate their ability to describe various features and the characteristics of particular topics (McHugh, 1997; Tompkins, 2005). Research into the notions of descriptive writing has centered on the use of descriptive strategies and mental pictures created during the process of writing. This work evaluated the ability of students to employ descriptive or sensory writing skills, by selecting sensory details, and using comparisons and examples. A descriptive writing rubric was used to assign writing samples a score ranging between 0 and 10 based on the following criteria drawn from the literature:

1. **Sensory Details:** Using sensory details and descriptions to help readers create a mental image and arouse reader interest

2. **Subject Focused:** Focusing on a specific subject
3. **Feelings:** Expressing the feelings of the writer
4. **Descriptors:** Specific descriptor words (such as precise nouns, vivid verbs, and descriptive adjectives) correctly/functionally, to describe appropriately and creatively
5. **Figurative Language:** Using figurative language (metaphor, simile) to portray people, places, events, objects, and things enabling readers to visualize what the writer describes.

Students were evaluated based on the blog entries they created following their exploration of the virtual world and discussion of their experiences. Currently, a great deal of interest has been focused on investigating how students respond to sensory input, how they use descriptors or other words, their use of metaphors and similes in writing, and the interest they show in completing writing tasks. A native English speaking assisted researchers in the assessment of the student's use of effective descriptors (stronger and weaker), and overall effectiveness of their writing. The written text was analyzed to investigate the research questions: (1) How will linking Second Life and Web 2.0 develop descriptive writing? (2) What are the characteristics of the students' descriptive writing?

A native English speaking assisted researchers in assessing the student's use of descriptors (strong or weak), and the overall effectiveness of the writing, including composition, style, sentence formation, usage, and mechanics. To ensure inter-rater reliability, two raters, who were instructors at the Department of English, were invited to evaluate the rubric prior to rating and verify agreement among the raters. Two raters assessed the descriptive writing of the four writers. Each rater assigned scores for the same descriptions using the categories in Holliway's (2000) terms: descriptive strategy and mental picture.

Scores were assigned for descriptions bi-weekly. The quantitative results varied according to theme and task, and the results showed a high degree of correlation with the qualitative data related to the writing attitudes and practices of the four students in answer the research question: What is the linkage effect on students' writing attitudes and practice?

## RESULTS

The follow-up empirical research contributed to our understanding of the writing processes adopted by EFL learners and the experiences they gained. We employed a triangulated multiple data collection method, including writing samples from blogs, interviews, and a post study attitudinal survey administered to determine the feelings of participants regarding synchronous interaction in SL and (descriptive) writing tasks. In summarizing the results, each descriptive task was addressed as it pertained to the feelings of the participants. The use of sensory details, descriptors, and figurative language varied according to the type of task as well as the individual traits of students. Additionally, the targeted EFL graduate students generally enjoyed the online learning activities and writing process and maintained positive learning and writing attitudes throughout the study.

### Results of the Writing Samples

This research investigated the descriptive writing according to five main points, including sensory details, feelings, subject focused, descriptors, and figurative language, expected in descriptive writing. A five-element, ten-score (0 to 10) descriptive writing rubrics assessed the writing and observed the descriptive language used.

Four students described a series of selected topics by listing characteristics, features, and examples, providing details of their perceptions of the entities they encountered in the virtual world. Students showed gains in their descriptive writing, while their scores varied across tasks. Overall writing proficiency was assessed using a writing rubric (total score ranged from 1to 4) to evaluate "composition," "style," "sentence formation," and "usage."

This research focused on four EFL graduate students (Chun, Wei, Pun, Gei) (pseudonyms) majoring in language education. Chun is a student exhibiting above average oral proficiency. Based on observational data, Chun showed a higher overall writing score than the others with a mean score of 3.8/4. Details of the descriptive writing scores included 7.3 on Sensory Details, 10 on Subject Focused, 9.7 on Feelings, 7.6 on Descriptors, 3.7 on Figurative Language on a scale of 10.0. (See Table 2. for descriptive writing scores.) In a comparison of the five elements of descriptive writing, all of the participants earned higher average scores on Feelings and Subject Focused, and lower average scores on Figurative Language.

Descriptive writing performance varied according to the type of task and the individual traits of the students. The results of scores from seven tasks selected at random showed that descriptors were used in most of the completed writing samples for tasks "Lunamaruna" and "Winterfest." Based on rubric scores following text analysis, the writing samples from the above two tasks showed the best descriptive writing, with a higher mean score (7.9 and 7.4 on a scale of 10.0) than the other tasks (Table 2.)

It was noted that the students also exhibited a high degree of motivation and positive attitudes in exploring SL, completing (pre-) writing tasks and creating blog entries. Although the students' motivation could not be measured, interviews, observations, and a student open-ended survey indicated student enjoyment during the learning and writing process.

## Analysis of Selected Writing Samples

This study selected and qualitatively analyzed writing samples featuring rich sensory details, visual images, and descriptors to explore the characteristics of descriptive writing and reveal new possibilities in this setting. The first sample (Blog Entry, Student-Chun, April 25, 2010) was written in response to "Lunamaruna" with an average description score of 8.8 (on a scale of 10.0). Below is Chun's description:

Chun's description for "Lunamaruna" (From Student's Blog):

*When I visited Lunamaruna, I was attracted by this cartoonish, fantasy, and mystery world. All of the buildings and materials were painted by pastel and watercolor. There were some colorful seaweed around the riverbank. A dolphin liked [-like] fountain was in the middle of the town square. The buildings were around the square and they all looked abnormal and leaned to one side. The ratio of the houses was strange and gave all the adventurers a special vision. But the sky was dark and had some mist and made me feel a little bit scared.*

*On the other side of the square, I saw three "flying" rays. The view was really special that I stopped for a while to enjoy this vision. I took some snapshots and tried to catch the best angle for the rays. When I arrived at the town square, I saw a pink dolphin sitting on a rocking chair with a white sailor hat and a pipe in his mouth. It reminds me of the cartoon character-Popeye:)*

*There was a sign introducing the puffer fish. I saw four brightly colored and vivid puffer fish swam freely there. I decided to walk closer and take a look at them. Again, the puffer fish scared me because they puffed themselves up suddenly. However, they all look nice and friendly. You can even ride on them.*

*Table 2. List of four students' descriptive writing scores of selected tasks*

| Name | # Task | 1 1st | 2 Banff | 3 Food | 4 WF | 5 Christ | 6 Lu | 7 Titanic | Total Score | Mean Score |
|---|---|---|---|---|---|---|---|---|---|---|
| Chun | **Sensory Details** | 2 | 9 | 7 | 9 | 8 | 9 | 7 | 51 | 7.3 |
| | **Subject Focused** | 10 | 10 | 10 | 10 | 10 | 10 | 10 | 70 | 10 |
| | **Feelings** | 8 | 10 | 10 | 10 | 10 | 10 | 10 | 68 | 9.7 |
| | **Descriptors** | 4 | 8 | 6 | 9 | 8 | 9 | 9 | 53 | 7.6 |
| | **Figurative** | 2 | 2 | 2 | 6 | 4 | 6 | 4 | 26 | 3.7 |
| | **Total Score** | 26 | 39 | 35 | 44 | 40 | 44 | 40 | | |
| | **Mean Score** | 5.2 | 7.8 | 7 | 8.8 | 8 | 8.8 | 8 | | |
| Wei | **Sensory Details** | 4 | 2 | 3 | 6 | 2 | 5 | 2 | 24 | 3.4 |
| | **Subject Focused** | 8 | 2 | 5 | 8 | 2 | 6 | 6 | 37 | 5.3 |
| | **Feelings** | 8 | 8 | 8 | 8 | 8 | 8 | 8 | 56 | 8 |
| | **Descriptors** | 4 | 5 | 6 | 7 | 3 | 5 | 6 | 36 | 5.1 |
| | **Figurative** | 2 | 0 | 0 | 5 | 2 | 4 | 2 | 15 | 2.1 |
| | **Total Score** | 26 | 17 | 22 | 34 | 17 | 28 | 24 | | |
| | **Mean Score** | 5.2 | 3.4 | 4.4 | 6.8 | 3.4 | 5.6 | 4.8 | | |
| Pun | **Sensory Details** | 2 | 4 | 5 | 7 | 7 | 6 | 6 | 37 | 5.3 |
| | **Subject Focused** | 2 | 8 | 8 | 8 | 8 | 8 | 8 | 50 | 7.1 |
| | **Feelings** | 8 | 8 | 4 | 8 | 4 | 7 | 4 | 53 | 7.6 |
| | **Descriptors** | 2 | 6 | 6 | 8 | 7 | 8 | 6 | 43 | 6.1 |
| | **Figurative** | 2 | 0 | 0 | 6 | 2 | 4 | 6 | 20 | 2.9 |
| | **Total Score** | 16 | 26 | 23 | 37 | 28 | 33 | 30 | | |
| | **Mean Score** | 3.2 | 5.2 | 4.6 | 7.4 | 5.6 | 6.6 | 6 | | |
| Gei | **Sensory Details** | 0 | 3 | 6 | 9 | 0 | 8 | 4 | 30 | 4.3 |
| | **Subject Focused** | 4 | 10 | 10 | 10 | 6 | 10 | 8 | 58 | 8 |
| | **Feelings** | 8 | 8 | 5 | 10 | 5 | 10 | 8 | 54 | 7.7 |
| | **Descriptors** | 5 | 5 | 2 | 8 | 2 | 7 | 4 | 33 | 4.7 |
| | **Figurative** | 1 | 2 | 1 | 5 | 2 | 8 | 2 | 21 | 3 |
| | **Total Score** | 18 | 28 | 24 | 42 | 15 | 43 | 26 | | |
| | **Mean Score** | 3.6 | 5.6 | 4.8 | 8.4 | 3 | 8.6 | 5.2 | | |
| Total | | 86 | 110 | 104 | 157 | 100 | 148 | 120 | | |
| Mean | | 4.3 | 5.5 | 5.2 | 7.9 | 5 | 7.4 | 6 | | |

*Note.* 1st stands for First Experience in SL; Banff stands for The Trip to Banff; Food stands for Canadian Food; WF stands for Winterfest; Christ stands for Christmas; Lu stands for "Lunamaruma"

*In this mission, I did learn a lot from Jason (instructor) and the other participants. Jason taught us some words to describe what we saw in the world and helped us to discuss some topics. I liked this world and it provided us a good chance to explore the new things. (Blog Entry, Student-Chun, April 25, 2010)*

Chun's description illustrates her attention to sensory details describing the characteristics of "Lunamaruna" such as "colorful seaweed," "cartoonish," "looked abnormal," and "sky was dark," to create a strong mental images for readers. Chun employed analogy and a figurative language device (simile), when she described a fountain, by comparing it directly to "a dolphin like fountain." She also wrote a character sketch using figurative language devices of personification and metaphor, "I saw a pink dolphin sitting on a rocking chair with a white sailor hat and a pipe in his mouth. This reminds me of the cartoon character-Popeye." Chun addressed the features of places, people, and objects which caught her attention on her virtual journey. She included color descriptors such as, "painted by pastel and watercolor," "pink," and "white." She also created spatial imagery by describing spatial relationships and layouts, such as "around the riverbank," and "in the middle of the town square," to produce a picture of the scene in the minds of readers. We noted the descriptors mentioned, used, and/or explained by instructor Jason or peers during the teacher-led prewriting activities, and discussions in SL and instructor's blog entries, influenced the quality of Chun's descriptions.

The collaborative learning and prewriting activities were highly valued, and the instructor's description of "Lunamaruna" exemplified supportive prewriting activity and blogs. The following quotations from the instructor's blog and a student's blog also illustrate the descriptive writing used to share the experiences of cultural immersion gained from SL Winterfest. The written descriptions of both the instructor and student describe a particularly special scene of a Christmas celebration from SL including "brightly-colored pairs of oversized Christmas ornaments."

## Winterfest (From Instructor's Blog)

*The world looked beautiful in the dark of night. The boughs of the evergreen trees were shrouded with snow, and silvery fairy trees sparkled with frost. Occasionally big snowflakes fell from the sky. The ice rink was bordered by a low stone wall. Brightly-colored pairs of oversized Christmas ornaments were placed at intervals along the top of this wall. A wooden bridge spanned the river that flowed nearby, and the dark hills stood off in the distance. I began to explore.*

The second sample (Blog Entry, Student-Gei, December 27, 2009) was written in response to "Winterfest" with an average score of 8.4 (on a scale of 10.0). Gei used a figurative language device (simile) by comparing Santa Claus to "a hot-air balloon" and hedging the description with "looked like." Gei attempted to create spatial imagery with "around a fixed point," incorporating Christmas celebration features such as "Santa Claus," "reindeers," "sleigh," and "presents." Gei's description demonstrated increased attention to virtual objects such as "a house made of gingerbread cookies, jelly, and candy," to draw the reader into the dream-like world associated with his child's dream (see Figure 3).

## Winterfest (From Student's Blog)

*When flying in the Prancer, I was attracted by a huge Santa Claus which looked like a hot-air balloon. It was revolving around a fixed point; almost everywhere in the Prancer can see his face. However, without seeing Santa Claus with his reindeers and sleigh is quiet strange so I started to find them.*

*After finding out Santa Claus with his reindeers and sleigh, I couldn't help sitting on his reindeer, shown on the picture. When I was a child, I wished to ride on the reindeer and sent presents with them. In reality, it's impossible, but I can make my dream come true here.*

*When walking around, I found a snowman and a house which made of gingerbread cookies, jelly and candy. (Blog Entry, Student-Gei, December 27, 2009) (see Figures 4 and 5)*

*Figure 3. Snapshot taken by an instructor in Dansher in SL*

*Figure 4. Snapshot taken by Gei in Prancer in SL*

*Figure 5. Snapshot taken by Gei in Prancer in SL*

## IMPLICATION AND DISCUSSION

These results have strong positive implications for integrating Web 2.0 tools with MUVEs for the development of motivation, attitude, and overall performance in creative writing. The empirical research centered on the processes involved in descriptive writing within a blended learning environment. The study was performed under the assumption that one may develop the characteristic features of descriptive writing while enhancing motivation and attitudes within a technologically sophisticated setting.

Students worked collaboratively in a team setting exploring, discussing, and role-playing in SL. In addition, they received and shared information via Web 2.0 tools during the prewriting phrase, and follow-up writing exercises served as a powerful tool to launch students on a journey of self-discovery. Through the implementation of instructor-guided writing groups of peers, students were encouraged to write blog entries independently, to share their feelings, ideas, and vision. At the same time, having to describe the sensory details obtained through observation of themselves and others, enables students to uncover and possibilities involved in the writing process and overcome difficulties. Resources gained through the discovery of a virtual environment inspire students to develop their writing skills as a means to share them with others.

A rubric was used to evaluate descriptive writing according to five characteristics using a ten point scale. The highest average score attained were for the tasks, "Winterfest" (8.8/10) and "Lunamaruna" (8.8/10), which provided prewriting aids rich in visual stimuli. The scores varied according to task, and the individual traits of participants; however, the scores revealed no significant differences over time, due to the limited time available. From analysis of the descriptive writing samples, it is clear that students learned to integrate imagery with figurative language including similes and metaphors, and employed descriptive writing strategies to draw in readers and share their impressions.

The findings also revealed that students earned higher average scores on Feelings and Subject Focused, and lower average scores on Figurative Language. Students faced far fewer difficulties in focusing on subjects and sharing their feelings and performed well in constructing spatial imagery; however, they showed relatively limited ability to use figurative language devices.

Learners demonstrated a high degree of motivation and unflagging enthusiasm for the process of learning languages through SL, in conjunction with Web 2.0 tools, and in particular through blogs.

*If there are some interesting things happened, I would like to write them done. Take SL missions for example, I like to write what I have heard and learned in blog. I also like to share my experiences with others…I think it is important for me to express my real thought by using various descriptions and words. I will try to use different words to express my feelings and experiences in my writing. (Open-Ended Survey, Student-Chun, August 27, 2010)*

During the process of composition, students developed their descriptive writing skills through self-discovery, sharing, and observing examples of writing from the blogs entries of their native English instructor and peers. Gei indicated, "Moreover, in order to improve my writing, I sometimes read others' article as a writing sample. By reading other's writings can improve not only my writing skill, but also my reading skill" (Open-Ended Survey, Student-Chun, August 27, 2010). By reviewing the writing of their instructor and peers, the students began improving their writing performance, sharing ideas, and becoming more independent, even as they simultaneously learned from their peers. The technologies created an atmosphere of self-discovery, cooperation among peers, and positive group dynamics, which helped to strengthen writing performance. These results make a strong case for the assertion that integrating MUVEs with Web 2.0 tools can be highly beneficial for EFL language learners.

## CONCLUSION AND FUTURE WORK

Based on current findings, this project designed and implemented an innovative and effective means to bolster the descriptive writing skills, motivation, and overall attitudes of EFL students. Nonetheless, whether or not we succeeded in increasing the quantity or transforming the quality of their descriptive writing remains to be seen. This will have to serve as a topic for further study.

Community writing groups are theoretically a form of collaborative learning, and one may engage in such a community through descriptive writing processes via Web 2.0 tools and/or through cultural learning within a MUVE. The possibility of combining such technologies was reinforced by the results of this study. In a future study, we will explore the possibility of integrating a new MUVE, developed by the research team in conjunction with Web 2.0 applications into a cultural learning environment.

## ACKNOWLEDGMENT

The research has been heavily supported by a grant from the Taiwan National Science Council. Correspondence concerning this article should be addressed to Ya-Chun Shih, Department of English, National Dong Hwa University, Taiwan. E-mail: yachunshih@mail.ndhu.edu.tw

## REFERENCES

Aguilar, F. R. (2007). Top of the pods: In search of a podcasting "pedagogy" for language learning. *Computer Assisted Language Learning*, *20*(5), 471–492. doi:10.1080/09588220701746047

Alm, A. (2006). CALL for autonomy, competence and relatedness: Motivating language learning environments in Web 2.0. *The JALT CALL Journal*, *2*(3), 29–38.

AVALON Project. (n.d.). *Communication and language learning models (Project Deliverable no.1)*. Retrieved October 1, 2010, from https://files.pbworks.com/download/HEPOBuMvfb/avalonlearning/33903754/WP2_Deliverable_1_Language_Learning_Models%20.pdf.

Barab, S. A., Thomas, M., Dodge, T., Carteaux, R., & Tuzun, H. (2005). Making learning fun: Quest Atlantis, a game without guns. *Educational Technology Research and Development*, *53*(1), 86–107. doi:10.1007/BF02504859

Black, J. (1993). *The effects of auditory and visual stimuli on tenth graders' descriptive writing*. (ERIC Document Reproduction Service No. ED364887). Retrieved October 1, 2010, from http://www.eric.ed.gov/PDFS/ED364887.pdf.

Campbell, A. (2003) Weblogs for use with ESL classes. *The Internet TESL Journal*, *9*(2). Retrieved October 1, 2010, from http://iteslj.org/Techniques/Campbell-Weblogs.html.

Corona, C., Spangenberger, S., & Venet, I. (1998). *Improving student writing through a language rich environment*. (ERIC Document Reproduction Service No. ED420860).

Decrem, B. (2006). *Introducing Flock Beta 1*. Flock official blog. Retrieved October 1, 2010, from http://www.flock.com/node/4500.

Dede, C., Ketelhut, D., & Ruess, K. (2006). *Designing for motivation and usability in a museum-based multi-user virtual environment*. Retrieved October 1, 2010, from http://www.gse.harvard.edu/~dedech/muvees/documents/AELppr.pdf.

Deutschmann, M., Panichi, L., & Molka-Danielsen, J. (2009). Designing oral participation in Second Life: A comparative study of two language proficiency courses. *ReCALL*, *21*(2), 206–226. doi:10.1017/S0958344009000196

Ducate, L., & Lomicka, L. (2009). Podcasting: An effective tool for honing language students' pronunciation? *Language Learning & Technology*, *13*(3), 66–86.

EVO project. (n.d.). *Home page*. Retrieved October 1, 2010, from http://evosessions.pbworks.com/w/page/10708567/FrontPage.

Franco, C. (2008). Using Wiki-based peer-correction to develop writing skills of Brazilian EFL learners. *Novitas-ROYAL*, *2*(1), 49–59.

Godwin-Jones, R. (2003). Blogs and Wikis: Environments for on-line collaboration. *Language Learning and Technology*, *7*(2), 12-16. Retrieved October 1, 2010, from http://llt.msu.edu/vol-7num2/emerging/default.html.

Hollingsworth, H., & Eastman, S. (1988). *Teaching writing in every class: A guide for grades 6-12*. Boston, MA: Allyn & Bacon.

Holliway, D. R. (2000). *It looks like a goose: Composing for the informational needs of readers*. (ERIC Document Reproduction Service No. ED439437). Retrieved October 1, 2010, from http://www.eric.ed.gov/PDFS/ED439437.pdf.

Hundsberger, S. (2009). *Foreign language learning in Second Life and the implications for resource provision in academic libraries*. Arcadia Fellowship Programme, Cambridge University Library. Retrieved October 1, 2010, from http://arcadiaproject.lib.cam.ac.uk/docs/second_life.pdf.

Kavaliauskienė, G. (2008). Podcasting: A tool for improving listening skills. *Journal of Teaching English with Technology*, *8*(4). Retrieved November 30, 2010, from http://www.tewtjournal.org/VOL%208/ISSUE%204/A%20WORD%20FROM%20A%20TECHIE.pdf.

Kern, R., & Warschauer, M. (2000). Introduction: Theory and practice of network-based language teaching . In Warschauer, M., & Kern, R. (Eds.), *Network-based language teaching: Concepts and practice* (pp. 1–19). Cambridge, UK: Cambridge University Press.

Kim, D. (2010). Incorporating podcasting and blogging into a core task for ESOL teacher candidates. *Computers & Education*, *56*(3), 632–641. doi:10.1016/j.compedu.2010.10.005

Lee, L. (2010). Exploring Wiki-mediated collaborative writing: A case study in an elementary Spanish course. *CALICO Journal, 27*(2).

Lim, K. Y. T. (2009). The six learnings of Second Life: A framework for designing curricular interventions in-world. *Journal of Virtual Worlds Research, 2*(1), 3–11.

Linden Research Inc. (n.d.). *Second Life*. Retrieved October 1, 2010, from http://secondlife.com/.

Lord, G. (2008). Podcasting communities and second language pronunciation. *Foreign Language Annals, 41*(2), 364–380. doi:10.1111/j.1944-9720.2008.tb03297.x

Maranto, G., & Barton, M. (2010). Paradox and promise: MySpace, Facebook, and the sociopolitics of social networking in the writing classroom. *Computers and Composition, 27*, 36–47. doi:10.1016/j.compcom.2009.11.003

McCarty, S. (2005). Spoken Internet to go: Popularization through podcasting. *JALT CALL Journal, 1*(2), 67–74.

McHugh, N. (1997). Teaching the domains of writing . In Olson, C. B. (Ed.), *Practical ideas for teaching writing as a process at the high school and college levels* (pp. 112–118). Sacramento, CA: California Department of Education.

McLellan, H. (1996). Virtual realities . In Jonassen, D. (Ed.), *Handbook of research for educational communications and technology*. New York, NY: Macmillan.

O'Bryan, A., & Hegelheimer, V. (2007). Integrating CALL into the classroom: The role of podcasting in an ESL listening strategies course. *ReCALL, 19*(2), 162–180. doi:10.1017/S0958344007000523

O'Reilly, T. (2005). *What is Web 2.0*? O'Reilly Network. Retrieved October 1, 2010, from http://www.oreillynet.com/pub/a/oreilly/tim/news/2005/09/30/what-is-web-20.html.

Peterson, M. (2010). Learner participation patterns and strategy use in Second Life: An exploratory case study. *ReCALL, 22*(3), 273–292. doi:10.1017/S0958344010000169

Pinkman, K. (2005). Using blogs in the foreign language classroom: Encouraging learner independence. *The JALT CALL Journal, 1*(1), 12-24. Retrieved October 1, 2010, from http://jaltcall.org/journal/articles/1_1_Pinkman.pdf.

Rosen, L., & Kato, K. (2006). *Building community, improving oral proficiency: A Wiki case study*. Poster session, ACTFL 2006. Retrieved Retrieved October 1, 2010, from http://www.actfl.org/files/ACTFL06handouts/Session371.pdf.

Shih, Y. C. (2010). Immersive language learning in collaborative virtual environments: The current status and possible trends . In Hai-Jew, S. (Ed.), *Virtual immersive and 3D learning spaces: Emerging technologies and trends*. Hershey, PA: IGI Global. doi:10.4018/978-1-61692-825-4.ch005

Stanley, G. (2006). Podcasting: Audio on the Internet comes of age. *Teaching English as a Second or Foreign Language, 9*(4). Retrieved October 1, 2010, from http://www-writing.berkeley.edu/TESL-EJ/ej36/int.html.

Sykes, J., Oskoz, A., & Thorne, S. L. (2008). Web 2.0, synthetic immersive environments, and mobile resources for language education. *CALICO Journal*. Retrieved October 1, 2010, from http://language.la.psu.edu/~thorne/SykesOskozThorne_CALICO_08.pdf.

Sze, P. (2006). Developing students' listening and speaking skills through ELT podcasts. *Education Journal, 34*(2), 115–134.

Talk with Me Project. (n.d.). *About the project*. Retrieved October 1, 2010, from http://www.talk-with-me.eu/cms/index.php?id=203.

Thomas, M. (Ed.). (2009). *Handbook of research on Web 2.0 and second language learning*. Hershey, PA: IGI Global Publishing. doi:10.4018/978-1-60566-190-2

Tompkins, G. E. (2005). *Language arts: Patterns of practice* (6th ed.). Upper Saddle River, NJ: Pearson.

Tuzun, H. (2004). *Motivating learners in educational computer games*. Unpublished dissertation, Indiana University, Bloomington, IN.

Vickers, H. (2007a). *SurReal language quests*. AvatarLanguages.com/Blog. Retrieved October 1, 2010, from http://avatarlanguages.com/blog/?p=14.

Vickers, H. (2007b). SurReal quests: Enriched, purposeful language learning in Second Life. *The Knowledge Tree*. Retrieved October 1, 2010, from http://kt.flexiblelearning.net.au/tkt2007/edition-15/surreal-quests-enriched-purposeful-language-learning-in-second-life.

Warren, S. (2006). Researching a MUVE for teaching writing: The Anytown experience. In C. Crawford et al. (Eds.), *Proceedings of Society for Information Technology and Teacher Education International Conference 2006* (pp. 759-764). Chesapeake, VA: AACE.

Warren, S., Dondlinger, M. J., Stein, R., & Barab, S. (2009). Educational game as supplemental learning tool: Benefits, challenges, and tensions arising from use in an elementary school classroom. *Journal of Interactive Learning Research, 20*(4), 487-505. Chesapeake, VA: AACE. Retrieved October 1, 2010, from http://www.editlib.org/p/28349.

Warren, S., Stein, R. A., Dondlinger, M. J., & Barab, S. A. (2008). A look inside a MUVE design process: Blending instructional design and game principles to target writing skills. *Journal of Educational Computing Research, 40*(3). Baywood Publishing Company.

Warren, S. J., Dondlinger, M. J., & Barab, S. A. (2008). A MUVE towards PBL writing: Effects of a digital learning environment designed to improve elementary student writing. [JRTE]. *Journal of Research on Technology in Education, 41*(1), 113–140.

## KEY TERMS AND DEFINITIONS

**Blog Assisted Language Learning (BALL):** Blog is an abbreviated form of Weblog ("web" for internet; and "log" for journal), and is a new application that is a current trend in language learning. Blogs facilitate collaborative language learning over the Internet and can inspire language teachers, especially writing teachers. A blog is a public web site set up by individual users to be edited, and updated with entries allowing for expression in the forms of text, graphics, audio, and video.

**Collaborative Virtual Environment (CVE):** CVE is the acronym for Collaborative Virtual Environment. CVEs, usually built in Virtual Reality Modeling Language (VRML), are created to support multi-user collaboration and interaction regardless of the distance, and have currently been used in educational settings. Participants are embodied in avatars and use chat boxes and/or voice chat to communicate with others in CVEs.

**Computer Assisted Language Learning (CALL):** CALL is the acronym for Computer Assisted Language Learning and is defined as (the study of) the use of computers in language learning and teaching. Computer technology in the language learning domain is a promising field in Information and Learning Technology, as well as in Language Instruction.

**Descriptive Writing:** Descriptive writing refers to portraying people, places, or objects vividly. Readers construct the meaning from the content the writer has described, and share in the writer's experiences.

**EFL:** EFL stands for English as a Foreign Language. English is taught to people who learn the language for different reasons in non-English-speaking countries.

**Language Learning:** Language learning involves the development of the four major language skills (reading, listening, writing, and speaking), with particular focus on those skills that are frequently used in daily life and/or academically.

**Multi-User Virtual Environments (MUVEs):** Multi-User Virtual Environments (MUVEs), also known as virtual worlds such as Second Life, refer to online three-dimensional environments created to facilitate multi-user synchronous interaction and immersion through incorporating networks, computer graphics, and sound. Users are embodied as avatars in the shared virtual environments and interact with one another through real-time text and/or voice chat.

**Second Life (SL):** Second Life © is a registered trademark of Linden Research, Inc. Second Life (SL) is a computer-generated three-dimensional multi-user virtual environment (MUVE). Users are called residents and are embodied as avatars who interact with one another through text chat, voice chat, avatar gestures, instant messaging, and notecards in SL. Second Life allows residents to discover a vast virtual world, socialize with others, trade virtual properties, and join events and activities held by various communities.

**Virtual Reality Assisted Language Learning (VRALL):** A computer- generated three-dimensional environment, such as Second Life, is used to assist language learning. VRALL is the new frontier in CALL. VRALL is the acronym for Virtual Reality Assisted Language Learning.

**Web 2.0:** The term "Web 2.0" originates from "a brainstorming session between O'Reilly and MediaLive International" (O'Reilly, 2005). Web 2.0, including web applications, such as blogs, wikis, video-sharing Web sites, is used to foster collaboration, interaction, communication and information sharing on the World Wide Web.

## ENDNOTES

1. Second Life © is a registered trademark of Linden Research, Inc. The mentioned trademarks, projects and virtual worlds in SL are respected properties of their owners.
2. Winterfest SL is scheduled for December every year. Events include ice skating, live music, a ski jump tournament, etc. They take place in various sites of SL.
3. Lunamaruna, located in Lennox Hill, SL, was designed and built by Scottius Polke.
4. The RMS Titanic is a project and virtual space in SL and the official website can be reached via http://www.titanicsecondlife.nl/pages/51034/RMS_Titanic.html.

# Chapter 9
# Applied Informal Problem-Solving through Self-Discovery Online:
## An Approach

**Shalin Hai-Jew**
*Kansas State University, USA*

## ABSTRACT

*People often refer to the World Wide Web (WWW) and the Internet to conduct ad hoc and informal problem-solving. Their success in their endeavors has depended on a wide range of information access and crowd-sourcing; deeper analysis of problems; and growing self-efficacy through acclimating into certain problem-solving groups (with attendant new identities) and the "takeaway" learning by abstracting the problem-solving process. This chapter suggests that a greater awareness of site and online resource designers about the steps of problem-solving may enhance the building of self-discovery learning affordances for every phase of the informal problem-solving process.*

## INTRODUCTION

*"Inquiry and technology-enhanced learning are a good marriage." – W.R. van Joolingen and Z.C. Zacharia (2009) in Chapter 2: "Developments in Inquiry Learning" in Technology-Enhanced Learning*

People around the world regularly access the World Wide Web (WWW) and Internet for support on a range of challenges. Some of their issues are simple ones—a quick check on a fact or a simple process. The users are asking close-ended questions with clear-cut answers. They want to know how to prepare a particular dish; use a particular tool; achieve a particular task; or solve a basic problem. These are common challenges in the so-called fast-growing DIY (do-it-yourself)-sphere.

Many bring more complex and high-magnitude problems to the Web. These involve more complex strategies and tools and information; these may take much longer time horizons to solve and many more resources and interventions to address. These challenges may involve potentially highly serious or dire effects. Some challenges may not be solvable. Some questions asked may not be

DOI: 10.4018/978-1-61350-320-1.ch009

Copyright © 2012, IGI Global. Copying or distributing in print or electronic forms without written permission of IGI Global is prohibited.

answerable. These users want to know how to handle more sizeable challenges—such as in handling financial, health, legal, or personal issues, for example. And still others pursue complex problems that require coordination among a wide number of individuals—such as issues in addressing environmental challenges, public health, economic disparities, and broad-based social justice issues. If the scope of problems may be conceptualized as a continuum from those requiring simple and fleeting solutions to complex ones (requiring deep and nonconventional exploration and long-term or even continuous attention), some ultimate mediated achievements may involve interdependent problem-solving of large-scale non-obvious problems through crowd-sourcing and collaborative virtual work. Those kinds of collaborations may ultimately contribute to the larger polities and environment. For many, the actual solution to the problem may be partially or fully achieved online. At every moment, there are many millions who are turning to the WWW and Internet for informal problem-solving.

Said another way, if A. Maslow's hierarchy of needs may be applied, people go online to deal with foundational physiological needs, safety; love and belonging, self-esteem, and self-actualization (in ascending order from lower-order to higher-order needs). Physiological needs may include the need for food, water, and sleep. In terms of safety, people need employment, access to resources, connections with family and friends, access to health, and access to property. In terms of love and belonging, people need social relationships and important primary intimate relationships. In terms of esteem, people need a sense of achievement and a respect for and from others. At the pinnacle of this pyramid is self-actualization, which consists of "morality, creativity, spontaneity, problem solving, lack of prejudice, acceptance of facts" ("Maslow's hierarchy of needs," Oct. 16, 2010). The WWW and Internet have become such an integrated part of people's lives that they often turn to these resources for needs at every level of Maslow's hierarchy of needs pyramid.

Even from the earliest days of the WWW, Tim Berners-Lee [creator of the hypertext transfer protocol or "http" with Robert Cailliau, a student at the European Organization for Nuclear Research (CERN)] envisioned a Web through which people of the world could come together to solve shared problems. In the ensuing decades since the Web's origins in 1989 - 1990, plenty of functionalities have enhanced the Web as a problem-solving tool.

The self-discovery element of the Web has not been as fully developed as possible for informal (and complex) problem-solving needs. Enormous amounts of physical information have been preserved in digital form and made available, and there are supportive communities and networks of learning. However, these elements are often cobbled together only by individual users.

There is a benefit for framing some parts of the Web and Internet as problem-solving spaces for a range of concerns—in order to enhance user self-discovery learning in the following ways:

1. Framing particular challenges as problem(s)-solution(s);
2. Offering a range of user tools to address defined problem-solving steps, and
3. Acclimating users into different communities to enhance their problem-solving knowledge and skills

Informal problem-solvers may benefit from more methodical and reasoned approaches in understanding their unique situations instead of proceeding in an instinctual, emotion, or ad hoc fashion. This "use case" of informal problem solving suggests particular benefits in terms of online designs.

A review of the literature on problem-based learning online will set the context for this chapter.

Then, a methodical model for problem-solving will be presented. The affordances and constraints of the current Web will be analyzed in the context of problem(s)-solution(s). Further exploration of problem-based learning designs online will contribute to enhanced usability and practical applications.

## A REVIEW OF THE LITERATURE

Colloquially, informal problem solving refers to the kind of troubleshooting and problem-solving required as a regular part of daily life. It is understood that such issues arise "in the wild" and not in a formal university or professional training environment. Problems arise that are related to work, family, social lives, academic studies, or leisure, and the troubleshooting and learning that follow are often personal and idiosyncratic.

Informal learning is often "haphazard and unconscious" learning (Kase, Carroll, Zhang, & Rosson, 2008, p. 3438). Such learning is not pre-packaged in a set curricular or social structure; it does not involve the earning of formal credit or official recorded acknowledgment. This instinct towards problem-solving and new learning is native to the human person, which is constantly engaging with the environment and with others—as a natural part of existence. Such learning tends to be quick, with many steps to traditional problem-solving models missed or assumed, without sufficient reflection.

Socially and academically, informal learning is sometimes situated as a reaction against the compartmentalized curricular and social structures of formal education systems. In informal settings, the learning is considered "fun" and much more freeform in which learners "collect and reflect" on various information and interactions between various diverse members of the public (Strohecker & Butler, 2004, p. 151). Theirs is a diverse solutions environment with an appropriation of ideas and strategies.

Informal learning not only affects individuals but also organizational learning among members who collectively generate and share knowledge to group challenges and then act on those shared decisions (Kase, Carroll, Zhang, & Rosson, 2008).

People engage informal problem-based learning for a variety of reasons. Some may want to solve a simple issue; others may want to change themselves through addressing perceived faults or short-comings; others may mix various motives—related to personal lives and professional engagements. Others are motivated by personal curiosity and a desire to learn. Many have a practical desire to improve their circumstances or environment. Others want to help people. Many desire to relieve the pressures or tensions of a difficult situation.

Informal learning outside the bounds of formal learning structures affects much longer spans of human life than their years in formal education. As the capabilities of the WWW and Internet have grown in terms of collecting, delivering, and archiving digital information in various forms; connecting people across space, time, cultures and languages; and maintaining memory, people are bringing more complex problems to be addressed through informal learning. As more complex issues are engaged, it's no longer as desirable to work through problem-solving by default instead of more methodical work. D. Schön and C. Argyris' work on theories-in-use show how many decisions are made without conscious acknowledgment of the assumptions (and values) underlying certain actions. Schön and Argyris' "double-loop learning" concept imbues the decision-making process with checks and double-checks to test and correct for errors and resistance to learning. This approach taps into deeper causal relationships in a culture and context to understand why certain decisions get made a particular way (and not in other ways) within a system. The double-loop learning approach taps into the tacit mental models at work to understand underlying realities. Arriving at deeper understandings of the informal and unstructured problem-solving process may enhance outcomes and increase people's and groups' abilities to face future problems.

Problem-solving may be conceptualized as a series of steps that may be somewhat recursive. Figure 1, "A Conceptualization of an Informal Problem-Solving Process" suggests that there are four basic steps that are involved in this process.

a. Problem Identification and Analysis
b. Solutions Identification and Analysis
c. Planning, Decision-making, and Action
d. Reflection, Abstracting, and Contributing

Within each of these processes are sub-steps as reflected in Figure 1.

More specifically, this conceptualization involves the following steps.

A. Problem Identification and Analysis
    1. Pre-Awareness
    2. Problem Definition and Scope
    3. Decision Criteria
    4. Deeper Problem Analysis
B. Solutions Identification and Analysis
    5. Solutions Brainstorming
    6. Internal and External Resources Analysis
    7. Defining Problem(s)-Solution(s) Stakeholders
    8. Solutions Analysis and Decision-making
C. Planning, Decision-making, and Action
    9. Planning
    10. Taking Strategic Action
    11. Assessing the Effects and Making Adjustments

*Figure 1. A conceptualization of an informal problem-solving process*

12. Final Evaluation of the Problem(s)-Solution(s) Endeavor

D. Reflection, Abstracting, and Contributing

13. Abstracting: Takeaways for Future Informal Problem-Solving
14. Improved Awareness and Capacity
15. Enhancing the Larger Environment

## WHAT IS INFORMAL PROBLEM SOLVING?

This section will highlight the work of more complex, informal problem-solving, and will highlight some of the extant affordances and enablements of the current Web (based on the Internet substructure).

Broadly, the WWW offers wide access to a range of information and expertise. It offers clearly defined processes for some types of problem solving. It offers access to information visualizations and tools that may strengthen users' sense of self-efficacy in addressing certain problems. It also enables synchronous and asynchronous access to a range of people with various levels of expertise and willingness to collaborate—around shared problems. The Web also features virtual human communities and networks of learners to build individual identities as parts of larger problem-solving groups (whether as open-source software developers, health-based communities, political groups, or writers, for example).

## PROBLEM IDENTIFICATION AND ANALYSIS

The "Problem Identification and Analysis" quadrant focuses on (1) Pre-Awareness; (2) Problem Definition and Scope; (3) Decision Criteria, and (4) Deeper Problem Analysis. Each of these stages may vary in length, and many may be highly fleeting. Essentially, this first quadrant involves the awareness of a problem and its parameters.

### Pre-Awareness

The initial stage involves pre-awareness of a problem (or set of interrelated problems). While the problem itself may be extant, with a range of signs and symptoms, the individual experiencing this may not be clear that there is an issue that needs addressing. Sometimes, a particular trigger for greater awareness may be information shared online. A "problem" here may be something that needs attention and effort to rectify, or it may be aspirational—a challenge which the individual would like to attain or achieve. Oftentimes, the pre-awareness changes to awareness when an individual experiences some dissatisfaction with the *status quo*. This change may occur suddenly or gradually.

### Problem Definition and Scope

Once an individual becomes aware that there is an issue, he or she often strives to understand the problem both locally and in a larger context. Locally, the scope of a problem may be ascertained with some of the following questions.

- What is the "problem"? What is *not* the problem? (Define the boundaries of the problem.)
- Why is this issue a "problem" or something that will need attention?
- What are some of the undesirable effects of this problem on my life?
- What are some of the undesirable effects of this issue on others' lives?

To understand the scope of a problem, individuals often conduct informal environmental scans to see if others are experiencing similar challenges. This larger context helps individuals to frame their understandings of their situations. This larger context offers perspective.

- How unusual is this problem in the larger context?
- What are social attitudes about this problem?
- What are different perspectives or angles applied to this problem?
- Where are the authoritative sources on this particular issue? What are the criteria for identifying authoritative sources?

The experiences of the individual with similar challenges may change how he or she perceives this challenge. R. N. Taylor (1975) explains that prior experiences "can either facilitate (positive transfer) or inhibit (negative transfer) problem solving, depending in part on the structure of the problem" (p. 22).

## Decision Criteria

Individuals often need to define their own central values in approaching the problem. These values differ and are based on the individual's personality, conscience, value systems, morals, and lifestyle. The decision criteria also involve the importance an individual puts on the particular problem-solution, because that affects the amount of effort and resources that may be used for that issue.

- Are there values issues at play in addressing this problem?
- Are there values in conflict? If certain approaches will result in conflictual values, which values are more critical than others?
- When is the problem sufficiently serious to address?
- What types of interventions will be considered ethical?
- How much responsibility does the individual have?
- How important is the problem, in terms of how many resources should be used in its solution?

## Deeper Problem Analysis

More complex problems often require a deeper sense of background and analysis. It may also help to understand the causative factors (precursors) of the problem as well as current and future implications of the problem, so the individual is not just addressing the problem's symptoms. This phase also involves examining how the issue relates to other potentially connected issues. Some questions that may be asked to define this include the following:

- How serious is the problem? What are some of these indicators of seriousness?
- How did this problem originate? What is the history of the problem?
- What may be causing the effects or symptoms of this problem?
- How entrenched is the problem?
- Are there related concurrent problems and issues? Is this problem stand-alone, or is it related to other challenges? If so, which ones?
- What elements in the environment affect the problem? Enable it? Support or constrain it?

Examples of more complex problems may be those that address systemic issues—such as policy implications on a society; individual health issues (which affect physiological and emotional systems); planning for a family's move to another country; and so on. Every challenge may have Tier 1 – Tier 3 implications, and how the individual conceptualizes and approaches the challenge may determine the challenge's magnitude (see Table 1).

Based on the above categories, a Tier 1 problem could be an endeavor like defining a word, finding a recipe, planning a party, troubleshooting how an object should work, or shopping for a particular object. A Tier 2 issue may involve individuals dealing with shared financial challenges; an environmental non-governmental or-

*Table 1. Informal problem-solving complexity*

| | Potential Implications | Time Span | Resource Use (Information, Functions) | Social Angles | Ethical / Moral Dimension |
|---|---|---|---|---|---|
| **Tier 3** | Society (macro scale) | Long-term | Substantial | Large Groups | High-value ethics |
| **Tier 2** | Others | Medium-term | Multiple Unrelated Sources | Small Groups | Medium-value ethics |
| **Tier 1** | Self (micro scale) | Short-term | Minimal, Single Source or Related Sources | Individual Only | Low-value ethics (or non-applicable) |

ganization (NGO) working to deal with an environmental challenge; an agency conducting an investigation of an individual or an organization; a journalist forming background understandings for a story, and so on. A Tier 3 issue may manifest as societal level concerns—whether social, political, legal, economic, or others.

## SOLUTIONS IDENTIFICATION AND ANALYSIS

The second quadrant, "Solutions Identification and Analysis," examines various options to addressing the issue and a consideration of whether a partial or even a full solution is possible. This section involves an examination of internal and external resources that may be brought to bear on the issue. This also looks at defining stakeholders to both the problem and potential solutions. This phase culminates with a selection from among the various options for the best effect.

### Solutions Brainstorming

The next step will be to generate a wide range of possible solutions, based on what the individual imagines and conceptualizes as well as what he or she finds others have done. The idea here is not to artificially close off any possible endeavor or mix of endeavors. The use of a "wide net" is to consider the widest range of options in order to have a wide range of choices to select from.

- What are all possible interventions—regardless of practicality or likelihood?
- What is a desired end state? Working backwards from this desired scenario, what are the endeavors that may build up to the potential solution?
- What are the odds that non-action will lead to a resolution of the situation or challenge?
- What are possible mitigating issues?
- What are the objectives or goals of a possible solution?

At this point, the individual is not considering the costs or benefits or impacts of the various solutions. This is only about dredging up all potential solutions.

### Internal and External Resources Analysis

In this step, the individual considers what internal and external resources are available. Resources may be conceptualized broadly as time, attention, finances, materials, equipment, physical resources, information, and analysis that may be used to address the problem. This is a first step in evaluating capabilities for making change. Understanding the individual's particular context is also a first step in defining the "degrees of freedom" that he or she may have in addressing the issue.

An internal resource refers to what an individual has access to typically. An external resource is one that is controlled or owned external to the individual but may be accessed with the agreement of others.

- How much time does he or she have to spend?
- How much mental energy and attention does the individual have to spend on the problem?
- How much money may be reasonably spent on this particular issue?
- What sorts of materials, equipment, and physical resources may be used?
- What information does the individual already have? How much more information will be needed for the implementation of an effective solution?
- What intellectual capabilities does the individual have to bring towards the problem?
- Are there external resources that may be brought to bear on the particular challenge?

## Defining Problem(s)-Solution(s) Stakeholders

This step involves the identification of others who may have some information or knowledge that affects the problem(s)-solution(s). Stakeholders are others with some overlapping or similar interests as the individual problem-solver; these stakeholders are potential allies, with potential shared benefits from particular efforts.

- Who are potential allies in this problem(s)-solution(s) endeavor? Who are non-allies, who may disagree with the potential problem(s)-solution(s)?
- What are the respective interests for the various stakeholder groups? The non-allies?
- What is the time frame considerations for these various stakeholders? The non-allies?
- What resources do these stakeholders have in this issue? The non-allies?
- What are possible benefits and possible challenges in partnering with each respective stakeholder or stakeholder group?
- What are possible ways to engage non-allies or to mitigate some of the potential anticipated resistance?
- What are the possible costs of coordination or partnering?

## Solutions Analysis and Decision-Making

This next phase considers the feasibility of various potential solutions. He or she may consider possible side effects or unintended consequences of particular solutions. He or she may also consider whether doing nothing at all may be another option. The various possible solutions may be weighted against a certain set of values, principles, and practices to see which one may work best for the individual, his or her social group ("authorizing environment"), and anticipated short-term and long-term effects.

- What types of interventions will be considered practical?
- What are their respective costs and benefits? Are there continuing costs? Are there hidden costs? Are there continuing benefits? Are these objectively measureable over time?
- What are the degrees of freedom which may be applied to possible solutions?
- What are some possible unintended consequences of each of the reasonable solutions? On what basis are these future projections made, and are these projections valid?

- Are there potential liabilities or harms in certain endeavors? Will there be attendant harms? The contravention of important values and principles?
- What were the bases for information collection to understand the problem and the various potential solutions? Are these bases valid?

P. Senge (1990) suggests that a systems view must take into consideration non-obvious relationships and effects. He shows well how systems respond with compensatory feedback (p. 58) for various endeavors, and short-term solutions may result in much longer-term challenges. He notes that the areas of highest leverage are often non-obvious to most participants in a system (p. 64).

Once a decision is made at the idea or "policy" level, the actual on-ground implementation affects the actual success and outcomes. That said, a decision may involve selecting the best strategies and tactics from the range of possible solutions. A solution may be tailor-made for a particular individual and circumstance.

## PLANNING, DECISION-MAKING, AND ACTION

This third quadrant focuses on applied decision-making and actions during the implementation of the solution.

### Planning

The planning phase offers a practical approach to implementing the selected solution.

- What specific actions should be taken? When? In what order? How?
- Which allies should be brought on board? Which non-allies should be addressed, if any? Should this task be an individual one, or a collaborative one?
- How will information be collected? Will it be shared?
- How will the endeavor be monitored for progress?

### Taking Strategic Action

This step involves the actual work of problem-solving. This step involves continual analysis and live decision-making during the work. This involves the spending of different resources.

For individuals, this will require higher order executive functions—including the application of the human will. Individuals may keep records of the progress. They may also use these records for self-encouragement (and positive internal self-talk) for the discipline necessary for follow-through.

At any time, there may have to be adjustments made—given new opportunities, new challenges, and the surprises and serendipity.

### Assessing the Effects and Making Adjustments

Complex endeavors require awareness of the environment and the challenge being addressed. Changes in plans, tactics, and resourcing will have to be made as necessary. Even the goals may have to be reconceptualized as new information comes in. Very few plans work exactly to the letter.

### Final Evaluation of the Problem(s)-Solution(s) Endeavor

After a partial or full solution has been achieved, an individual may analyze what the current *status quo* is in relation to the challenge. He or she may conduct a cost-benefits analysis of their actions and those of others. He or she may consider lessons learned—or what is transferable from this problem(s)-solution(s) experience.

## REFLECTION, ABSTRACTING, AND CONTRIBUTING

The fourth and last quadrant involves actions that are not often taken in informal problem-solving—the learning that came from that experience. In the problem-based learning methodology, Koschmann, Feltovich, Myers, and Barrows (1992) describe a mostly linear process (with some recursiveness) which runs as follows: problem formulation, self-directed learning, problem reexamination, abstraction, and reflection (p. 33). Of special interest is the importance of the abstraction and reflective learning from the process.

### Abstracting: Takeaways for Future Informal Problem-Solving

The step of abstracting learning from the problem-solving process is a way of generalizing from the specific case or experience of dealing with a specific problem. In this process, an individual has optimally understood underlying problem dynamics more deeply; he or she has a deeper understanding of the challenges of the situation; he or she understands the resources available, the allies in the environment, and strategies for harnessing those tools to solve the problem.

The act of abstracting then is to draw out the lessons learned and to see what may apply to future or similar challenges. This step involves the generalizing and articulating of observations for a more considered, orderly, and effective problem-solving approach.

- What was non-obvious initially in the problem(s)-solution(s) situation?
- What tools were necessary, and which were unnecessary? And why?
- Did the nature of the problem change over time, and if so, why? And what relevant lessons may be derived from an observation of those changes?
- In terms of the steps in the process taken, was the order of the steps correct? Could those steps be improved? If so, how?
- Would earlier interventions have been more effective? Would different combinations of resource applications made a difference in the ultimate outcomes?
- Are there more effective ways to anticipate what can go wrong? Are there contingency plans that need to be made?
- Should there be others with different skill sets to address potential issues?
- Are there better ways to measure progress in this problem(s)-solution(s) situation?
- What may be done to improve this process?

In the same way that learners draw transferable "deep learning" from scenarios that demand drawing from existing knowledge and everyday experiences (Iqbal & Every, 2005, p. 262), abstracting demands that problem-solvers apply an analytical lens to their experiential learning.

### Improved Awareness and Capacity

This phase highlights the reality that individuals that have gone through a problem(s)-solution(s) cycle related to a particular issue may be more sensitively attuned to any recurrence of the problem. They have increased awareness; they have a stronger skill set or capacity in dealing with similar challenges in the future. These benefits may be extended by making the lessons more explicit and sharing them with others.

### Enhancing the Larger Environment

In the ethos of the Connected Web, people who use its resources and connections to others should return and contribute to that same space and community. They give back by sharing their expertise and encouraging others who are dealing with their own problem(s)-solution(s). Strategies and approaches are refined with the sharing of rich methods of arriving at solutions. The contributions of a community to this shared space may result in greater social resilience and impact in handling similar challenges. Lessons learned in one area of human endeavor may be applied to those of others, for greater effect.

## SOME CURRENT DESIGNED AFFORDANCES FOR PROBLEM-BASED LEARNING ONLINE

The current Web offers distributed affordances for the problem(s)-solution(s) process: (1) Problem Identification and Analysis; Solutions Identification and Analysis; Planning, Decision-making, and Action; and Reflection, Abstracting, and Contributing. Because these affordances may benefit a number of stages of the process, the affordances will be discussed broadly

### Access to Information

One major affordance of the Web involves access to information of various kinds and origins. Information that may have been considered protected is now widely available—such as remote sensing satellite images. People may also request tailored information through social sites—and access crowd-sourced information. Language translation tools have enabled wide access of information originating in foreign languages.

Plenty of sites offer step-by-step problem(s)-solution(s) for a range of daily life issues. New-generation search engines have continued improving search functions, with specialized tailoring based on user assessments of what the search tools surfaced. A few collections of case-based problem-solving exist in particular fields, along with scaffolded reasoning activities (Kolodner, Hmelo, & Narayanan, 1996).

Tools that plumb not only the so-called Surface (or Public) Web but also the Invisible (or Deep) Web surface many more types of information, even those hosted on sites that require authentication or membership or registration to access. The Invisible Web also contains plenty of information that may only be called up through dynamic searches and involve information that is not just hosted statically.

The growing sophistication of search engines to plumb both the Visible and Invisible (Deep) Web will enable orders-of-magnitude more information than is currently available. The algorithms used to surface information will both become more thorough but also more selective (customized) in terms of helping human users find what they are looking for. The information that was considered "dark" and inaccessible in the recent past will likely be brought into the light.

### What's Lacking?

There are few problems-solution cases available online that deal with more complex problem(s)-solution(s). These cases would require appropriate resources to support individuals working through their own unique situations. These would also have to provide supports without creating legal liabilities.

### Visualization

The Web now contains a variety of ways to visualize (visually depict and observe) complex information. These external representations help users better grasp a particular situation. One common example involves the depictions of complex meso-scale weather systems moving through a region or social migration patterns across a human landscape or an epidemiologic outbreak across multiple countries expressed on a world map. Such visualizations may also address theoretical concepts, such as a scientist's conceptualization of evolution or a projected planetary system or an abstract principle. Economic statistics and relationships may be depicted visually to show the magnitudes of differences between different data sets.

Improved understandings of particular situations [depicted in simulations or virtual worlds or "digital learning ecosystems" (Ficheman & Lopes, 2008)] may help self-discovery problem solvers better grasp their challenges; it may also help them feel more confident about pursuing particular solutions. Many can get real-time information about the issues they are addressing and so tailor their solution.

### What's Lacking?

Visualizations tend to be general, or they are tailored to shared human endeavors instead of unique individual progress. However, some programs enable individuals to track their progress at weight loss or financial management or fund-raising. Dedicated visualizations to help individuals with their problems-solutions would enhance problem-solving.

## Social Supports

Constructivist approaches to problem(s)-solution(s) are myriad on the Web. There are social groups for wide ranges of personal and professional interests and for life challenges. These online communities not only provide expertise, but they also involve relational support. These environments offer environments for experts and non-experts; they help individuals acclimate into certain identities that support problem-solving—such as identifying with a community of open-source course material learners in a particular field (Wiley & Henson, 2006).

There are online social structures to help people collaborate around knowledge contents for digital repositories, digital libraries, and around open-source learning materials and modules. Individual problem-solvers may collaborate around shared endeavors, such as through image- or audio- or video-sharing sites. They may interact around digital artifacts, such as objects in digital libraries or digital poster sessions for online conferences.

### What's lacking?

A methodical approach to the building of problem-solving communities would create a more coherent experience and enhance the experience.

Socio-technical infrastructures, those which bring together people through technical means, are widely used for social networking, but problem-solving is a distant byproduct of sub-groups within such spaces. Having more dedicated problem-solution spaces would be important.

## Virtual Environments

The WWW features many immersive spaces (like purely textual knowledge-sharing spaces to multi-sensory 3D virtual worlds) where problem-solving individuals may immerse in a particular culture. Foreign-language learners may "hang out" in virtual worlds where he or she may converse with native speakers of the language in environments that simulate real-world spaces.

These spaces apply a kind of selective fidelity in their design—to highlight the salient aspects of the community. In knowledge spaces, the information ontologies (structures) specify what is considered important for the learning and the identities. In immersive worlds, the designed environment and presential aspects of the digital avatars communicate much about the spaces. For example, some online spaces simulate healthcare environments for learners to problem-solve how to communicate with patients or how to diagnose potential health issues or how to conduct simple surgeries (often with tactual interaction devices).

Online communities often provide shared virtual environments for cognitive scaffolding. Individuals can experiment with their acclimation into a certain identity, such as a user of a particular software or a developer of particular code. Human-embodied avatars may be the vehicles through which people experience new roles—in areas of interest. These virtual spaces offer ways into acclimating into new experiences and identities.

### What's Lacking?

Many virtual environments engage learners in indirect and inductive logic ways. They do not explicitly draw out the problem-solution aspects of the learning. Having more structures to capture the learning and to have users record and reflect on their own learning would enhance the uses of these spaces for problem-solving. In addition, most simulations are designed for specific types of learning, which makes it harder for serendipitous and purely experiential learning, which may be more achievable in other real-world contexts. The artificiality of virtual world environments (limited physics, limited gravity, limited artificial intelligence agents, limited natural language interactivity, and some degree of predictability) makes it hard for more than a limited range of predefined learning.

## Self Management Tools

A critical part of problem-solving for self-discovery learners is to be able to approach the problem methodically, with access to the appropriate information and resources. Online sites may define the problem-solving experience with a kind of coherence that may promote appropriate decision-making and actions.

Separate stand-alone sites offer ways to individuals to record information (in journals or on personalized sites). If used appropriately, they may offer help in long-term problem-solving—by raising individual self-awareness and offering ways to record progress—but there is very little in the way of specific tools for a problem(s)-solution(s) situation.

Having portable tools for ubiquitous mobile devices would also be helpful. The location-sensitive aspects of these devices may also be harnessed for real-time information exchanges, decision-making, sampling the environment, and recording problem-solving observations—in lived, activity spaces. The exploratory environment may well be the real-world one, with digital information overlays.

This also raises the question of how to create long-term persistence, when the drop-out rate on many human problem-solving endeavors is so high.

### What's Lacking?

Problem-solving requires a way to structure accurate understanding of the problem and then practical ways to structure decision-making and actualizing solutions. More research may be necessary to reconceptualize what learners need for informal learning (Hsi, Crowley, Duschl, Finke, King, & Sabelli, 2004, p. 12).

# INTEGRATIVE DESIGN FOR FUTURE INFORMAL PROBLEM-SOLVING

Individuals who go to the Web as part of a problem-solving endeavor will often use a variety of resources for their work. The Web though may be structured more powerfully to frame problems-solutions. It may offer a wider range of tools and sites for problem-solving steps—in a coherent fashion. These tools need to be designed in highly flexible ways to accommodate the wide range of individuals engaging in problem-solving. Sites that may acclimate users into various communities to enhance their problem-solving knowledge and skills would be helpful, but there should also be a core federated identity which an individual can use to bring together their various endeavors.

Negative learning, or learning inaccurate information and practices, is a concern in problem-solving spaces. Even when information is explicitly described, people may misinterpret that information, or they may apply that information in inappropriate ways. This means potential risks for uses of problem-solution sites, and it may mean legal liabilities to the hosts of those particular sites. There may be instructional designs and legal disclaimers to prevent some negative learning or inappropriate analysis and choices and actions.

Real-time and ubiquitous supports may be designed for specific types of problem-solving in the way that decision-support systems are used today.

There may be complex checklists that help users consider relevant information in various steps of the problem-solving process. There may be models on how to abstract knowledge from the problem(s)-solution(s) experience to benefit others in similar endeavors.

Lastly, it would be important to have ways to measure the efficacies of problem(s)-solution(s) spaces that employ self-discovery learning.

## CONCLUSION

Informal problem-solving may be understood to be a recursive process involving four quadrants of steps: (1) Problem Identification and Analysis; (2) Solutions Identification and Analysis; (3) Planning, Decision-making, and Action, and (4) Reflection, Abstracting, and Contributing. Each of the steps within these quadrants may benefit from purposive design to enhance self-discovery learning.

There are numerous endeavors to try to create coherence from the disparate elements on the WWW. Using a problem(s)-solution(s) approach has already been done for many types of simple problems, but raising the stakes and building structures that enable more complex problems-solutions and collaborative problem-solving endeavors would improve the Web's usability as a practical resource for numerous informal users.

Specifically, what designs may help people become aware that they have an issue to address? What structures may be created to help people understand the scope of a particular problem? How may people's unique decision criteria be surfaced meaningfully? What tools may enhance people's ability to analyze a problem in more relevant depth? What tools may broaden human abilities to brainstorm potential solutions? How may human decision-making be enhanced for informal complex problem-solving? What social tools may help people connect with others with like interests and similar needs? What socio-technical tools may enhance people's abilities to collaborate with each other and to share resources? How may the problem-solving sequences be formulated and encourage user persistence? How may people's reflection be enhanced in this process? How may people's self-management and self-efficacy in regards to informal problem-solving be enhanced? And finally, how may non-obvious problem(s)-solution(s) and underlying effects be surfaced for a broader audience?

## ACKNOWLEDGMENT

Thanks to R. Max, who engages in all sorts of problem-solving with excellent results.

## REFERENCES

Ficheman, I. K., & Lopes, R. de D. (2008). Digital learning ecosystems: Authoring, collaboration, immersion and mobility. In Proc*eedings of the Interaction Design and Children* (IDC 2008), (pp. 9–12.) Chicago, IL: ACM.

Hsi, S., Crowley, K., Duschl, R., Finke, C. L., King, H., & Sabelli, N. (2004). Models of learning and theories of practice for informal learning environments. In Pro*ceedings of the International Conference on Learning Sciences,* (pp. 12–15). Santa Monica, CA: Association of Computing Machinery.

Iqbal, R., & Every, P. (2005). Scenario based method for teaching, learning and assessment. In Pro*ceedings of Special Interest Group for Information Technology Education* (SIGITE 2005) (pp. 261–266). Newark, NJ: ACM.

Kase, S. E., Carroll, J. M., Zhang, Y., & Rosson, M. B. (2008). Sustainable informal IT learning in community-based nonprofits. In Pro*ceedings of CHI2008,* (pp. 2335–3440). Florence, Italy: ACM.

Kolodner, J. L., Hmelo, C. E., & Naranyanan, N. H. (1996). Problem-based learning meets case-based reasoning. In Pro*ceedings of the 1996 International Conference on Learning Sciences*, Evanston, Illinois, (pp. 188–195).

Koschmann, T. D., Feltovich, P. J., Myers, A. C., & Barrows, H. S. (1992). Implications of CSCL for problem-based learning. *Sigcue Outlook, 21*(3), 33. doi:10.1145/130893.130902

*Maslow's hierarchy of needs*. (2010, Oct. 16). Wikipedia. Retrieved on October 16, 2010, from http://en.wikipedia.org/wiki/Maslow%27s_hierarchy_of_needs.

Senge, P. M. (1990). *The fifth discipline: The art and practice of the learning organization*. New York, NY: Doubleday Currency.

Strohecker, C., & Butler, D. (2004). The informal informing the formal to form new models of learning. In Pro*ceedings of the IDC 2004*, (pp. 151–152). College Park, MD: ACM.

Taylor, R. N. (1975). Perception of problem constraints. *Management Science, 22*(1), 22–29. doi:10.1287/mnsc.22.1.22

Wiley, D., & Henson, S. (2006). An initial characterization of engagement in informal social learning around MIT OCW. In Pro*ceedings of the International Conference of the Learning Sciences* (ICLS 2006), Bloomington, Indiana, (pp. 832–837).

## KEY TERMS AND DEFINITIONS

**Authorizing Environment:** The influential individuals surrounding a decision-making that constrain his or her choices by having opinions and preferences of their own.

**Decision Support System:** A decision strategy (such as a decision-tree) that informs decision-making at various junctures.

**Double-Loop Learning:** A concept of reflection and verification of information and clean lines of logic for more effective decision-making, based on collaborative research by D. Schon and C. Argyris.

**Environment:** The surrounding context, ecology.

**Implementation:** The performing of a certain plan-of-action.

**Informal:** Casual, ill-structured, unofficial, irregular.

**Invisible Web:** The so-called Deep Web consists of the additional parts of the Web that is not available on the "surface" (searchable by Web browsers); this Web consists of databases and other contents that often lie behind an authentication layer which allows access through subscriptions or some sorts of registration (The Surface Web is said to contain some 167 Terabytes of information while the Invisible Web is estimated to consist of about 91,000 terabytes, many orders of magnitude larger than what can be found on the Surface Web.).

**Juncture:** A critical point in time, a state of crisis, a point at which important decision-making should be made.

**Problem-Based Learning (PBL):** A trans-disciplinary framework for learning which is based around specific challenges in a field and which require the calling up of a range of information and actions.

**Scaffolding:** A temporary structure to enhance the effectiveness of learning (in order to accommodate the learner in whatever level of cognitive readiness for learning that he or she is at, from novice / amateur to expert levels).

**Surface Web:** The easily accessible Visible Web that may be accessed using Web browsers and search engines.

**Systems Theory:** The framework or conceptualization of a system as consisting of interdependent and interacting parts, with non-linear and complex interactions and non-obvious causes and effects.

**Transfer:** The application of one model onto another situation or circumstance or problem.

**Use Case:** A hypothetical or actual scenario used in software engineering to describe how a system functions in response to a specific human need; multiple use cases are used to determine the functional requirements of a system for initial design and future iterations.

# APPENDIX

| Steps to Informal Problem-Solving | Problem(s)-Solution(s) Topic / Scenario | Projected Uses of the Web |
|---|---|---|
| **A. Problem Identification and Analysis** | | |
| *1. Pre-Awareness* | | |
| *2. Problem Definition and Scope* | | |
| *3. Decision Criteria* | | |
| *4. Deeper Problem Analysis* | | |
| **B. Solutions Identification and Analysis** | | |
| *5. Solutions Brainstorming* | | |
| *6. Internal and External Resources Analysis* | | |
| *7. Defining Problem(s)-Solution(s) Stakeholders* | | |
| *8. Solutions Analysis and Decision-making* | | |
| **C. Planning, Decision-making, and Action** | | |
| *9. Planning* | | |
| *10. Taking Strategic Action* | | |
| *11. Assessing the Effects and Making Adjustments* | | |
| *12. Final Evaluation of the Problem(s)-Solution(s) Endeavor* | | |
| **D. Reflection, Abstracting, and Contributing** | | |
| *13. Abstracting: Takeaways for Future Informal Problem-Solving* | | |
| *14. Improved Awareness and Capacity* | | |
| *15. Enhancing the Larger Environment* | | |

**Note:** This table offers a way to begin to conceptualize how the Web may be better harnessed to achieve a problem(s)-solution(s) functionality.

Section 4

# Design Strategies for Self-Discovery Learning

# Chapter 10
# Design Guidelines for Self-Assessment Support for Adult Academic Distance Learning

**Maria Menendez Blanco**
*Open University of the Netherlands, The Netherlands*

**Gerrit C. van der Veer**
*Open University of the Netherlands, The Netherlands*

**Laura Benvenuti**
*Open University of the Netherlands, The Netherlands*

**Paul A. Kirschner**
*Open University of the Netherlands, The Netherlands*

## ABSTRACT

*This contribution focuses on adult distance learning. Based on experiences at the Open University of the Netherlands we investigate specific problems that our students have with self-assessment and metacognition while studying. Starting from a literature review and complementing this with available student data from our teaching research center, we developed a conceptual framework that was iteratively adjusted and assessed by a questionnaire study and interviews. This allowed us to develop design guidelines for self-assessment support in distance learning environments. These guidelines were reviewed by experts. The input from the experts was used to modify the guidelines and iterate until they were considered complete. Tangible designs (i.e., mock-ups) for each of the self-assessment methods were proposed. These tangible designs were prototyped for later evaluation. Finally, we provide our conclusions and propose recommendations for actual application and systematic design.*

DOI: 10.4018/978-1-61350-320-1.ch010

Copyright © 2012, IGI Global. Copying or distributing in print or electronic forms without written permission of IGI Global is prohibited.

## INTRODUCTION

This chapter aims at providing grounded design-guidelines for self-assessment support for learners. The application domain, adult academic distance learning, is based on our context of work: The Open University of the Netherlands (OUN), a Dutch university for adult distance learning. Our university is funded by the government to make higher education accessible to anyone with the necessary aptitudes and interests, regardless of formal qualifications. Students can study at their own pace and at their own venue. Therefore, OUN students are a heterogeneous group of learners with diverse goals and needs. Flexibility and learning independence in study activities are among the main motivations for studying at the OUN. Lack of interaction and feeling of isolation are some of the disadvantages associated to distance learning, and OUN teachers generally consider this one of the main reasons for the low graduation rates in comparison to those at "traditional" Dutch universities.

In order to keep the type of students in mind, as well as to reason about their needs, we developed a set of personas, based on what our university statistics tell us about relevant student characteristics such as age, employment, family context, location, educational background, learning activities, and learning goals.

### Sonja

Sonja is 23 years old and works as a waitress in a town in Flanders, Belgium. She started working when she finished high school. She works every day from noon until 10:00 PM which does not leave her too much spare time. Last year she decided that she would like to change her job and start working as a therapist in a help-center close to her town. That's why she joined the OUN and started studying Psychology. She has been studying for ten months and has successfully completed almost all of the courses in the first year of Psychology. She wants to obtain her Bachelor's degree in three years and maybe then continue to complete a Master's degree in Pedagogy.

### Marta

Marta is 47 years old, is married, and has two young children. She works as a civil servant at the provincial level dealing with environmental regulatory policy who had studied environmental science but lacks the Law and Policy.

She is really good at her job. However, she has a weak point: legal issues. Although she had a class in Law during her secretarial education, she often lacks the necessary knowledge to understand the complex problems of the company and she has to ask her colleagues for help. Some months ago she decided to study Law at the OUN. It would be nice to obtain a Bachelor degree, maybe she could even get a better job, but her main priority is to obtain knowledge which she can apply to her daily work-related problems.

### Peter

Peter is 76 years old. He used to work as a Professor of Math at the Technical University Eindhoven but now he is happily retired. He has plenty of free time and he likes to spend it taking care of his garden, going for walks in the woods, and growing vegetables and cooking them. He is very keen on natural sciences and would like to know more about so that he can better understand the physical environment that he so enjoys. That's why he decided to take some courses at the OUN. He does not want to obtain a degree, but he enjoys reading the texts sitting in the garden with a cup of tea.

### Dirk

Dirk is 45 years old. He is married and has a little baby. He works in a large IT company in Amsterdam as a consultant. During the 15 years he has been working at the company, he has obtained extensive knowledge in Databases, programming and other IT skill, however he does not have a certificate which proves it. He would like to obtain an official document which shows his knowledge and that's why he decided to join the Computer Science Master's degree program at the OUN. Although he does not have a lot of free time, he tries to study as consistently as possible so as to graduate as quickly as possible. He thinks this is a good opportunity to improve his professional life by either looking for a better job or obtaining a promotion with his current company.

## BACKGROUND

OUN students are adults with a broad age range (18 to 75). Most have full time jobs and families which take up most of their time. Among the most common motivations to study at the OUN are: obtain a promotion in one's current job, get a better job, obtain a degree to certify knowledge obtained through years of experience, or simply to become more knowledgeable on a subject of interest. But working on your own can also have drawbacks. Lack of interaction and feelings of isolation are often stated disadvantages associated with distance learning. Interaction between students and with the teacher is good for maintaining motivation, getting feedback, discussing ideas, and assessing one's knowledge. The self-assessment of knowledge is the focus of our study. In particular, we study how to support students' self-assessment by helping them to "know what they know" (i.e., metacognition). The problems we are attacking are generic for adult distance learning and, thus, solutions need to be applicable in a broad variety of adult academic learning situations, as long as interactive systems, and, in some cases, internet connection, are available.

Our approach to design is based on an analysis of available relevant literature on self-assessment and metacognition, and on archival OUN student data, gathered by CELSTEC, the Center for Learning Sciences and Technologies (section 1). From the resulting insight we developed a conceptual model, refined this from a student survey study, and supported our results with additional interviews (section 2). Our design approach starts with the development of guidelines that were reviewed by experts in adult teaching. The input from the experts was used to modify the guidelines, allowing us to iterate until these were considered complete (section 3). The next step consisted of a tangible design (i.e., mock-ups as well as interactive prototypes) that was iteratively developed with empirical assessment (section 4). In the final section we provide our conclusions and suggestions for application in the context of adult distance learning environments.

## SELF-ASSESSMENT AND METACOGNITION: A LITERATURE SURVEY COMPLEMENTED BY SOME OPEN UNIVERSITY DATA

Self-assessment is a broad concept which can be interpreted in different ways depending on what the focus of the assessment is. According to Boud (1995), self-assessment has two essential components. The first component relates to the identification of standards and criteria for judging the quality of the work. The second refers to the judgment of the extent to which the standards and criteria have been reached. A different approach by Paris and Paris (2001) considers self-assessment to consist of the learners' evaluation and appraisal of their competences and performance in the process of learning. This approach relates self-assessment to the concept of metacognition. Metacognition has been identified as one of the most important factors affecting learning (Mok et al, 2006). It can be defined as *thinking about thinking* (Wellman, 1985) or *knowing what you know*. In our design approach, we follow Paris and Paris, focusing on the development of a framework to support self-assessment in adult distance education by supporting the development of metacognition. The following overview shows the topics related to self-assessment and metacognition that we identified from our survey and selected as a start for our design.

## Support Learners in their Self-Reflection

Self-reflection can be defined as the thinking reflexively or thinking about oneself. Self-reflection is related to metacognition in that it provides understanding of what one knows, and a way of improving metacognitive strategies through the examination of how a task was performed (Metacognition and reflection, 2006). Schön (1983) states that a reflective thinker is aware of her/his own knowledge and lack of knowledge. Supporting learners' self-reflection can also have collateral positive effects since it is related to performance improvement and learner motivational beliefs (Means et al, 2009).

## Provide Instructional Guidance

Theoretical approaches like andragogy (Knowles, 1970) suggest that adult learning should be independent and self directed. It has, however, been proven that providing novice learners with support and guidance during the learning process is a more effective and efficient approach to learning (Kirschner, Sweller & Clark, 2006).

Teachers' support can be classified in metacognitive, procedural, contextual and technical. Metacognitive support includes presenting relationships between concepts, explaining rationale for tasks and activities, and encouraging the development of relationships among participants. Students might need help in procedural support: searching, organizing, and representing the information provided as well as in clarifying the course contents. Teachers can guide learners by adding, elaborating and correcting information; content support. Finally, due to the special case of online education, learners might need technical support about the learning environment. The results of an empirical study with adult students in an online course show the importance of all of the kinds of support in the development of metacognitive skills (Rimor, Reingold, & Kalay, 2006).

At the OUN, student data are regularly collected. In a recent study (Puls & van den Munkhof, 2010) 786 respondents answered between 60% and 95% of each question. Of these, 60% registered in a Bachelor or Master degree curriculum, 40% taking one or more Bachelor or Master level courses), .students were asked to indicate their satisfaction with specific aspects of distance education. Aspects such as "content of written study material," "printing quality," and "course offering" were judged satisfactory by more than 80% of the respondents and "training content," "content consistency," "examination procedures," "examination content," and "electronic learning environment" by more than 60%. On the other hand, "guidance" and "study advice" were among the lower rated features, with only 40% scoring them as satisfactory. To determine which aspects need more guidance, students were asked to indicate if they would like to receive guidance in 13 different areas. The top three areas where students noted that guidance would be appreciated were "study coaching," "building their individual curriculum," and "monitoring the study" (each indicated by between 37 and 39% of the respondents).

## Individualized Instruction

Individualized instruction is defined as a technique where the pace, content, and method are tailored to the individual needs of each learner (StateUniversity.com, 2010). Individualized instruction has been reported to have a positive effect in the performance and motivational beliefs of the learners (U.S. Department of Education, 2009).

The role of individualized instruction in the development of metacognition has been studied by Azevedo et al (2005). In their research, they discuss the use of scaffolding methods in Computer Based Learning Environments (CBLE) as a metacognitive tool for enhancing student learning. This research provides the empirical basis for the design of CBLE as metacognitive tool to foster students in their learning of challenging science topics (Means et al, 2009).

According to the definition above, tailoring the method used in the learning environment is also linked to the concept of individualized instruction. It deals with how instruction is structured and managed for different learners. The different instructional structures can, for example, be designed by based upon the learners' different learning styles: "the composite of characteristic cognitive, affective, and physiological factors that serve as relatively stable indicators of how a learner perceives, interacts with, and responds to the learning environment" (Keefe, 1979, p. XX). Learning environments which address different learning styles can influence learner performance, satisfaction (Dunn et al, 1995; Kirchen, 2007), and metacognitive skill development (Shannon, 2008).

## Collaborative Learning

Collaborative learning can enhance the development of metacognitive skills (Sandi-Urena, Cooper & Stevens, 2010). Larkin (2006) explains this in that "asking questions to oneself can begin by being questioned by others" (p. 23). Researchers have found evidence of metacognition development during collaborative work (Larkin) and through the practice of collective metacognitive activities (Case, Gunstone, & Lewis, 2001; Georghiades, 2006). There is evidence (Sandi-Urena, Cooper and Stevens) that metacognition skills obtained through collaboration with peers can be transferred to the individual solution of an unrelated and independent task.

Although collaborative learning has great potential, some researchers are skeptical about using asynchronous discussion groups, especially in the way these are managed by teachers and the participation rates.

Puls and Van den Munkhof (2010) report on the current situation regarding collaborative learning at the OUN. Asked about the expected value of discussion groups, students indicated that they were a way to acquire additional insight, additional explanations and share educational experiences. However, concerns regarding the usefulness of discussions groups surface at the OUN because most of the students do not use the discussion groups, and other students experienced that discussion groups did not fulfill their expectations. To better understand this, student coaches and teachers from different faculties at the OUN were asked why discussion groups fail. They reported that they felt that there is not enough intervention from the teachers and, due to the lack of time and difference of timetable among students, discussions were not as smooth as they wished and did not provide immediate feedback that the students feel they need.

## Plan and Monitor the Learning Process

Planning and monitoring are regulative processes. They do not directly yield knowledge, as do transformative processes, but are necessary to manage the discovery process (de Jong and van Joolingen, 1998).

Planning strategies relate positively to success in learning (Azevedo, 2005), perceived control of time, job satisfaction, and health, and relate negatively to stress (Claessens et al, 2007). Planning and monitoring is also related to the development of metacognitive skills because metacognition occurs when learners plan, monitor, and evaluate their own cognitive behavior in a learning environment (Sandi-Urena, Cooper, & Stevens, 2010). Students appreciate support in planning and monitoring their learning process (Alexander, 2001).

Time management is an important planning and monitoring strategy. Although it has been reported that adult students have better developed time-management skills than younger students (Trueman & Hartley, 1996), lack of time is still an important issue for them (Dunn et al, 1995). Helping adult students to profit most of their available time can positively influence their learning.

## Strengthen Learner's Self-Efficacy

Bandura (1977) introduced the concept of self-efficacy, which refers to a person's perceived ability to attain a desired outcome (i.e., the feeling one has that she/he can do what is asked of her/him). People with high levels of self-efficacy focus their energy on analyzing and resolving problems. People with low self-efficacy get worried about evaluation, doubt their skills and abilities, and anticipate failure before investing effort in problem solving (Bandura & Wood, 1989).

A study on the relationship between self-efficacy, metacognition and performance revealed that metacognition and performance are mediated by self-efficacy. This suggests that students with effective metacognitive strategies also have strong beliefs about their ability to successfully perform a task (Coutihno, 2008). Supporting learners in the development of their metacognitive skills will help them increase their levels of self-efficacy and improve learning outcomes.

# A CONCEPTUAL MODEL FOR THE SUPPORT OF METACOGNITION

After choosing topics related to self-assessment and metacognition, we developed an online questionnaire to investigate possible relationships between the topics (e.g., Is the level of self-reflection related to the level of guidance needed?) and other potentially relevant variables (e.g., Is the level of guidance needed related to the previous level of education?).

The questionnaire consists of three parts. Part 1 dealt with background variables such as age, previous level of education, hours of study and faculty of study. Part 2 referred to the selected topics. Each topic was mapped to one or more questions. The variables from the questionnaire can be classified in three groups according to their role in the metacognitive process:

- **Facts**, skills and behaviors variables, containing: time available for study, level of education, student attitude, and time management skills. These variables can not be influenced externally.
- **Means variables** that hypothetically can influence the development of metacognitive skills: teacher feedback, resources offered, and adapted exercises. These variables can be externally influenced (e.g., by design).
- **Goal variables**, selected as indicators of metacognitive skills.

The final part was an open-ended question where students were asked to write any further comment they might have.

Table 1 shows the variables in Part 2 along with actual questions (translated from Dutch). Figure 1 shows how these variables feature in our original hypothetical conceptual model to support metacognition.

The questionnaire was sent to 288 bachelor and master students and was completed by 102. Goodman and Kruskal's gamma (1979) was used to determine the correlation between variables. The upper right half of Figure 2 shows the significant correlations (95% confidence level) between the answers from the questionnaire. The height of a correlation coefficient is visualized by the saturation and diameter of the circle. The only significant negative correlations are between job time and study time, between time management skill and procrastination, and between procrastination and know criteria.

The correlation structure challenged us to reconsider our hypothetical conceptual model.

*Table 1. Variables (Bold face) and the actual questions (italic) in the questionnaire*

| Variable | Question |
|---|---|
| **Time available** | |
| Job time | *How many hours do you work per week?* |
| Study time | *How many hours do you study per week?* |
| **Previous education** | |
| Level of education | *Level of education* |
| *Time management* | |
| Time management skills | *While studying for a course, I know how to manage my time* |
| Procrastination | *I tend to postpone exams because I am not sure I am ready to pass* |
| **Student attitude** | |
| I collaborate | *I collaborate with other students during a course (through discussion groups)* |
| Preference for teacher collaboration | *I want teachers to participate in the collaboration* |
| Preference for real time | *When collaborating with students on-line I prefer to use real time collaboration (Skype, chats)* |
| Preference for non real time | *When collaborating with students on-line I prefer to use non-real time collaboration (discussion groups, forums)* |
| **Means to support metacognition** | |
| Teacher feedback | *I receive enough feedback from the teacher* |
| Offer resources | *While studying for a course the offered material (text, tutorials, examples) covers my needs* |
| Adapted exercises | *The exercises given during a course are adapted to my knowledge (they are neither too easy nor too difficult)* |
| **Goals of metacognition in learning** | |
| Know strengths and weaknesses | *While studying for a course, I can identify my weak and strong points in the subject* |
| Know criteria | *It is clear what I have to study to pass a course* |
| Know source location | *When I need further information on a topic, I know where to find it.* |
| Self assessment | *My expected score after finishing an exam matches the actual score I get* |

*Figure 1. Original (hypothetical) model to support metacognition*

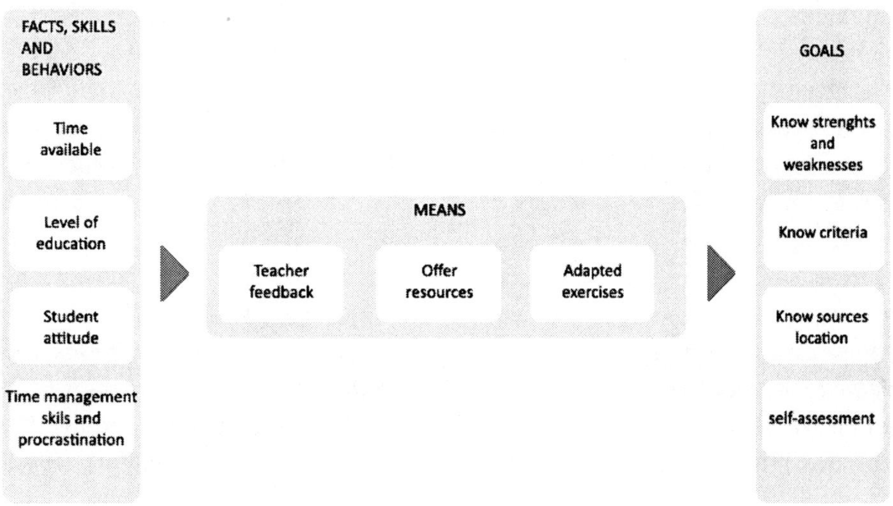

*Figure 2. Significant correlations (size and saturation of circle indicate strength of correlation) between the answers to the questionnaire*

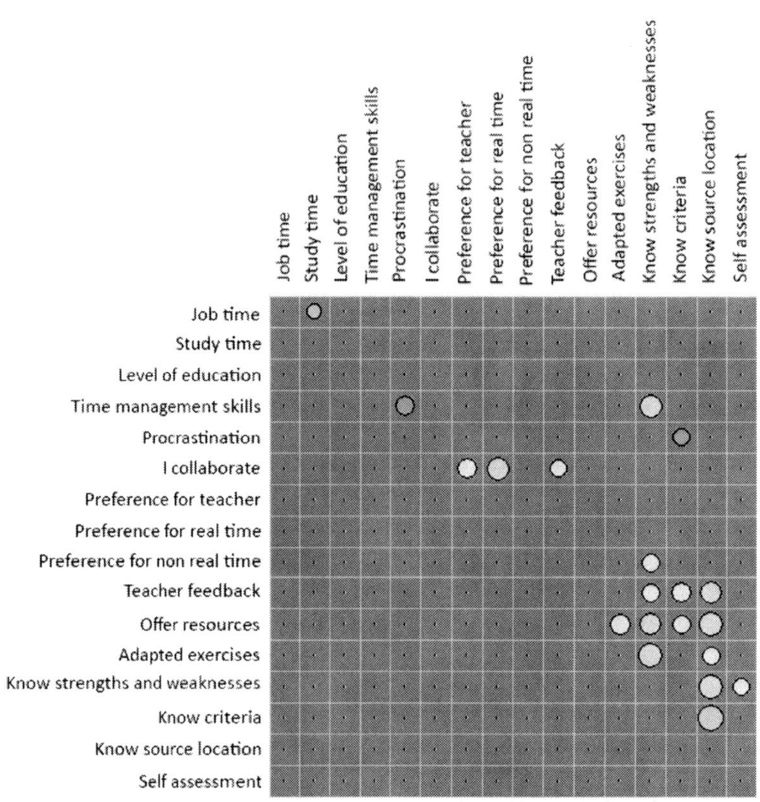


## Facts, Skills, and Behaviors

These variables depend directly on the situation and state of the student and are the input of our metacognition model. *Time available* is a set of variables which includes the variables *study time* and *job time*. Understandably, the number of job hours is negatively correlated to the number of study hours. Students who spend more time working have less time to study. The variables *study time* and *job time*, together with the variable *level of education* are facts that can not be influenced.

This turns out not to be a serious problem because no significant correlations were found between *study time*, *job time* and *level of education* and any of the other variables. The means required by the learner to develop metacognitive knowledge and metacognitive skills do not strongly depend either on the hours spent in studying or working, or on the previous level of education. As these variables are not significantly correlated with any other, they can be removed from the model (Figure3).

*Student attitude*, *time management skills and procrastination* are variables and sets of variables which can be indirectly influenced. *Student attitude* refers to the learner's attitude towards collaboration in the learning environment. It is composed of a set of variables which includes: *I collaborate*, *preference for teacher*, *preference for real-time* and *preference for non-real time*. *I collaborate* relates to the participation of students in discussion groups and forums. This variable is positively correlated with *preference for teacher*

*Figure 3. Simplified model to support metacognition*

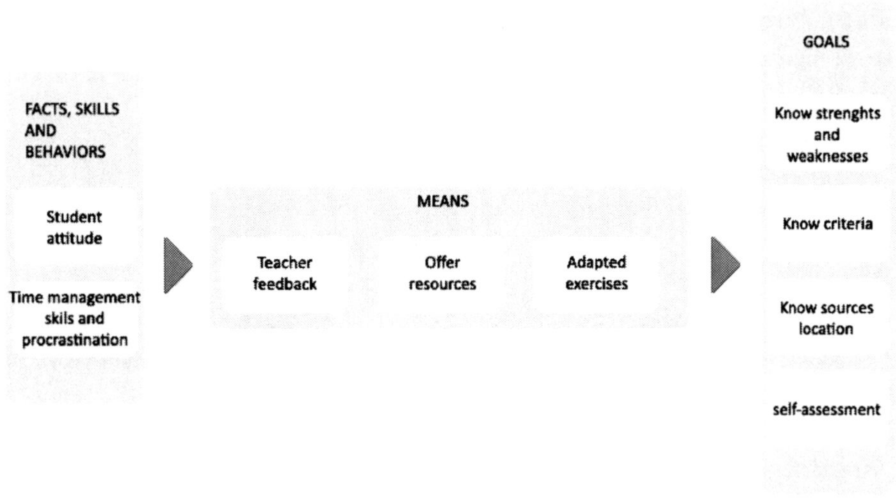


and *preference for real time*; γ is .39 and .55 respectively. There is a significant correlation between *I collaborate* and the variable *teacher feedback (γ= .34)*. Students who collaborate in the discussion groups and forums think that the level of teacher feedback is enough.

As stated earlier, students at the OUN complain about the low level of feedback from teachers. This along with the results from our questionnaire show that most students do not participate in the discussion groups. As collaboration is positively correlated with teacher feedback, redesigning the current way of collaboration into a tailored service which supports collaboration among learners can help to solve the problem of perceived low feedback.

From the results of the questionnaire it is not clear whether the positive correlation between *I collaborate* and *enough feedback* is due to the interaction of students with teachers in the discussion groups and forums, or because collaboration among students decreases the amount of feedback needed from the teacher.

*Time management* is a set of variables which includes *time management skills* and *procrastination*. *Time management skills* is positively correlated to *know strength and weaknesses* (γ=.57) and negatively correlated to procrastination (γ= – .41). *Procrastination* is not only negatively correlated to *time management skills* but also to *know criteria (γ= - .33)*.

## Means Variables

The 'means' variables are *teacher feedback*, *offer resources*, and *adapted exercises*. These variables are ways (i.e., the means) to influence learners' metacognition. Significant correlations were found between means and goals variables, which will be further explained.

## Goals Variables

The 'goals' variables are *known strengths and weaknesses*, *know criteria*, *know sources location* and *self-assessment*. These variables are metacognition indicators and need to be supported to develop metacognition. *Know sources location* is positively correlated with *know criteria* (γ=.72) and with *know strengths and weaknesses* (γ=.6). The correlations between 'means' variables and 'goal' variables give insight into how the development of metacognitive knowledge can be supported. The positive correlations between these variables were:

- *Teacher feedback* is positively correlated to *know source location (γ=.53), know criteria (γ=.4)*, and *know strengths and weaknesses (γ=.35)*.
- *Offer resources* positively correlates to *know source location (γ=.60), know strengths and weaknesses (γ=.51)*, and *know criteria (γ=.38)*.
- Providing *adapted exercises* correlates positively to *know strengths and weaknesses (γ=.64)* and *know source location (γ=.38)*.

In conclusion, the results from the questionnaire show that the attitude towards learning, behavior in learning, the need for material, teacher feedback and adapted exercises, and metacognition knowledge do not depend either on the level of education, or on time spent in studying or working. Time management skills help avoid the tendency to postpone exams and to support metacognition knowledge development. The metacognition indicators are correlated with the level of feedback provided by the teacher, the offered material and the exercises adapted to the individual needs of the learner. These results indicate that the metacognition in learners can be externally supported.

## Developing Deeper Insight

The student questionnaire yielded useful information about OUN students and the relationships between variables. However, it also triggered questions such as: "What are the desired features of a time-management tool?", "What are the reasons for choosing between practice exams and online quizzes?", and "How can we support collaboration among students?" Interviews were conducted to obtain further insight on those topics and qualitative data on self-assessment practices. Based on availability we interviewed two Master's students in Computer Science, one participant of a single course (on Databases) and a student in Psychology. These extensive interviews consisted of three parts. First, the students were asked to identify the main challenges faced by OUN students. Then, they were presented with four scenarios showing personas studying at the OUN using a new interface which integrates some of the features discussed in the previous sections (i.e., time management, collaborative learning, self- assessment through quizzes, practice exams with teacher feedback, and progress tracking). The students were asked to give their opinion for each of the new features. Finally, students were asked to share their own personal self-assessment methods.

Time management, personal circumstances which interfere with the study, concentration, and motivation are the main challenges identified by the students. It became clear that time management is not a problem because of a lack of time-management skills but because there is little time available. Students are not positive about a time-management tool which is considered more of a burden than a help. It seems the students get annoyed by having to switch tasks because it hinders task completion. However, were positive about using management tools when working in groups. Setting milestones, allocating tasks and keeping track of the group members' holidays are some of the suggested features.

The interviews revealed that collaboration is important. Discussion groups are useful for the students, even if they almost never participate (i.e., vicarious learning). The students really appreciate face-to-face meetings, and participate in the classes organized in the Study Centers (i.e., physical locations spread around main cities in The Netherlands where students can meet with other students and teachers, take exams, and/or use the OUN library). Students told us that teacher feedback can be helpful but is not really necessary. One student pointed out that teachers can be overwhelmed if they are asked to be really involved into the learning process. Some students prefer to collaborate with colleagues who they already know. One student liked studying with colleagues because he is not "*alone with the book*."

Students identified practice exams as the most valuable self-assessment method. They point out that the level of difficulty of the exams should be aligned with the level of difficulty in the actual test. They commented that the current practice exams only show whether the answer is right or wrong but do not provide further information. ("*you can just see what its wrong and you can not learn from it*," "*what you do not understand you can not find it out*"). Quizzes were also identified as useful. They would use the quizzes to assess their knowledge after a set of chapters. Some students proposed providing extra credit to those students whose performance in the "after chapters" quizzes is good. All students were positive about adaptive quizzes that provide instantaneous and personalized feedback.

The students also reported other ways of self-assessment that they developed through experience. Some ask other students to review their reports; others initiate face-to-face meetings which they find useful to "*know what you know*." Some students reported that when they have to deliver a report they wait a few days after finishing it before delivering. In the mean time they spend time on unrelated things such as sports and after a few days they read it again.

All students were positive about having a service which allows them to see their progress. They described such a service as "*nice*" and "*useful*." Currently, few courses allow this. Some students reported that they use third-party applications to track their progress when the service is not provided. Most reported that they kept track of the hours spent to complete a course. While courses provide an indication of the time needed to complete the course, students complained about underestimation. One student suggested including a feature which would point out the weak points ("*The best thing would be that the system could warn you by some Artificial Intelligence: Please look at this kind of equations because you have a problem with them*").

## From Model to Design

From the questionnaire and interviews we learnt that OUN students are self-directed learners. Most of them claim to have good self-reflection skills and that they are able to accurately assess their knowledge. OUN students' main challenges are lack of time, personal circumstances which interfere with study, concentration and motivation. While they are aware of the usefulness of time management,, in practice it is hard to keep up with the schedule because of individual circumstances which interfere with study. The platform used to schedule their tasks should not influence their time availability. They would appreciate a service which allows them to set the schedule when working in groups. Some of the options suggested are: set milestones, allocate tasks and set availability.

Procrastination is not an issue for most of the students. Only minority tends to postpone exams for a "good" reason: they are not sure whether they are able to pass though they would appreciate a service which allows them to follow their progress and identify their weak points.

Students appreciate practice exams and quizzes. The exams are a good method to assess global knowledge on a subject. However, the current way of presenting the answers does not take advantage of its potential. The exams should not be a mechanical way to assess knowledge but a supportive tool which promotes learning and reasoning. Quizzes are seen as a useful way of assessment "on the go." Most students would like to have a quiz after each, or at least after a set of chapters to assess their knowledge development.

Collaboration has been identified as successful for developing metacognition and is an important issue at the OUN. Discussion groups, which are one of the current ways of collaboration provided by the OUN, are not successful; students think that discussion groups are useful but do not participate. Some of the reasons why students do not use discussion groups are:

- **Fear to fail:** Some students think that their level of knowledge is lower than the active participants of the forums.
- **Preference for alternative ways of interacting with peers:** Some students prefer other ways of collaboration such as face-to-face meetings with peers, on-campus classes, phone or e-mail.
- **Preferences for known peers:** Some students prefer interacting with known colleagues.

In the on-line questionnaire, students requested enhancing collaboration. Some students are proactive in creating support groups and reported alternative methods to collaborate. Most of the interviewed students have alternative ways, not provided by the OUN, to collaborate with peers. Collaboration with the teacher is also important, though it is not considered as essential as collaboration with peers. We conclude, thus, that meetings with the teacher could be reduced to on-campus classes every few months, to exchange of e-mails or to specific appointments to solve problems if peer contacts exist.

The information gathered from literature and the conclusions from our field research were input to the creation of a set of guidelines to support self-assessment. The starting point was the initial list of six topics related to the development of metacognition and self-assessment:

- Support learners in their self-reflection
- Provide instructional guidance
- Individualize instruction
- Support collaborative learning
- Plan and monitor the learning process
- Strengthen learner self efficacy

We consider these topics "initial clusters." After reviewing all the information gathered (literature, reports by CELSTEC, answers to the questionnaire, and interviews with experts and students), we identified topics, practices and recommendations related to self-assessment and metacognition. If the practice was related to one of the existing clusters, we added it into the cluster. If it did not, we created a new cluster and iterated. When all sources were reviewed, each cluster was labeled by a sentence which described the topics, practices, and recommendations it contained. Finally, each cluster became one guideline and the topics, practices, and recommendations included in the cluster were recorded as information related to the guideline.

## GUIDELINES TO SUPPORT SELF-ASSESSMENT

These guidelines aim to help professionals in adult education design distance learning environments which support self-assessment and development of metacognition. In our opinion, these guidelines are a valuable contribution since they are a compilation of good practices obtained through a combination of theoretical research and supporting empirical data. Obviously, every course and group of learners is different. Education professionals use their expertise to adapt our guidelines to the individual needs of the specific course. Notice that each guideline is supported by references which point to existing literature, interviews, and/or reports by CELSTEC.

1 Create a Safe Learning Environment.
   1.1 Provide students with a safe environment where they feel free to express themselves, to ask questions (Hamilton, 1996; Porter, 1997), to experiment, and to fail (Chen, 1997; Spitzer, 1998; Interviews with OUN students and experts).
2 Provide Easy to Learn/Use Interfaces.
   2.1 Mental fatigue and lack of time are the main challenges identified by students and education experts (Interviews with OUN students and Experts; Mok et al, 2006). These characteristics make time and effort optimization a priority in adult distance education, and do not make learners struggle with the interface.
3 Thoughtfully Design the Learning Environment.
   3.1 Provide structured and clear learning context. A good design can improve the quality of the learning environment by structuring the visual and interactive display of learning contexts to facilitate metacognition (Kirsh, 2005).
   3.2 Adapt the content, format, infrastructure and strategy to the individual needs of the course (Pahl, 2003).
   3.3 Create a flexible learning environment which can be used by learners with different learning styles.
      - Address different learning styles by presenting material in multiples modes such as text, graphics and audio (Cercone, 2008; Bangert, 2004; van der Veer, 1989).
      - Learners struggle to develop metacognition skills due to lack of awareness of their own learning process (Shannon, 2008). Proving learners with material presented in multiple modes can help them find out which presentation style fits them best (e.g. book versus text and pictures on screen versus video, icons vs. words, pre-structured data vs. searchable data collections).
      - Learners' achievements and satisfaction benefit from learning environments where their learning style is addressed (Dunn et al, 1995; Kirchen, 2007).
4 Provide Feedback/Guidance Throughout the Learning Process.
   4.1 Provide meaningful and in-time feedback.
      - Appropriate teacher feedback in online courses helps students develop metacognitive skills (Reingold and Rimor, 2008). Also, feedback is more effective when delivered near the time a task is performed (Kluger & DeNisi, 1996). Immediate feedback can be a motivation factor in online education (Danchak, 2002).
   4.2 Provide guidance during the learning process.
      - Teacher's support is related to the development of metacognitive skills in learners (Rimor, Reingold & Kalay, 2006).
      - Minimally guided instruction is less effective and efficient than instructional approaches that support learners during the learning process (Kirschner, Sweller and Clark, 2006). The level of support can be reduced as the learner's level of expertise increases.
      - Keep timely contact with learners. Learners need support and appreciate teachers following their progress (Puls & van den

Munkhof, 2010; Interviews met OUN students and experts.

5 Promote Self-Assessment.

5.1 Self-assessment is related to developing of metacognitive skills (Ibabe & Jauregizar, 2010) as well as to other skills such as critical thinking, self-reflection, and problem solving (Dochy, Segers, & Sluijsmans, 1999; Segers & Dochy, 2001; Thompson, Pilgrim, & Oliver, 2005).

5.2 Provide self-assessment throughout the whole learning process. Continuous self-assessment yields better outcomes than post course self-assessment or no use of self-assessment (Lopez & Kossack, 2007).

5.3 Provide different ways of self-assessment to cover all stages of the learning process.

- Using computer based-quizzes as formative self-assessment method benefits learners (Wellman, 1985; Brusilovsky & Sosnovsky, 2005; Hunter, 2007). Quizzes can be proposed at the end of a chapter or set of chapters.
- Practice exams have been identified as a good method for self-assessment before a summative evaluation (Interviews with OUN students and experts).
- Collaboration among learners and with teachers can help students assess their knowledge throughout the whole learning process (Interviews with OUN students and experts; Sandi-Urena, Cooper, & Stevens, 2010).
- Real-life cases. Presenting examples that represent real-life problems helps set goals and supports development of metacognition that helps learners evaluate future applications of knowledge and skills (Lim and Moore, 2002).

6 Promote Collaborative Learning.

6.1 Collaboration is an effective way of enhancing metacognition (Interviews with OUN students and experts; Sandi-Urena, Cooper, & Stevens, 2010) and can affect learning effectiveness of distance adult learners (Rovai, 2001; Ragan, 1999).

6.2 Provide learners with different ways of collaboration.

- Discussion groups and forums (asynchronous). Teachers can participate in the discussion but it should also be possible for learners to discuss without teacher's intervention (Interviews with OUN students and experts).
- Chats (synchronous).
- Choose between asynchronous and synchronous collaboration depending on the nature of the course and learner preferences (Interviews with OUN students and experts).
- Facilitate setting up face to face meetings among students and/or with the teacher (Interviews with OUN students and experts; (Mok et al, 2006)).
- Provide the infrastructure required to set up video conferences.

6.3 Do not promote competition among learners (Sheridan, 1989).

6.4 Facilitate the creation of small collaborative groups (de Jong & van Jolingen, 1998). Students are generally unwilling to use discussion threads to collaborate

(Interviews with OUN students and experts; Mok et al, 2006; Dunn et al, 1995; Kleinman & Enting, 2002), regardless of their experience with electronic communication (McDonald, Dorn, & McDonald, 2004). Students feel more comfortable and find it safer to ask, answer, contribute and discuss within small groups (Interviews with OUN students and experts).

6.5 Collaboration is good for motivation which also influences the cognitive process (Danchak, 2002).

7 Promote Time Management.

7.1 Lack of time, mental fatigue, and individual circumstances which interfere with the study are aspects affecting study (Interviews with OUN students and experts; Mok et al, 2006). Time management relates positively to perceived control of time, job satisfaction, and health, and negatively to stress (Claessens et al, 2007). Helping learners manage their time can have a positive effect in the learning process.

7.2 Specify the goals of the course and highlight the important issues (Mok et al, 2006).

7.3 Provide learners with estimations of time needed to solve an exercise or understand a chapter (Interviews with OUN students and experts; Mok et al, 2006).

7.4 Provide learners with time management and task allocation services when working in groups (Interviews with OUN students and experts).

8 Progress Tracking

8.1 Visualize the learner's progress in the course. Learners' capability of monitoring what they do and modifying their learning strategies according to it is related to metacognition knowledge (Boud, 1995). Furthermore, using monitoring strategies in online course can help maintain motivation (Chang, 2007).

8.2 Set milestones. Progressive calendar deadlines help avoid procrastination and improve self-fulfillment (Liu et al, 2005; McLoughlin, 2002). It also helps self-reflection (interviews with OUN students and experts).

9 Keep up Motivation.

9.1 In distance education, it is often difficult to maintain motivation because learners might feel isolated or feel that their effort is not recognized (Interviews with OUN students and experts). As motivation influences behavior (Malhotra, Galletta, & Kirsch, 2008), it is desirable to maintain motivation to have a positive attitude for learning.

9.2 Creating a sense of community can help maintain motivation (Rovai, 2002).

9.3 Recognize learners' effort. Rewarding effort and persistence helps in the learning process towards mastering a subject (Schraw & Dennison, 1994).

9.4 Use real life examples. Adult learners need to learn "in order to cope more satisfyingly with real-life tasks or problems" (Knowles, 1980). Providing real cases can raise motivation as well as prompt discussion and support self-reflection.

## TANGIBLE DESIGNS

In this section we provide an example of how to use the guidelines by creating tangible designs which use them. The most learning specific guidelines related to self-assessment, collaboration, time management and progress tracking (guidelines 5 – 8) were directly mapped into four tangible designs or services (sections 4.1 – 4.4). The rest of the guidelines were considered generic recommendations to be applied whenever relevant during the design of the services.

To place the tangible designs in context, we created an imaginary course. The nature and content is irrelevant here because—at this stage—we are interested in understanding how to apply and transform the concepts in the guidelines into tangible designs.

## Tangible Designs to Support Self-Assessment

Self-assessment is a broad concept which refers to the involvement of learners in making judgments about their own learning, their achievements and the outcomes of their learning (Boud & Falchikov, 1989). Formative assessment is a way of assessment which contributes to student learning (Roberts, 2006), usually by using feedback (Sadler, 1989). Based on the interviews with students and experts we selected two types of formative assessment: training exams and quizzes.

- **Practice exams** are sets of questions which refer to information about any part of the material. We identified two approaches to this kind of formative assessment:

The first can be called an iterative formative assessment. Students take the exam at any time, identify weak points, study those weak points and retake the exam. Theoretically, the number of correct answers will increase as the student iterates, indicating progress.

A second approach, more popular with students, is to use such exams, without iteration. After each practice exam, learners have the option to check the correct answers.

We created a flexible design that allows students to take both types of practice.

- **Quizzes** are sets of questions which refer to a particular piece of the material. Based on the questionnaire and interviews, we determined that learners have a strong preference for taking quizzes after a set of chapters. Our services are designed to prompt learners to complete quizzes after a set of chapters.

Based on learner preferences, the practice exams and quizzes provide elaborate answers, links to further material and information about which part of the course the question refers to. Relevant types of questions found in the literature[1] are:

- Multiple Choice (MC)
- Multiple Response (MR)
- Alternate choice, a two items MC
- True-false
- Multiple true-false
- Matching, a set of options followed by a set of matching statements, questions or phrases
- Context dependent item set: a scenario, vignette, table, chart, graph followed by a single item.

Some question types might be stronger related to the development of metacognition than others. Experts' opinions and previous studies (Crips and Ward, 2005) suggest that questions which have multiple right answers depending on the context might help in the development metacognitive skills because answering such questions requires critical thinking which is related to developing metacognitive skills.

In a previous study (Hunter, 2007) students reported problems with a system that simply reported that their answer was wrong. We attempted to mitigate this effect by explicitly indicating when the learner's answer is right. If the answer is wrong, the system provides an explanation of the correct answer, links to further material and a link to which part of the course the question refers to (Figure 4).

In the interviews with experts and students, two other kinds of self-assessment exercises worth

*Figure 4. A quiz could be located at the end of any chapter in the course. After the student checked his choice of answer (B in this case) the system shows which answer(s) could be correct, explicitly indicating the conditions for teach answer to be correct. In addition, the system provides pointers to additional information.*

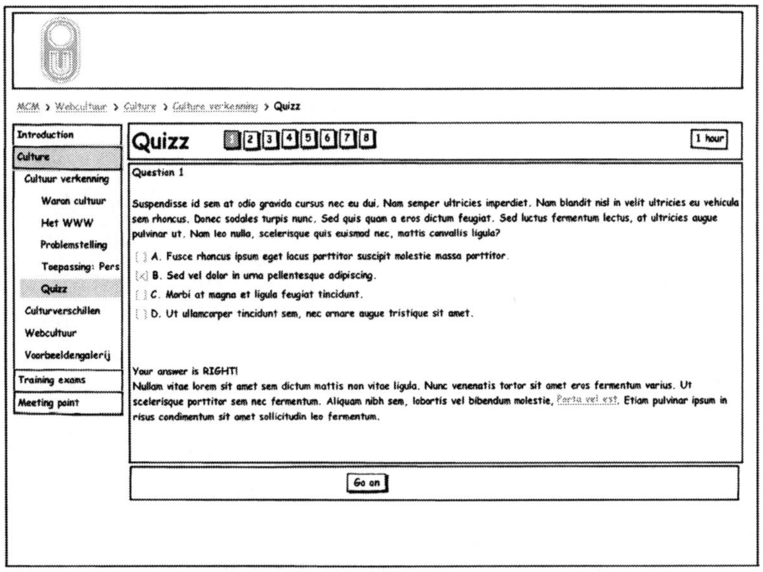


mentioning were offered, namely "real-life case exercises" and "worked-out examples." Real-life examples present situations from the real world and can be approached either individually or together with peers. This kind of exercises should prompt critical thinking and student discussions. Worked-out examples consist of the formulation of a problem and the steps needed to reach a solution. In some cases, learning from stepping through worked out examples can be more effective than be left alone solving a problem (Renkl, Atkinson, & Mier, 2000). Such exercises can also prompt discussion among students and with the teacher since there can be multiple correct answers depending on the assumptions. We propose that these kinds of exercises should be embedded into the material.

## Tangible Designs to Promote Collaborative Learning

Collaboration has been identified as a way to support the development of metacognition. Although the OUN provides ways to collaborate with other students and with teachers, the data gathered shows that participation is low. In spite of the low participation, students are aware of the potential benefits of collaboration and request more support in promoting collaboration with peers, especially face-to-face. The current ways of collaboration provided by the OUN are not tailored to the needs of the students. Some of the possible flaws are:

- The discussion groups are experienced as impersonal
- They barely support setting up face-to-face meetings
- Students prefer collaboration with people they trust

- Students do not feel engaged and the discussion groups become static
- Most students have to log into the learning management system to see posts in the discussion groups
- Some students are afraid to participate in the discussion groups because they think they might ask something irrelevant

We propose redesigning the current way of collaboration by providing services which are easy to use, personal, make students feel safe, facilitate setting up of face-to-face meetings, facilitate creation of small groups, support dynamic collaboration, support synchronous and asynchronous collaboration, and engage learners. The proposed tangible designs are:

- **Contextual discussions that appear at the bottom of each piece of learning material.** Students can comment and ask questions about the material presented in that page. We feel that this is an easy and fast way to collaborate with other students. Also, because it is possible to make anonymous comments, students should not be afraid to comment. Teachers can take part in the discussion to resolve doubts or correct misunderstandings.
- **General discussion groups aimed at solving questions about general issues such as doubts about the syllabus, examinations dates, and interface problems.** This general discussion group could be introduced at the beginning of the course together with an introductory video. In the video, the teacher may give a brief explanation of what the course is about, what is expected from the students and what they can expect from the teacher. We expect this video will help engage students and make the interface more personal.
- **Meeting point is a virtual space which provides various services to support student collaboration.** The services proposed are:
  - **Chat provides real-time (synchronous) collaboration.** Students can chat with other students in their contact list. New contacts can be added by providing the email address or through the study-buddy service (explained below).
  - **Sticky notes (seeFigure 5) provide informal collaboration among students.** It tries to mimic the situation of an on-campus class where students stick notes on a memo-board. Similarly, students can add sticky notes to a canvas. The notes have a color code which indicates the nature of the note: question, material, comment or other. Furthermore, it improves the functionality provided by the physical memo-boards by allowing students to attach files to the sticky note. This way of collaboration aims at providing an informal, fast, and intuitive way to leave short messages and prompt students to share their interpretations and summaries of the material.
- **Study-buddy (seeFigure 6) helps students to find other students to collaborate with.** Users can look for buddies based on variables such as geographical distance, number of common subjects, type of study (i.e., single course, Bachelor or Master), or kind of preferred collaboration (i.e., no preference, on-line or face to face). Students can decide whether they want to be found by others by indicating this in their settings. Students can check other students' profiles, send messages, and add them as buddies. New buddies are

*Figure 5. Whenever wanted, a student could go to the "meeting point" and choose "Sticky notes." Here the student can add color coded sticky notes indicating "comments," "questions," "material," or "other." With each new note the student can upload a PDF if needed. Also, for each new note the study should indicate whom should be allowed inspecting the note: "general" (meaning all buddies in his course group), "Private" (only the student herself), or any group the student has created (in this example there is a group "Utrecht CS"). New groups can be created by clicking on "Create Group."*

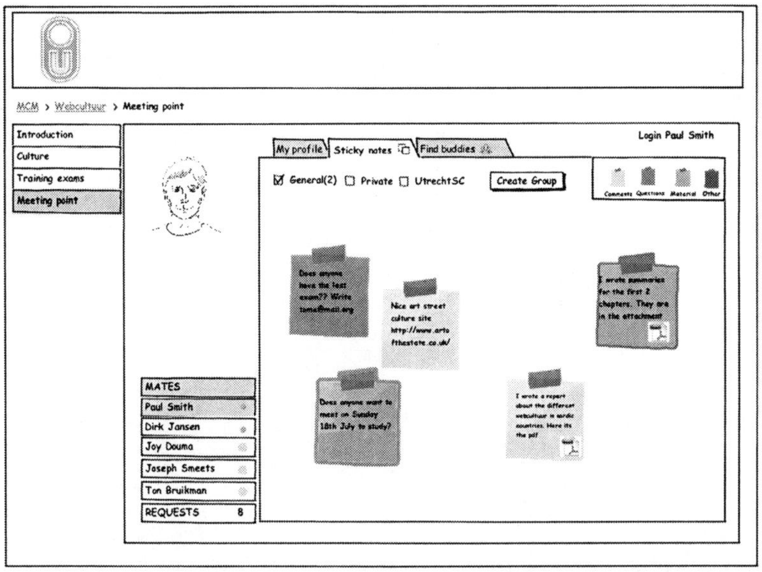


automatically added as chat contacts. This service was developed by a group of Bachelor students from the OUN Faculty of Computer Science.

## Tangible Designs to Promote Time Management

Lack of time is a major problem the OUN student faces. Based on the questionnaires and interviews we deteremined that this type of students have well developed time-management skills and would not appreciate a time-management tool to schedule static study plans. Instead, they want something to help them assess the time needed to reach their short-term goal (e.g., finish the chapter), and save time. We provide an estimation of the time needed for all the pieces of material, exercises, quizzes and practice exams. Also, we provide tools to highlight and comment on the text and save it (Figure 7). We expect students to highlight and comment on the material which will help them save time the next time they study.

Finally, we also provide a calendar which can be used individually or in groups. Group members can set milestones, events, and tasks and share them with the rest of the group.

## Tangible Designs for Progress Tracking

The questionnaire revealed that most students would appreciate a service which allows them to track their progress. Most of the interviewed students tracked their progress using external applications. A few courses provide services which allow students to track their progress. We propose two ways to track learner progress. First, the interface shows—in each piece of the material—how many single content items the student has studied and

*Figure 6. Another facility of "Meeting point" is "find buddies," where a student can identify members of his course group based on criteria like distance (e.g., in Miles), number of common courses or subjects, type of study (single course, Bachelor, Master), type of contact (on line, face to face), etc. The figure shows the student has just clicked "mates."*

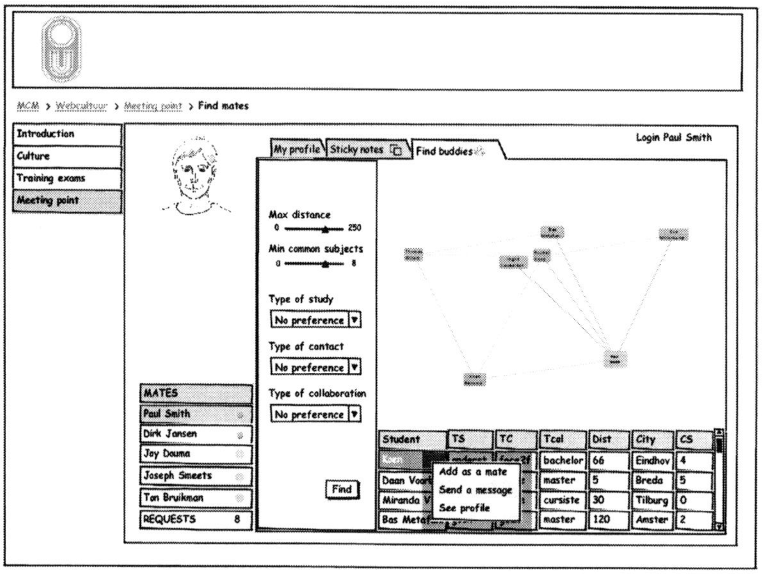


*Figure 7. This example shows how a student has highlighted some parts of the content and added a comment. The student can decide to check "I have seen this slide" right under the content. In that case the indication of how much of the content of this section ("Het WWW") has been studied. In the menu on the left, for each content section a color code indicates the amount studied so far.*

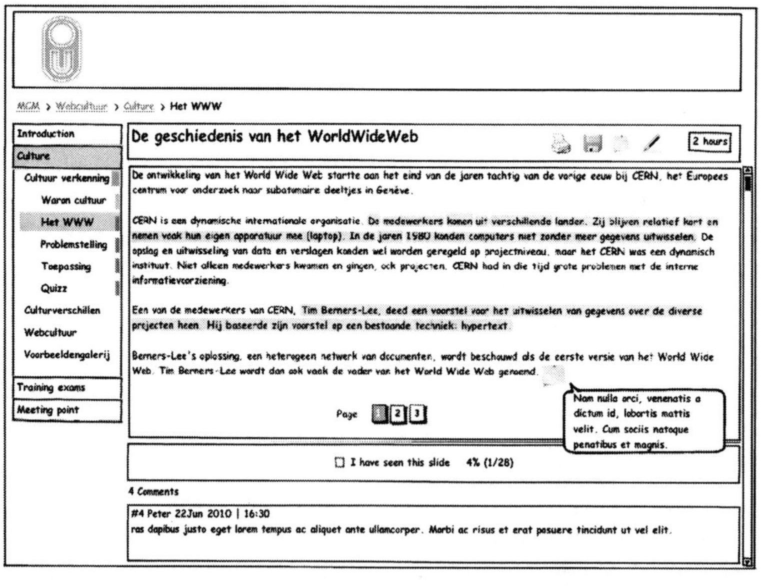

how many still need to be covered. Single content items are pieces of learning material which fit in one screenshot and contain information related to the course such as text, video clips, or images. The system keeps track of how many single content items the student has covered by keeping track of a check that a student may tick in the box "I have seen this slide" underneath the main content space on the screen.

Also, students can inspect their general progress by checking the progress tracker (Figure 8). Here they can find information about the material already covered, the practice exams and quizzes taken and how many hours they have spent logged into the system. Tracking hours spent logged in provides students with an estimation of their study time. However, this estimation might not be accurate because of idle-time where the students are logged in but are not studying. Also, students might study parts of the material by reading downloaded material or parts of books. If the concept evaluation shows that students appreciate this service, further research needs to be done on how to keep track of the time students have spent studying.

## Prototype Assessment

After creating mock-ups for each of the tangible designs, we created a video prototype illustrating how the services work and what is possible in the interface. This video prototype was intended to help gain insight in conceptual issues of the tangible designs. For the prototype evaluation, we invited OUN students and people who fit the profile of an adult distance learning student. First, we showed them the video and then conducted semi-structured interviews where we asked about general issues of the prototype. The questions asked during the interview were related to visibility, acceptability, likeability, and understanding

*Figure 8. The Meeting point also allows students to manage "My profile." Here they are able to inspect their overall progress on Reading material, Quiz exercises, Training exams, each relative to the total amount available. In addition this overview shows the Hours spend online with the course so far in relation to estimated average number of hours needed.*

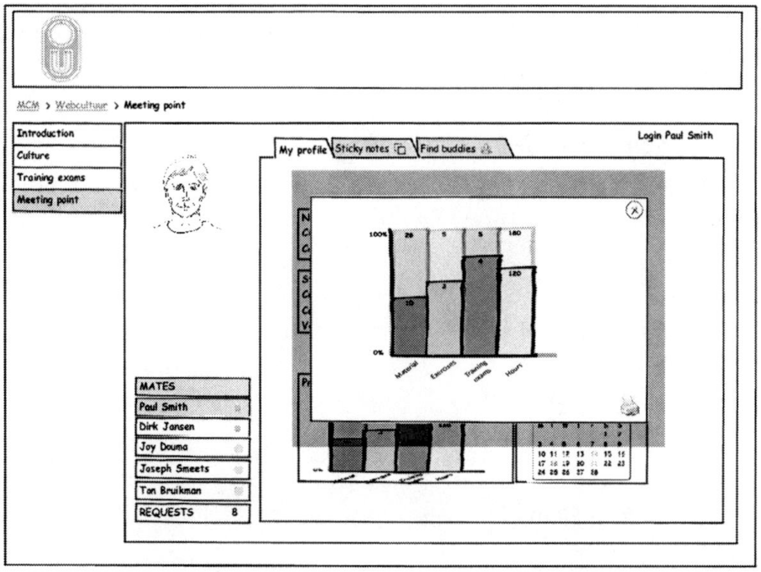

of the services as well as user opinions about the approach followed to map the concepts to tangible designs. The interview videos were analyzed and participant quotes were coded according to the service and area they were related. In this section we provide a comprehensive list of the results, with supportive quotes, arranged by service:

## Self-Assessment

Most of the interviewed users liked the practice exams and quizzes. They appreciated that the system provides elaborate answers, links to further material and information about which part of the course the question relates to. Some suggested including contextual discussions in the quizzes and practice exams (*"It would be interesting to put the forum inside the exams," "a place to go deeper than just the question and the answer, and that's important"*).

## Collaboration

Contextual discussions were well accepted (*"I think it is better to have it there in the material, in the specific part because if you put everything together it gets kind of cluttered"*). However, depending on the context of the course, just text might be not enough (*"It would be nice if the amount of media that you can put in those forums would be a bit more sophisticated than just text," "Maybe it would also be nice to be able not only to type text but also to sketch or draw to or put an arrow or a circle"*).

Contextual discussions are good to keep up motivation (*"It would be comforting for me if there was something that I didn't understand, to know I was not the only one who had difficulties," " You can see if more people have problems with the same question or in the same topic"*).

Communicating with other students by chat can be distracting and time-consuming. (*"When I think about studying I first try to do it myself before looking if somebody else is chatting or posting questions. I may have to turn it off, but I probably won't do that so it's better if it's not there," "I have to work, I have got a husband, I have got many things to do (...) I'm not going to chat with other students"*).

Although users like the visual approach of the sticky notes (*"I thought the color coding was nice," "the post-it notes look nice," "with that way of presenting, using sticky notes, it's more realistic"*), there are some issues related to them:

- Organization:
  "It can be a bit fuzzy"
  "What happens when you have many sticky notes? They could be cluttered"
  "Maybe you could have a feature where you select several notes and you turn this into a forum, so you move them to another space."
- Relevance:
  "When you receive a lot of information but you don't know what to do with it because it is too messy and you don't know what relates to what and if it is relevant";
  "You could have a kind of system where you can see what you want and hide what you don't want to see";
  "It would be nice to give more preference to some notes than to others";
  "Maybe I write something that people consider useless and it's taking the same space as something which may be very important."
- Development through time:
  "What happens when you are at the University for two years? How many of those sticky notes would you have? ";
  "I have some doubts about the organization: which ones are more recent, which ones should appear and how it will evolve over time."

- Misuse:
  "Sometimes these things get abused by people. Some people might use the sticky notes to have a conversation, while they should have this conversation through another channel."

Using sticky notes for two different purposes (i.e., commenting on your own material and posting messages in the common board) can be confusing. Some users thought that the sticky notes used to comment a piece of the material were somehow related to the sticky notes used to communicate with other students. This led to misunderstandings such as that the sticky notes used in parts of the material could be shared with other students.

The acceptance and likeability of the finding buddies service may depend on the needs of the students. (*"I would find it interesting and desirable," "I would like people to find me more than I would like to find people," "Usually I don't need other people to discuss the material," "I don't see people, I just see names"*).

There were concerns regarding the role of the teacher in the collaboration and the trustfulness of the person they collaborate with (*"You cannot confirm whether that information is right or not," "When I want to know something, I ask the professor. I don't ask another person because usually I think maybe I'm better than them"*). Most of the students like to collaborate with a small group of peers which they trust.

Reasons for not collaborating are lack of time (*"Maybe if I had more time, I would do that"*) or not knowing/trusting with whom you are collaborating with.

## Time Management

Highlight and comment was broadly accepted among the interviewed users. Many users suggested adding a functionality which would allow them to gather the highlighted text and obtain a single document out of all the pieces. (*"I would like to click one button to save all the highlighted parts in the paper," "There should be an option that allows me to grab only the marked things and to print those together, so I have a kind of summary"*).

Most users were positive about the calendar. Feelings of being observed or bother by constantly switching tasks was not an issue for the interviewed users (*"Even if the system does not tell you, you know that you are behind schedule anyway," "I think it's a nice reminder, it's not a bother"*)

The teacher could also help by setting milestones in the calendar like exams and deadlines for exercises (*"It could be useful that the teacher himself puts some deadlines", "One thing is how you organize your time, other thing are the deadlines which are not up to you"*).

The acceptance and likeability of providing an estimation of the time needed were diverse. Some users thought that it would be very useful (*"Sometimes you are reading stuff and you do not know how long it will be," "I have to stop and later it takes more time to try remember the stuff," "I can set some personal goals for time to help time management"*) but others thought they were not appropriate (*"How many hours the teacher think you should spend and how many are spent, if I was a teacher I would never say that" "I would not give such expectations to people because maybe it is unfair"*).

## Progress Tracker

The progress tracker was generally well accepted among the students (*"I think the progress tracker is important for the discipline you need"*), although some students showed concerns about the privacy issues of this service (*"It might bother me if it was telling others also"*)

This service could be further developed by showing more detailed information (*"If I could get a journal of my activities rather than just a very general statistical overview then I would think this was quite useful"*) and using individual information of the learners (*"It could be useful but it has to be somehow related," "maybe the system could suggest, you were supposed to read 40 pages and you read 30 and it gives you a kind of new schedule. From now on you don't have to read 10 pages per day but you have to read 12," "If I can see that I cover more material on Tuesday and more material on Wednesday then maybe I can also think why that was and correct stuff about my routine and the way I work with the site"*)

## CONCLUSION AND SUGGESTIONS FOR DESIGN AND APPLICATION

Self-assessment is important for learning and particularly important for adult distance learning since studying at a distance might negatively influence in the ability to assess one's knowledge. "Knowing what you know" (i.e., metacognition) plays an important ole in self-assessment and is the focus of this research. The development of metacognition can be externally influenced by teacher feedback, resources offered during the course, and exercises adapted to individually acquired knowledge. No correlations were found between time available or level of education, and variables related to the development of metacognition, which suggests that the development of metacognition can be equally supported regardless of the time available or the previous level of education of the learner.

Quizzes and training exams are the most popular and appreciated self-assessment methods. Quizzes and practice exams with elaborated answers and further information about the topic targeted in the question are highly appreciated by students because they *"can learn from the answers."* Providing questions with multiple correct answers depending on the context is a valid and valuable method to support the development of metacognition.

Collaboration is an important issue in the development of metacognition. The interviews with users reaffirm what the literature suggests: development of metacognitive skills can be supported by collaborating with other students. The presented tangible designs aim to overcome this problem by creating dynamic, safe, and easy to use ways of collaboration as well as supporting the set up of face-to-face meetings. Users liked the proposed designs and perceived them as an added value to a web-based course. However, design issues arose related to sorting, storing, and visualizing the evolution across time with the sticky notes. We recommend systematic research and assessment on these issues to accompany actual design.

In general, the adult students have well-developed time-management skills but their lack of time makes them frequently run behind schedule. Some students use time-management tools. However, due to often interfering circumstances which force them to constantly modify their schedule, these tools frequently become more a burden than a help. The interviewed users did not perceive our time-management support (i.e., providing estimations of the time needed, highlighting and commenting on the material, and calendar) as a bother. Instead, these were perceived as useful and convenient for time-management.

The progress tracker was broadly accepted among the interviewed students and during evaluation of the prototype. However, possible privacy issues were signaled during the evaluation. Students do not want other students to be able to see their progress. These results reassert that the guidelines suggesting "not promoting competition among students" and "providing a safe environment" are important when designing learning environments. It is important that students securely know which information they are sharing and how to modify their sharing options.

This research provides a base for the creation of self-assessment support in distance learning.

Modern technology allows this support and facilitation even if the learners differ in learning styles, learning context, and learning goals. Our guidelines, based on literature and accumulated empirical research, can be implemented in usable support tools. Our current version of the prototypes for this should be considered only the start.

After this initial exploration and evaluation of the services, we should be aware not all issues are covered.

First of all, the current analysis is mainly based on self-report survey data. A next step has to be to validate our findings against additional data like analysis of graduation rates after implementation of our self-assessment support. We will also need to collect and analyze demographic correlations of grades / attrition / participation with survey responses.

Secondly, we suggest future studies on possible adaptations, among which could be:

- Provide a main navigation menu with a clear structure so students can easily identify the different parts of the course and the provided services: (1) Introduction; (2) Content; (3) Practice exams; and (4) Meeting point.
- Allow students to create a single file which contains all the highlighted parts of the material. This file can be saved and printed.
- Add contextual discussion groups to the quizzes and practice exams.
- Add more options to the contextual discussions, such as formulas, drawings, or audio files.
- Allow teachers to set milestones in student calendars.
- Develop the functionality of the progress tracker. Show a more detailed picture of the learning progress, provide recommendations based on the individual progress of the learner, and relate the current and previous progress are some of the suggestions given by the users.
- Define a way to organize, manage through time and give preference to the sticky notes. The similarity between sticky notes used to comment on pieces of the material and sticky notes used as an informal way of collaboration led to misunderstandings about the functionality of both services. We think this is caused by, both, similar appearance and use of the same name to refer to different services. Changing the name and the appearance of the functionalities will prevent misunderstandings.
- Conduct further research on the "Find buddies" service. The current (working) prototype is developed by OUN students for a specific Bachelor project. Research has to be done on issues relevant to search-parameters for the context of application. Privacy issues also need to be addressed.

After new design like the ones suggested above, perform user testing—preferably interviewing students—and iterate as needed. Implement the prototyped services and test the new design incorporated in an actual course. A feasible testing method is the Success Case Method (SCM), an evaluation technique developed by Brinkerhoff (2003). Initially, it was used to investigate why some practices were working for some individuals but not for others. SCM is particularly useful for assessing social practices, outcomes and impacts in areas which are difficult to quantify. SCM has been successfully applied in the evaluation of services developed for distance higher learning at the Open University in UK. It relies on the hypothesis that the majority of the data collected follows a normal distribution, with examples of 'absolute success' and 'absolute failure' at the extreme ends. The core of the distribution contains what the majority perceives as 'satisfactory.' However, the method focuses on the extreme ends to assess the main success and failures of the system. The SCM evaluation technique is based on five steps:

1. Developing models of what 'success' and 'non-success' mean. These models should be thoughtfully developed. Variables to measure success and non-success should be related to metacognition development indicators. To measure the development of metacognition it is important to have a control group.
2. Identifying the success and non-success cases by questionnaires to the students.
3. Identifying students at the extremes.
4. Interviewing those students.
5. Documenting the findings and providing recommendations.

This method is suitable even if it requires many respondents to answer a relatively long list of questions (which can be done through e-mail or web based tools), since it requires only a small group of students to be actually interviewed. We experienced that it is easy to obtain students' feedback from questionnaires, but hard to contact remote adult students face-to-face.

## REFERENCES

Alexander, S. (2001). E-learning developments and experiences. *Education + Training, 43*(4/5), 240–248. doi:10.1108/00400910110399247

Azevedo, R. (2005). Using hypermedia as a metacognitive tool for enhancing students learning? The role of self regulated learning. *Educational Psychologist, 40*(4), 199–209. doi:10.1207/s15326985ep4004_2

Bandura, A. (1977). Self-efficacy: Toward a unifying theory of behavioral change. *Psychological Review, 84*, 191–215. doi:10.1037/0033-295X.84.2.191

Bandura, A., & Wood, R. E. (1989). Effect of perceived controllability and performance standards on self-regulation of complex decision making. *Journal of Personality and Social Psychology, 56*, 805–814. doi:10.1037/0022-3514.56.5.805

Bangert, A. W. (2004). The seven principles of good practice: A framework for evaluating online teaching. *The Internet and Higher Education, 7*, 217–232. doi:10.1016/j.iheduc.2004.06.003

Boud, D. (Ed.). (1995). *Enhancing learning through self assessment*. London, UK: Kogan Page Limited.

Boud, D., & Falchikov, N. (1989). Quantitative studies of self-assessment in higher education: A critical analysis of findings. *Higher Education, 18*, 529–549. doi:10.1007/BF00138746

Brinkerhoff, R. O. (2003). *The success case method: Find out quickly what's working and what's not*. San Francisco, CA: Berrett-Koehler.

Brusilovsky, P., & Sosnovsky, S. (2005). Engaging students to work with self-assessment questions: A study of two approaches, *Proceedings of 10th Annual Conference on Innovation and Technology in Computer Science Education* (pp. 251-255). New York, NY: ACM Press.

Case, J., Gunstone, R., & Lewis, A. (2001). Students' metacognitive development in an innovative second year chemical engineering course. *Research in Science Education, 31*, 313–335. doi:10.1023/A:1013113807788

Cercone, K. (2008). Characteristics of adult learners with implications for online learning design. *AACE Journal, 16*(2), 137–159.

Chang, M. (2007). Enhancing web-based language learning through self-monitoring. *Journal of Computer Assisted Learning, 23*(3), 187–196. doi:10.1111/j.1365-2729.2006.00203.x

Chen, L.-L. (1997). Distance delivery systems in terms of pedagogical considerations: A reevaluation. *Educational Technology*, (July/August): 34–37.

Claessens, B. J. C., Van Eerde, W., Rutte, C. G., & Roe, R. A. (2007). A review of the time management literature. *Personnel Review*, *36*(2), 255–276. doi:10.1108/00483480710726136

Coutihno, S. (2008). Self-efficacy, metacognition, and performance. *North American Journal of Psychology*, *10*(1), 165–172.

Crips, V., & Ward, C. (2005, July). *The PePCAA Project: Formative scenario-based CAA in psychology for teachers*. Paper presented at the Ninth International Computer Assisted Assessment Conference, Loughborough University.

Danchak, M. (2002). Bringing affective behavior to e-learning. *The Technology Source*, MIVU, September/October 2002. Retrieved September 30, 2010, from http://technologysource.org/article/bringing_affective_behavior_to_elearning/.

De Jong, T., & van Joolingen, W. R. (1998). Scientific discovery learning with computer simulations of conceptual domains. *Review of Educational Research, 68,* 179-201.

Dochy, F., Segers, M., & Sluijsmans, D. (1999). The use of self-, peer- and co-assessment: A review. *Studies in Higher Education*, *24*(3), 331–350. doi:10.1080/03075079912331379935

Dunn, R., Giggs, S. A., Olson, J., Beasley, M., & Gorman, B. S. (1995). A meta-analytic validation of the Dunn and Dunn Model of learning preferences. *The Journal of Educational Research*, *88*(6), 353–362. doi:10.1080/00220671.1995.9941181

Georghiades, P. (2006). The role of metacognitive activities in the contextual use of primary pupils' conceptions of science. *Research in Science Education, 36*(1–2), 29. doi:10.1007/s11165-004-3954-8

Goodman, L. A., & Kruskal, W. H. (1979). *Measures of association for cross classifications*. New York, NY: Springer-Verlag.

Hamilton, D. (1996). *Learning about education: An unfinished curriculum*. Bristol, UK: Open University Press.

Hunter, A. (2007, September). *Using an online formative assessment framework to enhance student engagement: A learning outcomes approach.* Paper presented at the 15th Improving Student Learning Symposium, Trinity College, Dublin, Ireland.

Ibabe, I., & Jauregizar, J. (2010). Online self-assessment with feedback and metacognitive knowledge. *Higher Education*, *59*(2), 243–258. doi:10.1007/s10734-009-9245-6

Keefe, J. W. (1979). Learning style: An overview. In *NASSP's Student learning styles: Diagnosing and prescribing programs* (pp. 1–17). Reston, VA: National Association of Secondary School Principals.

Kirchen, J. (2007). Investigating learning styles in the online educational environment. In *Proceedings of the 8th ACM SIGITE Conference on Information Technology Education (SIGITE '07)* (pp. 127-134). New York, NY: ACM Digital Library.

Kirschner, P. A., Sweller, J., & Clark, R. E. (2006). Why minimal guidance during instruction does not work: An analysis of the failure of constructivist, discovery, problem-based, experiential, and inquiry-based teaching. *Educational Psychologist*, *41*(2), 75–86. doi:10.1207/s15326985ep4102_1

Kirsh, D. (2005). Metacognition, distributed cognition and visual design. In Gardenfors, P., Johansson, P., & Mahwah, N. J. (Eds.), *Cognition, education, and communication technology* (pp. 147–180). Mahwah, NJ: L. Erlbaum Associates.

Kleinman, J., & Entin, E. (2002, April). Comparison of in-class and distance-learning students' performance and attitudes in an introductory computer science course. *The Journal of Computing in Small Colleges*, *17*(2), 206–219.

Kluger, A. N., & DeNisi, A. (1996). The effects of feedback interventions on performance: A historical review, a meta-analysis, and a preliminary feedback intervention theory. *Psychological Bulletin*, *119*, 254–284. doi:10.1037/0033-2909.119.2.254

Knowles, M. (1970). Andragogy: An emerging technology for adult learning. In Tight, M. (Ed.), *Education for adults: Adult learning and education*. London, UK: Croom Helm.

Knowles, M. S. (1980). *The modern practice of adult education: From andragogy to pedagogy*. Englewood Cliffs, NJ: Cambridge Adult Education.

Larkin, S. (2006). Collaborative group work and individual development of metacognition in the early years. *Research in Science Education*, *36*, 7–27. doi:10.1007/s11165-006-8147-1

Lim, E. L., & Moore, D. L. (2002). Problem-solving in geometry: Comparing the effects of non-specific instruction and conventional worked examples. *Educational Psychology: An International Journal of Experimental Educational Psychology*, *22*(5), 591–612.

Liu, X., Bonk, C. J., Magjuka, R. J., Lee, S., & Su, B. (2005). Exploring four dimensions of online instructor roles: A program level case study. *Journal of Asynchronous Learning Networks*, *9*(4), 29–48.

Lopez, R., & Kossack, S. (2007). Effects of recurring use of self-assessment in university courses. *The International Journal of Learning*, *14*(4), 203–216.

Lumana. (2006). *Metacognition and reflection*. Retrieved 30 September, 2010, from http://www.lumana.com/Education_Director_Website/Personal_Projects/Instructional_Design/research/Metacognition/Chapter2_Gama.pdf.

Malhotra, Y., Galletta, D., & Kirsch, L. (2008). How endogenous motivations influence user intentions: Beyond the dichotomy of extrinsic and intrinsic user motivations. *Journal of Management Information Systems*, *25*(1), 267–299. doi:10.2753/MIS0742-1222250110

McDonald, M., Dorn, B., & McDonald, G. (2004). A statistical analysis of student performance in online computer science courses. In *Proceedings of the 35th SIGCSE Technical Symposium on Computer Science Education* (pp. 71–74). New York, NY: ACM Press.

McLoughlin, C. (2002). Learner support in distance and networked learning environments: Ten dimensions for successful design. *Distance Education*, *23*, 149–162. doi:10.1080/0158791022000009178

Means, B., Toyama, Y., Murphy, R., Bakia, M., & Jones, K. (2009). *Evaluation of evidence-based practices in online learning: A meta-analysis and review of online-learning studies*. Washington, DC: U.S. Department of Education.

Mok, M. M. C., Lung, C. L., Cheng, D. P. W., Cheung, R. H. P., & Ng, M. L. (2006). Self-assessment in higher education: experience in using a metacognitive approach in five case studies. *Assessment & Evaluation in Higher Education*, *31*(4), 415–433. doi:10.1080/02602930600679100

Pahl, C. (2003). Managing evolution and change in web-based teaching and learning environments. *Computers & Education*, *40*(2), 99–114. doi:10.1016/S0360-1315(02)00100-8

Paris, S. G., & Paris, A. H. (2001). Classroom applications of research on self-regulated learning. *Educational Psychology, 36*(2), 89–101. doi:10.1207/S15326985EP3602_4

Porter, L. R. (1997). *Creating the virtual classroom distance learning with the Internet.* New York, NY: John Wiley & Sons.

Puls, J., & van den Munkhof, R. (2010). *Studentinzicht VII.* Heerlen, The Netherlands: Open Universiteit CELSTEC.

Ragan, L. C. (1999). Good teaching is good teaching: An emerging set of guiding principles and practices for the design and development of distance education. *Cause/Effect, 22*(1). Retrieved September 30, from http://net.educause.edu/ir/library/html/cem/cem99/cem9915.html.

Reingold, R., & Rimor, R. (2008). Instructor's scaffolding in support of student's metacognition through a teacher education online course - A case study. *Journal of Online Interactive Learning, 7*(2), 139–151.

Renkl, A., Atkinson, R. K., & Maier, U. H. (2000). From studying examples to solving problems: Fading worked-out solution steps helps learning. In L. Gleitman & A. K. Joshi (Eds.), *Proceeding of the 22nd Annual Conference of the Cognitive Science Society* (pp. 393–398). Mahwah, NJ: Lawrence Erlbaum Associates, Inc.

Rimor, R., Reingold, R., & Kalay, A. (2006, July). *The relationship between students' metacognition and instructor's scaffolding in online academic courses.* Paper presented at the 2nd Meeting of EARLI SIG 16 Metacognition, University of Cambridge, Faculty of Education, Cambridge, UK. Retrieved September 15, 2006, from http://www.educ.cam.ac.uk/download/MetacogAbstr.pdf.

Roberts, T. S. (2006). The use of multiple choice tests for formative and summative assessment. *ACM International Conference Proceeding Series, 165,* 175–180.

Rovai, A. (April, 2002). Building sense of community at a distance. *International Review of Research in Open and Distance Learning (IRRODL), 3*(1). Retrieved September 30, 2010, from http://www.irrodl.org/index.php/irrodl/article/viewArticle/79/152.

Rovai, A. P. (2001). Building classroom community at a distance: A case study. *Educational Technology Research and Development, 49*(4), 33–48. doi:10.1007/BF02504946

Sadler, D. R. (1989). Formative assessment and the design of instructional systems. *Instructional Science, 18,* 119–144. doi:10.1007/BF00117714

Sandi-Urena, S., Cooper, M. M., & Stevens, R. H. (2010). Enhancement of metacognition use and awareness by means of a collaborative intervention. *International Journal of Science Education, 33*(3).

Schön, D. A. (1983). *The reflective practitioner.* New York, NY: Basic Books.

Schraw, G., & Dennison, R. S. (1994). Assessing metacognitive awareness. *Contemporary Educational Psychology, 19,* 143–154. doi:10.1006/ceps.1994.1013

Segers, M., & Dochy, F. (2001). New assessment forms in problem-based learning: The value-added of the students' perspective. *Studies in Higher Education, 26*(3), 327–343. doi:10.1080/03075070120076291

Shannon, S. (2008). Using metacognitive strategies and learning styles to create self-directed learners. *Wayne State College Institute for Learning Styles Journal, 1,* 14-28.

Sheridan, J. (1989). Rethinking andragogy: The case for collaborative learning in continuing higher education. *Journal of Continuing Higher Education, 37*(2), 2–6. doi:10.1080/07377366.1989.10401167

Spitzer, D. R. (1998). Rediscovering the social context of distance learning. *Educational Technology*, (March/April): 52–56.

StateUniversity.com. (2010). *Individualized instruction - Pace, method, content, examples of individualized instruction, final issues.* Retrieved September 30, 2010, from http://education.stateuniversity.com/pages/2085/Individualized-Instruction.html.

Thompson, G., Pilgrim, A., & Oliver, K. (2005). Self-assessment and reflective learning for first year university geography students: A simple guide or simply misguided? *Journal of Geography in Higher Education, 29*, 403–420. doi:10.1080/03098260500290959

Trueman, M., & Hartley, J. (1996). A comparison between the time-management skills and academic performance of mature and traditional-entry university students. *Higher Education, 32*(2), 199–215. doi:10.1007/BF00138396

U.S. Department of Education. (2009). *Evaluation of evidence-based practices in online learning: A meta-analysis and review of online learning studies.* U.S. Department of Education Office of Planning, Evaluation, and Policy Development Policy and Program Studies Service. Retrieved September 30, 2010, from http://www.educause.edu/Resources/EvaluationofEvidenceBased-Pract/174235.

van der Veer, G. C. (1989). Individual differences and the user interface. *Ergonomics, 32*, 1431–1449. doi:10.1080/00140138908966916

Wellman, H. M. (1985b). The origins of metacognition. In Forrest-Pressley, D. L., MacKinnon, G. E., & Waller, T. G. (Eds.), *Metacognition, cognition and human performance* (*Vol. 1*, pp. 1–31). Orlando, FL: Academic Press.

# Chapter 11
# Unconstrained Walking Plane to Virtual Environment for Non-Visual Spatial Learning

**Kanubhai K. Patel**
*Ahmedabad University, India*

**Sanjay Kumar Vij**
*Sardar Vallabhbhai Patel Institute of Technology, India*

## ABSTRACT

*We have integrated the treadmill-style locomotion interface, called the unconstrained walking plane (UWP), with virtual environment (VE) to enhance spatial learning. This setting allows for a new type of experience, whereby participants with visual disability can explore VE for unattended non-visual spatial learning (NSL) and to develop cognitive maps of it. Although audio and haptic interface has been studied for NSL, nothing is known about the use of locomotion interface for supporting NSL. The structure and control mechanism of the device are presented. Discussion of advantages and limitations of the interface are given. Different types of locomotion interface to virtual environment with their constraints and benefits are discussed briefly. The purpose of the current study is to evaluate the efficacy of the UWP for VE exploration which leads to enhancement of unattended spatial learning and thereby enhancing the mobility skills of visually impaired people (VIP). We report an experiment that investigates the efficacy of UWP for VE exploration during turning and straight walking mode.*

## INTRODUCTION

Every year about hundred thousand new blind cases are added to an estimated 314 million visually impaired people in the world, 45 million of them are blind. It includes around 15 million from India. The inability to travel independently around and interact with the wider world is one of the most significant handicaps that can be caused by visual impairment or blindness, second only to the inability to communicate through reading and writing. The difficulties in the mobility of visually impaired people in new or unfamiliar locations are caused by the fact that spatial information is not

DOI: 10.4018/978-1-61350-320-1.ch011

Copyright © 2012, IGI Global. Copying or distributing in print or electronic forms without written permission of IGI Global is prohibited.

fully available to them as against it being available to sighted people. Visually impaired people (VIP) are thus handicapped to gather this crucial information, which leads to great difficulties in generating efficient cognitive maps of spaces and, therefore, in navigating efficiently within new or unfamiliar spaces. Consequently, many blind people become passive, depending on others for assistance. More than 30% of the blind do not ambulate independently outdoors (Clark-Carter, D., Heyes, A., & Howarth, C., 1986; Lahav, O., & Mioduser, D., 2003).

This constraint can be overcome by providing some means to generate cognitive mapping of spaces and of the possible paths for navigating through these spaces virtually, which are essential for the development of efficient orientation and mobility skills. Reasonable number of repeated visits to the new space leads to formation of its cognitive map subconsciously. Thus, a good number of researchers focused on using technology to simulate visits to a new space for building cognitive maps. It need not be emphasized that the strength and efficiency of cognitive map building process is directly proportional to the closeness between the simulated and real-life environments. However, most of the simulated environments reported by earlier researchers don't fully represent reality. The challenge, therefore, is to enhance and enrich simulated environment so as to create a near real-life experience.

The fundamental goal of developing virtual environment for VIP is to complement or replace sight by another modality. The visual information therefore needs to be simplified and transformed so as to allow its rendition through alternate sensory channels, usually auditory, haptic, or auditory-haptic. One of the methods to enhance and enrich simulated environment is to use virtual reality along with advanced technologies such as computer haptics, brain-computer interface (BCI), speech processing and sonification. Such technologies can be used to provide learning environment to visually impaired people to create cognitive maps of unfamiliar areas. We present various research studies including ours for communicating spatial knowledge to VIP and evaluating it through virtual environment (VE), and thereby enhancing spatial behaviour in real environment. Different types of locomotion interface to virtual environment with their constraints and benefits are discussed briefly. Virtual environment provides for creation of simulated objects and events with which people can interact. Essentially, virtual environment allows users to interact with a computer-simulated environment. Users can interact with a virtual environment either through the use of standard input devices such as a keyboard, joystick and mouse, or through multi-modal devices such as a wired glove, the Polhemus boom arm, or else locomotion interfaces.

A locomotion interface is an input-output device to simulate walking interactions with virtual environments without restricting human mobility in a confined space such as a room. The locomotion interface is used to simulate walking from one location to another location. The locomotion interface can make a person participate actively in virtual environments and feel real spatial sense by generating appropriate unconstrained walking plane or ground surfaces.

The device is needed to be of a limited size, allow a user to walk on it and provide a sensation as if he is walking on an unconstrained walking plane. Locomotion interface with unidirectional as well as omni-directional treadmills create infinite surface by use of motion floors. But realization of the motion floors requires bulky or complex drive mechanism, thereby restricting practical use of locomotion interfaces. Secondly, it presents a problem of stability. As a result, such devices induce a kind of fear psychosis leading to difficulties in cognitive map formation. We have proposed a locomotion interface which reduces to a minimum these constraints. Our proposed design of a locomotion interface to the virtual environment for mobility learning is aimed at building improved cognitive map thereby enhancing mobility skills of persons with limited vision. A major design goal is to allow VIP to walk safely on the device with a limited size, and to give them the sensation of walking on an unconstrained walking plane. The device proposed by us uses manual treadmill with handles to provide support, if required, thus allowing walking with assured stability.

To the best of our knowledge, no researcher has used treadmill-styled locomotion interface to enhance the spatial learning of VIP. Even though in the use of VE with the visually impaired person, the visual channel is missing, the other sensory channels can still lead to benefits for VIP as they engage in a range of activities in a simulator relatively free from the limitations imposed by their disability. In our proposed design, they can do so in safe manner. We describe the design of a locomotion interface to VE to acquire spatial knowledge and thereby to structure cognitive maps of an area. Non-visual virtual environment is used to provide spatial information to VIP and prepare them for independent travel. The locomotion interface is used to simulate walking of visually impaired. The device is needed to be of a limited size, allow a user to walk on it and provide a sensation as if he is walking on an unconstrained plane.

Locomotion interface with unidirectional as well as omni-directional treadmills create infinite surface by use of motion floors. But realization of the motion floors requires bulky or complex drive mechanism, thereby restricting practical use of locomotion interfaces. Secondly, it presents a problem of stability, especially while using these interfaces for simulating virtual walking of visually impaired people for spatial learning through virtual environments. As a result, such devices induce a kind of fear psychosis leading to difficulties in exploring virtual environment and thereby in cognitive map formation. A design of locomotion interface which reduces to a minimum these constraints is presented by first undertaking a literature review of the material existing in the area of locomotion interfaces and computer science. Our proposed design of a locomotion interface to the virtual environment for spatial learning is aimed at providing unconstrained walking plane for building improved cognitive map and thereby enhancing mobility skills of persons with limited vision. A major design goal is to allow visually impaired people to walk safely on the device with a limited size, and to give them the sensation of walking on an unconstrained plane. The device proposed by us uses manual treadmill with handles to provide support, if required, thus allowing walking with assured stability.

We believe that by incorporating perspectives from cognitive and experimental psychology, mechanical and electronics engineering, to computer science, this chapter will appeal to a wide range of audience - particularly computer engineers concerned with assistive technologies; professionals interested in locomotion interface to the virtual environments, including computer engineers, architect, city-planner, cartographer, high-tech artists, and mobility trainer; and psychologists involved in the study of spatial cognition, cognitive behaviour, and human-computer interfaces.

## LOCOMOTION INTERFACE

Figure 1 shows the overall diagram of human walking interactions with locomotion interface in computer simulated virtual environments. When a human walks on the locomotion interface, the walking motions of the human are recognized by several sensors such as motion trackers attached to the human body, and force sensors mounted on the locomotion interface. Then, the sensed information is used by the locomotion interface for generation of infinite unconstrained surfaces for continuous walking and the virtual environments for scene update according to motions of the human walking. Then, by feedback of visual and locomotion information, a human can immerse into virtual environments.

*Figure 1. Walking interaction using a locomotion interface*

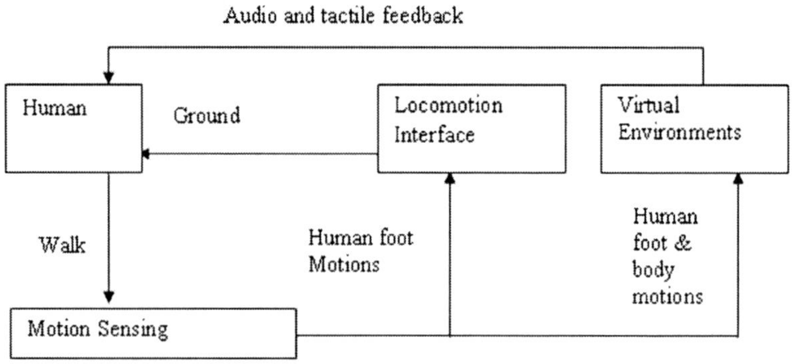


Locomotion interface can be used in several application fields such as virtual design, training, exercises, and walking rehabilitation. Locomotion interface can be used to help designers by providing a walk through modeled buildings, airplanes, ships, etc. Moreover, it can be applied to train fire fighters or army personnel, which are very difficult to do in real situations. For entertainment purpose, it can be used for winter sports such as ski and skates as well as general exercise such as promenade. Without locomotion interface, it is difficult to fabricate various terrain models. More applications using locomotion interfaces are well summarized in (Hollerbach, 2002).

Good number of devices has been developed over the last two decades to integrate locomotion interfaces with virtual environments. We have categorized the most common virtual locomotion approaches as follow:

1. Treadmills-style interface (Darken, Cockayne & Carmein, 1997; Hollerbach, Xu, Christensen, & Jacobsen,2000; Iwata & Yoshida, 1999; De Luca, Mattone, & Giordano, 2007),
2. pedaling devices (such as bicycles or unicycles) (Iwata & Fuji, 1996),
3. walking-in-place devices (Sibert, Templeman, Page, Barron, McCune & Denbrook, 2004; Whitten et al, 2008),
4. the motion foot pad (Iwata, Yano, Fukushima, & Noma, 2005),
5. actuated shoes (Iwata, Yano, & Tomioka, 2006),
6. the string walker (Iwata, Yano, & Tomiyoshi, 2007), and
7. Finger walking-in-place devices.

Treadmills in general cancel human walking motions by moving belts in the direction opposite to that of the human walking. The Sarcos Treadport (Christensen et. al., 2000) with linear treadmills allows a user to walk, run, and kneel at level ground or slopes. In addition, due to the mechanical tether that provided missing inertial forces, it is not possible to make the acceleration phase of locomotion energetically equivalent to the ground locomotion without applying forces to the body. Darken et al. (Darken et al., 1997) developed omni-directional treadmill (ODT) that is composed of two independent roller-belts, which are made from approximately 3400 separate rollers. But, it was reported that the walking on the ODT was not stable due to a misalignment between the direction of forward motion and the centering motion of the belt. Iwata (Iwata, 1999) developed omni-directional walking device using "Torus Treadmill," which is composed 12 sets of treadmills connected side-by-side and driven in a perpendicular direction. Mechanically, even though these 2D treadmills can allow the user to perform turning motions on these interfaces, they are highly complex and have difficulties in generating fast upright motions.

Wang et. al (Wang et. al., 2003) suggested the powered offset caster transmission to realize the omni-directional motion. Casters are placed on the top of a large piece of cloth material and move the cloth in a planar motion (x, y, and theta). Also, the deformable belt system of ATR's treadmill systems (Noma et. al., 2000) was suggested to allow uneven slopes to be displayed.

The basic idea used in these approaches is that a locomotion interface should cancel the user's self motion in a place to allow the user to move in a large virtual space. A treadmill can cancel the user's motion by moving its belt in the opposite direction. Its main advantage is that it does not require a user to wear any kind of devices as required in some other locomotion devices. However, it is difficult to control the belt speed in order to keep the user from falling off. Some treadmills can adjust the belt speed based on the user's motion. There are mainly two challenges in using the treadmills. The first one is the user's stability problem while the second is to sense and change the direction of walking. The belt in a passive treadmill is driven by the backward push generated while walking. This process effectively balances the user and keeps him from falling off.

The problem of changing the walking direction is addressed by Brooks, F. P. Jr., (1986) and Hirose, M. & Yokoyama, K., (1997), who employed a handle to change the walking direction. Iwata, H. & Yoshida, Y., (1997) developed a 2D infinite plate that can be driven in any direction and Darken, R. P., Cockayne, W.R., & Carmein, D., (1997) proposed an Omni directional treadmill using mechanical belt. Noma, H. & Miyasato, T., (1998) used the treadmill which could turn on a platform to change the walking direction. Iwata, H. & Fujji, T., (1996) used a different approach by developing a series of sliding interfaces. The user was required to wear special shoes and a low friction film was put in the middle of shoes. Since the user was supported by a harness or rounded handrail, the foot motion was canceled passively when the user walked. The method using active footpad could simulate various terrains without requiring the user to wear any kind of devices.

Other than treadmill-style interface, pedaling devices (Brogan, 1997) with an instrumented bicycle was employed to simulate the effect of going up or down hills. Iwata and Fujii suggested sliding machines (Iwata & Fuji, 1996) that utilize shoes with low-friction films on the soles and a brake pad on the toe to stop swing phase. Roston and Peurach (Roston & Peurach, 1997) proposed a "Whole Body Display" that has 3-dof motions. They utilized 3-dof parallel device driven by sliders. Iwata (Iwata, 1999) developed the "Gait Master" that consists of two 3-dof (x, y, and z) Gough-Stewart Platforms and a turntable. Even though the Gait Master utilized high rigidity and multi-DOF motion of a parallel device, the available stride distance is only 30cm, which is not large enough to allow natural walking with upright walking motion. Schmidt et al. (Schmidt et al., 2002) suggested a serial-parallel hybrid robotic walking simulator for neurological rehabilitation with 3-dof motions of sagittal plane at each foot. The device was composed of 2-dof translational parallel mechanisms, on which an electric motor was used to provide one rotation. Noma (Noma & Miyasato, 1998; Noma & Miyasato, 1999) suggested the turning strategy to change the walking direction by using a treadmill platform mounted on a turntable. The user's turning motions during walking were canceled by rotating the turntable of the interface according to user's feet motion in swing phase. However, since their device had limitation for rotation angle, the system should stop and return the device to the neutral position when rotation approaches the limit. Bouguila et al. (Bouguila et al., 2003) developed the turntable type locomotion interface which can generate tilt motion with three air cylinders mounted beneath the turntable. But, their device couldn't allow a user to do real walking on the interface since the device couldn't cancel the forward or backward motions as well as lateral motions.

For various surfaces, Slater et al. (Slater et al., 1995) proposed locomotion sensing in virtual environments by "walking in place." Their device was used to recognize the gesture of walking using a position sensor and a neural network. For simulation of various walking surfaces, Hollerbach et al., (Hollerbach et al., 2001) simulated a slope display by utilizing mechanical tether and treadmill since treadmills through their tilt mechanisms are typically too slow to present fast slope changes. Similarly, by adding a force to the waist with a mechanical tether, realistic side slopes and stairs can be simulated (Hayward & Hollerbach, 2002; Hollerbach, 2003).

## UNCONSTRAINED WALKING PLANE

Good number of locomotion interfaces to virtual environment (VE) have been developed over the last two decades (as described in previous section). None of these provides natural or near-natural walking, as these devices demand use of special gadgets such as strings, shoes, etc. While, treadmill-style locomotion interface with unidirectional as well as omni-directional treadmills create infinite surface by use of motion floors, they typically have:

1. Bulky or complex drive mechanism,
2. Stability problem, and
3. Problem of loud noise.

The bulky or complex drive mechanism restricts the practical use of this locomotion interface, stability problem results in the induction of fear psychosis to the user, and loud noise leads to feeling of irritation and it interferes in receiving the contextual help and instructions.

It is intuitively clear that exploring VE by natural walking is likely to build the cognitive map more effectively and efficiently. So, we have designed and developed a novel treadmill-style locomotion interface, called unconstrained walking plane (UWP), which facilitates VE exploration through near-natural walking. Also it does not require a user to wear any kind of devices, as required in most of other locomotion devices. The proposed UWP uses manual treadmill with handles to provide need-based support, thus allowing natural walking with assured stability.

To the best of our knowledge, no researcher has used treadmill-style locomotion interface to enhance the spatial learning of visually impaired people (VIP). Also no research has been conducted to investigate the influence of locomotion interface with VE for spatial learning by VIP. Our novel design of UWP is not only simple, safe, and stable but also it is very effective and a low-cost device.

Its simplicity of design coupled with supervised multi-modal training facility makes it an effective device for spatial learning and thereby enhancing the mobility skills of VIP. It facilitates VIP in developing cognitive maps of new and unfamiliar places through VE exploration, so that they can visit such places independently with confidence. Various other advantages of our proposed UWP are presented later in this chapter.

### Mechanical Structure of Unconstrained Walking Plane

Figure 2 shows the schematic view of the UWP which is based on thorough understanding of the human gait.

As shown in Figure 2, UWP consists of three major parts:

1. A motor-less treadmill,
2. A mechanical rotating base, and
3. A block containing AC motor (0.5 HP) and gearbox.

*Figure 2. Mechanical structure of unconstrained walking plane. There are three major parts in the figure: (a) A motor-less treadmill, (b) mechanical rotating base, and (c) block containing Servo motor and gearbox to rotate the mechanical base.*

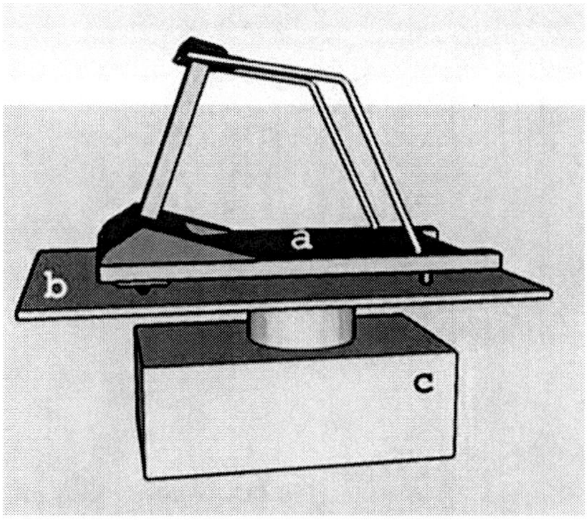


The device's upper platform (mechanical rotating base) is 48" in length and 30" wide with an active surface measuring 48" X 24." We use motor-less (manual) treadmill, which is place on this mechanical rotating base. An AC motor (0.5 HP) along with gear box, are lying under the mechanical rotating base (see Figure 3). The rotation of platform, along with treadmill and user standing on it, is carried by the gearbox and AC motor.

A typical manual treadmill passively rotates backward as the user moves forward on its surface. Advantages of this non-motorized movement include:

1. It is an almost silent operation with negligible-noise during straight movement.
2. The backward movement of treadmill is synchronized with forward movement of user leading thereby a jerk-free motion.
3. It allows the trainee to stop walking, which is detected by non-movement of belt. In case a trainee stops before completing the full path, our system guides her for further movement.

When a user wants to take turn, Rotation Controller turns the whole treadmill, with user standing or walking on it, on mechanical rotating base (see Figure 4). This ensures that the user can place next footstep on the treadmill's belt. The rotation of platform is carried out using an AC motor, lying under the mechanical rotating base along with gear box. Our device also provides an emergency switch for manually stopping the device as a safety measure. The side handle support provides the feeling of safety and stability to the person thereby eliminating all kinds of fears (except fear of failure), resulting in efficient and effective formation of cognitive maps.

## Control Principle of Unconstrained Walking Plane

Locomotion involves walking and manoeuvring.

Belt of treadmill of device moves in backward or forward direction as user walks in forward or backward direction, respectively, on the treadmill. This is an adaptive, non-motorized, movement of treadmill giving full sense of stability.

For manoeuvring, which involves turning and side-stepping, the whole treadmill is rotated in the desired direction on mechanical rotating base (see Figure 4).

*Figure 3. Mechanical structure of UWP (side view)*

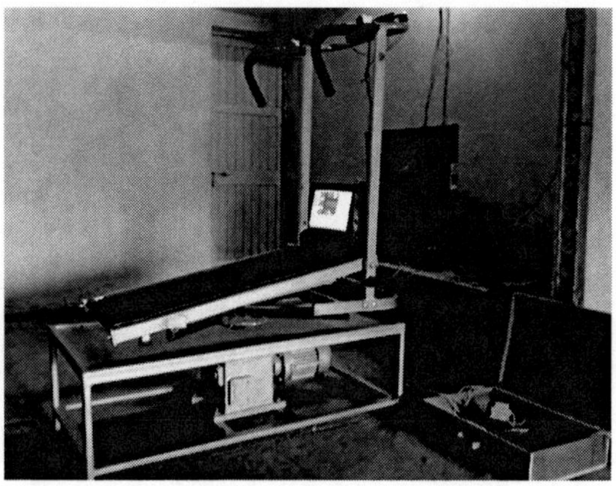

*Figure 4. Blind participant exploring VE using UWP*

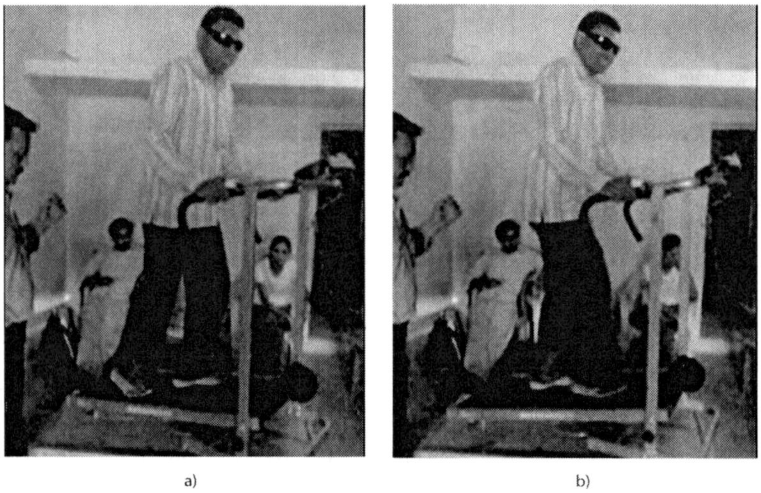


In initial design of our locomotion device, maneuvering involves turning and side-stepping both. Our Rotation control system determines not only user's intention to take a turn, but also the direction and desired angle to rotate the whole treadmill in particular direction on mechanical rotating base. Human beings subconsciously place their foot at angular direction whenever they intend to take a turn. Therefore, the angular positions of the feet on the treadmill are monitored to determine user's intention to take a turn, the direction of turn, and desired angle (at granularity of 15°). The belt of treadmill contains mat on which 24 stripes along the direction of motion, at a distance of 1" between two stripes are placed. Below each stripe, there are position sensitive sensors (PSS) that sense the position of feet from which the angles of feet can be derived.

## Turning

As shown in Figure 5, when foot is on more than three strips then user wants to take a turn and treadmill should be rotated in the direction of user's intention. If middle strip of new step is on left side of middle strip of previous footstep then rotation is on left side and if middle strip of new step is on right side of middle strip of previous footstep then rotation is on right side.

## Side-Stepping

When each foot is on three strips then compare distance between current and the previous foot positions to determine whether side-stepping has taken placed or not. If it is more than a threshold value, the side-stepping has taken placed otherwise there is no side-stepping as shown in Figure 6. If it is within threshold value then that is a normal walk and no action is taken.

*Figure 5. Rotation of treadmill for veer left turn (i.e. 45°) (a) position of treadmill before turning (b) after turning*

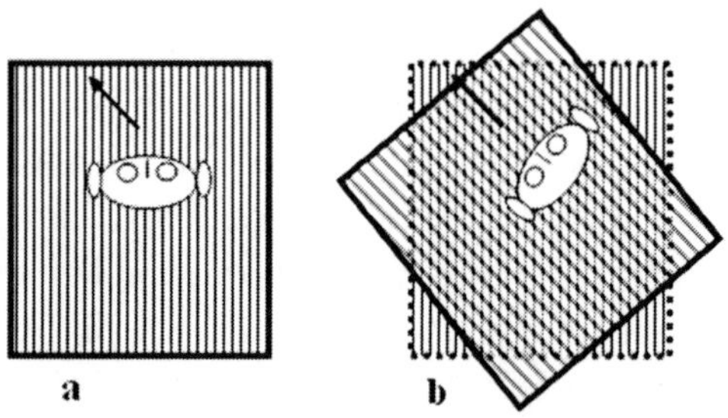

*Figure 6. Rotation of treadmill for side-stepping (i.e. $15^O$) (a) before side-stepping and (b) after side-stepping*

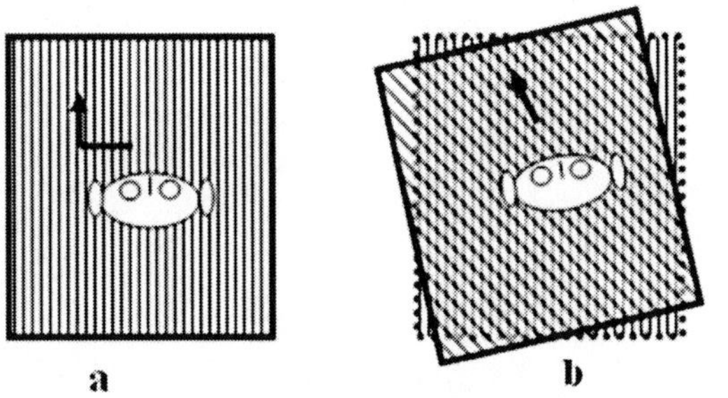


After determining the direction and angle of rotation, appropriate signals are sent to AC motor to rotate in the desired direction by given angle and, accordingly, the platform rotates. This process ensures that the user places the next footstep on the treadmill itself, and do not go off the belt.

## ALGORITHM FOR TURNING AND SIDE-STEPPING

Our algorithm (Algorithm 1), to find the direction and angle of turning, is based on

1. Number of strips pressed by left foot (nl),
2. Number of strips pressed by right foot (nr),
3. Distance between middle strips of two feet (dist), and
4. Threshold for the distance between middle strips of two feet.

The outputs are direction (Left Turn - lt, Right Turn - rt, Left Side-stepping - ls, or Right Side-stepping - rs), and angle of turn. Different possible cases of turning and sidestepping are shown in Figure 7.

The speed of rotation of the upper platform (r) measured in angle/sec is computed from average foot step size (f) in inches and relative velocity (v) that is speed of walking in inches/sec.

$r = (\lambda * v) / f$, Here $\lambda$ is constant.

## MODULAR STRUCTURE OF UWP SOFTWARE

The modular structure of software for the UWP is shown in Figure 8. Main Controller is used for initiating the system, which activates three controllers meant for different purposes:

*Figure 7. Various Cases Of Turning And Side Stepping*

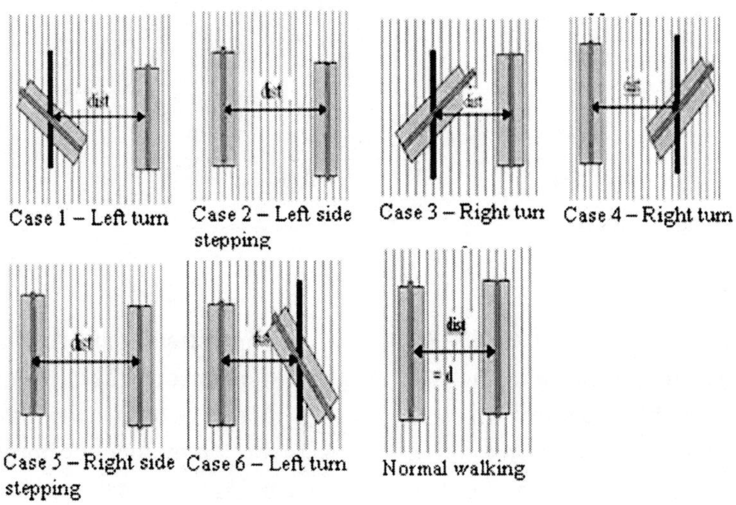

*Algorithm 1. For turning and side-stepping*

```
If (nl>3) && (dist>d) then   //Case-1
find θ
left_turn = true //i.e. return lt
elseif (nl==3) && (dist>d) then //Case-2
Θ = 15°
left_side_stepping = true //i.e. return ls
elseif (nl>3) && (dist<d) then //Case-3, rare case
find θ
right_turn = true //i.e. return rt
elseif (nr>3) && (dist>d) then //Case-4
find θ
right_turn = true //i.e. return rt
elseif (nr==3) && (dist>d) then //Case-5
Θ = 15°
right_side_stepping = true //i.e. return rs
elseif (nr>3) && (dist<d) then //Case-6, rare case
Find θ
left_turn = true //i.e. return lt
End if
```

*Figure 8. Modular structure of software for UWP*

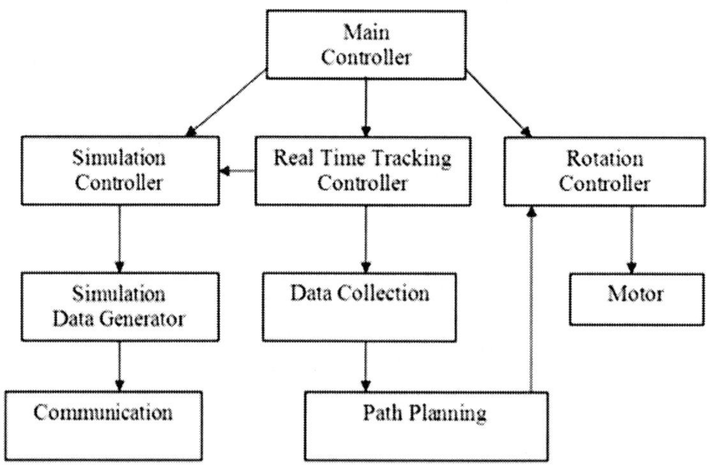


1. Real Time Tracking Controller tracks the user's movement and feeds the tracking information to Simulation Controller. It also sends the data to the Data Collection module, which store the data (received from control circuitry), into the database.
2. Simulation Controller maps the participant's movement to the movement of Avatar in VE. It also generates the information and sends to Communication module to convey the information to the participant. This information is used to plan the path for providing various instructions.

3. Rotation Controller sends the signal to motor to rotate in specific direction, which in result rotates the upper platform (with treadmill) on mechanical rotating base.

## System Architecture

Our system allows visually impaired persons to navigate virtually using a locomotion interface. It is not only closer to real-life navigation as against using the tactile map, but it also simulates the distance and the directions more accurately than the tactile maps. The functioning of a locomotion interface to navigate through virtual environment has been explained in previous sections. Computer-simulated virtual environment showing few major pathways of a college is shown in Figure 9. The user (trainee) chooses starting location and destination, and navigates by standing and walking on our locomotion interface physically. The current position indicator (referred to as cursor in this section) moves as per the movement of the user on locomotion interface.

There are two modes of navigation, first is – Guided navigation, that is navigation with system help and environment cues for creating cognitive map and, second is – Unguided navigation, that is navigation without system help and only with environment cues. During unguided navigation mode, the data of the path traversed by the user (i.e. trainee) is collected and assessed to determine the quality of cognitive map created by the user as a result of training.

In the first mode of navigation, the Instruction Modulator guides the visually impaired person through speech by describing surroundings, guiding directions, and giving early information of a turning, crossings, etc. Additionally, occurrence of various events such as (i) arrival of a junction, (ii) arrival of object(s) of interest, etc. are signaled through vibration using consumer-grade devices and by sound through speakers or headphones. Whenever the cursor is moved onto or near an object, its sound and force feedback features are activated, and a corresponding specific sound or a pre-recorded message is heard by the participant.

*Figure 9. Screen shot of computer-simulated 2-D environments*

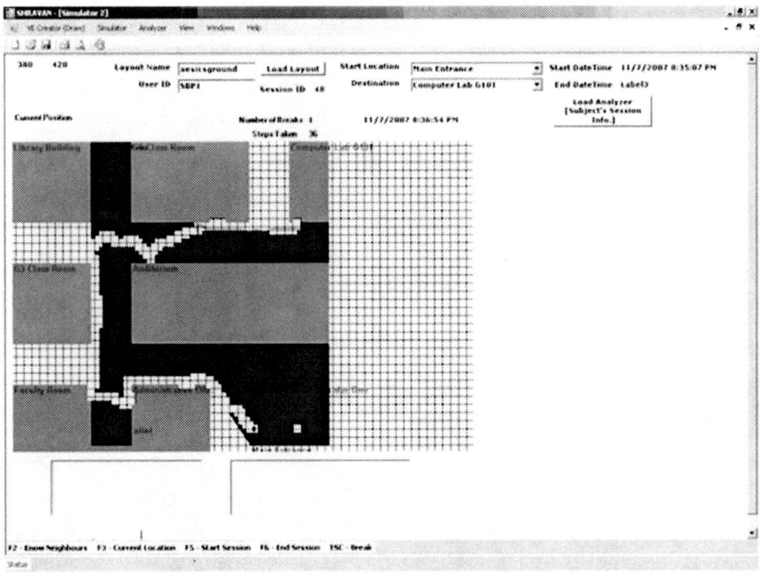

Participant can also get information regarding orientation and nearby objects, whenever needed, through help keys. The Simulator also generates vibration and audible alert when the participant is approaching any obstacle. During training, the Simulator continuously checks and records participant's navigating style (i.e. normal walk or drunkard/random walk) and the path followed by the user when encountered with obstacles.

Once the user gets confident and memorizes the path and landmarks between source and destination, he navigates by using second mode of navigation that is without system's help and tries to reach the destination. The Simulator records participant's navigation performance, such as path traversed, time taken and number of steps taken to complete this task. It also records the sequence of objects encountered on the traversed path and the positions where he seemed to have some confusion (and hence took relatively longer time). The Data Collection module keeps receiving the data from foot position sensors, which is sent to VR system for monitoring and guiding the navigation. Feet position data are also used for sensing the user's intention to take a turn, which is directed to the Motor Planning (Rotation) module to rotate the treadmill.

## ADVANTAGES OF UWP

The advantages of the UWP are as follows:

1. Assistive Technology point-of-view:
    - It simulates virtual walking and provides natural walking experience.
    - It enables VIP to navigate VE, which results in the formation of cognitive maps very efficiently and effectively without any hindrance.
    - It solves instability problem during walking by enabling non-jerking motion and by providing supporting rods.
    - No special training is required by user to walk on it.

As it is treadmill-style locomotion, it is more adaptive by user in the sense of operation. It is not required to wear or load any devices or materials on body parts.

2. Locomotion Interface Device point-of-view:
    - It is simple to operate and easy to maintain due to its simple design.
    - Risks of false signals to control system due to electrical noise are also eliminated.
    - It is of moderate weight due to use of manual treadmill and optimally designed gearbox and mechanical rotating base.
    - It is cost effective.
    - It simulates the distance and directions more accurately than the tactile maps and other devices.

## ORIGINALITIES AND CONTRIBUTIONS OF THE UWP

The originalities and contributions of the UWP (proposed and developed by us) can be summarized under the following three categories:

1. Mechanical (hardware)
    - Modular design
    - Mechanical rotating base - omni-directional locomotion interface.
    - Control unit - Controls rotation.
    - Novel 2-dof parallel mechanisms with single platform for foot motions - More natural foot motions.
2. Control (software)
    - Modular structure of software.
    - Control software captures movement data and controls rotation of the device on participant's request for turning.

3. Systems (applications)
    - Locomotion interface - 360° Walking simulations by using single interface.
    - Non-visual Spatial Learning -
        - Generation of natural trajectories of foot movements.
        - Natural walking experience.
        - Handling of guided and unguided navigation.
        - Evaluation of the quality of spatial learning.

## EXPERIMENTAL DESIGN AND METHODOLOGY

This study was designed to investigate the usability of the UWP as locomotion interface to VE by examining the sensitivity of each of the five common metrics of locomotion interface (i.e. naturalness, safety, control, presence and overall satisfaction of the participants). It was also aimed to determine whether UWP can simulate an unconstrained walking to navigate a large space both during straight walking and turning.

### Design

The independent variables (two): (i) trial number, and (ii) walking period (i.e. straight walking or turning motion).

The dependent variables (nine): (i) time taken to complete the given task, (ii) the number of times help taken, (iii) the number of times help provided, (iv) the number of pauses taken, (self-reported) (v) sense of naturalness, (vi) safety, (vii) control, (viii) sense of presence, and (ix) overall satisfaction of the participants.

### Procedure

The participants were given initial instructions to ride on the treadmill and the way they should walk over it. They were advised to walk at normal speed as they generally walk. Each participant was asked to perform exploration task 4 times. The task assigned to the participants included at least two turns.

After the last trial, participant were asked a set of questions so as to get ratings (between 1 and 5) for each of five parameters (naturalness, safety, control, presence, and overall satisfaction) during straight walking and turning motions. These ratings are based on 5-point Likert scale (i.e., 1 represents "Strongly disagree," 2-"Disagree," 3- "Neutral," 4-"Agree," and 5 representing "Strongly agree").

### Results and Discussion

#### Hypothesis 1

- **Ho:** *UWP provides overall satisfaction for VE exploration during straight walking as well as during turning motion.*
- **Ha:** *UWP does not provide overall satisfaction for VE exploration during straight walking as well as during turning motion.*

The participants' responses to the questionnaire are presented in Table-1 given below, which are also depicted in Figure 10 and Figure 11. We applied t-test on the above data. As per t-test, there is 95% confidence level (5% significance level) that population mean will approximately range between 4 (representing "Agree") and 5 (representing "Strongly agree") for all five parameters during straight walking and turning motion both. This statistics show that population mean for all the parameters is between 4 and 5 (i.e. all the participants agree and some participants strongly agree on all the five parameters). Thus the overall satisfaction level is high during straight walking as well as during turning.

The paired samples t-test was used to analyze the statistical significance of the two modes of navigation. Since the degree of freedom (dof) is

*Figure 10. Feedback for UWP (Straight walking)*

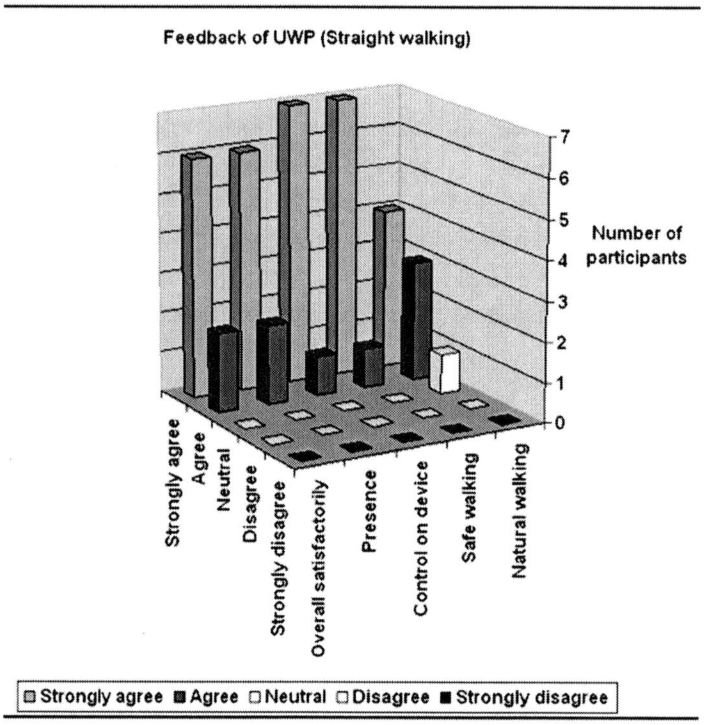


*Figure 11. Feedback for UWP (Turning)*

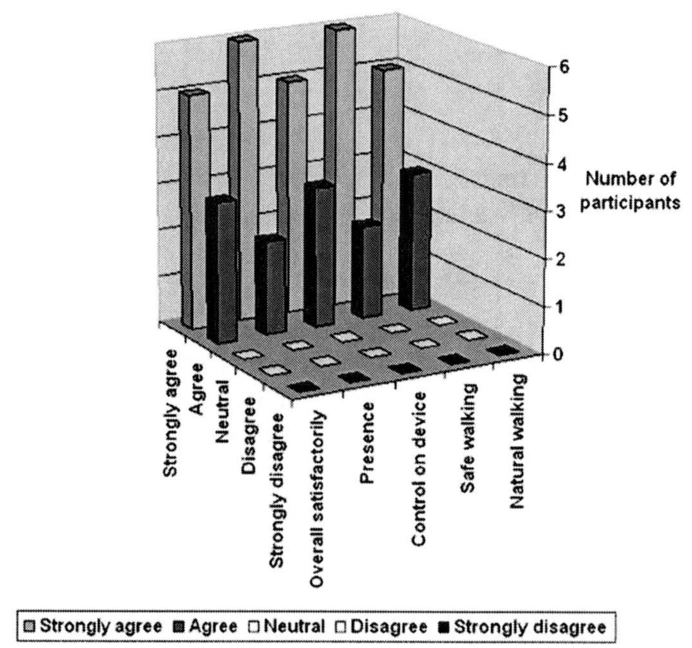

7 in this case, t-test table value for dof = 7 is compared with the computed t-value (shown as T7).

Significant difference was not found for each of the following parameters (refer Table 1):

1. T7 = 0.71 < 2.365 ($t_{0.05}$) for Sense of naturalness,
2. T7 = 0.46 < 2.365 ($t_{0.05}$) for safe walking,
3. T7 = 1.07 < 2.365 ($t_{0.05}$) for control on device,
4. T7 = 0 < 2.365 ($t_{0.05}$) for the sense of presence, and
5. T7 = 0.49 < 2.365 ($t_{0.05}$) for overall satisfaction.

We observe that the calculated values are less than t-test table values for all the parameters. Thus we can say that there is no significant difference in overall satisfaction during straight walking and turning. And we have already shown above that the overall satisfaction level is better than 'high' for each of two navigation modes (i.e. straight walking and turning). Thus we can say with 95% confidence that the null hypothesis is accepted.

## Hypothesis 2

- **Ho:** UWP is not effective for VE exploration.
- **Ha:** UWP is effective for VE exploration.

The null hypothesis (Ho) effectively implies that there is no difference between means of Trial-1 and Trial-4 samples.

In order to evaluate whether UWP is also effective (in addition to being acceptable) for VE exploration, the Trial-1 and Trial-4 values of the four parameters have been collected and shown in Table-2, which are also depicted in Figure 12.

T7 is computed using the paired samples t-test to analyze the statistical significance of post-exploration gains. The t-test table value for dof = 7 and α = 0.05 is compared with the computed t-value (shown as T7) for all the four parameters as shown below:

1. T7 = 4.55 > 2.365 ($t_{0.05}$) in time taken,
2. T7 = 10.92 > 2.365 ($t_{0.05}$) in number of times help taken,
3. T7 = 15.05 > 2.365 ($t_{0.05}$) in number of times help provided, and
4. T7 = 11.97 > 2.365 ($t_{0.05}$) in pauses taken to complete the exploration task.

Since the calculated values are more than table values for all the parameters, the null hypothesis is rejected. Thus, there is a significant difference (improvement) in Trial-4 as against Trial-1 performances of the user. That is, we can say with 95% confidence that the participants have been benefited by the VE exploration using UWP or

*Table 1. Feedback statistics for the experimental study*

| Participant | Parameters | Straight walking | | | | Turning | | | | |
|---|---|---|---|---|---|---|---|---|---|---|
| | | Mean | SD | T7 | | Mean | SD | T7 | | T7 |
| | | | | Min | Max | | | Min | Max | |
| BFS (8 in No., dof = 7) | Sense of naturalness | 4.38 | 0.74 | 3.79 | 4.95 | 4.62 | 0.51 | 4.11 | 5.13 | 0.71 |
| | Safe Walking | 4.50 | 1.41 | 3.39 | 5.60 | 4.75 | 0.46 | 4.29 | 5.20 | 0.46 |
| | Control on device | 4.88 | 0.35 | 4.59 | 5.15 | 4.62 | 0.51 | 4.11 | 5.13 | 1.07 |
| | Sense of Presence | 4.75 | 0.46 | 4.38 | 5.11 | 4.75 | 0.46 | 4.38 | 5.11 | 0 |
| | Overall satisfaction | 4.75 | 0.46 | 4.38 | 5.11 | 4.62 | 0.51 | 4.11 | 5.13 | 0.49 |

*Figure 12. Pre-post VE exploration difference*

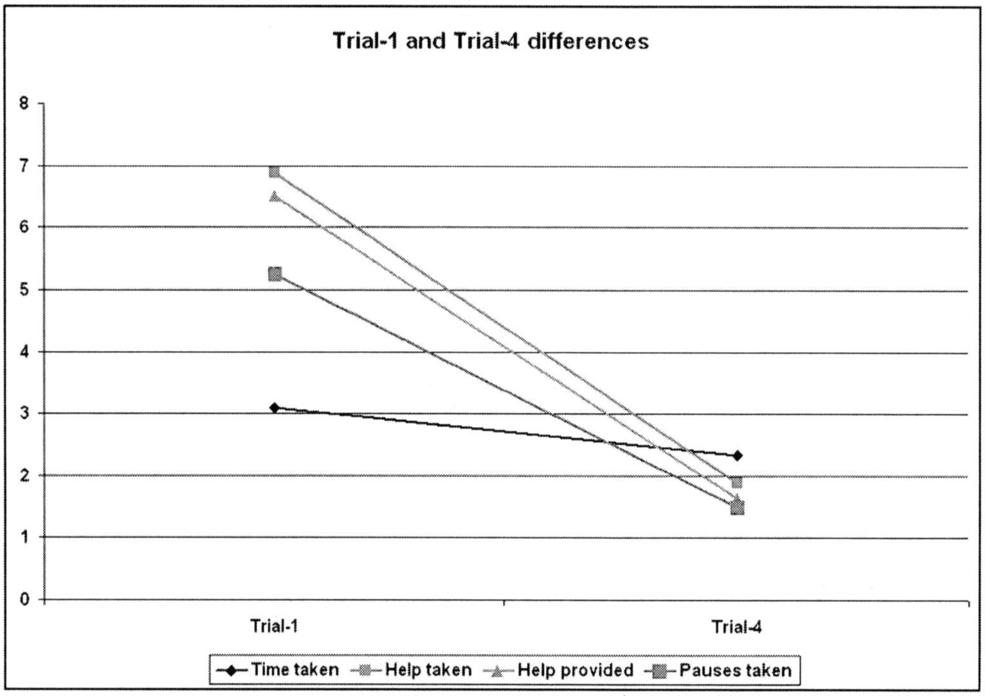


*Table 2. Descriptive statistics measures for the experimental study*

| Participant | Parameters | Trial 1 | | Trial 4 | | T7 |
|---|---|---|---|---|---|---|
| | | Mean | SD | Mean | SD | |
| BFS (8 in No., dof = 7) | Time taken (in minutes) | 3.09 | 0.38 | 2.34 | 0.27 | 4.55 |
| | Number of times help taken | 6.88 | 0.99 | 1.88 | 0.83 | 10.92 |
| | Number of times help provided | 6.50 | 0.76 | 1.63 | 0.52 | 15.05 |
| | Number of times pauses | 5.25 | 0.71 | 1.50 | 0.53 | 11.97 |

alternatively we can say that the UWP is an effective technique of VE exploration to perform natural walking with full immersion and realism during straight walking as well as during turning motion.

To sum up, we can say that participants can create cognitive maps of an area, localize the landmarks and there is significant improvement in spatial learning of the BFS participants after getting training on our system.

## DISCUSSION AND FUTURE DIRECTIVES

This chapter presents an unconstrained walking plane to facilitate visually impaired persons in developing mental maps of new and unfamiliar places, so that they can navigate through such places with ease and confidence. The proposed device although is of limited size but it gives a user the sensation of walking on an unconstrained plane. Its simplicity of design coupled with supervised multi-modal training facility makes it an effective device for virtual walking simulation. We tried to design a loud-less non-motorized locomotion device that helps user to hear the audio guidance and feedback including contextual help of virtual environment. In fact, absence of mechanical noise reduces the distraction during training thereby minimizing the obstructions in the formation of mental maps. The specifications and detailing of the design were based on the series of interactions with selected visually impaired people. We have conducted the experimental study with 8 blind-folded persons. Authors do not intend to claim that their proposed device is the ultimate one. Our proposed unconstrained walking plane simulates the virtual walking and assist in formation of cognitive maps of an area. One known limitation of our device is its inability to simulate movements on slopes. We plan to take up this enhancement in our future work.

## REFERENCES


Bouguila, L., Iwashita, M., Hirsbrunner, B., & Sato, M. (2003). Virtual locomotion interface with ground surface simulation. *Proc. of the International Conference on Artificial Reality and Telexistence*, ICAT'03.

Brogan, D. C., Metoyer, R. A., & Hodgins, J. K. (1997). *Dynamically simulated characters in virtual environments* (p. 216). SIGGRAPH Visual Proc.

Brooks, F. P., Jr. (1986). Walk through- A dynamic graphics system for simulating virtual buildings. *Proc. of 1986 Workshop on Interactive 3D Graphics*, (pp. 9-21).

Christensen, R. R., Hollerbach, J. M., Xu, Y., & Meek, S. G. (2000). Inertial-force feedback for the treadport locomotion interface. *Presence (Cambridge, Mass.)*, *9*(1), 1–14. doi:10.1162/105474600566574

Clark-Carter, D., Heyes, A., & Howarth, C. (1986). The effect of non-visual preview upon the walking speed of visually impaired people. *Ergonomics*, *29*(12), 1575–1581. doi:10.1080/00140138608967270

Darken, R. P., Cockayne, W. R., & Carmein, D. (1997). The omni-directional treadmill: A locomotion device for virtual worlds. *Proc. of UIST'97*, (pp. 213-221).

De Luca, A., Mattone, R., & Giordano, P. R. (2007). Acceleration-level control of the CyberCarpet. *2007 IEEE International Conference on Robotics and Automation*, Roma, I, (pp. 2330-2335).

Earnshaw, R. A., Gigante, M. A., & Jones, H. (Eds.). (1993). *Virtual reality systems*. Academic Press. Hayward, R. C., & Hollerbach, J. M. (2002). Implementing virtual stairs on treadmills using torso force feedback. *Proc. of IEEE Int'l Conf. on Robotics and Automation*, (pp. 586-591).

Hirose, M., & Yokoyama, K. (1997). Synthesis and transmission of realistic sensation using virtual reality technology. *Transactions of the Society of Instrument and Control Engineers*, *33*(7), 716–722.

Hollerbach, J. M. (2002). Locomotion interfaces. In Stanney, K. M. (Ed.), *Handbook of virtual environments technology* (pp. 239–254). Lawrence Erlbaum Associates, Inc.

Hollerbach, J. M., Checcacci, D., Noma, H., Yanaida, Y., & Tetsutani, N. (2003). Simulating side slopes on locomotion interfaces using torso forces. *Proc. of 11th Haptic Interfaces for Virtual Environment and Teleoperator Systems*, (pp. 247-253).

Hollerbach, J. M., Mills, R., Tristano, D., Christensen, R. R., Thompson, W. B., & Xu, Y. (2001). Torso force feedback realistically simulates slope on treadmill-style locomotion interfaces. *The International Journal of Robotics Research, 20*, 939–952. doi:10.1177/02783640122068209

Hollerbach, J. M., Xu, Y., Christensen, R., & Jacobsen, S. C. (2000). Design specifications for the second generation Sarcos Treadport locomotion interface. *Haptics Symposium, Proc. ASME Dynamic Systems and Control Division, DSC-Vol. 69-2*, Orlando, Nov. 5-10, 2000, (pp. 1293-1298).

Hollins, M. (1989). *Understanding blindness: An integrative approach*. Lawrence Erlbaum Associates.

Iwata, H. (1999). The Torus Treadmill: Realizing locomotion in VEs. *IEEE Computer Graphics and Applications, 19*(6), 30–35. doi:10.1109/38.799737

Iwata, H., & Fujji, T. (1996). Virtual preambulator: A novel interface device for locomotion in virtual environment. *Proc. of IEEE VRAIS'96*, (pp. 60-65).

Iwata, H., Yano, H., Fukushima, H., & Noma, H. (2005). CirculaFloor. *IEEE Computer Graphics and Applications, 25*(1), 64–67. doi:10.1109/MCG.2005.5

Iwata, H., Yano, H., & Tomioka, H. (2006). *Powered shoes*. SIGGRAPH 2006 Conference DVD (2006).

Iwata, H., Yano, H., & Tomiyoshi, M. (2007). *String walker*. Paper presented at SIGGRAPH 2007.

Iwata, H., & Yoshida, Y. (1997). Virtual walk through simulator with infinite plane. *Proc. of 2nd VRSJ Annual Conference*, (pp. 254-257).

Iwata, H., & Yoshida, Y. (1999). Path reproduction tests using a Torus Treadmill. *Presence (Cambridge, Mass.), 8*(6), 587–597. doi:10.1162/105474699566503

Lahav, O., & Mioduser, D. (2003). A blind person's cognitive mapping of new spaces using a haptic virtual environment. *Journal of Research in Special Educational Needs, 3*(3), 172–177. doi:10.1111/1471-3802.00012

Lynch, K. (1960). *The image of the city*. Cambridge, MA: MIT Press.

Medina, E., Fruland, R., & Weghorst, S. (2008). VIRTUSPHERE: Walking in a human size VR hamster ball. In *Proceedings of the Human Factors and Ergonomics Society 52nd Annual Meeting* (pp. 2102-2106). New York, NY: HFES.

Noma, H., & Miyasato, T. (1998). *Design for locomotion interface in a large scale virtual environment. ATLAS: ATR Locomotion interface for active self motion*. 7th Annual Symposium on Haptic Interfaces for Virtual Environment and Teleoperator Systems. The Winter Annual Meeting of the ASME. Anaheim, USA.

Noma, H., & Miyasato, T. (1998). Design for locomotion interface in a large scale virtual environment, ATLAS: ATR Locomotion interface for active self motion. *ASME-DSC, 64*, 111–118.

Noma, H., & Miyasato, T. (1999). A new approach for canceling turning motion in the locomotion interface. *ATLAS, ASME-DSC, 67*, 405–407.

Noma, H., Sugihara, T., & Miyasayo, T. (2000). Development of ground surface simulator for Tel-E-Merge System. *Proc. of IEEE-Virtual Reality 2000 Conference*, (pp. 217-224).

Roston, G. P., & Peurach, T. (1997). A whole body kinesthetic display device for virtual reality applications. *Proc. of IEEE Int'l Conf. on Robotics and Automation*, (pp. 3006-3011).

Schmidt, H., Sorowka, D., Hesse, S., & Bernhardt, R. (2002). Design of a robotic walking simulator for neurological rehabilitation. *IEEE/RSJ Int. Conf. On Intelligent Robots and Systems*, (pp. 1487-1492).

Shingledecker, C. A., & Foulke, E. (1978). A human factors approach to the assessment of mobility of blind pedestrians. *Human Factors*, *20*, 273–286.

Sibert, L., Templeman, J., Page, R., Barron, J., McCune, J., & Denbrook, P. (2004). *Initial assessment of human performance using the gaiter interaction technique to control locomotion in fully immersive virtual environments. (Technical Report)*. Washington, DC: Naval Research Laboratory.

Slater, M. (1995). Taking steps: The influence of a walking metaphor on presence in virtual reality. *ACM Transactions on Computer-Human Interaction*, *2*(3), 201–219. doi:10.1145/210079.210084

Wang, Z., Bauernfeind, K., & Sugar, T. (2003). Omni-directional treadmill system. *Proc. of 11th Haptic Interfaces for Virtual Environment and Teleoperator Systems*, (pp. 367–373).

## KEY TERMS AND DEFINITIONS

**Omni-Directional Treadmill:** A device that allows a person to perform locomotive motion in any direction. The ability to move in any direction is how these treadmills differ from their basic counterparts (that permit only unidirectional locomotion). Omni-directional treadmills are employed in immersive virtual environment implementations to allow unencumbered movement within the virtual space through user self-motion.

**Pedaling Device:** Pedaling devices with an instrumented bicycle were employed to simulate the effect of going up or down hills.

**String Walker:** A type of locomotion interface device to simulate walking using Strings.

**Virtual Environment:** VE provides for creation of simulated objects and events with which people can interact. The definitions of VE, although wide and varied, include a common statement that VE creates the illusion of participation in a synthetic environment rather than going through external observation of such an environment.

**Walking in Place:** A motion platform may be entirely avoided by measuring walking in place. A different set of muscles is employed than in walking forward, but an advantage is a potentially lower cost system.

# Chapter 12
# Engaging Learners in the Digital Age through Self-Discovery Learning

**Ramesh C Sharma**
*University of Guyana, Guyana*

**Paul Kawachi**
*Open University of China, China*

## ABSTRACT

*The development of social networking, Web 2.0, and virtual worlds has opened new avenues for online collaborative communication. For learners in this digital age, there is a need to devise new models and metaphors to examine the learner and teacher interactions with technologies and for models which can help in designing effective and innovative learning interventions. In this chapter we examine some models and discuss how learners can be guided to become engaged in self-discovery learning.*

## INTRODUCTION

One of the hallmarks of the digital age is online education or e-learning. Almost all types of educational settings have employed e-learning, some with low-cost technology and others with expensive technology. The learning experiences are acquired by learners with the help of ICT (information and communication technologies) tools which develop, deliver, support and evaluate learning content. Not only at the institutional level, at the individual level also, e-learning (in one form or another) is being used. Institutions have adopted the ICT mechanisms either as solitary or complementary mode for offering educational services to the learners. Mishra (2001) called it a "new generation of distance education" (p.2) as it comprises the best of both mediums: asynchronous (print-based) and synchronous (tele-learning). There are different terms we use to describe e-learning, like web-based learning, Internet-based learning, virtual education, blended learning,

DOI: 10.4018/978-1-61350-320-1.ch012

Copyright © 2012, IGI Global. Copying or distributing in print or electronic forms without written permission of IGI Global is prohibited.

online learning etc. Whatever the name we give to it, it offers asynchronous and synchronous forms of interactions between the teachers and learners. Becta (2008) and the European Commission (2008) in their reports also predicted a seamless interchange of classroom interactions and collaborations with ubiquitous and ambient technologies. If we look at the developments in technologies (Pea & Wallis, cited in Borgman et al. 2008:13) whereby simple face-to-face instruction was supported with radio, television and telephone and then networked computers to the use of web 2.0 and social networking in education, Pea & Wallis report, "We can now interact at a distance, accessing complex and useful resources in ways unimaginable in early eras.' These technologies have altered the ways the students were engaged in learning either by the teacher or by the student alone.

The 2011 Horizon Report (Johnson et al. 2011) identified the highest ranking challenge as digital media literacy which continues to rise in importance as a key skill in every discipline and profession (p.3). It recognizes that the Internet technologies have increasingly facilitated interactions and collaboration in such a way that teams now work together to address the issues which are not easy for a single worker to resolve alone. There is a great surge in user-generated content, new ideas, information and opinions are coming forward on all possible themes that we need to sift through a mountain of information on a weekly or daily basis (p.4). Thus there is a change in the way we communicate, access information, collaborate and socialise with peers and colleagues. Thus dynamic learning environments have been developed which engage the learners for learning through self-discovery. An examination of Web 2.0 technologies will reveal that they have great pedagogic value (Conole, 2009a) for example, Web 2.0 technologies have shifted the focus from individual to social, blogging is good for reflective thinking, Virtual or 3D immersive world software or gaming is good for experiential learning. However, studies also indicate a gap between the potential these technologies have and the real utility or practical value from the use of these technologies (Conole, 2009b; Conole & Culver, 2009). Oblinger & Oblinger (2005) also reported a lack of understanding among the learners on how to use technologies for academic purposes which was later found to be still valid by other research by Kennedy et al. (2008).

## ENGAGING LEARNERS

As explained above, e-learning courses are everywhere and on all possible subject areas. To help students take full advantage of these e-learning courses, we use all sorts of media-mix: quizzes, video, tests, links to extra resources etc. Hazel Associates (2005) projected that by 2015 the online higher education market would exceed $69 billion and found it to be the fastest growing sub-sector in global education market. In an urge to be technologically advanced (some with proper thinking and some without any thought) educational institutions and teaching community adopted online education in its rudimentary form where the lecture notes and presentations were uploaded onto institutional servers. These measures failed to engage students as reported by Weigel (2000) that these lacked any pedagogical considerations, rather being " little more than an exercise of posting on the Internet an enhances syllabus that includes lecture content, reading assignments and practice tests along with using discussion groups and e-mails to respond to students questions." This disappointment was also echoed by Carr-Chellman and Duchastel (2000) related to effectiveness of web courses:

*It is also evident that many online courses lack basic design consideration and that the web is simply being used as a medium for delivery of instructions created within another framework. Such transposition from one medium to another*

*Table 1. Online practices*

| Integrated | Mixed / Blended | Independent |
|---|---|---|
| Supplement to face-to-face teaching | Complement to face-to-face teaching | Alternate to face-to-face teaching |

*may have some value in reaching certain outreach goals, but it also run serious risks of diluting the original instruction and possibly rendering it ineffective (p.229).*

If we examine the usage pattern of online education practices (Mason, 1998; Mitra, 1999; Berge, Collins and Dougherty, 2000; Mayes, 2000), we can put them in three categories (Table 1).

In whatever way the online education practices are used, trends showed a need for a paradigm shift from teacher to student centered learning; from simply passing on knowledge to constructions of knowledge and collaboration (Salmon, 2000; Bates, 2001; Laurillard, 2002). Hence for the students to be engaged into learning successfully they need a set of new skills, knowledge, talents and competencies (Ryan and Woodward, 1997; Salmon, 2000). Berge (2001) and Willis (1992) recommended suitable induction and orientation programmes for the learners enabling them to adjust with these digital practices for effective engagement. Different strategies have been suggested for engaging learners in digital environments: constructivism (Oliver, 1999; Hung, 2001; Hung and Nichani, 2001); web-constructivism (Basiel, 1999); learning by doing (Schank, 1997), problem-based learning (Barrows, 1994), case-based learning (Lynn, 1996; Chen et al, 2006), learning by designing (Naidu, Anderson, and Riddle, 2000), and role-play-based learning (Ip, and Linser, 1999) and an eclectic approach in instructional design for web-based learning (Mishra, 2002). Sharma and Mishra (2007) suggested *Experience-Reflect-Interact-Construct* (ERIC) model for learner engagement in digital environments (see Figure 1).

This model postulates that the system must provide learning *experiences* to the learners to be accessed anytime and anywhere. These experiences may include anything ranging from listening to audio, watching video, web resources or animations and simulations. After obtaining certain experiences, as a matter of *a priori*, the learner *reflects*. This stage leads the learner to *interact* (synchronously and asynchronously). Last phase of the model is leading to *construction* of knowledge (by various means like projects, presentations, independent or collaborative work activities etc).

The above cited studies indicate different strategies for engaging learners, it was also found that learners may have impoverished knowledge or idea about different strategies on what learning is and how it occurs (Hofer, Yu and Pintrich, 1998). Although all learners self-engage, they may do it with varying degrees thus leading to a variation in their learning (Jamieson-Noel, 2004). Given these concerns with learners' engagement, lets examine different approaches or models of how students can be self-engaged by highlighting how instructional models can be designed or which methods could be adopted resulting in improved learning outcomes.

## SELF-DISCOVERY THROUGH GAME-BASED LEARNING

The 2011 Horizon report identified six technologies which have fast emerged as having greatest potential for teaching, learning and creative enquiry. These technologies are e-books, mobile telephones, augmented learning, game-based

*Figure 1. ERIC model (Sharma & Mishra, 2007)*

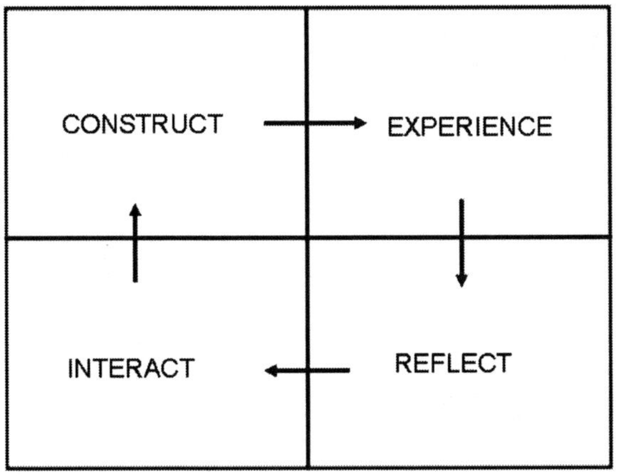


learning, gesture-based computing, and learning analytics. The Horizon report classified these on the basis of their potential into some time frame when they shall move closer or be a part of mainstream education like mobile telephones and electronic books are put in 'on the near-term horizon' group meaning thereby within the next 12 months that students, faculty and staff would adopt them heavily. The 2011 Horizon Report identified game-based learning as one of the fast emerging technologies in education to enhance collaboration, problem solving and procedural thinking (p.5). Game-based learning (which is placed as the second adoption on the horizon) is expected to be in the mainstream as widespread adoption within two to three years. These games can be educational or commercial and from the participation point of view can be from single-player to massively multiplayer online games and alternate reality games.

## Critical Thinking Skills through Self-Discovery

There are various models dealing with learning critical thinking skills, two are notable: Dewey (1933) and Brookfield (1987).

Dewey proposed five phases for reflective or critical thinking:

1. suggestions, in which the mind leaps forward to a possible solution;
2. an intellectualization of the difficulty or perplexity that has been felt (directly experienced) into a problem to be solved, a question for which the answer must be sought;
3. the use of one suggestion after another as a leading idea, or hypothesis, to initiate and guide observation and other operations in collection of factual material;
4. the mental elaboration of the idea or supposition (reasoning, in the sense in which reasoning is a part, not the whole, of inference); and
5. testing the hypothesis by overt or imaginative action.

Brookfield proposed also five phases to develop critical thinking:

1. a triggering event;
2. an appraisal of the situation;
3. an exploration to explain anomalies or discrepancies;
4. developing alternative perspectives; and
5. integration of alternatives in ways of thinking or living.

These two models have the limitation of creating a scaffold. Kawachi (2003b) proposed a model for learning critical thinking using multimedia which is summarized in Table 2 and expounded below. It has been validated in theory (Kawachi, 2005), and in practice in open distance universities in fifteen countries (Kawachi, 2003a). The presented Design for Multimedia in Learning (DML) Model translates conventional theoretical models of learning into an efficient practical design for use in the multimedia educational environment. This new Model has four distinct stages, and is directly underpinned by Moore's (1993) Theory

*Table 2. The four stages of the Kawachi multimedia learning model*

| Stage | Tasks |
|---|---|
| Stage 1 Cooperative and Synchronous Media | Activation of prior knowledge and recall of relevant schema, sharing prior knowledge, giving extension and expansion |
| Stage 2 Collaborative and Asynchronous Media | Determine and discover reasoning underlying prior knowledge |
| Stage 3 Collaborative and Asynchronous Media | Consider the merits and demerits of other alternative perspectives and chose a way forward to explore |
| Stage 4 Cooperative and Synchronous Media | Test out new way experientially in familiar contexts and then in new contexts |

of Transactional Distance which tries to measure the psychological distance between the student and the information to be learnt.

In Stage 1, learning occurs in a group cooperatively, gathering and sharing information and fostering a learning community. The starting level for many online courses is at this greatest transactional distance (S- D-) characterised by no structure imposed or directed by the tutor (fully responsive to the student) and with no educative dialogue.

Here we use the letters S and D to refer to:

- **S (Structure)** denotes the educative structure imposed by the teacher, textbook or institution
- **D (Dialogue)** denotes the educative guiding conversation (not idle or social chat)

Each student can contribute his or her own prior knowledge to a group shared forum, and all transactions are reciprocally beneficial. This situation is cooperative learning in a group. Initial self-introductions, own contexts, expectations and reasons for participating are topics here. Especially when more purposeful, the transactions that are occurring could be described in practice as 'brainstorming,' and synchronous computer-mediated communications are most suited to this activity. The education provider could give administrative or non-academic counselling support including personal comments here (which being non-educative remain as D-) to increase responsiveness to individual needs (moving from S- through to Stage 2 with S+) which can serve to motivate students (see Moore, 1993, p.29, note 2).

In Stage 2 at a desirable next level of less transactional distance, some structure should be introduced by the tutor, symbolised as S+ D- in which there is still no expert input from the tutor. Here the tutor can initiate the discussion by eliciting an opinion and then request clarification or supportive elaboration. There is added Structure and collaborative interactions among the students and content. This Stage is characterised by the students questioning the content, by theorising or lateral-thinking to generate and develop metaphors or create new ideas, and these supported by argument satisfying the educative demand of the institution. The demand for rationality is the added Structure. Some time is needed for reflection here, and asynchronous modes such as email and a bulletin board are appropriate (see for example Yakimovicz & Murphy, 1995). However, current studies show that new social software applications such as Wikis or shared Google Docs can be used synchronously here (see Figure 2).

In Stage 3 at the next level of even less transactional distance, the tutor engages the students with guiding comments in what Holmberg (1983) has described as a Guided Didactic Conversation, helping the students achieve the course structural requirements of understanding the general concepts to be learnt (D+ S+). Where this conversation is the aesthetic stance reading and interacting cognitively with an assigned text then

*Figure 2. Kawachi multimedia learning model*

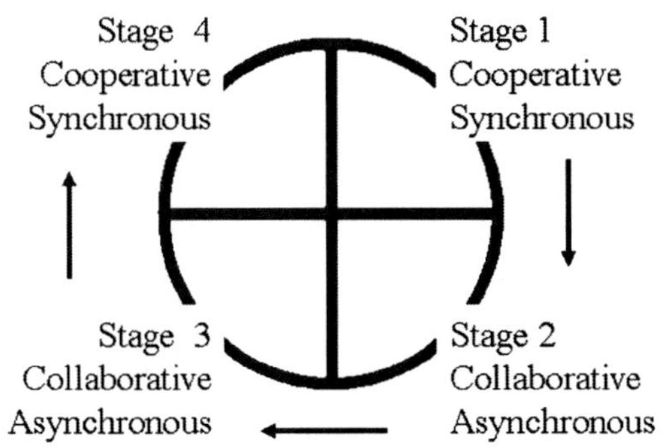


this is Internal Didactic Conversation. The tutor or the text poses questions, and students defend their formulations. This Stage is characterised by hypotheses testing and logical straight-forward thinking—termed 'vertical' thinking in contrast to 'lateral' thinking—associated with problem-solving, and is collaborative. Since the tutor is likely unfamiliar with the distant student's foreign and individual context, the tutor can be an equal participant in this process of co-discovery and hypotheses testing. The tutor can provide input (D+) pro-actively to guide the collaborative process by commenting expertly positively with opinions suggesting ways forward to be explored such as the set text or other books or resources or negatively with counter-opinions to keep the discussion on track (keeping Structure S+). Asynchronous mode is ideal here, to allow sufficient time for cognitive connections and co-construction of new non-foundational knowledge. As in Stage 2, recently developed advanced technologies such as Wikis could be used collaboratively here synchronously.

In Stage 4 at the optimum level of lowest transactional distance, interactivity is characterised by experiential learning and is cooperative, and at minimum transactional distance (D+ S-), in synchronous mode and with teaching dialogue to assist the students to reflect on their studies. The tutor can be fully responsive to the student's wants and fully participate with maximum dialogue. There is no direct counter-opinion, and the activity is cooperative – eliciting, valuing and sharing what has been gained (newly acquired knowledge). Maximum dialogue would suggest here that synchronous communications be used. Other experts or stakeholders may participate in these synchronous discussions. Educative discussions may be a cooperative review of the course, perhaps inviting the course-writer to be online in synchronous conferencing. Another forum may be the student presenting a summary of what has been learnt to a real conference.

While the DML Model serves as a comprehensive model for engaging students in self discovery learning using multimedia and advanced learning technologies to achieve critical learning and develop as lifelong learners, few students actually proceed beyond Stage 2 or 3 – both the collaborative stages. Concerning the use of the world-wide-web and multimedia to promote students' learning, Herrington & Oliver (1999) have reported that the higher-order thinking (of Stage 3 and Stage 4 here) was supported by using a situated-learning framework for relating the discussion to the student's own context. When using multimedia in situated learning, there was much less lower-order discussion and less social chat (Herrington & Oliver, 1999), indicating multimedia could be applied to move students from Stage 1 to Stages 2 and 3. The implication here is that increasing the use of multimedia might have helped younger students cope better with the collaborative Stage 3.

## ENGAGING LEARNERS THROUGH MINIMALLY INVASIVE EDUCATION (MIE)

The Hole-in-the-wall experiment (conducted in 1999 in India) is one of the world famous experiments to showcase that unsupervised children, without any planned instructional intervention, were able to acquire a certain level of computer literacy. These children were able to self-engage themselves towards learning certain skills (Mitra and Rana, 2001). Mitra and Rana addressed this approach as MIE as it was based on free access and minimal intervention. they suggest that although this approach was specific to learning of computing skills, it can easily be adopted for many other subjects as well. Mitra et al (2005) defined minimally invasive education as a pedagogic method that uses the learning environment to generate an adequate level of motivation to induce learning in groups of children, with minimal, or no, intervention by a teacher."

In this experiment, computers were placed in a room, usually mounted on wall (hence the name "hole-in-the-wall") with easy access to children. The success of this experiment lies in proving that children can learn with minimum intervention and by constructing their own learning environments. The experiment further revealed that when children engaged themselves into learning, certain learning strategies emerged: trial and error, role of rehearsal in learning, practice and drill, self discovery, and continuous dialogue with peer. Dangwal and Kapur (2009) reported, "MIE research confirms the view that young children learn most efficiently when they are engaged in interaction, rather than in merely receptive or passive activities, as has been observed in formal schooling practices." (p.19)

## ENGAGING THROUGH SIMULATED EXPERIMENTS IN VIRTUAL LABORATORIES

Developing heuristic skills in the students through simulated experiments has been found to be useful for those situations where students are expected to carry out experiments which are either expensive or dangerous (Nedic et al, 2003 ; Sahin, 2006). The computer generated model which emulates the real life like situation is known as simulation. The students can try out different variables to find the solution of a problem as it provides a safe environment. A virtual laboratory is another example where the learners perform operations on computers which they may be doing otherwise in real life on real objects. Here the learner is provided with a complete experience of working in a real laboratory. Howard Hughes Medical Institution has done pioneer work by developing "the Transgenic Fly," "The Bacterial Identification Lab," "The Cardiology Lab," "The Neurophysiology Lab" and "The Immunology Lab" where the learners carry out experiments and develop hands on skills through working on the Internet and computer systems.

### Web 2.0/Social Networking/ Wiki and Learner Engagement

Web 2.0 offers many services pertaining to different areas like social networking, collaboration, content sharing in terms of photo sharing or document sharing or video sharing etc. Some of the key Web 2.0 services are:

- Blogs
- Wikis
- RSS and syndication
- Tagging and social bookmarking
- Multimedia sharing
- Audio blogging and podcasting
- Newer Web 2.0 services and applications

Web 2.0 tools and Social networking sites (SNS) (like Facebook) are one of the captivating tools which engages people in staying in touch with friends, family and colleagues, sharing ideas, news, photos, videos etc. Such social networking sites allow people to post messages (can be about anything, education, sports, religion, politics etc) either for every one to see or there may be private communications. These also allow for creating Groups for people working or interested in common theme.

A wiki is a certain kind of blog. While a blog has serial entries according to date much like a diary, a wiki can be built up both horizontally in breadth and vertically in depth, while being fairly time independent. Since pages can be added for increasing breadth, and more hypertext links and details can be added to any pre-existing page for increasing the depth, wikis are therefore considered to be synchronous collaborative tools, and potentially effective as such in learner engagement. Wikis are considered to be synchronous collaborative tools since they are continually being updated by users (Schwartz, Clark, Cossarin, & Rudolph, 2004; and Boulos, Maramba, & Wheeler 2006).

It is noteworthy that wikis are not yet part and parcel of university learning management systems such as Moodle or Blackboard. Rather, they are standalone applications to build an open knowledge database accessed through any browser on the internet. Wikis are interlinked with each other so that the MIT wiki has pages by Cornell University as well as links to password-protected copyrighted library sites. In his paper on the topic of Social Applications for e-learning Dalsgaard (2006) argues that learning management systems (LMSs) are not designed for student-student(s) group learning tasks. When LMSs are for example used for student-student interactions through text-messaging chat-rooms, they are slow and cumbersome. As a result, we believe LMS do not achieve the potential of providing virtual spaces for learning (chat rooms are 99% unused), Such LMS virtual spaces can help with certain discussions for deciding a schedule or negotiating a syllabus.

The issue of whether wikis can be used for collaborative learning balances on the point of what level of learning is being done. During construction, contributors offer their own ideas cooperatively, although the finished product is unknown by anyone and so the overall process can be considered collaborative construction through cooperative sharing. Children in school can learn from wikis as a resource of reasonably-reliable current knowledge, in a one-way cooperative delivery mechanism; wikis rarely offer conflicting or contrasting opinions within a same page – any incoming knowledge usually displaces the 'weaker' earlier contributions, sadly, and to our loss. University students might also access wikis for up-to-date knowledge – especially since hardback textbooks are so expensive nowadays. A certain level of learner engagement and maturity is essential if wikis are to be effective collaborative learning spaces (Seely Brown and Adler, 2008). This would move us on to the concept of learner autonomy. Seely Brown and Adler (2008) suggest that these web 2.0 tools (SNS, blogs, and wikis etc) has created a new form of participatory medium which is ideal for learning in digital age. There is a whole set of researches available which suggest that Web 2.0 tools have effect on learning, there are issues also which may affect the engagement of learners with technologies. Kirkwood & Price (2005) commented that access to ICT is a challenge for the learners and thus they are required to share computing and communication facilities with others. They advised that course design should not be over-dependent upon ICT. Self-discovery learning can be successful when the students are self-aware and self-critical, honest about themselves and open to criticism and feedback (Mason & Rennie, 2008).

## CONCLUSION

Like radio and television that were first used in education about forty years ago, the Internet and multimedia technologies are here to stay in the field of education. Not all institutions are online, yet it is true that perhaps all now use some form or other of electronic technology known as e-learning. In many cases this is used to organize administration, teaching and delivery of content. Overall e-learning has not shown any significant improvements in level or quality of learning achieved. e-Learning has however made learning easier for most students and enabled multitudes of students to gain learning experiences and opportunities that would not have been possible without

these new tools. One key reason why e-learning has not demonstrated improved learning is that many conventional teachers and of course the students themselves do not know how to employ e-learning efficiently. If the students can access class video then they chose to stay at home in bed. We need a way for using e-learning to enhance the cognitive learning processes—not to replace old ways but to augment them. This is why the Model for Multimedia Learning is advocated here. It functions essentially to reduce the psychological transactional distance between the individual student and the content to be learnt. It also coaches the student in what to do next and why—to increase learner autonomy and absolutely foster discovery learning. Without such a Model, students remain stuck in a Facebook social stage without moving on to the collaborative transactional stages for learning. The Model acts as e-learning scaffolding to each student, and to teachers and institutions. Virtual laboratories, simulations and other types of e-learning need structure to succeed. The Model for Multimedia Learning provides exactly this structure.

## REFERENCES


Barrows, H. S. (1994). *Problem-based learning applied to medical education. School of Medicine*. Springfield, IL: Southern Illinois University.

Basiel, A. (1999). *Applied formative evaluation in the Web-based environment.* MPhil. Thesis in Computing Science, Middlesex University, London.

Bates, T. (2001). *National strategies for e-learning in post-secondary education and training*. Paris, France: UNESCO, IIEP.

Becta. (2008). *Harnessing technology: Next generation learning 2008-14*. Becta, Coventry. Retrieved on 2 December, 2010, from http://publications.becta.org.uk/display.cfm?resID=37348&page=1835.

Berg, Z., Collins, M., & Dougherty, K. (2000). Design guidelines for web-based courses. In Abby, B. (Ed.), *Instructional and cognitive impacts of web-based education* (pp. 32–40). Hershey, PA: Idea Group. doi:10.4018/978-1-878289-59-9.ch002

Berge, Z. (Ed.). (2001). *Sustaining distance training*. San Francisco, CA: Jossey-Bass.

Borgman, C., et al. (2008). *Fostering learning in the networked world: The cyberlearning opportunity and challenge*. National Science Foundation. Retrieved on 3 December, 2010, from http://www.nsf.gov/pubs/2008/nsf08204/nsf08204.pdf.

Boulos, M. N. K., Maramba, I., & Wheeler, S. (2006). Wikis, blogs and podcasts: A new generation of web-based tools for virtual collaborative clinical practice and education. *BMC Medical Journal, 6*(41). Retrieved on July 10, 2010, from http://www.biomedcentral.com/content/pdf/1472-6920-6-41.pdf.

Brookfield, S. D. (1987). *Developing critical thinkers: Challenging adults to explore alternative ways of think and acting*. San Francisco, CA: Jossey-Bass.

Carr-Chellman, A., & Duchastel, P. (2000). The ideal online course. *British Journal of Educational Technology, 31*(3), 229–241. doi:10.1111/1467-8535.00154

Chen, C. C., Rong-An, S., & Harris, A. (2006). The efficacy of case method teaching in an online asynchronous learning environment. *International Journal of Distance Education Technologies, 4*(2), 72–86. doi:10.4018/jdet.2006040106

Conole, G. (2009a). *Personalisation through technology-enhanced learning*. Keynote at the E-Portfolio June 2009 Conference: Innovation, Creativity and Accountability, City University, London.

Conole, G. (2009b). Research methodological issues with researching the learner voice. In Hin, L. T. W., & Subramaniam, R. (Eds.), *Handbook of research on new media literacy at the K-12 level: Issues and challenges* (pp. 669–682). Hershey, PA: IGI Global. doi:10.4018/978-1-60566-120-9.ch042

Conole, G., & Culver, J. (2009). The design of Cloudworks: Applying social networking practice to foster the exchange of learning and teaching ideas and designs. *Computers & Education*, *54*(3).

Dalsgaard, C. (2006). Social software: e-Learning beyond learning management systems. *European Journal of Open, Distance and E-Learning*. Retrieved July 10, 2010, from http://www.eurodl.org/materials/contrib/2006/Christian_Dalsgaard.htm.

Dangwal, R., & Kapur, P. (2009). Learning through teaching: Peer-mediated instruction in minimally invasive education. *British Journal of Educational Technology*, *40*(1), 5–22. doi:10.1111/j.1467-8535.2008.00863.x

De Freitas, S., & Conole, G. (2010). The influence of pervasive and integrative tools on learners' experiences and expectations of study. In Sharpe, R., Beetham, H., & De Freitas, S. (Eds.), *Rethinking learning for a digital age: How learners are shaping their own experiences*. New York, NY: Routledge.

Dewey, J. (1933). *How we think: A restatement of the relation of reflective thinking to the educative process*. Lexington, MA: D.C. Heath and Company.

European Commission. (2008). *An updated strategic framework for European cooperation in education and training*. Communication from the Commission to the European Parliament, the Council, the European Economic and Social Committee and the Committee of the Regions (December). Retrieved on 2 December, 2010, from http://ec.europa.eu/education/lifelong-learning-policy/doc28-en.htm.

Hazel Associates. (2005). *Global e-learning opportunity for U.S. higher education*. Retrieved from http://www.hezel.com/globalreport/.

Herrington, J., & Oliver, R. (1999). Using situated learning and multimedia to investigate higher-order thinking. *Journal of Educational Multimedia and Hypermedia, 8*(4), 401-422. Retrieved on 6 December, 2010, from http://dl.aace.org/9172.

Hofer, B., Yu, S., & Pintrich, P. (1998). Teaching college students to be self-regulated learners. In Schunk, D., & Zimmerman, B. J. (Eds.), *Self-regulated learning: From teaching to self-reflective practice* (pp. 57–88). New York, NY: The Guilford Press.

Holmberg, B. (1983). Guided didactic conversation in distance education. In Sewart, D., Keegan, D., & Holmberg, B. (Eds.), *Distance education: International perspectives* (pp. 114–122). London, UK: Croom Helm.

Hung, D. (2001). Design principles for web-based learning: Implications for Vygotskian thought. *Educational Technology*, *41*(3), 33–41.

Hung, D., & Nichani, M. (2001). Constructivism and e-learning: Balancing between the individual and social levels of cognition. *Educational Technology*, *41*(2), 40–44.

Ip, A., & Linser, R. (1999). *Web-based simulation generator: Empowering teaching and learning media in political science.* Retrieved from http://www.roleplaysim.org/papers/rpsg.htm.

Jamieson-Noel, D. (2004). *Exploring task definition as a facet of self-regulated learning*. Unpublished Doctoral Dissertation, Simon Fraser University.

Johnson, L., Smith, R., Willis, H., Levine, A., & Haywood, K. (2011). *The 2011 Horizon Report*. Austin, TX: The New Media Consortium.

Kawachi, P. (2003a). Asia-specific scaffolding needs in grounded design e-learning: Empirical comparisons among several institutions. *Proceedings of the 17th Annual Conference of the Asian Association of Open Universities,* Bangkok 12-14 Nov.

Kawachi, P. (2003b). Choosing the appropriate media to support the learning process. *Journal of Educational Technology*, *14*(1 & 2), 1–18.

Kawachi, P. (2005). Empirical validation of a multimedia construct for learning. In Mishra, S., & Sharma, R. (Eds.), *Interactive multimedia in education and training* (pp. 158–183). Hershey, PA: IDEA Group.

Kennedy, G., Judd, T. S., Chruchward, A., Gray, K., & Krause, K. (2008). First year students' experiences with technology: Are they really digital natives. *Australasian Journal of Educational Technology*, *24*(1), 108–122.

Kirkwood, A., & Price, L. (2005). Learners and learning in the twenty-first century: What do we know about students' attitudes towards and experiences of information and communication technologies that will help us design courses? *Studies in Higher Education, 30*(3), 257–274. doi:10.1080/03075070500095689

Laurillard, D. (2002). *Rethinking university teaching: A conversational framework for the effective use of learning technologies*. London, UK: Routledge. doi:10.4324/9780203304846

Lynn, L. E. (1996). *What is the case method? A guide and casebook*. Japan: the Foundation for Advanced Studies on International Development.

Mason, R. (1998). Models of on-line courses. *ALN Magazine, 2*(2). Retrieved 24 March, 2011, from http://www.aln.org/publications/magazine/v2n2/mason.asp.

Mason, R., & Rennie, F. (2008). *E-learning and social networking handbook: Resources for higher education*. New York, NY: Routledge.

Mayes, T. (2000). *Pedagogy, lifelong learning and ICT*. Retrieved on 16 December, 2010, from http://www.ipm.ucl.ac.be/ChaireIBM/Mayes.pdf.

Mishra, S. (2001). *Designing online learning*. COL Knowledge Series. Vancouver, Canada: The Commonwealth of Learning. Retrieved on 19 November, 2010, from http://www.col.org/Knowledge/ks_online.pdf.

Mishra, S. (2002). A design framework for online learning environments. *British Journal of Educational Technology*, *33*(4), 493–496. doi:10.1111/1467-8535.00285

Mitra, S. (1999). Virtual institutions in the Indian subcontinent. in Farrell, G. (Ed.), *The development of virtual education: A global perspective* (pp. 125-134). Vancouver, Canada: The Commonwealth of Learning.

Mitra, S., Dangwal, R., Chatterjee, S., Jha, S., Bisht, R., & Kapur, P. (2005). Acquisition of computing literacy on shared public computers: Children and the "hole in the wall.". *Australasian Journal of Educational Technology*, *21*(3), 407–426.

Mitra, S., & Rana, V. (2001). Children and the Internet: Experiments with minimally invasive education in India. *British Journal of Educational Technology*, *32*(2), 221–232. doi:10.1111/1467-8535.00192

Moore, M. (1993). Theory of transactional distance. In Keegan, D. (Ed.), *Theoretical principles of distance education* (pp. 22–38). London, UK: Routledge.

Naidu, S., Anderson, J., & Riddle, M. (2000). The virtual print exhibition: A case of learning by designing. In Sims, R., O'Reilly, M., & Sawkins, S. (Eds.), *Learning to choose: Choosing to learn (short papers and works in progress)* (pp. 109–114). Lismore, Australia: Southern Cross University Press.

Nedic, Z., Machotka, J., & Nafalski, A. (2003). Remote labs versus virtual and real labs. Paper published in the *Proceedings of the 33rd ASEE/ IEEE Frontiers in Education Conference*, November 5-8, 2003.

Oblinger, D. G., & Oblinger, J. L. (Eds.). (2005). Educating the Net generation. Boulder, CO: Educause. Retrieved on 3 December, 2010, from http://www.educause.edu/educatingthenetgen.

Oliver, R. (1999). Exploring strategies for online teaching and learning. *Distance Education, 20*(2), 240–254. doi:10.1080/0158791990200205

Ryan, M., & Woodward, L. (1997). *Impact of computer mediated communication (CMC) on distance tutoring*. In ED-MEDIA & ED-TELECOM World Conference June 1998, Freiburg, Germany. AACE.

Sahin, S. (2006). Computer simulations in science education: Implications for distance education. *Turkish Online Journal of Distance Education, 7*(4).

Salmon, G. (2000). *E-moderating: The key to teaching and learning online*. London, UK: Kogan Page.

Schank, R. (1997). *Virtual learning: A revolutionary approach to building a highly skilled workforce*. New York, NY: McGraw-Hill.

Schwartz, L., Clark, S., Cossarin, M., & Rudolph, J. (2004). Educational wikis: Features and selection criteria. *International Review of Research in Open and Distance Learning, 5*(1). Retrieved July 10, 2010, from http://www.irrodl.org/index.php/irrodl/article/view/163/692.

Sharma, R. C., & Mishra, S. (2007). *Cases on global e-learning practices: Successes and pitfalls*. Hershey, PA: Idea Group Publishing.

Smith, J. L., Smith, R., Willis, H., Levine, A., & Haywood, K. (2011). *The 2011 Horizon Report*. Austin, TX: The New Media Consortium.

Weigel, V. (2000). E-learning and the tradeoff between richness and the reach in higher education. *Change, 33*(5), 10–15. doi:10.1080/00091380009605735

Whitton, N. (2010). *Learning with digital games: A practical guide to engaging students in higher education*. New York, NY: Routledge.

Willis, B. (1992). *Strategies for teaching at a distance*. (ERIC Document Reproduction Service No. ED351008).

Yakimovicz, A. D., & Murphy, K. L. (1995). Constructivism and collaboration on the internet: Case study of a graduate class experience. *Computers & Education, 24*(3), 203–209. doi:10.1016/0360-1315(95)00015-E

# Chapter 13
# Addressing the "Commitment Problem": Driving Long-Term Persistent Focus in Self-Discovery Learning (A Thought Experiment)

**Shalin Hai-Jew**
*Kansas State University, USA*

## ABSTRACT

*Self-discovery learning, theoretically, can apply to the extreme ends of human endeavor—the acquisition and maintenance of in-depth expertise over long periods of time. Long-term persistence and focus have always been difficult challenges, even with the enabling structures of educational and career tracks. The inherent unstructuredness and informal aspects of self-discovery learning may make it harder for people to maintain long-term focused interests and investments in their learning. However, the creation of social collaborative work spaces for communities (and networks) of practice and the wide accessibility of various data sets online may be the nascent elements of more elite enabling spaces that may address the "commitment problem" for long-term persistent attention. This chapter proposes a draft survey based on the research to learn more about long-term informal discovery learning online.*

## INTRODUCTION

The world has crossed the Rubicon: the affordances of the Internet and Web have radically changed how people learn and acquire skill sets. These technologies have become indispensable in human learning. The enormous informational-access affordances and broad social connectivity of the persistent and pervasive information and communication technologies (ICT) substructure theoretically enable long-term self-discovery learning. Self-driven learning may lead to the creation and evolution of expertise in some fields

DOI: 10.4018/978-1-61350-320-1.ch013

Copyright © 2012, IGI Global. Copying or distributing in print or electronic forms without written permission of IGI Global is prohibited.

that may be complementary to work interests or engaging lives. The current structure of the Internet and World Wide Web (WWW) may not offer sufficient structured guidance for self-discovery learners.

*Web-based learning, per se, is not inherently student-centered in nature. Rather, it may be externally-directed, student-directed, free-choice, or combinations of each" (Berge & Mrozowski 2001; Bernard, et al. 2004, as cited in Hannafin, Hannafin, & Gabbitas, 2009, p. 768).*

The development of human expertise requires plenty of societal resources—in terms of educational systems and career paths. Yet, even with these societal structures supporting human endeavors, long-term focus and persistence has been a difficult challenge. High schools and universities face student retention challenges; work places also have a number of their employees moving on to other positions, in other fields. Specific nurturing environments have to exist for people to express their inherent tendency to autonomously seek out and pursue novelty and challenges. Because self-discovery learning is self-driven and often informal, this type of learning may be harder to create in a persistent way over the long-term. Self-discovery and inquiry-based learning refer to independent learners who acquire learning based on their own motivations. In the Web environment, such learners have to take important responsibilities to direct their own learning.

*During student-centered learning, the individual assumes responsibility for determining learning goals, monitoring progress toward meeting goals, adjusting or adapting approaches as warranted, and determining when individual goals have been adequately addressed. This can be particularly challenging while learning from the World-Wide Web, where billions of resources address a variety of needs. The individual must identify which tools and resources are available and appropriate, how to assemble them, and how to manage and support their unique learning goals (Hannafin, Hannafin, & Gabbitas, 2009, p. 767).*

In the present day, people develop expertise based on the support of their formal education—with access to plenty of information resources and human expert-guidance. There are workplace supports for expert skill-set development, with formalized training systems, required training, and hands-on assigned work. In addition, some idiosyncratic job descriptions (created for individuals) enable individuals to pursue even more idiosyncratic skill sets on a regular basis. These trainings are set in place to deal with the varying risk levels of critical skills losses in professional organizations given employee turnover and the growing complexity of difficult problems (Carley, 1992). In addition to higher education programs and work places, another generally untapped social engine of expertise development involves informal self-discovery learning. Given the criticality of connecting higher education with professional work lives, informal self-discovery acquisition of complex skill sets may be an important middle ground to enhance human capabilities. The informal learning may augment the formal learning structures. Figure 1, "Informal and Formal Learning Tracks for Life-long Learning," shows informal learning as one track in learning, but with more solid predominance of formal learning tracks—from higher education and work-based learning and acquisition of expertise.

Figure 1 shows a circuitous, interrupted, semi-linear, non-linear approach to informal acquisition of expertise. In fact, it may be interpreted that people may be unconsciously acquiring learning that forms a skill set potentially even without pre-planning.

Using informal learning for the building of a complex skill set is no easy feat, with so much information that is competing for people's attention in the present day. Henry James is reported to have cited the saying that "genius is nothing

*Figure 1. Informal and formal learning tracks for life-long learning*

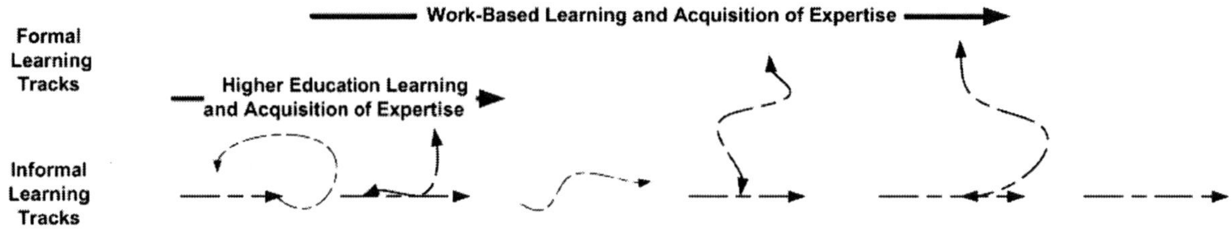


but a power of sustained attention," and that concept may apply. People have limited attentional resources and constraints on their information processing or cognition (Dukas, 2002). From the limited data, people "generate clues implicitly and explicitly" about the world (Horvitz, Kadie, Paek, & Hovel, 2003, p. 52). People are incapable of taking in the totality of their experiences; without selective attentional filtering, people would go into information overload (Gallagher, 2009), and they would have a harder time orienting themselves. This focus will be important in the long term, with competing life demands. Such learner self-regulation for the development of a complex expertise will require a future time perspective of the utility value of the particular learning and the delay of gratification and a resistance to a wide-ranging array of distractions (Bembenutty & Karabenick, 2004). The future time perspective must necessarily affect proximal sub-goals in order to offer further inducements to learners to stay on track (Miller & Brickman, 2004). In the same way that "change blindness" may make individuals blind to fundamental changes in their environment, and various distracters and mental models may make learners unable to see when they are moving off-course in their learning.

The maintenance of long-term focus can be challenging. Then, too, without the motivation of a scaffolding structure—a university that may confer a degree or a workplace that may confer a livelihood and social status—individuals who respond to external motivations and incentives may have a harder time maintaining the investment and focus to continue learning. Learners may experience incongruities between their own learning preferences and the presentation and teaching-and-learning modes offered. Further, acquiring new skill sets and knowledge bases can be highly challenging, especially at the beginning when critical faculties in the particular domain field may be non-existent. Long-term endeavors may well be interrupted by moments of non-effort, during which there is a large decay of knowledge and a potential loss of momentum. Long-term learner resilience may be a critical factor to try to build into the virtual spaces.

Amateurs are individuals who want to learn a subject matter only to a limited degree; novices are those who aspire to expertise eventually but are starting out with little domain information; experts are those who have learned a field thoroughly. They understand the critical concepts, principles, practices, and inter-relationships between these elements in a field. They can make sophisticated troubleshooting observations, judgment calls, and decisions in that domain. They can bring together complex bodies of knowledge and arrive at appropriate solutions. Experts are often able to innovate in a field.

There is a high contrast between the thought processes and abilities of novices and experts-in decision-making and problem-solving. Experts have been shown to have recognition-primed decision-making in which "rapid, intuitive decisions based on recognizing critical features of dynamic performance situations" are made (Fadde, 2009, p. 359). Experts often bring more complex framing of issues from multiple points-of-view than non-experts. Some researchers offer five invariants of expertise:

*First, experts, by definition, know more about their domain than do novices. Second, experts not only know more, but their knowledge is better organized. Third, on the basis of their greater knowledge and better organization, experts perform better than novices in domain-related tasks. Fourth, experts' skill is domain specific: There is very little transfer to unrelated domains. Finally, there are also many situations in which experts do not excel (Bédard & Chi, 1992, pp. 138 - 139).*

Ways to confound experts include the following: "by selecting a task in which interpreting the problem at a deeper level may interfere with problem solving, and by selecting a task for which a standard response may be inappropriate" (Bédard & Chi, 1992, p. 138). A tendency for people to "self-herd" (guide themselves) and justify their prior actions may lock them into habituating poor behaviors in problem-solving even though their initial decisions were based on hot-state emotions (Ariely, 2010). Novices tend to try to minimize risk in their work and "work backwards" (backward induction or reasoning backwards in time) towards a solution; by contrast, experts will tend to "work forward" to a solution even though that approach involves higher risk:

*Working forward is riskier than working backward in problem solving because operations are executed without first checking to see if they lead toward the goal. It seems more intelligent to organize the problem solving around the goal. Why, then, do experts work forward? It seems that working forward is more efficient if the problem solver knows enough about the domain to recognize the problem type (Bédard & Chi, 1992, p. 137).*

Experts bring a sense of history and complexity to their work; they can draw on a large repertoire of problem representations and types; they have knowledge of a broader range of applicable contexts. They may work more speedily, and they may apply deeper levels of details. Novices approach problem-solving with some limits. For example, those who are interrupted in their tasks were found to perform their work slower, commit more errors, make worse decisions, and express more negative emotions (Iqbal, Adamczyk, Zheng, & Bailey, 2005, p. 311). Experts themselves though may fall into rigid decision-making. They may fail to take into account the full breadth of relevant information. They may not have kept up with changes in their respective fields.

Modern peoples—impelled by a range of passions—may have multiple areas of expertise over their lifetime. Individuals have different learning preferences. They approach informal learning with a range of motivations and learning styles. Traditionally, informal learning has been applied for short-term and brief learning. By contrast, world-class expertise requires some 10,000 hours usually distributed over 10 years (Gladwell, 2008). Expertise in one area is not broadly transferable to another; rather, it is often task-specific and does not mean proficiency in other domains (Bédard & Chi, 1992, p. 138). To consciously apply learning from one domain to another, it requires the work of "mindful abstraction" (Salomon & Perkins, 1989, as cited in Maclellan, 2005, p. 133). Learners have to generalize the concepts from one learning context to another, with varying efficacy and applicability.

What may transfer is the skill level in self-regulation and learning of new contents in new circumstances—which may be somewhat transferable. These skills may include the practical abilities to research, to seek out experts and to invite their support, and to structure learning; they may include the ability to promote self-initiative and to regulate learning moods. This may include the meta-cognition of when the learner has reached absorptive capacity and how to back off for emotional renewal before moving forward.

Expertise is a complex concept, and its definition varies across domain fields. Mastery in a particular domain may be defined in a mix of factors: the depth of information knowledge (declarative and procedural); the applicable skill sets; the acculturation into a particular field; the depth of experiential learning, and even social recognition of that expertise. Specialization is defined as "the degree to which an individual, group, or organization performs a narrow range of activities" (Schilling, Vidal, Ployhart, & Marangoni, 2003, p. 39). Expertise is not generally conceptualized in a broad-based generalist way. Achieving this mastery may vary, with different time-to-acquisition for certain skill sets and likely high variances among learners who are informally pursuing these skill sets. Learners likely will experience a kind of "equifinality" with variant learning approaches that would result in mastery; in other words, there is often not just one successful approach in acquiring mastery of a complex skill set.

Over long time periods, focused informal learning may be characterized by discontinuities and punctuated equilibrium—moments of advanced progress interspersed with less active periods or even periods of no progress; in other words, there may be periods of continuity and discontinuity. These learning phases may seem random to the learner. They may comprise an orderly progression of progress. There may be periods of high enthusiasm against a back drop of relative calm. The "burn rate" of resources may affect how much an informal learning endeavor may be continue, in part, dependent on the replenishment of resources. In the same way that engagement with a game may offer cycles of "contemplation and engagement" in different rhythms (Marsh, Nitsche, Liu, Chung, Bolter, & Cheok, 2008, p. 99), long-term informal learning sequences and learning curves may manifest in different ways and with different rhythms. Certain periods in the learning cycle may be more opportune for interruptions than others, in the same way that interruption during an engaging task is more optimal during "periods of low mental workload" (Iqbal, Adamczyk, Zheng, & Bailey, 2005, p. 311). Long-term expertise development will require the organization of the learning around lived lives. Individuals with meta-cognition and self-regulation may have more skills to know when to deeply focus and when to just "float" or pull back from the action. "Perceptual expertise is at the heart of our everyday competence in the world," writes J. Richeimer (2000). The control of that expertise may enable people to expand their learning and engagement with the world. They may have more self-control in terms of mustering resources to invest in learning endeavors. They may have the self-efficacy to engage in the creative frictions and cross-fertilization of ideas that may enhance their work.

The core question is how to shape spaces on the WWW to encourage the long-term development of self-driven expertise. The flip-side of this argument has been to create learner-centered online learning experiences—by tailoring learning to particular learner profiles, learner cultures, learner language preferences, and their particular developmental needs. This particular approach here emphasizes the need to create internal learner resilience in the face of learning that may be challenging, culturally difficult, and not particularly customized to the learners' needs—all of which may be expected to happen in a lifelong learning pursuit or in the creation of complex expertise. Further, this concept of designing for long-term learner persistence does not require that the discovery learning only exist virtually but may involve some supports from the physical world—in a virtual and physical world synergistic give-and-take. This approach is not exclusive to virtual or fully-online spaces.

For the purposes of this chapter, the acquisition of expertise will be generally understood to fall into four main processes. The first phase involves initiation into a particular field through an intriguing experience, reading, or personality. The second phase involves the acquisition of the understandings and skill sets that are critical for expertise in a field. The third phase involves the proper acquisition of in-depth knowledge, interactions, experiences, and other aspects that enable high-level understandings in the field. The ultimate level of expertise is understood here as the ability to be able to innovate in that domain—by applying existing ideas in new ways, by coming up with new ideas and theories, and by contributing new research to the field. Within each of these phases, there are critical decisions to be made, resourcing to be done, and important efforts—to achieve particular aims. Throughout these endeavors, there may be issues of optimal pacing—when to escalate particular times of learning and when to de-escalate.

The assumed learning in this context is non-trivial and divergent learning, including learning in fields that are as-yet not fully matured (potentially) or discovered (concepts, ontologies, value systems practices, histories, main thinkers, and other elements). This work may involve creating new theories in a field and then testing the concepts, as well as offering alternate theorizing (Weick, 1989). The finer points of each of the above phases will be addressed in the body of the chapter.

This work also has implications for life-span learning, particularly the times when adult learning is most intense and effective—during the traditional higher education years, early in a career, throughout a working life, and possibly after retirement. It may help to define what the different needs are at the different life-span phases. It may also help to understand the different mixes of complex motivations at different phases—in terms of both intrinsic and extrinsic rewards. For long-term endeavors, people often need to perceive a sense of continuing intrinsic reward in their pursuits. They need to structure their lives, in a sense, for the contexts that would be nourishing of those interests. Pink (2009) asserts that those who are intrinsically motivated achieve larger successes in the long term:

*Intrinsically motivated people usually achieve more than their reward-seeking counterparts. Alas, that's not always true in the short term. An intense focus on extrinsic rewards can indeed deliver fast results. The trouble is, this approach is difficult to sustain. And it doesn't assist in mastery—which is the source of achievement over the long haul. The most successful people, the evidence shows, often aren't directly pursuing conventional notions of success. They're working hard and persisting through difficulties because of their internal desire to control their lives, learn about their world, and accomplish something that endures. (p. 79)*

This understanding is intuitive because the world itself does not offer extrinsic rewards continually. The reinforcements from the world are hit-and-miss and often non-existent.

This chapter first offers a literature review of the acquisition of expertise, informal learning, and some insights on designed socio-technical spaces for learning. As a thought experiment, this chapter explores the theoretical potential for shaping some virtual spaces to enhance the long-term development of expertise. These may be stand-alone tools, amalgamated tools, dedicated environments for specific development of informal expertise in particular fields, or generalized socio-technical environments. It proposes a draft survey to gather more information from direct informal learners about their needs on the Internet. This then suggests certain socio-technical affordances that may be pursued to enhance this potential.

## LITERATURE REVIEW

A brief literature review will examine the metaphor of selective attention and focal vision to highlight the challenge of long-term persistence in self-discovery learning. This will also examine some of the ICT affordances that may contribute to long-term informal acquisition of expertise.

The role of human attention has been deeply studied in terms of perception of digital media. Human attention is not random; rather, attention is used to focus on information-rich content for particular purposive uses, such as collecting necessary information, evaluating a situation, making a decision, or taking action (Canosa, 2009).

Attention is said to generally be of two types: bottom-up attention begins with details that draw human perception, which brings human attention and sense-making (and interpretation); top-down attention is an executive front-brain function that purposively deploys the brain's and sensory system's resources (often starting with organizing structures and drilling down to specific details). Bottom-up attention refers to objects that attract human attention and interest. In viewing still images, people's visual attention is drawn to human faces and faces in general. It is drawn to bright colors. It is drawn to what is perceived as salient. People may perceive the gist of a scene in milliseconds. In multi-sensory environments, people's attention is drawn to motion and action, to faces, to bright color contrasts, to sound sources, to sudden appearances of light, and to recognizable forms. Top-down attention refers to the "executive function" of the human brain, both cognition (thinking) and affect (emotions), which purposively focuses on particular information. People's expectations and mental models of a certain event have been shown to affect what they actually see and perceive. What is attended to is often "amplified" (enhanced by "sensory gain") by the human brain and made more noticeable and memorable (Hillyard, Vogel, & Luck, 1998, p. 1257).

The power to see an opportunity, which will change human decision-making and behaviors, stem from so-called "chance discovery"—and this involves an awareness of a particular event or situation and its significance—or what is called "perspective taking" (Oehlmann, 2002, pp. 3 -4). A fresh learning opportunity which aligns with self-discovery learner interests may be such a "chance discovery," to a learner has to be empowered with a certain informed perspective in order to identify it as such.

Human minds work with the energy signals (light waves, sound waves) and molecules (tastes and smells) and pressures (touch) from the environment to co-render reality. Certain signals from the world may be amplified or suppressed based on human attention and the perception of salience for survival (Michaels & Carello, 1981). The human mind captures more sensory information than it can process at one time. Attention does drive perception by focusing on some signals and dampening the effects of other signals; it helps the human mind interpret unclear signals and situational ambiguities. Attention informs cognition and sense-making. The human mind contributes to perceptual coherence by filling in information gaps.

In the same way that focal vision (the image at the center of human vision as compared to the periphery) is much more high-resolution than peripheral vision (a phenomenon known as the "eccentricity effect"), the objects at the center of human attention and focus are more clearly captured and understood than those in the mental periphery. Unattended channels still automatically capture information which may be recovered by retroactive attentional focus (and other mental exercises), but such information tends to be incomplete and even inaccurate.

Some aspects of the human mind are less suited for long-term self-driven learning and acquisition of expertise. Recent research suggests that the human mind wanders about 30 percent of the time into "imaginary rambles" during all activities except sex (Killingsworth & Gilbert, 2010, as cited in Bower, 2010, p. 1). While such mental wanderings may lead to darker moods, some types of imagination work may lead to creative problem-solving. The creativity literature has examples of inventors who slept on design problems and woke up with solutions that came to them in dreams. Creativity also comes into play when learners branch out to interdisciplinary fields that may inform their primary areas of work.

## Suitable Domain Fields

Clearly, not all domain fields would be suitable for informal expertise acquisition. Some factors in domain fields would render them inappropriate for informal learning:

- Those that involve potential harm or risk in decision-making (Collins & Evans, 2002);
- Those that are too complex and nuanced;
- Those that are insufficiently mature or defined;
- Those that require expensive equipment or locales;
- Those that are highly regulated in terms of procedures, ethics, and other aspects

Certain types of complex domain fields may be more suitable for the integration of informal learners. Currently, those domain fields with defined and focused skill sets seem more appropriate for informal learning. For example, there are computer languages. Complementary skill sets—like writing, public speaking—may also be easier to acquire informally. Hobbyist interests (like some recreational sports, games, and collecting) also seem more intuitively aligned for informal expertise.

## Long-Term Focus and Persistence in Self-Discovery Learning

To structure this approach, the informal acquisition of expertise is conceptualized as falling into four main phases. The first phase involves initiation into a particular domain field; the second phase involves immersion in that field; the third phase involves the acquisition and practice of expertise in that field, and the fourth phase is conceptualized as the ability to innovate as an expert in the field. Figure 2, "The Informal Acquisition of Expertise in a Domain," offers a straightforward conceptualization of four general phases of expertise acquisition through informal learning.

The simple developmental structure may vary in terms of the finer details in particular fields of expertise. At any point in the process (conceptualized here as critical junctures), people may choose to veer off and pursue another path. They may choose to delve deeper in the topic and potentially condense the time needed to achieve certain levels of proficiency. Dual-use types of learning (or multi-use learning) may enhance the learning speed. There may be substitutable experiences that may add progressive gain to the work. They may take a hiatus from their endeavors. This pathway is non-deterministic, but ultimately, it has to be somewhat enduring in time for the building of complex expertise.

This depiction is purposively general in order to accommodate as many possibilities as possible. Such acquisition of expertise paths should be much more defined and specific for particular task pathways.

## PHASE 1: INITIATION

## The Phase

Phase 1, Initiation, generally describes the introduction of a particular field to a person that may light intellectual curiosities that may evolve into a long-term committed learning endeavor that results in domain mastery. People may form an interest in a field from any aspect of the field—its periphery, its core; its proponents (inventors, historical figures, instructors, practitioners, and other learners); its practices; the fictional portrayals of a field, and any number of other points-of-entry. They may begin addressing pre-conceived notions of a domain-field. This stage is critical to capture the attention of learners and to also maintain sufficient interest that they would delve further into the learning.

*Figure 2. The informal acquisition of expertise in a domain*

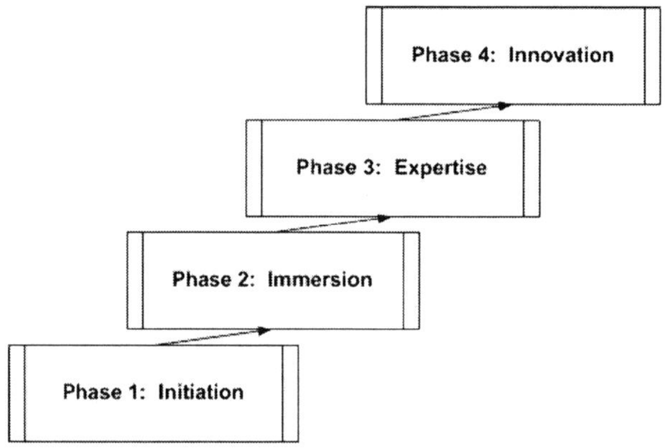


For complex tasks, Weick (1984) proposed the importance of "small wins" (accomplishments) to build the individual's sense of self-efficacy (self-confidence about what he or she can do) and sense that their endeavors will have an impact. Ideally, systems should instill that sense of confidence in learners. In a sense, there is a zero-sum aspect to all endeavors because of opportunity costs. An endeavor that requires a certain amount of energy and skill will draw away the same resources from another endeavor.

Novices in a particular field may need a sense of purpose and a defined path on their way to developing expertise. They have to be able to see achievable sub-tasks, not only for self-encouragement but to help them progress in the field. In a way, learning a complex skill set involves the development of human identities and the forming of complex modernly-skilled human beings. New learners have to be able to visualize themselves as a functioning member of a particular professional or educational or hobbyist or other community based on that interest.

Encouragement from respected others may also provide the intra-psychological supports that may benefit initiation into particular learning, based on social cognition and constructivist theories. While discovery learning requires self-passion and self-drive, the support of others may be a critical motivational element in the hard work of new learning. People's needs to share new insights and to get help on basic questions may be supported in virtual spaces.

## Current Information and Communication Technologies (ICT) Affordances

The extant technologies that may enhance initiation may be any of the following as stand-alone tools or as combined ones. Current knowledge spaces offer informational and multimedia entrée into particular topics. These spaces include more traditional spaces like digital repositories, referatories, and digital libraries. There are websites that offer wide distribution of information. Knowledge building sites like wikis, public encyclopedias, and blogs, collect more timely sorts of information. New tools to "scrape" information from sites and to skim data from the WWW, the Invisible Web (databases that have contents that are dynamically delivered and so are not as easily findable using current-stage Web browsers), and the Internet, there are plenty of information extraction tools that may add fresh insights to a particular topic. Search tools have a degree of built-in serendipity and play for diverse search results.

Various socio-technical systems (like learning/course management systems and other computer-supported collaborative work spaces) involve back-end data aggregators to enable the identification of rich data streams. In the same way, site analytics tools enable analysis of user visits to a site. Micro-blogging sites may be analyzed for real-time "global consciousness" based on text analysis. Various online data analysis tools—quantitative, qualitative, and mixed methods—enrich the value of statistical information.

Recommender systems may be focused to customize searches for individuals or may tap crowd-sourcing as a way to direct users to particular resources. Really Simple Syndication (RSS) feeds and tagging features may help learners identify potentially relevant resources for their investigations of particular fields. These tools all lower the perceived and real costs-of-entry.

These various affordances may enable naïve learners to start forming deeper understandings and points of reference. They may start creating foundational understandings—of schemas or ontologies in particular fields. They may be better grounded in what is plausible and what is, by contrast, magical thinking. They may start developing a better sense of the signal from the noise. They may develop a sense of what negative learning is and be able to avoid misconceptions.

In their initiation, they may form a clearer sense of their actual capabilities versus idealized ones. They may also develop some self-discipline in terms of self-regulation of learning in the field. Naïve learners may also start forming senses of what is peripheral information—some of which is relevant—and others of which are interdisciplinary sources that may or may not have relevance.

The variety of social spaces—virtual immersive ones, social networking spaces, as well as those specifically designed for co-learning and co-work—enable a wide range of collaborative and individualistic learning and work. These virtual environments enable mixed types of learning—automated as well as human-facilitated ones. These virtual communities are enhanced by the wide accessibility of various data sets online, with a range of in-discipline information as well as interdisciplinary data. Virtual communities have sprung up around open-source building of software and shared interests. These communities may offer access to expertise and shared collegial interests that may enhance the building of more complex skill sets. They also offer access to audiences and consumers of ideas, communications, and innovations by individuals in the field. Virtual spaces may enable people to seek out able allies to help in the endeavors.

The WWW enables a range of informational visualizations that may spark fresh conceptualizations of information and analytical depth. There are simulations that people may experience through their human-embodied avatars in order to gain intuitive understandings in a kind of situated cognition. Such spaces are also used to help people acclimate into a particular professional environment. Some simulations involve designed and scripted environments (such as biological ecosystems) which may be directly experienced for various experiential learning.

## Potential Design Issues

To build on the current ICT structures and affordances, it would be critical to help learners structure and customize their approaches to new learning in new fields. This would suggest that self-discovery learners need a clearer sense of their own meta-cognition learning. Self-discipline and self-regulation tools that may make their learning more coherent would be helpful. These include record-keeping tools in the cloud that are maintained over time that may be repositories of their learning, as they move from challenge to challenge, inquiry to inquiry. Insights may oftentimes be fleeting and transient, and having a way of capturing those concepts is important for review and potential later use. The idea is to have as few frictions as possible to achieve learning efficiencies through online "accelerants" and "incubators." Also, there should be lowered barriers to accessing particular resources to support this long-term endeavor. User interfaces may be designed to better guide in-the-moment learning. Explicit guidance may minimize cognitive load demands (Kirschner, et al., 2006, as cited in Hannafin, Hannafin & Gabbitas, 2009, p. 772).

Virtual social spaces may be enhanced with easier finding of others with like interests and the building of trust between members.

Those in particular fields that are more readily accessible for the informal acquisition of expertise may create direct appeals to certain learners to develop specific skill sets. Such targeted communications and outreaches may appeal to a particular type of individual. Researchers suggest that "abstract and highly structured knowledge domains" like statistics, computer programming, and math, may require more directive rather than indirect trial-and-error fully-independent self-discovery (Budé, Imbos, Wiel, Broers, & Berger, 2009, p. 25) .

Novice and amateur learners in a field may benefit from some form of priming. This priming may disabuse them of mythologies that may get in the way of the new learning. It may also prepare their minds for the particular learning that they will engage in.

The design of help-seeking tools may enhance the new learner experience, to not only expand the "zone of proximal development" (to use Vygotsky's term) but also to encourage further risk-taking and affordances in the learning.

## PHASE 2: IMMERSION

### The Phase

Phase 2, Immersion, focuses on the moment when a learner has decided to commit to a certain learning domain. This phase assumes that the learners may make time in their lives and set aside resources (time, energy, and others) to pursue focused informal learning. This phase may use formal learning structures, too, such as higher education courses or work-place opportunities, but with the main originating impetus as an informal approach. This phase involves the deeper acquisition of relevant knowledge. This also involves the necessary hands-on practices for deeper development of applied skills within the particular domain. The immersion phase involves the development of the proper mindset and skills to query the field—by formulating the appropriate questions and then pursuing the necessary knowledge appropriately.

Yakel and Torres (2003) describe the importance of three main skill sets in terms of pursuing information: domain knowledge, antifactual literacy (the ability to differentiate truth from fiction; the ability to apply critique; the ability to analyze), and what they call "archival intelligence" ("the ability to interpret records and assess their value as evidence" and the knowledge of "archival principles, practices, and institutions"; the differentiation between primary sources "and their surrogates") (Yakel & Torres, 2003, p. 52). The ability to sift information for what is relevant is a critical foundational step towards new learning. They may be able to engage the cross-fertilization of ideas for more complex thinking in a particular field—for more complicated sense-making.

Another important aspect in immersion is to surface tacit knowledge as it is being acquired, so learners are consciously aware of their own developing ideas and knowledge. Various ICT tools for this include those that enhance rumination and self-reflection.

Another factor in Phase 2 involves the learners' exposures of themselves to various constructive experiences that enhance their learning. This also assumes the creation of social ties to others who are critical to the learning endeavors; this assumes negotiating social relationships to enhance the learning.

At some level, self-regulation also matters—the application of short-term memory and long-term memory affordances. Past performances likely have some impact on future decisions and performance. Learners need to apply their executive functions to managing their own learning. Learners will have to troubleshoot and problem-solve challenges in their learning trajectory. On the one hand, they will have to pace their learning appropriately so as not to lose motivation; they must maintain speed and altitude so that their endeavor does not stall.

Learners, over time, will need to prioritize their learning tasks. They will have to make critical decisions of when to press ahead and when to veer off a particular course. Self-learners in this phase have to engage complex logistics. They have to decide which learning paths make sense for themselves. They may consider others' defined paths but also make adjustments for their own learning styles. They need to decide when to transition to peripheral or parallel or complementary areas of interest.

They also need to consider when they are ready for hands-on practice. They need to create the circumstances in which they can apply their new learning and get feedback on their performance (whether that feedback is automated, from peer learners, or from subject matter experts). They also need to find feedback loops for helpful insights for their own learning. As their learning becomes more sophisticated, they may engage in trouble-shooting, problem-solving, and even project work within the field—all of which may extend their skill sets.

They also have to identify and use the ICT tools that will enable their work. With fast-moving changes in this area, the learning is likely fairly constant if learners want to use a range of tools. Phase 2 may well be one of the most challenging phases because of the depth of sustained work required.

## Current ICT Affordances

Similar to Phase 1, the diversity of information resources also enhances Phase 2. Some digital libraries have been building collaborative tools to bring together co-researchers and co-learners to collaborate around information. The social connections to others, the availability of virtualized experiences, the abilities to visualize important information, all enhance Phase 2.

Web 2.0 technologies enable individuals to tag resources that they may want to revisit and archive publications listings for anytime access. This type of electronic memory and access enhance the efficiencies of learning.

The ability to strengthen learner self-reflection through the digital recording of observations (in the cloud and otherwise) enhances the immersion in a particular field. In digital laboratories, there are often electronic journals to capture insights from the experiments. These are tools that may enhance the acquisition of learning and also some meta-cognition. Learners may get a sense of their own interests and strengths. They may correct errors in their own learning when they come across mutually-exclusive conflicting information. They may identify areas of self-improvement in their learning. This enhances the ability to manage personal knowledge. Some tools enable spatial layouts of the mental models, for those for whom visual learning is more effective.

The uses of virtual immersive worlds built around certain communities of practice and networks of practice help learners acclimate to a field. The ease-of-entry (and participation) and ease-of-exit to these communities are strengths and weaknesses; they allow open experimentation for self-discovery learners, but they do not necessarily encourage long-term engagements and participation. Virtual spaces also help them define and enact their fresh identities in part by their new acquired knowledge and skill sets. Some social networking sites enable the creation of sub-groups, which users may self-identify to and join. Some algorithms have been created to surface individuals' hidden interests based on their messaging (such as email messaging) in order to identify nascent emerging communities of interest—to see if individuals want to purposively pursue virtual interactions.

ICT that enables learners to test out their ideas through trial-and-error learning (such as in some immersive simulations) may enhance hands-on practice.

The availability of live webinars and live conferences also broadens the learners' accesses to professionals in various fields and their access to information. The popularity of digital poster sessions enables asynchronous access to important data, as well.

Co-learners may collaborate with others in virtual spaces, particularly those dedicated to certain types of dedicated knowledge. Dyads, small teams, and even larger ones may be formed for mutual learning benefits. The networking of various individuals has allowed for the creation of much larger virtual teams than have been described in the human teaming research literature.

## Potential Design Issues

One ICT affordance currently missing for immersions in particular subject areas is designed coherence. Currently, people pursuing self-discovery learning in certain areas have to tap into diverse resources and socio-technical affordances. They have to maintain their own internal sense of coherence in their skills and learning acquisitions. Having designed and dedicated sites around particular interests may enhance the informal development of such skill sets.

Some tools have endeavored to define expertise and to create a sense of trust for those who claim expertise. Peer review in professional journals is one way of establishing the bona fides of various professionals. However, there are still many gaps in identifying true expertise. Even harder is the establishment of benevolent helps from experts to novice and amateur learners in a field.

Immersions would benefit from safe spaces with guaranteed securities and privacy for evolving learning and ideas. While there are some back-channel ways to communicate, learners are not deeply encouraged to take risks or to share nascent thoughts in public spaces—in part because of the culture of disrespecting others in various public forums. Trust relationships may enable higher levels of collaboration and co-learning, and these maybe only exist in safer contexts such as those in select higher education and possibly workplace contexts, with more rules of engagement and supervisory oversight.

# PHASE 3: EXPERTISE

## The Phase

Phase 3, Expertise, describes a stage in which the learner has internalized and mastered the critical knowledge of a field; a sense of the domain's history; research strategies in the field; the ability to engage in some of the practices of the field; and the values and principles of the field. They understand that the field is limited, and they also are aware of some of the peripheral interdisciplinary aspects. They are able to make professional judgment calls and decisions in the domain field, even when they differ from others' viewpoints. They have professional relationships to others in the field, and they have some measure of an identity in the field.

Another way to conceptualize mastery is as an elusive state is that is never achieved. Pink (2009) uses an algebraic concept of an asymptote—a straight line that a curve approaches but never quite reaches (pp. 126 – 127). A self-discovery learner is always in approach mode but never in full attainment. This concept is captured also in the "low floor, high ceiling" concept—the idea that the simple things in a field are easy to begin learning, but the complex aspects are impossible (which is analogous to the straight line that is never quite achieved by the approaching curve). That straight line is the concept of idealized mastery. The curve is the level of individual expertise approaching mastery—but never quite fulfilling that aim.

### Current ICT Affordances

At the expert level, learners will run up against the limits of information on the WWW and Internet. They will be aware that there is information which they do not have access to, and which is not broadly public. The long-term persistence of digital artifacts and WWW / Internet memory (through caching) enables a critical sense of continuance of expertise in a particular field. The vibrancy of the informal and formal communities supporting particular learning domains may offer rich information and new research in a particular field, which enables the growth and deepening of expertise.

The persistent memory of cloud spaces may enable a kind of building of a sense of developmental history in the building of an expert knowledge base and skill set. The capturing of knowledge of how others learn may create a "bread crumb trail" of learning for learners with similar needs or profiles.

The prevalence of foreign language translator tools and transliteration tools enable easier potential collaborations between peoples of different cultures and backgrounds.

### Potential Design Issues

One critical design issue is to offer opportunities for experts to practice their skills. For many, the practice has to be proprioceptive and in-the-physical-world. For others, the practice may be done virtually, such as through the dissemination of original widgets, apps, software tools, and code online.

A more effective identity regime to validate human identities would be important to enhance the interrelationships between those with expertise. It may become harder and harder to evolve an expert skill set without access to other experts. The acquisition of an expert skill set shows that skills are part of the co-evolution of the self, and the self does have a manifestation and a presence on the Web (for many in the world).

## PHASE 4: INNOVATION

### The Phase

Phase 4, Innovation, is a step above expertise because this is expertise-in-action—to the point of contributing new insights to the domain field. This assumes not only an internalized complex mastery of a domain but the ability to innovate, articulate, and externalize their new insights. This phase also assumes the ability to self-critique—to see where weaknesses exist in one's particular work. Innovation assumes knowledge of the extant information in a domain field and in related contiguous domain fields, and the ability to contribute something novel.

Such innovative thinkers may be able to remix known facts. They may be able to conduct meta-analyses and draw out fresh insights from the known information. They may be able to apply deductive logic and apply principles to particular specific circumstances. They may be able to apply abductive logic (inferential guessing to arrive at an explanatory hypothesis), which involves the drawing of conclusions from the real and offering a hypothesis and testing that hypothesis against the real (to best represent real-world realities). The work of innovation also depends in part of the imagination, applied to particular domain information, to emerge with something new. To strengthen the adoption of innovations, such thinkers also need to be able to reach out to a wider audience to support adoption of their work.

For creativity, the maintenance of positive affect increases the range of attentional selection

(Rowe, Hirsch, & Anderson, 2007). That said, the long-term orientation of research and development (R&D) in corporations are the most difficult to reward although some incentives are designed to "focus employees' attention on long-term results" (Steers, Porter, & Bigley, 1996, p. 558).

### ICT Affordances

Various digital tools enhance human brainstorming through listing, doodling, the cross-fertilization of information, randomization and designed serendipity, and conceptualizing; the persistence of such tools and the resulting artifacts may support the capture of critical information and enhance human long-term memory.

One large affordance of innovators in ICT is the widespread popularity of peer-edited professional journals—which offer a public or semi-public test-bed space for experts to test their research and works.

The wide availability of authoring tools that enable fairly easy self-expression—through image editing, video editing, digital drawing, and other forms—lowers the cost-of-entry for digital publication and distribution. Many such tools also are free in the cloud or are downloadable.

### Potential Design Issues

One of the most critical pieces missing for innovators is the protection of intellectual property. Innovators should have the right to be rewarded for their work before it goes into the public domain. The wide abuses of copyright online may be disincentivizing to true innovators.

## DESIGNING SOCIO-TECHNICAL SYSTEMS FOR INFORMAL EXPERTISE ACQUISITION

Socio-technical spaces (spaces where people interact with others through mediating technologies) and other ICT tools may be brought in to amplify and complement human endeavors and capabilities in the pursuit of expertise of complex skill sets. The research and design of such spaces will need to be precise and accurate for the proper building of the necessary infrastructures, but users will not have to be necessarily transparent for all (Mackenzie, 2003). Encapsulated complexities may make such systems more usable.

### An Early Functionalities Features-List

A basic design tenet begins with a features list of functionalities. These functionalities may fit non-exclusively in different phases. Some early ideas for this list could include the following enablements for users of the various tools and socio-technical spaces that promote the long-term acquisition of complex expertise.

#### Phase 1: Initiation

- Explore early interests (via broad sampling);
- Identify others who have shared interests and areas of expertise;

#### Phase 2: Immersion

- Coordinate one's own schedule and activities;
- Pursue relevant information, digital resources, and virtual experiences;
- Connect with relevant real-world events, individuals, and groups;
- Acculturate into a particular domain-field;
- Evolve a sense of identity (internal and external) in a domain-field;
- Experience serendipity and adventure in self-learning;
- Interact with relevant virtual communities and networks of learning at the user's level of comfort and self-revelation;

- Acquire and analyze possible (multiple and alternate) paths in the self-learning process (with appropriate decision-supports for effective decision-making);
- Find support and self-motivation in moments of discouragement, setbacks, and low or negligible returns;
- Understand one's level of learning at each phase of learning;
- Form a sense of coherence about the learning, even when one is using mobile devices in circumstances of high-interruption;

### Phase 3: Expertise

- Maintain necessary privacy as needed;
- Collaborate with trusted others;
- Maintain a personal archive of learning and some personal "institutional memory" of the acquisition of expertise;
- Experience a sense of freedom, adaptability, choice, and non-coercion in the learning;

### Phase 4: Innovation

- Share findings in an open-source way when desired (and build a legacy of contributions);
- Form ideas and directions for fresh innovations;
- Formulate new and original research;
- Acquire rewards, credit, and legal protections for original innovations;
- Find the others to hand-off the work to once a learner knows he or she has taken a work as far as he or she can.

The design of socio-technical spaces that would support and enable long-term acquisition of expertise in various fields will have to be done with a sense of accountability. The resources created should also be fully transparent, with all assumptions of the model fully clarified to users. There are questions of how to design to mitigate unintended consequences, such as potentially misleading learners or leading them off-course (of their own objectives). The unique pursuit of learning in respective fields will most certainly result in a wider range of functionalities for defined fields. This features-list serves as a mere start.

### The Evolution of the "Informal Long-Term Self-Discovery Learning Acquisition of Expertise" (ILSLAE) Survey

A draft survey, titled "Informal Long-Term Self-Discovery Learning Acquisition of Expertise" Survey, was created in order to query people on their lived experiences with such acquisition of expertise. At the time of publication, this survey had not yet gone through validity assessment or deployment. A next step in this research will involve the evolution of this instrument and its deployment (see Appendix).

## FUTURE CONSIDERATIONS

The building of ICT tools and spaces and devices to enhance the acquisition of expertise through informal self-discovery learning is a broad and difficult challenge. Learners have diverse skills and disparate needs at different times in their long-term learning. They may have different needs based on training, cultural understandings, language backgrounds, and personalities.

While there is relevant research, there is plenty of room for the capturing of even more information that may inform this endeavor. More needs to be known about life-span learning and high-demand expert-level skill sets. Are there developmental windows during which certain learning and skills must be achieved? Are certain types of information and skill sets more attainable than others, and if so, why? Are there certain personality types that are more prone to long-term self-discovery learning in the pursuit of complex skill sets? What are the main barriers facing such learners, and how may those barriers be mitigated?

Further, what technologies may complement human endeavors? Which technologies (and their applications) may hinder human learning endeavors? Is there a time when the expertise has evolved beyond a need for ICT resources, or are ICT resources a lifetime necessity? Should long-term self-discovery learning be more structured or less structured? When would a model be too prescriptive or regimented, and on the contrary, when would it be too freeform?

In various cultural contexts, are there unique learner needs? If so, what would cause these differences? How should these differences be addressed in the design of tools to support long-term discovery learning?

The requirements of expert skill sets are complex and generally unmapped, with unclear time-to-acquisition of different skill sets. It may help to design a dedicated multi-function space as a longitudinal test case of this concept of the acquisition of expert skill sets.

In cases where individual pursuits of further learning have sparked group learning endeavors and projects, what factors led to the evolutions of such virtual communities? (Raymond, 1999, as cited in Koru & Tian, 2004). How can individuals do proper hand-offs or plan "succession" for their work once they have reached the limits of their own contributions? (Raymond, 2003, p. 9).

## CONCLUSION

This chapter offers a thought experiment about the acquisition of complex skill sets through informal self-discovery learning. It highlights some extant ICT tools that may enhance such long-term endeavors. This suggests ways to build technological tools and virtual socio-technical spaces with a closer eye to long-term and complex self-learning, to complement known human strengths and weaknesses in regards to learning and skills acquisitions.

## ACKNOWLEDGMENT

Without realizing it, I have been noticing the learners who are comfortable learning off-track and without formal structures—for the hard work of acquisition of expertise and for achieving creativity. I had not realized how difficult and daring that sort of off-ranch learning is until now. I hope this chapter might be an encouragement for those willing to create new learning paths for unique insights. Thanks to R. Max.

## REFERENCES

Ariely, D. (2010). *The upside of irrationality: The unexpected benefits of defying logic at work and at home*. New York, NY: HarperCollins.

Bédard, J., & Chi, M. T. H. (1992). Expertise. *Current Directions in Psychological Science*, *1*(4), 135–139. doi:10.1111/1467-8721.ep10769799

Bembenutty, H., & Karabenick, S. A. (2004). Inherent association between academic delay of gratification, future time perspective, and self-regulated learning. *Educational Psychology Review*, *16*(1), 35–57. doi:10.1023/B:EDPR.0000012344.34008.5c

Bower, B. (2010, Nov. 12). Many unhappy returns for wandering minds. *Science News. U.S. News & World Report*, 1–3.

Budé, L., Imbos, T., Wiel, M. W. J. d., Broers, N. J., & Berger, M. P. F. (2009). The effect of directive tutor guidance in problem-based learning of statistics on students' perceptions and achievement. *Higher Education*, *57*, 23–36. .doi:10.1007/s10734-008-9130-8

Canosa, R. L. (2009). Real-world vision: Selective perception and task. *ACM Transactions on Applied Perception, 6*(2), 11:1–11:34.

Carley, K. (1992). Organizational learning and personnel turnover. *Organization Science, 3*(1), 20–46. doi:10.1287/orsc.3.1.20

Collins, H. M., & Evans, R. (2002). The third wave of science studies: Studies of expertise and experience. *Social Studies of Science, 32*(2), 235–296. doi:10.1177/0306312702032002003

Dukas, R. (2002). Behavioural and ecological consequences of limited attention. *Philosophical Transactions of the Royal Society of London, 357*, 1539–1547. .doi:10.1098/rstb.2002.1063

Fadde, P. J. (2009). Instructional design for advanced learners: Training recognition skills to hasten expertise. *Educational Technology Research and Development, 57*(3), 359–376. .doi:10.1007/s11423-007-9046-5

Gallagher, W. (2009). *Rapt: Attention and the focused life* (pp. 1–244). New York, NY: The Penguin Press.

Gladwell, M. (2008). *Outliers: The story of success*. New York, NY: Little, Brown and Company.

Hannafin, M., Hannafin, K., & Gabbitas, B. (2009). Re-examining cognition during student-centered, Web-based learning. *Educational Technology Research and Development, 57*, 767–785. .doi:10.1007/s11423-009-9117-x

Hillyard, S. A., Vogel, E. K., & Luck, S. J. (1998). Sensory gain control (amplification) as a mechanism of selective attention: Electro-physiological and neuroimaging evidence. *Philosophical Transactions of the Royal Society of London: Biological Sciences, 353*(1373), 1257–1270. doi:10.1098/rstb.1998.0281

Horvitz, E., Kadie, C., Paek, T., & Hovel, D. (2003). Models of attention in computing and communication: From principles to applications. *Communications of the ACM, 44*(3), 52–59. doi:10.1145/636772.636798

Iqbal, S. T., Adamczyk, P. D., Zheng, X. S., & Bailey, B. P. (2005). Toward an index of opportunity: Understanding changes in mental workload during task execution. In the *Proceedings of Human-Computer Interaction, CHI* 2005: Portland, Oregon, (pp. 311–320).

Koru, A. G., & Tian, J. (2004). Defect handling in medium and large open source projects. *IEEE Software, 21*(4), 54–61. doi:10.1109/MS.2004.12

Mackenzie, A. (2003). These things called systems: Collective imaginings and infrastructural software. *Social Studies of Science, 33*(3), 365–387. doi:10.1177/0306312703033003

Maclellan, E. (2005). Conceptual learning: The priority for higher education. *British Journal of Educational Studies, 53*(2), 129–147. doi:10.1111/j.1467-8527.2005.00287.x

Marsh, T., Nitsche, M., Liu, W., Chung, P., Bolter, J. D., & Cheok, A. D. (2008). Film informing design for contemplative gameplay. In the *Proceedings of the Sandbox Symposium*, Los Angeles, California, (pp. 99–106).

Michaels, C. F., & Carello, C. (1981). *Direct perception* (pp. 1–200). Englewood Cliffs, NJ: Prentice-Hall, Inc.

Miller, R. B., & Brickman, S. J. (2004). A model of future-oriented motivation and self-regulation. *Educational Psychology Review, 16*(1), 9–33. doi:10.1023/B:EDPR.0000012343.96370.39

Oehlmann, R. (2002). Metacognitive and computational aspects of chance discovery. *New Generation Computing, 21*(2003), 3–12. Ohmaha, Ltd. and Springer-Verlag.

Pink, D. H. (2009). *Drive: The surprising truth about what motivates us* (pp. 79, 126–127). New York, NY: Riverhead Books.

Raymond, E. S. (2003). The cathedral and the bazaar. *First Monday*. Retrieved from http://rfrost.people.si.umich.edu/courses/SI110/readings/IntellecProp/Cathedral-Bazaar.pdf.

Rowe, G., Hirsh, J. B., & Anderson, A. K. (2007). Positive affect increases the breadth of attentional selection. *Proceedings of the National Academy of Sciences of the United States of America*, *104*(1), 383–388. doi:10.1073/pnas.0605198104

Schilling, M. A., Vidal, P., Ployhart, R. E., & Marangoni, A. (2003). Learning by doing something else: Variation, relatedness, and the learning curve. *Management Science*, *49*(1), 39–56. doi:10.1287/mnsc.49.1.39.12750

Steers, R. M., Porter, L. W., & Bigley, G. A. (1996). *Motivation and leadership at work* (6th ed., p. 558). Boston, MA: McGraw Hill.

Weick, K. E. (1984). Small wins: Redefining the scale of social problems. *The American Psychologist*, *39*(1), 40–49. doi:10.1037/0003-066X.39.1.40

Weick, K. E. (1989). Theory construction as disciplined imagination. *Academy of Management Review*, *14*(4), 516–531.

Yakel, E., & Torres, D. A. (2003). AI: Archival intelligence and user expertise. *The American Archivist*, *66*(1), 51–78.

## KEY TERMS AND DEFINITIONS

**Archive:** A digital storage space of digital objects.

**Articulation:** The verbal expression of an idea or feeling.

**Asymptote:** An algebraic construct of a straight line which is approached by a curve, which never touches the line.

**Attention:** The act of concentrating the mind on a particular issue; a high state of concentration.

**Collaboration:** The act of working together with other people on a shared project.

**Expertise:** A high level of mastery in a particular domain field, interdisciplinary domain fields, or area of study.

**Findable:** The ability to be identified and searched out, as in a digital object.

**Imagination:** The forming of mental images of something that is not present or real.

**Inquiry-Based Learning:** A learner-centered type of learning that focuses on the posing of questions or problems and their answers and solutions (respectively); the seeking of information based around a specific question.

**Persistence:** The act of lasting through time; continuance.

**Searchable:** The characteristic of digital repositories that enable the finding of particular and specific resources.

**Self-Discovery Learning:** Learner-directed and learner-driven learning.

**Socio-Technical Space:** Web-mediated spaces that enable human socializing, interactivity, shared work, knowledge exchange, and other functionalities.

## APPENDIX

### Informal Long-Term Self-Discovery Learning Acquisition of Expertise (ILSLAE) Survey

Informal learning involves any sort of learning that you've pursued on your own without direct formal support from a higher education degree program or workplace environment. This survey is about the uses of informal learning to develop complex skill-sets to the level of mastery. If you have attained expertise in any field through informal learning—and have used the Internet and Web as part of that learning—then please proceed with this survey.

1. What made this topic of your informal learning meaningful to you? Why did you decide to pursue this learning in depth?
2. How long did it take you to acquire the level of "mastery"? (Please define this in months and years.)
3. How much resource investment did you put into acquiring expertise? (Money? Material resources?)
4. Did you use the Internet and World Wide Web to support your learning? If so, how so? Please check all that apply. If you used the Internet and WWW in other ways, please write that into the blank below.
   Communications
   Web conferencing
   Research
   Socializing
   Collaboration
   Virtual experiences
5. Did you ever consider stopping your informal learning endeavor? What were critical points in your decision-making about whether to continue with this learning or not? Please describe those moments.
6. Did you miss some of the supports of either a college setting or a workplace setting for your learning? If so, what parts did you miss?
7. What tasks did you engage in to evolve your expertise? (Please check all that apply.)
   Inter-Communications
   Email
   Microblogging
   Human-embodied digital avatar interactions
   Live web conferencing
   Digital poster sessions
   Collaborations
   Virtual work spaces
   Hands-on Practice
   Direct practicing of skills (design, writing, research, or others)
   Research and Information Gathering
   Researching information
   Conducting your own primary interviews and experiments and other direct research
   Soliciting information online such as through surveys

Socializing
Joining virtual community groups
Formal Guidance
Contact with experts
Feedback from crowd-sourcing
Feedback from informal communities
Semi-Formal Trainings
Taking online classes or trainings
Using digital learning objects
Reading research
Virtual Experiences
Experiencing online virtual spaces / virtual worlds
Going through simulations
Experiencing self-discovery learning spaces
Visualizing information in new ways

8. Of these activities, which were the most critical for you in the development of your expertise? Why?
9. Were there moments where you made great progress? If so, what led to this expansion of your learning and your skills? What sorts of experiences most enhanced the development of your skill set? Why?
10. Are there new tools or virtual spaces that could be designed that could enhance your engagement with informal learning? If so, what? Why?

# Compilation of References


Adamo-Villani, N., & Johnson, E. (2010). Virtual heritage applications: The 3D tour of MSHHD. *Proc. of ICCSIT 2010 - International Conference on Computer Science and Information Technology*, April 28-30, Rome.

Adamo-Villani, N., Johnson, E., & Penrod, T. (2009). Virtual reality on the Web: The 21st Century project. *Proc. of M-ICTE 2009 - V Int. Conf. on Multimedia and Information and Communication Technologies in Education*, 22-24 April, Lisbon, (pp. 622-626).

Adobe. (2010). *Flash 3D graphics*. Retrieved from http://help.adobe.com/en_US/Flash/10.0_UsingFlash/WS3D3F757E-6EEB-4f6b-BC7F-BE8F94D329E1.html.

Agency for Healthcare Research and Quality. (2002, April). Preventing disability in the elderly with chronic disease. *Research in Action, 3*. AHRQ Publication No. 02-0O18. Retrieved October 13, 2010, from http://www.ahrq.gov/research/elderdis.htm.

Aguilar, F. R. (2007). Top of the pods: In search of a podcasting "pedagogy" for language learning. *Computer Assisted Language Learning, 20*(5), 471–492. doi:10.1080/09588220701746047

Aldrich, C. (2009). *The complete guide to simulations and serious games: How the most valuable content will be created in the age beyond Gutenberg to Google*. Pfeiffer.

Alexander, S. (2001). E-learning developments and experiences. *Education + Training, 43*(4/5), 240–248. doi:10.1108/00400910110399247

Alm, A. (2006). CALL for autonomy, competence and relatedness: Motivating language learning environments in Web 2.0. *The JALT CALL Journal, 2*(3), 29–38.

American Cancer Society. (2007). *The society in Second Life*. Retrieved October 8, 2010, from http://www.cancer.org/InYourArea/HighPlainsHawaiiPacific/AreaHighlights/the-society-in-second-life.

Ames, C. (1992). Classroom goals, structures, and student motivation. *Journal of Educational Psychology, 84*(3), 261-271. Retrieved September 30, 2010, from http://www.unco.edu/cebs/psychology/kevinpugh/motivation_project/resources/ames92.pdf.

Andreas, K., Tsiatsos, T., Terzidou, T., & Pomportsis, A. (2010). Fostering collaborative learning in Second Life: Metaphors and affordances. *Computers & Education, 55*(2), 603–615. doi:10.1016/j.compedu.2010.02.021

Ariely, D. (2010). *The upside of irrationality: The unexpected benefits of defying logic at work and at home*. New York, NY: HarperCollins.

AVALON Project. (n.d.). *Communication and language learning models (Project Deliverable no. 1)*. Retrieved October 1, 2010, from https://files.pbworks.com/download/HEPOBuMvfb/avalonlearning/33903754/WP2_Deliverable_1_Language_Learning_Models%20.pdf.

Azevedo, R. (2007). Understanding the complex nature of self-regulatory processes in learning with computer-based learning environments: An introduction. *Metacognition and Learning, 2*, 57–65..doi:10.1007/s11409-007-9018-5

Azevedo, R. (2005). Using hypermedia as a metacognitive tool for enhancing students learning? The role of self regulated learning. *Educational Psychologist, 40*(4), 199–209. doi:10.1207/s15326985ep4004_2

Baggetun, R., & Wasson, B. (2006). Self-regulated learning and open writing. *European Journal of Education, 41*(3/4), 453–472. doi:10.1111/j.1465-3435.2006.00276.x

Bainbridge, W. S. (2007). The scientific research potential of virtual worlds. *Science*, *317*(5837), 472. doi:10.1126/science.1146930

Bandura, A. (1977). *Social learning theory*. Englewood Cliffs, NJ: Prentice-Hall.

Bandura, A. (1977). Self-efficacy: Toward a unifying theory of behavioral change. *Psychological Review*, *84*, 191–215. doi:10.1037/0033-295X.84.2.191

Bandura, A., & Wood, R. E. (1989). Effect of perceived controllability and performance standards on self-regulation of complex decision making. *Journal of Personality and Social Psychology*, *56*, 805–814. doi:10.1037/0022-3514.56.5.805

Bangert, A. W. (2004). The seven principles of good practice: A framework for evaluating online teaching. *The Internet and Higher Education*, *7*, 217–232. doi:10.1016/j.iheduc.2004.06.003

Barab, S. A., Thomas, M., Dodge, T., Carteaux, R., & Tuzun, H. (2005). Making learning fun: Quest Atlantis, a game without guns. *Educational Technology Research and Development*, *53*(1), 86–107. doi:10.1007/BF02504859

Barrows, H. S. (1994). *Problem-based learning applied to medical education. School of Medicine*. Springfield, IL: Southern Illinois University.

Bartlett, F. (1932). *Remembering: A study in experimental and social psychology*. Cambridge University Press.

Basiel, A. (1999). *Applied formative evaluation in the Web-based environment.* MPhil. Thesis in Computing Science, Middlesex University, London.

Bates, T. (2001). *National strategies for e-learning in post-secondary education and training*. Paris, France: UNESCO, IIEP.

Beard, L., Wilson, K., Morra, D., & Keelan, J. (2009). A survey of health-related activities on second life. *Journal of Medical Internet Research*, *11*, 2. doi:10.2196/jmir.1192

Becta. (2008). *Harnessing technology: Next generation learning 2008-14*. Becta, Coventry. Retrieved on 2 December, 2010, from http://publications.becta.org.uk/display.cfm?resID=37348&page=1835.

Bédard, J., & Chi, M. T. H. (1992). Expertise. *Current Directions in Psychological Science*, *1*(4), 135–139. doi:10.1111/1467-8721.ep10769799

Beitz, B., Brewer, G., & Kirby, S. (1993). Educating consumers about universal design. *Journal of Extension*, *31*(1) Article 1IAW5. Retrieved from http://www.joe.org/joe/1993spring/iw5.php.

Bembenutty, H., & Karabenick, S. A. (2004). Inherent association between academic delay of gratification, future time perspective, and self-regulated learning. *Educational Psychology Review*, *16*(1), 35–57. doi:10.1023/B:EDPR.0000012344.34008.5c

Berg, Z., Collins, M., & Dougherty, K. (2000). Design guidelines for web-based courses. In Abby, B. (Ed.), *Instructional and cognitive impacts of web-based education* (pp. 32–40). Hershey, PA: Idea Group. doi:10.4018/978-1-878289-59-9.ch002

Berge, Z. (Ed.). (2001). *Sustaining distance training*. San Francisco, CA: Jossey-Bass.

Cognition and Technology Group at Vanderbilt. (1996). Looking at technology in context: A framework for understanding technology and education research. In Berliner, D. C., & Calfee, R. C. (Eds.), *The handbook of educational psychology* (pp. 807–840). New York, NY: Macmillan.

Bicknell-Holmes, T., & Hoffman, P. S. (2000). Elicit, engage, experience, explore: Discovery learning in library instruction. *RSR. Reference Services Review*, *28*(4), 313–322. doi:10.1108/00907320010359632

Bieber, M., Im, I., Rice, R., Goldman-Segall, R., Paul, R., Stohr, E., et al. (2002). Toward knowledge sharing and learning in virtual professional communities. In R. H. Sprague (Ed.), *Proceedings of the 35th Annual Hawaii International Conference on System Sciences* (vol. 8, pp. 2843-2852). Los Alamitos, CA: IEEE Computer Society.

Bijker, W. (1995). *Of bicycles, Bakelites, and bulbs: Toward a theory of sociotechnical change*. Cambridge, MA: MIT Press.

Bird, S. (2010, Feb. 25). *RE: 28.space mysteries* [web log comment]. Retrieved from http://www.nasatalk.com/blog/article/bylines/99-nasa-stem-educators-conference/627-28.html.

Black, J. (1993). *The effects of auditory and visual stimuli on tenth graders' descriptive writing.* (ERIC Document Reproduction Service No. ED364887). Retrieved October 1, 2010, from http://www.eric.ed.gov/PDFS/ED364887.pdf.

Blogger. (2010, August). *Blogger home page*. Retrieved September 12, 2010, from http://www.blogger.com.

Blood, R. (2004). How blogging software reshapes the online community. *Communications of the ACM, 47*(12), 53–55. doi:10.1145/1035134.1035165

Blueman, M. (2010, Feb. 25). *RE: 2nd Annual NASA STEM Educators Workshop Series* [web log comment]. Retrieved from www.nasatalk.com.

Bode, B. (1929). *Conflicting psychologies of learning.* New York, NY: Heath.

Boland, R. J., Tenkasi, R. V., & Te'eni, D. (1994). Designing information technology to support distributed cognition. *Organization Science, 5*(3), 456–475. doi:10.1287/orsc.5.3.456

Boone, K. M., Sleichter, L., Miller, R., & Breiner, S. (2007). Perceptions and preferences of extension programming and sources among extension users and non-users: 10 Kansas counties. *Journal of Extension, 45*(6), Article 6RIB1. Retrieved from http://www.joe.org/joe/2007december/rb1.php.

Borek, A., McLaren, B. M., Karabinos, M., & Yaron, D. (2009). How much assistance is helpful to students in discovery learning? In U. Cress, V. Dimitrova, & M. Specht (Eds.), *The Proceedings of EC-TEL 2009, LNCS 5794*, (pp. 391–404). Berlin, Germany: Springer-Verlag.

Borgman, C., et al. (2008). *Fostering learning in the networked world: The cyberlearning opportunity and challenge*. National Science Foundation. Retrieved on 3 December, 2010, from http://www.nsf.gov/pubs/2008/nsf08204/nsf08204.pdf.

Boud, D. (Ed.). (1995). *Enhancing learning through self assessment*. London, UK: Kogan Page Limited.

Boud, D., & Falchikov, N. (1989). Quantitative studies of self-assessment in higher education: A critical analysis of findings. *Higher Education, 18*, 529–549. doi:10.1007/BF00138746

Bouguila, L., Iwashita, M., Hirsbrunner, B., & Sato, M. (2003). Virtual locomotion interface with ground surface simulation. *Proc. of the International Conference on Artificial Reality and Telexistence*, ICAT'03.

Boulos, M. N. K., Hetherington, L., & Wheeler, S. (2007). Second life: An overview of the potential of 3-D virtual worlds in medical and health education. *Health Information and Libraries Journal, 24*, 233–245. doi:10.1111/j.1471-1842.2007.00733.x

Boulos, M. N. K., Maramba, I., & Wheeler, S. (2006). Wikis, blogs and podcasts: A new generation of web-based tools for virtual collaborative clinical practice and education. *BMC Medical Journal, 6*(41). Retrieved on July 10, 2010, from http://www.biomedcentral.com/content/pdf/1472-6920-6-41.pdf.

Bower, B. (2010, Nov. 12). Many unhappy returns for wandering minds. *Science News. U.S. News & World Report*, ▪▪▪, 1–3.

Bowman, D. A., Koller, D., & Hodges, L. F. (1997). Travel in immersive virtual environments: An evaluation of viewpoint motion control techniques. *Proc. of VRAIS '97 - Virtual Reality Annual International Symposium*, Albuquerque, NM, 1997.

Bransford, J. D., Brown, A. L., & Cocking, R. R. (1999). *How people learn: Brain, mind, experience, and school.* Washington, DC: National Academies Press. Retrieved from http://books.nap.edu/catalog/6160.html.

Brinkerhoff, R. O. (2003). *The success case method: Find out quickly what's working and what's not*. San Francisco, CA: Berrett-Koehler.

Brna, P. (1987). Confronting dynamics misconceptions. *Instructional Science, 16*, 351–379. doi:10.1007/BF00117752

Broadribb, S., & Carter, C. (2009). Using Second Life in human resource development. *British Journal of Educational Technology, 40*(3), 547–550. doi:10.1111/j.1467-8535.2009.00950.x

Brogan, D. C., Metoyer, R. A., & Hodgins, J. K. (1997). *Dynamically simulated characters in virtual environments* (p. 216). SIGGRAPH Visual Proc.

Bronack, S. (2006). Learning in the zone: A social constructivist framework for distance education in a 3-dimensional virtual world. *Interactive Learning Environments*, *14*(3), 219–232. doi:10.1080/10494820600909157

Brookfield, S. D. (1987). *Developing critical thinkers: Challenging adults to explore alternative ways of think and acting*. San Francisco, CA: Jossey-Bass.

Brooks, F. P., Jr. (1986). Walk through- A dynamic graphics system for simulating virtual buildings. *Proc. of 1986 Workshop on Interactive 3D Graphics*, (pp. 9-21).

Brossoie, N., Roberto, K. A., Willis-Walton, S., & Reynolds, S. (2010). *Report on baby boomers and older adults: Information and service needs*. Blacksburg, VA: Virginia Polytechnic Institute and State University, Center for Gerontology.

Brusilovsky, P., & Sosnovsky, S. (2005). Engaging students to work with self-assessment questions: A study of two approaches, *Proceedings of 10th Annual Conference on Innovation and Technology in Computer Science Education* (pp. 251-255). New York, NY: ACM Press.

Budé, L., Imbos, T., Wiel, M. W. J. d., Broers, N. J., & Berger, M. P. F. (2009). The effect of directive tutor guidance in problem-based learning of statistics on students' perceptions and achievement. *Higher Education*, *57*, 23–36..doi:10.1007/s10734-008-9130-8

Bures, E. M., Abrami, P. C., & Amundsen, C. (2000). Student motivation to learn via computer conferencing. *Research in Higher Education*, *41*(5), 593–621. doi:10.1023/A:1007071415363

Butler, D. L., & Winne, P. H. (1995). Feedback and self-regulated learning: A theoretical synthesis. *Review of Educational Research*, *65*(3), 245–281.

Calongne, C. M. (2008). Educational frontiers: Learning in a virtual world. *EDUCAUSE Review*, *43*(5).

Campbell, A. (2003) Weblogs for use with ESL classes. *The Internet TESL Journal*, *9*(2). Retrieved October 1, 2010, from http://iteslj.org/Techniques/Campbell-Weblogs.html.

Candy, P. C. (1991). *Self-direction for lifelong learning*. San Francisco, CA: Jossey-Bass Publishers.

Canosa, R. L. (2009). Real-world vision: Selective perception and task. *ACM Transactions on Applied Perception*, *6*(2), 11:1–11:34.

Carey, R., & Bell, G. (1997). *The annotated VRML-97 reference manual*. Reading, MA: Addison-Wesley.

Carley, K. (1992). Organizational learning and personnel turnover. *Organization Science*, *3*(1), 20–46. doi:10.1287/orsc.3.1.20

Carr-Chellman, A., & Duchastel, P. (2000). The ideal online course. *British Journal of Educational Technology*, *31*(3), 229–241. doi:10.1111/1467-8535.00154

Case, J., Gunstone, R., & Lewis, A. (2001). Students' metacognitive development in an innovative second year chemical engineering course. *Research in Science Education*, *31*, 313–335. doi:10.1023/A:1013113807788

Castronova, J. (2002). *Discovery learning for the 21st century: What is it and how does it compare to traditional learning in effectiveness in the 21st century?* Retrieved September 10, 2010, from http://teach.valdosta.edu/are/Litreviews/vol1no1/castronova_litr.pdf.

Cavalli, E. (2008, December 23). *World of Warcraft hits 11.5 million users*. Retrieved July 4, 2010, from http://www.wired.com/gamelife/2008/12/world-of-warc-1/.

Centers for Disease Control and Prevention. (2010). *The health communicator's social media toolkit*. Retrieved October 18, 2010, from www.cdc.gov/healthcommunication/.

Centers for Disease Control and Prevention. (n.d.) *Virtual worlds*. Retrieved October 2, 2010, from http://www.cdc.gov/SocialMedia/Tools/VirtualWorlds.html.

Cercone, K. (2008). Characteristics of adult learners with implications for online learning design. *AACE Journal*, *16*(2), 137–159.

Chang, M. (2007). Enhancing web-based language learning through self-monitoring. *Journal of Computer Assisted Learning*, *23*(3), 187–196. doi:10.1111/j.1365-2729.2006.00203.x

Chapman, B. (2008). Learning technology primer. In Biech, E. (Ed.), *ASTD handbook for workplace learning professionals* (pp. 383–406). Danvers, MA: ASTD Press.

Chen, L.-L. (1997). Distance delivery systems in terms of pedagogical considerations: A re-evaluation. *Educational Technology*, (July/August): 34–37.

Chen, C. C., Rong-An, S., & Harris, A. (2006). The efficacy of case method teaching in an online asynchronous learning environment. *International Journal of Distance Education Technologies*, *4*(2), 72–86. doi:10.4018/jdet.2006040106

Chittaro, L., & Ranon, R. (2007). Web3D technologies in learning, education and training: Motivations, issues, opportunities. *Computers & Education*, *49*, 3–18. doi:10.1016/j.compedu.2005.06.002

Christensen, R. R., Hollerbach, J. M., Xu, Y., & Meek, S. G. (2000). Inertial-force feedback for the treadport locomotion interface. *Presence (Cambridge, Mass.)*, *9*(1), 1–14. doi:10.1162/105474600566574

Claessens, B. J. C., Van Eerde, W., Rutte, C. G., & Roe, R. A. (2007). A review of the time management literature. *Personnel Review*, *36*(2), 255–276. doi:10.1108/00483480710726136

Clark, R. C., & Mayer, R. E. (2008). *E-learning and the science of instruction: Proven guidelines for consumers and designers of multimedia learning*. San Francisco, CA: Pfeiffer.

Clark-Carter, D., Heyes, A., & Howarth, C. (1986). The effect of non-visual preview upon the walking speed of visually impaired people. *Ergonomics*, *29*(12), 1575–1581. doi:10.1080/00140138608967270

Coffman, T., & Klinger, M. B. (2008). Utilizing virtual worlds in education: The implications for practice. *International Journal of Social Sciences*, *2*(1), 29–33.

Cohen, N. (2008, September 15). Don't buy that textbook, download it free. *New York Times (NY Edition)*, C3.

Collins, H. M., & Evans, R. (2002). The third wave of science studies: Studies of expertise and experience. *Social Studies of Science*, *32*(2), 235–296. doi:10.1177/0306312702032002003

Connexions. (2008). *Connexions: About us*. Retrieved October 16, 2008, from http://cnx.org/aboutus/.

Connexions. (2010). *Connexions home page*. Retrieved July 10, 2010, from http://cnx.org/.

Conole, G., & Culver, J. (2009). The design of Cloudworks: Applying social networking practice to foster the exchange of learning and teaching ideas and designs. *Computers & Education*, *54*(3).

Conole, G. (2009b). Research methodological issues with researching the learner voice. In Hin, L. T. W., & Subramaniam, R. (Eds.), *Handbook of research on new media literacy at the K-12 level: Issues and challenges* (pp. 669–682). Hershey, PA: IGI Global. doi:10.4018/978-1-60566-120-9.ch042

Conole, G. (2009a). *Personalisation through technology-enhanced learning*. Keynote at the E-Portfolio June 2009 Conference: Innovation, Creativity and Accountability, City University, London.

Cooke, C. C., Yearns, M. H., & Martin, P. (2005). Aging in place: Home modifications among rural and urban elderly. *Housing and Society*, *32*(1), 85–105.

Corona, C., Spangenberger, S., & Venet, I. (1998). *Improving student writing through a language rich environment*. (ERIC Document Reproduction Service No. ED420860).

Cortez, B. (2010, Feb. 23). *RE: 3.mapping the moon with WALL-E* [web log comment]. Retrieved from http://www.nasatalk.com/index.php?option=com_resource&controller=article&article=723&category_id=99&Itemid=147.

Coutihno, S. (2008). Self-efficacy, metacognition, and performance. *North American Journal of Psychology*, *10*(1), 165–172.

Covington, M., & Mueller, K. (2001). Intrinsic versus extrinsic motivation: An approach/avoidance reformulation. *Educational Psychology Review*, *13*(2). Retrieved September 20, 2010, from http://www.unco.edu/cebs/psychology/kevinpugh/motivation_project/resources/covington_mueller01.pdf.

Crips, V., & Ward, C. (2005, July). *The PePCAA Project: Formative scenario-based CAA in psychology for teachers*. Paper presented at the Ninth International Computer Assisted Assessment Conference, Loughborough University.

Dale, S. (2010, May). *Cultivating knowledge through communities of practice*. Paper presented at the Congreso Internacional EDO 2010.

Dalgarno, B., & Harper, B. (2004). User control and task authenticity for spatial learning in 3D environments. *Australasian Journal of Educational Technology, 20*(1), 1–17.

Dalgarno, B., & Lee, M. J. W. (2010). What are the learning affordances of 3-D virtual environments? *British Journal of Educational Technology, 41*(1), 10–32. doi:10.1111/j.1467-8535.2009.01038.x

Dalgarno, B., Hedberg, J., & Harper, B. (2002). The contribution of 3D environments to conceptual understanding. *Proc. of ASCILITE*, 2002, New Zealand.

Dalsgaard, C. (2006). Social software: e-Learning beyond learning management systems. *European Journal of Open, Distance and E-Learning*. Retrieved July 10, 2010, from http://www.eurodl.org/materials/contrib/2006/Christian_Dalsgaard.htm.

Danchak, M. (2002). Bringing affective behavior to e-learning. *The Technology Source*, MIVU, September/October 2002. Retrieved September 30, 2010, from http://technologysource.org/article/bringing_affective_behavior_to_elearning/.

Danforth, M. P. D. (2009). Development of virtual patient simulations for medical education. *Journal of Virtual Worlds Research, 2*(2).

Dangwal, R., & Kapur, P. (2009). Learning through teaching: Peer-mediated instruction in minimally invasive education. *British Journal of Educational Technology, 40*(1), 5–22. doi:10.1111/j.1467-8535.2008.00863.x

Darken, R. P., Cockayne, W. R., & Carmein, D. (1997). The omni-directional treadmill: A locomotion device for virtual worlds. *Proc. of UIST'97*, (pp. 213-221).

De Clerck, N. M. (2010). Children, wired: For better and for worse. *Neuron, 67*(5), 692–701. doi:10.1016/j.neuron.2010.08.035

De Freitas, S. (2010). Learning as immersive experiences: Using the four□dimensional framework for designing and evaluating immersive learning experiences in a virtual world. *British Journal of Educational Technology, 41*(1), 69–85. doi:10.1111/j.1467-8535.2009.01024.x

De Freitas, S., & Neumann, T. (2009). The use of exploratory learning for supporting immersive learning in virtual environments. *Computers & Education, 52*(2), 343–352. doi:10.1016/j.compedu.2008.09.010

De Freitas, S., & Conole, G. (2010). The influence of pervasive and integrative tools on learners' experiences and expectations of study. In Sharpe, R., Beetham, H., & De Freitas, S. (Eds.), *Rethinking learning for a digital age: How learners are shaping their own experiences*. New York, NY: Routledge.

De Jong, T. (2005). The guided discovery principle in multimedia learning. In Mayer, R. E. (Ed.), *The Cambridge handbook of multimedia learning*.

De Jong, T., & van Joolingen, W. R. (1998). Scientific discovery learning with computer simulations of conceptual domains. *Review of Educational Research, 68,* 179-201.

De Luca, A., Mattone, R., & Giordano, P. R. (2007). Acceleration-level control of the CyberCarpet. *2007 IEEE International Conference on Robotics and Automation*, Roma, I, (pp. 2330-2335).

De Lucia, A. (2009). Development and evaluation of a virtual campus on Second Life: The case of SecondDMI. *Computers & Education, 52*(1), 220–233. doi:10.1016/j.compedu.2008.08.001

Dean, D., & Kuhn, D. (2007). Direct instruction vs. discovery: The long view. *Science Education, 91*(3), 384–397. doi:10.1002/sce.20194

Decrem, B. (2006). *Introducing Flock Beta 1*. Flock official blog. Retrieved October 1, 2010, from http://www.flock.com/node/4500.

Dede, C. (Ed.). (1998). *Introduction. Association for Supervision and Curriculum Development (ASCD) Yearbook: Learning with technology* (pp. v–x). Alexandria, VA: Association for Supervision and Curriculum Development.

Dede, C. (2009). Immersive interfaces for engagement and learning. *Science, 323*(5910), 66. doi:10.1126/science.1167311

Dede, C., Ketelhut, D., & Ruess, K. (2006). *Designing for motivation and usability in a museum-based multiuser virtual environment*. Retrieved October 1, 2010, from http://www.gse.harvard.edu/~dedech/muvees/documents/AELppr.pdf.

Deitz, M. E., Mulford, J., & Case, K. (2009). The Utah house: An effective educational tool and catalyst for behavior change? *Building and Environment, 44*, 1707–1713. doi:10.1016/j.buildenv.2008.11.007

Denis, G., & Jouvelot, P. (2005). *Motivation driven educational game design: Applying best practices to music education.* Retrieved September 28, 2010, from http://citeseerx.ist.psu.edu/viewdoc/download?doi=10.1.1.59.7687&rep=rep1&type=pdf.

dePaula, R., & Rischer, G. (2005). *Knowledge management: Why learning from the past is not enough!* (pp.21 – 53). Retrieved February 13, 2010, from http://l3d.cs.colorado.edu/~gerhard/papers/km-final-2005.pdf.

Deutschmann, M., Panichi, L., & Molka-Danielsen, J. (2009). Designing oral participation in Second Life: A comparative study of two language proficiency courses. *ReCALL, 21*(2), 206–226. doi:10.1017/S0958344009000196

Dewey, J. (1933). *How we think: A restatement of the relation of reflective thinking to the educative process.* Lexington, MA: D.C. Heath and Company.

Dickey, M. D. (2003). Teaching in 3D: Pedagogical affordances and constraints of 3D virtual worlds for synchronous distance learning. *Distance Education, 24*(1), 105–121. doi:10.1080/01587910303047

Dillenburg, P. (2000). Virtual learning environments. *Proc. of EUN Conference 2000 - Workshop on Virtual Learning Environments.*

Dochy, F., Segers, M., & Sluijsmans, D. (1999). The use of self-, peer- and co-assessment: A review. *Studies in Higher Education, 24*(3), 331–350. doi:10.1080/03075079912331379935

Doignon, J. P., & Falmagne, J. C. (1999). *Knowledge spaces.* Springer-Verlag. doi:10.1007/978-3-642-58625-5

Douglass, R. T., Little, M., & Smith, J. w. (2005). *Building online communities with Drupal, phpBB, and WordPress.* Apress.

Downing, E. (2010, Feb. 25). *RE: 6.NASA eClips: NASA Launchpad* [web log comment]. Retrieved from http://www.nasatalk.com/blog/article/bylines/99-nasa-stem-educators-conference/720-6-nasa-eclips-nasa-launchpad.html.

Driscoll, D. M. (2009). The death of the professor: Dialogue education's learning focus. *Journal of Extension, 47*(5), Article 5TOT2. Retrieved from http://www.joe.org/joe/2009october/tt2.php.

Driver, R., Asoko, H., Leach, J., Mortimer, E., & Scott, P. (1994). Constructing scientific knowledge in the classroom. *Educational Researcher, 23*(7), 5–12.

DuBois, N. F., & Staley, R. K. (1997). A self-regulated learning approach to teaching educational psychology. *Educational Psychology Review, 9*(2), 171–197. doi:10.1023/A:1024792529797

Ducate, L., & Lomicka, L. (2009). Podcasting: An effective tool for honing language students' pronunciation? *Language Learning & Technology, 13*(3), 66–86.

Dukas, R. (2002). Behavioural and ecological consequences of limited attention. *Philosophical Transactions of the Royal Society of London, 357*, 1539–1547.. doi:10.1098/rstb.2002.1063

Dunn, R., Giggs, S. A., Olson, J., Beasley, M., & Gorman, B. S. (1995). A meta-analytic validation of the Dunn and Dunn Model of learning preferences. *The Journal of Educational Research, 88*(6), 353–362. doi:10.1080/00220671.1995.9941181

Earnshaw, R. A., Gigante, M. A., & Jones, H. (Eds.). (1993). *Virtual reality systems.* Academic Press. Hayward, R. C., & Hollerbach, J. M. (2002). Implementing virtual stairs on treadmills using torso force feedback. *Proc. of IEEE Int'l Conf. on Robotics and Automation*, (pp. 586-591).

ELATEWiki. (2009, March 28). *E-learning paths.* Retrieved July 10, 2010, from http://www.elatewiki.org/index.php/E-Learning_Paths.

ElateWiki. (2010, September). *TubeRadio.FM.* Retrieved September 30, 2010, from http://www.elatewiki.org/index.php/TubeRadio.FM.

Esteves, M. (2010). Improving teaching and learning of computer programming through the use of the Second Life virtual world. *British Journal of Educational Technology, 42*(4).

European Commission. (2008). *An updated strategic framework for European cooperation in education and training*. Communication from the Commission to the European Parliament, the Council, the European Economic and Social Committee and the Committee of the Regions (December). Retrieved on 2 December, 2010, from http://ec.europa.eu/education/lifelong-learning-policy/doc28-en.htm.

EverNote. (2010, September). *EverNote home page*. Retrieved September 22, 2010, from http://www.evernote.com.

EVO project. (n.d.). *Home page*. Retrieved October 1, 2010, from http://evosessions.pbworks.com/w/page/10708567/FrontPage.

Experience Project. (2010, December 13). *Experience Project home page*. Retrieved December 13, 2010, from http://www.experienceproject.com.

eXtension. (2008). *Community of practice handbook*. Retrieved September 12, 2010, from http://about.extension.org/wiki/Handbook_Introduction.

eXtension. (2009). *Return on investment annual report*. Retrieved September 8, 2010, from http://about.extension.org/mediawiki/files/7/7f/EXtension_annual_report_09.pdf.

eXtension. (2010). *About*. Retrieved September 8, 2010, from http://www.extension.org/main/about.

Fadde, P. J. (2009). Instructional design for advanced learners: Training recognition skills to hasten expertise. *Educational Technology Research and Development*, *57*(3), 359–376..doi:10.1007/s11423-007-9046-5

*FastTalk*. (2010, September). Retrieved September 16, 2010, from http://www.webtransitions.com/components-discussion.asp.

Ficheman, I. K., & Lopes, R. de D. (2008). Digital learning ecosystems: Authoring, collaboration, immersion and mobility. In the *Proceedings of the Interaction Design and Children* (IDC 2008), (pp. 9–12.) Chicago, IL: ACM.

Finkeldei, S. (2011). *K-State online learning management system: Development, tools and uses*. Kansas State University Axio Learning internal document, January 2011.

Fitzpatrick, J. (2009, May 10). *Five best journaling tools*. Retrieved August 20, 2010, from http://lifehacker.com/5246819/five-best-journaling-tools.

Foreman, N., Stanton-Fraser, D., Wilson, P. N., Duffy, H., & Parnell, R. (2005). Transfer of spatial knowledge to a two-level shopping mall in older people, following virtual exploration. *Environment and Behavior*, *37*, 275–292. doi:10.1177/0013916504269649

Forterra Systems. (2010). *Website*. Retrieved from http://www.forterrainc.com/.

Fosnot, C. T. (2005). *Constructivism: Theory, perspectives, and practice* (2nd ed.). New York, NY: Teachers College Press.

Franco, C. (2008). Using Wiki-based peer-correction to develop writing skills of Brazilian EFL learners. *Novitas-ROYAL*, *2*(1), 49–59.

Franz, N. (2007). Adult education theories: Informing cooperative extension's transformation. *Journal of Extension, 45*(1), Article 1FEA1. Retrieved from http://www.joe.org/joe/2007february/a1.php.

Franz, N., Garst, B. A., Baughman, S., Smith, C., & Peters, B. (2009). Catalyzing transformation: Conditions in extension educational environments that promote change. *Journal of Extension, 47*(4), Article 4RIB1. Retrieved from http://www.joe.org/joe/2009august/rb1.php.

Freedman, V. A., Agree, E. M., Martin, L. G., & Cornman, J. C. (2005). Trends in the use of assistive technology and personal care for late-life disability, 1992-2001. *The Gerontologist*, *46*(1), 124–127.

FreeMind. (2010, September). *FreeMind home page*. Retrieved September 11, 2010, from http://freemind.sourceforge.net/wiki/index.php/Main_Page.

Fruhlinger, J. (2010, November 28). *9 technologies that were ahead of their time*. Retrieved December 12, 2010, from http://www.pcworld.com/article/211779/1999_live_journal.html.

Fullwood, D. E. (2010, Feb. 25.). *RE: 10.Buzz Lightyear* [web log comment]. Retrieved from http://www.nasatalk.com/index.php?option=com_resource&controller=article&article=716&category_id=99&Itemid=147.

Fullwood, D. E. (2010, Mar. 1). *RE: 13.NASA Educator Resource Center Network* [web log comment]. Retrieved from http://www.nasatalk.com/index.php?option=com_resource&controller=article&article=711&category_id=99&Itemid=147.

Gallagher, W. (2009). *Rapt: Attention and the focused life* (pp. 1–244). New York, NY: The Penguin Press.

Georghiades, P. (2006). The role of metacognitive activities in the contextual use of primary pupils' conceptions of science. *Research in Science Education, 36*(1–2), 29. doi:10.1007/s11165-004-3954-8

Gerrior, S. A., & Crocoll, C. C. (2008). USDA CSREES' role in broadening support for an aging nation. *Journal of Extension, 46*(1), Article 1COM2. Retrieved from http://www.joe.org/joe/2008february/comm2.php.

Gerstein, J. (2009). Beyond the game: Quest Atlantis as an online learning experience for gifted elementary students. *Journal of Virtual Worlds Research*, •••, 403.

Gijlers, H., & Jong, T. d. (2005). The relationship between prior knowledge and students' collaborative discovery learning processes. *Journal of Research in Science Teaching, 42*(3), 264–282. doi:10.1002/tea.20056

Girvan, C., & Savage, T. (2010). Identifying an appropriate pedagogy for virtual worlds: A communal constructivism case study. *Computers & Education, 55*(1), 342–349. doi:10.1016/j.compedu.2010.01.020

Gitlin, L. N., Earland, T. V., Piersol, C. V., & Shaw, G. (2010). Enhancing quality of life in functionally vulnerable older adults: From randomized trial to standard care. *Generations (San Francisco, Calif.), 34*(1), 84–87.

Gladwell, M. (2008). *Outliers: The story of success*. New York, NY: Little, Brown and Company.

Gleicher, H., Lindenberg, D., & Sumter, S. (2008). *Troops and family care fund feasibility study*. Retrieved September 27, 2010, from www.montgomerycountymd.gov/.

Godwin-Jones, R. (2003). Blogs and Wikis: Environments for on-line collaboration. *Language Learning and Technology, 7*(2), 12-16. Retrieved October 1, 2010, from http://llt.msu.edu/vol7num2/emerging/default.html.

Goodman, L. A., & Kruskal, W. H. (1979). *Measures of association for cross classifications*. New York, NY: Springer-Verlag.

Gorsky, P., & Finegold, M. (1992). Using computer simulations to restructure students' conceptions of force. *Journal of Computers in Mathematics and Science Teaching, 11*, 163–178.

Grapevine Talk. (2010, July 28). *GrapevineTalk homepage*. Retrieved July 28, 2010, from http://grapevinetalk.com/index.html.

Greater Midwest Region of the National Network/National Library of Medicine. (2010). *Health and medicine in Second Life*. Retrieved October 8, 2010, from http://healthinfoisland.blogspot.com/.

Grune-Yanoff, T., & Weirich, P. (2010). The philosophy and epistemology of simulation: A review. *Simulation & Gaming, 41*(1), 20–50. doi:10.1177/1046878109353470

Hai-Jew, S. (2011). (Forthcoming). Creating an emotionally resilient virtual student community at K-State [A case study]. *The University Life Café*.

Hai-Jew, S. (2008b). Scaffolding discovery learning spaces. *Journal of Online Learning and Teaching, 4*(4), 533–548. Retrieved from http://jolt.merlot.org/vol4no4/hai-jew_1208.htm.

Hai-Jew, S. (2008a). Designing discovery learning spaces [PowerPoint presentation]. In S. Hai-Jew (Ed.), Scaffolding discovery learning spaces. *Journal of Online Learning and Teaching, 4*(4), 533-548. Retrieved from http://jolt.merlot.org/vol4no4/Self%20Discovery%20Learning%20Spaces.ppt.

Hamilton, D. (1996). *Learning about education: An unfinished curriculum*. Bristol, UK: Open University Press.

Hannafin, M., Hannafin, K., & Gabbitas, B. (2009). Re-examining cognition during student-centered, Web-based learning. *Educational Technology Research and Development, 57*, 767–785..doi:10.1007/s11423-009-9117-x

Hansen, M. (2008). Versatile, immersive, creative and dynamic virtual 3-D healthcare learning environments: A review of the literature. *Journal of Medical Internet Research, 10*(3). doi:10.2196/jmir.1051

Harper, B., Squires, D., & McDougall, A. (2000). Constructivist simulations: A new design paradigm. *Journal of Educational Multimedia and Hypermedia*, *9*(2), 115–130.

Hart, J. (2008, July 28). *Jane's pick of the day selected by Jane Hart of the Centre for Learning & Performance Technologies*. Retrieved December 13, 2010, from http://janeknight.typepad.com/pick/2008/07/questler.html.

Hayes, G. (2006). *Virtual worlds, Web 3.0 and portable profiles*. Retrieved February 2, 2008, from http://www.personalizemedia.com/virtual-worlds-web-30-and-portable-profiles.

Hazel Associates. (2005). *Global e-learning opportunity for U.S. higher education*. Retrieved from http://www.hezel.com/globalreport/.

Heider, F. (1958). *The psychology of interpersonal relations*. New York, NY: John Wiley & Sons. doi:10.1037/10628-000

Herrington, J., & Oliver, R. (1999). Using situated learning and multimedia to investigate higher-order thinking. *Journal of Educational Multimedia and Hypermedia, 8*(4), 401-422. Retrieved on 6 December, 2010, from http://dl.aace.org/9172.

Hersh, M. A., & Johnson, M. A. (2008). On modeling assistive technology systems-Part I: Modeling framework. *Technology and Disability*, *20*, 193–215.

Hillyard, S. A., Vogel, E. K., & Luck, S. J. (1998). Sensory gain control (amplification) as a mechanism of selective attention: Electro-physiological and neuroimaging evidence. *Philosophical Transactions of the Royal Society of London: Biological Sciences*, *353*(1373), 1257–1270. doi:10.1098/rstb.1998.0281

Hirose, M. (2006). Virtual reality technology and museum exhibit. *The International Journal of Virtual Reality*, *5*(2), 31–36.

Hirose, M., & Yokoyama, K. (1997). Synthesis and transmission of realistic sensation using virtual reality technology. *Transactions of the Society of Instrument and Control Engineers*, *33*(7), 716–722.

Hmelo, C., & Williams, S. M. (Eds.). (1998). Special issue: Learning through problem solving. *Journal of the Learning Sciences*, *7*(3), 4.

Hofer, B., Yu, S., & Pintrich, P. (1998). Teaching college students to be self-regulated learners. In Schunk, D., & Zimmerman, B. J. (Eds.), *Self-regulated learning: From teaching to self-reflective practice* (pp. 57–88). New York, NY: The Guilford Press.

Hoge, C. W., McGurk, D., Thomas, J. L., Cox, A. L., Engle, C. C., & Castro, C. A. (2008). Mild traumatic brain injury in U.S. soldiers returning from Iraq. *The New England Journal of Medicine*, *358*, 453–463. doi:10.1056/NEJMoa072972

Hollerbach, J. M., Mills, R., Tristano, D., Christensen, R. R., Thompson, W. B., & Xu, Y. (2001). Torso force feedback realistically simulates slope on treadmill-style locomotion interfaces. *The International Journal of Robotics Research*, *20*, 939–952. doi:10.1177/02783640122068209

Hollerbach, J. M. (2002). Locomotion interfaces. In Stanney, K. M. (Ed.), *Handbook of virtual environments technology* (pp. 239–254). Lawrence Erlbaum Associates, Inc.

Hollerbach, J. M., Checcacci, D., Noma, H., Yanaida, Y., & Tetsutani, N. (2003). Simulating side slopes on locomotion interfaces using torso forces. *Proc. of 11th Haptic Interfaces for Virtual Environment and Teleoperator Systems*, (pp. 247-253).

Hollerbach, J. M., Xu, Y., Christensen, R., & Jacobsen, S. C. (2000). Design specifications for the second generation Sarcos Treadport locomotion interface. *Haptics Symposium, Proc. ASME Dynamic Systems and Control Division, DSC-Vol. 69-2*, Orlando, Nov. 5-10, 2000, (pp. 1293-1298).

Hollingsworth, H., & Eastman, S. (1988). *Teaching writing in every class: A guide for grades 6-12*. Boston, MA: Allyn & Bacon.

Hollins, M. (1989). *Understanding blindness: An integrative approach*. Lawrence Erlbaum Associates.

Holliway, D. R. (2000). *It looks like a goose: Composing for the informational needs of readers*. (ERIC Document Reproduction Service No. ED439437). Retrieved October 1, 2010, from http://www.eric.ed.gov/PDFS/ED439437.pdf.

Holmberg, B. (1983). Guided didactic conversation in distance education. In Sewart, D., Keegan, D., & Holmberg, B. (Eds.), *Distance education: International perspectives* (pp. 114–122). London, UK: Croom Helm.

Homes for Our Troops. (2009). *Homes for our Troops 2009 annual report*. Retrieved September 27, 2010, from http://www.homesforourtroops.org/.

Horiguchi, T., & Hirashima, T. (2001). The role of counter-examples in discovery learning environment: Awareness of the chance for learning. In the *Proceedings of JSAI 2001 Workshops, LNAI 2253* (pp. 468 – 474). Berlin, Germany: Springer-Verlag.

Horvitz, E., Kadie, C., Paek, T., & Hovel, D. (2003). Models of attention in computing and communication: From principles to applications. *Communications of the ACM, 44*(3), 52–59. doi:10.1145/636772.636798

Houser, A., Gibson, M. J., & Redfoot, D. L. (2010, September). *Trends in family caregiving and paid home care for older people with disabilities in the community: Data from the National Long-Term Care Survey*. Washington, DC: AARP Public Policy Institute. Retrieved October 13, 2010, from http://assets.aarp.org/rgcenter/ppi/ltc/2010-09-caregiving.pdf.

Hsi, S., Crowley, K., Duschl, R., Finke, C. L., King, H., & Sabelli, N. (2004). Models of learning and theories of practice for informal learning environments. In the *Proceedings of the International Conference on Learning Sciences,* (pp. 12–15). Santa Monica, CA: Association of Computing Machinery.

Huang, H. M. (2010). Investigating learners' attitudes toward virtual reality learning environments: Based on a constructivist approach. *Computers & Education, 55*(3). doi:10.1016/j.compedu.2010.05.014

Huitt, W. (2001). Motivation to learn: An overview. *Educational Psychology Interactive*. Valdosta, GA: Valdosta State University. Retrieved July 25, 2010, from http://www.edpsycinteractive.org/col/motivation/motivate.html.

Hundsberger, S. (2009). *Foreign language learning in Second Life and the implications for resource provision in academic libraries*. Arcadia Fellowship Programme, Cambridge University Library. Retrieved October 1, 2010, from http://arcadiaproject.lib.cam.ac.uk/docs/second_life.pdf.

Hung, D. (2001). Design principles for web-based learning: Implications for Vygotskian thought. *Educational Technology, 41*(3), 33–41.

Hung, D., & Nichani, M. (2001). Constructivism and e-learning: Balancing between the individual and social levels of cognition. *Educational Technology, 41*(2), 40–44.

Hunter, A. (2007, September*). Using an online formative assessment framework to enhance student engagement: A learning outcomes approach.* Paper presented at the 15th Improving Student Learning Symposium, Trinity College, Dublin, Ireland.

Ibabe, I., & Jauregizar, J. (2010). Online self-assessment with feedback and metacognitive knowledge. *Higher Education, 59*(2), 243–258. doi:10.1007/s10734-009-9245-6

Ip, A., & Linser, R. (1999). *Web-based simulation generator: Empowering teaching and learning media in political science.* Retrieved from http://www.roleplaysim.org/papers/rpsg.htm.

Iqbal, R., & Every, P. (2005). Scenario based method for teaching, learning and assessment. In the *Proceedings of Special Interest Group for Information Technology Education* (SIGITE 2005) (pp. 261–266). Newark, NJ: ACM.

Iqbal, S. T., Adamczyk, P. D., Zheng, X. S., & Bailey, B. P. (2005). Toward an index of opportunity: Understanding changes in mental workload during task execution. In the *Proceedings of Human-Computer Interaction, CHI* 2005: Portland, Oregon, (pp. 311–320).

Iwata, H. (1999). The Torus Treadmill: Realizing locomotion in VEs. *IEEE Computer Graphics and Applications, 19*(6), 30–35. doi:10.1109/38.799737

Iwata, H., Yano, H., Fukushima, H., & Noma, H. (2005). CirculaFloor. *IEEE Computer Graphics and Applications, 25*(1), 64–67. doi:10.1109/MCG.2005.5

Iwata, H., & Yoshida, Y. (1999). Path reproduction tests using a Torus Treadmill. *Presence (Cambridge, Mass.), 8*(6), 587–597. doi:10.1162/105474699566503

Iwata, H., & Fujji, T. (1996). Virtual preambulator: A novel interface device for locomotion in virtual environment. *Proc. of IEEE VRAIS'96*, (pp. 60-65).

Iwata, H., & Yoshida, Y. (1997). Virtual walk through simulator with infinite plane. *Proc. of 2nd VRSJ Annual Conference*, (pp. 254-257).

Iwata, H., Yano, H., & Tomioka, H. (2006). *Powered shoes.* SIGGRAPH 2006 Conference DVD (2006).

Iwata, H., Yano, H., & Tomiyoshi, M. (2007). *String walker*. Paper presented at SIGGRAPH 2007.

Jackson, P. (1995). On the place of narrative in teaching. In McEwan, H., & Egan, K. (Eds.), *Narrative in teaching, learning, and research* (pp. 3–23). New York, NY: Teachers College Press.

Jamieson-Noel, D. (2004). *Exploring task definition as a facet of self-regulated learning*. Unpublished Doctoral Dissertation, Simon Fraser University.

Jang, S. J. (2009). Exploration of secondary students' creativity by integrating web-based technology into an innovative science curriculum. *Computers & Education*, *52*(1), 247–255. doi:10.1016/j.compedu.2008.08.002

Janta, K. (2010, Feb. 7). *RE: RE: 2nd Annual NASA STEM Educators Workshop Series* [web log comment]. Retrieved from http://www.nasatalk.com/index.php?option=com_resource&controller=article&article=578&category_id=2&Itemid=0.

Janta, K. (2010, Feb. 26). *RE: 8.paper plate Astronomy* [web log comment]. Retrieved from http://www.nasatalk.com/index.php?option=com_resource&controller=article&article=718&category_id=99&Itemid=147.

Jarmon, L. (2009). An ecology of embodied interaction: Pedagogy and homo virtualis. *Journal of Virtual Worlds Research*, *2*(1).

Java 3D. (2010). *Home page.* Retrieved from https://java3d.dev.java.net/.

Jiang, Z., & Potter, W. D. (1994). A computer microworld to introduce students to probability. *Journal of Computers in Mathematics and Science Teaching*, *13*(2), 197–222.

Johnson, C. M. (2009). Virtual worlds in health care higher education. *Journal of Virtual Worlds Research*, *2*(2).

Johnson, L., Smith, R., Willis, H., Levine, A., & Haywood, K. (2011). *The 2011 Horizon Report*. Austin, TX: The New Media Consortium.

Johnson, C. (2001). A survey of current research on online communities of practice. *Internet and Higher Education, 4*. Retrieved February 26, 2011, from http://citeseerx.ist.psu.edu/viewdoc/download?doi=10.1.1.106.5848&rep=rep1&type=pdf.

Johnson, L. F., & Levine, A. H. (2009). *Virtual worlds inherently immersive, highly social learning spaces*. Retrieved September 16, 2010, from http://Immersive_Learning-Johnson_and_Levine.pdf.

Johnstone, S. (2005). *Open educational resources serve the world.* Retrieved December 12, 2010, from http://www.educause.edu/apps/eq/eqm05/eqm0533.asp.

Jonassen, D. (1991). Objectivism versus constructivism: Do we need a new philosophical paradigm? *Educational Technology Research and Development*, *39*, 5–14. doi:10.1007/BF02296434

Joo, Y.-J., Bong, M., & Choi, H.-J. (2000). Self-efficacy for self-regulated learning, academic self-efficacy, and Internet self-efficacy in Web-based instruction. *Educational Technology Research and Development*, *48*(2), 5–17. doi:10.1007/BF02313398

Journal, E. Inc. (n.d.). *Welcome to the Journal of Extension*. Retrieved September 1, 2010, from http://www.joe.org/index.php.

Kafai, Y. B. (1995). *Minds in play: Computer game design as a context for children's learning*. Hillsdale, NJ: Erlbaum.

Kangassalo, M. (1994). Children's independent exploration of a natural phenomenon by using a pictorial computer-based simulation. *Journal of Computing in Childhood Education*, *5*(3/4), 285–297.

Kase, S. E., Carroll, J. M., Zhang, Y., & Rosson, M. B. (2008). Sustainable informal IT learning in community-based nonprofits. In the *Proceedings of CHI 2008*, (pp. 2335–3440). Florence, Italy: ACM.

Kavaliauskienė, G. (2008). Podcasting: A tool for improving listening skills. *Journal of Teaching English with Technology*, *8*(4). Retrieved November 30, 2010, from http://www.tewtjournal.org/VOL%208/ISSUE%204/A%20WORD%20FROM%20A%20TECHIE.pdf.

Kawachi, P. (2003b). Choosing the appropriate media to support the learning process. *Journal of Educational Technology*, *14*(1 & 2), 1–18.

Kawachi, P. (2005). Empirical validation of a multimedia construct for learning. In Mishra, S., & Sharma, R. (Eds.), *Interactive multimedia in education and training* (pp. 158–183). Hershey, PA: IDEA Group.

Kawachi, P. (2003a). Asia-specific scaffolding needs in grounded design e-learning: Empirical comparisons among several institutions. *Proceedings of the 17th Annual Conference of the Asian Association of Open Universities,* Bangkok 12-14 Nov.

Kaye, H. S., Yeager, P., & Reed, M. (2008). Disparities in usage of assistive technology among people with disabilities. *Assistive Technology*, *20*(4), 194–203. doi:10.1080/10400435.2008.10131946

Kazmierski, J. (2010, December 2). *May the source be with you.* Retrieved December 12, 2010, from http://www.unogateway.com/may-the-source-be-with-you-1.1817794.

Keefe, J. W. (1979). Learning style: An overview. In *NASSP's Student learning styles: Diagnosing and prescribing programs* (pp. 1–17). Reston, VA: National Association of Secondary School Principals.

Kennedy, G., Judd, T. S., Chruchward, A., Gray, K., & Krause, K. (2008). First year students' experiences with technology: Are they really digital natives. *Australasian Journal of Educational Technology*, *24*(1), 108–122.

Kerka, S. (2000). Incidental learning. *Trends and Issues Alert No.18*. Retrieved from http://www.eric.ed.gov/PDFS/ED446234.pdf.

Kern, R., & Warschauer, M. (2000). Introduction: Theory and practice of network-based language teaching. In Warschauer, M., & Kern, R. (Eds.), *Network-based language teaching: Concepts and practice* (pp. 1–19). Cambridge, UK: Cambridge University Press.

Kim, T., & Axelrod, S. (2005). Direct instruction: An educators' guide and a plea for action. *Behavior Analyst Today*, *6*(2), 111.

Kim, D. (2010). Incorporating podcasting and blogging into a core task for ESOL teacher candidates. *Computers & Education*, *56*(3), 632–641. doi:10.1016/j.compedu.2010.10.005

Kirchen, J. (2007). Investigating learning styles in the online educational environment. In *Proceedings of the 8th ACM SIGITE Conference on Information Technology Education (SIGITE '07)* (pp. 127-134). New York, NY: ACM Digital Library.

Kirkwood, A., & Price, L. (2005). Learners and learning in the twenty-first century: What do we know about students' attitudes towards and experiences of information and communication technologies that will help us design courses? *Studies in Higher Education*, *30*(3), 257–274. doi:10.1080/03075070500095689

Kirschner, P., Sweller, J., & Clark, R. (2006). Why minimal guidance during instruction does notwork: An analysis of the failure of constructivist discovery, problem-based, experiential, and inquiry-based teaching. *Educational Psychologist*, *41*, 75–86. doi:10.1207/s15326985ep4102_1

Kirsh, D. (2005). Metacognition, distributed cognition and visual design. In Gardenfors, P., Johansson, P., & Mahwah, N. J. (Eds.), *Cognition, education, and communication technology* (pp. 147–180). Mahwah, NJ: L. Erlbaum Associates.

Klahr, D., & Nigam, M. (2004). The equivalence of learning paths in early science instruction: Effects of direct instruction and discovery learning. *Psychological Science*, *15*, 661–667. doi:10.1111/j.0956-7976.2004.00737.x

Kleinman, J., & Entin, E. (2002, April). Comparison of in-class and distance-learning students' performance and attitudes in an introductory computer science course. *The Journal of Computing in Small Colleges*, *17*(2), 206–219.

Kluger, A. N., & DeNisi, A. (1996). The effects of feedback interventions on performance: A historical review, a meta-analysis, and a preliminary feedback intervention theory. *Psychological Bulletin*, *119*, 254–284. doi:10.1037/0033-2909.119.2.254

Knowles, M. S. (1980). *The modern practice of adult education: From andragogy to pedagogy*. Englewood Cliffs, NJ: Cambridge Adult Education.

Knowles, M. (1970). Andragogy: An emerging technology for adult learning. In Tight, M. (Ed.), *Education for adults: Adult learning and education*. London, UK: Croom Helm.

Kohn, A. (1993). Rewards versus learning: A response to Paul Chance. *Phi Delta Kappan, 74*, 783–787. Retrieved September 25, 2010, from http://www.li.suu.edu/Library/Circulation/Ellington/eled3200meRewardsVersusLearningFall02.pdf.

Kolodner, J. L., Hmelo, C. E., & Naranyanan, N. H. (1996). Problem-based learning meets case-based reasoning. In the *Proceedings of the 1996 International Conference on Learning Sciences*, Evanston, Illinois, (pp. 188–195).

Korakakis, G., Pavlatou, E. A., & Spyrellis, N. (2009). 3D visualization types in multimedia applications for science learning: A case study for 8th grade students in Greece. *Computers & Education, 52*(2), 390–401. doi:10.1016/j.compedu.2008.09.011

Koru, A. G., & Tian, J. (2004). Defect handling in medium and large open source projects. *IEEE Software, 21*(4), 54–61. doi:10.1109/MS.2004.12

Koschmann, T. D., Feltovich, P. J., Myers, A. C., & Barrows, H. S. (1992). Implications of CSCL for problem-based learning. *Sigcue Outlook, 21*(3), 33. doi:10.1145/130893.130902

Koznov, D., & Pliskin, M. (2009). Computer-supported collaborative learning with mind-maps. In *Communications in Computer and Information Science* (*Vol. 17*, pp. 478–489). Springer.

Lahav, O., & Mioduser, D. (2003). A blind person's cognitive mapping of new spaces using a haptic virtual environment. *Journal of Research in Special Educational Needs, 3*(3), 172–177. doi:10.1111/1471-3802.00012

Land, S. M. (2000). Cognitive requirements for learning with open-ended learning environments. *Educational Technology Research and Development, 48*(3), 61–78. doi:10.1007/BF02319858

Lang, A. S., & Kobilnyk, D. (2009). Visualizing atomic orbitals using Second Life. *Journal of Virtual Worlds Research, 2*(1).

Larkin, S. (2006). Collaborative group work and individual development of metacognition in the early years. *Research in Science Education, 36*, 7–27. doi:10.1007/s11165-006-8147-1

Laurillard, D. (2002). *Rethinking university teaching: A conversational framework for the effective use of learning technologies*. London, UK: Routledge. doi:10.4324/9780203304846

Lave, J., & Wenger, E. (1991). *Situated learning: Legitimate peripheral participation (learning in doing: Social, cognitive and computational perspectives)*. Cambridge, UK: Cambridge University Press.

Lavine, R. (2005). Guided discovery learning with videotaped case presentation in neurobiology. *Journal of the International Association of Medical Science Educators, 15*(4). Retrieved February 1, 2011, from www.iamse.org/member/article/volume15-1/15-1-4-7.pdf.

Lee, L. (2010). Exploring Wiki-mediated collaborative writing: A case study in an elementary Spanish course. *CALICO Journal, 27*(2).

Lemke, J. (1993). Hypermedia and higher education. *Interpersonal Computing and Technology, 1/2*.

Lesko, C. J., & Hollingsworth, Y. (2010). Compounding the results: The integration of virtual worlds with the Semantic Web. *Journal of Virtual Worlds Research, 2*(5).

Lévy, P. (1997). *L'intelligence collective: Pour une anthropologie du cyberspace*. La Decouverte.

Liccardi, I., Ounnas, A., Pau, R., Massey, E., Kinnunen, P., & Lewthwaite, S. … Sarkar, C. (2007). The role of social networks in students learning experiences. *ACM SIGCSE Bulletin, 39*(4). Retrieved February 25, 2011, from http://portal.acm.org/ft_gateway.cfm?id=1345442&type=pdf&CFID=11918280&CFTOKEN=72547543.

Lim, K. Y. T. (2009). The six learnings of Second Life: A framework for designing curricular interventions in-world. *Journal of Virtual Worlds Research, 2*(1), 3–11.

Lim, E. L., & Moore, D. L. (2002). Problem-solving in geometry: Comparing the effects of non-specific instruction and conventional worked examples. *Educational Psychology: An International Journal of Experimental Educational Psychology, 22*(5), 591–612.

Lin, F., Lin, S., & Huang, T. (2008). Knowledge sharing and creation in a teachers' professional virtual community. *Computers & Education, 50*(3), 742–756. doi:10.1016/j.compedu.2006.07.009

Linden Lab. (2010). *Home page.* Retrieved from http://lindenlab.com/.

Linden Research Inc. (n.d.). *Second Life*. Retrieved October 1, 2010, from http://secondlife.com/.

Linden Research, Inc. (2010). *System requirements.* Retrieved October 5, 2010, from http://secondlife.com/support/system-requirements/.

Linebarger, D. L., & Walker, D. (2005). Infants' and toddlers' television viewing and language outcomes. *The American Behavioral Scientist*, *48*, 624–645. doi:10.1177/0002764204271505

Liu, X., Bonk, C. J., Magjuka, R. J., Lee, S., & Su, B. (2005). Exploring four dimensions of online instructor roles: A program level case study. *Journal of Asynchronous Learning Networks*, *9*(4), 29–48.

LiveJournal. (2010, September). *LiveJournal home page*. Retrieved September 22, 2010, from http://www.livejournal.com.

Livingstone, D., & Kemp, J. (2006). Putting a Second Life "metaverse" skin on learning management systems. *Proc. of the Second Life Education Workshop at the Second Life Community Convention*, (pp. 13-18).

Lloyd, W. A. (1922). *Extension workers creed.* Retrieved September 22, 2010, from http://espnational.com/index.php?option=com_content&view=article&id=71:extension-professionals-creed&catid=59&Itemid=57.

Locke, L. (2010, November 24). *Scribd stats: New social dashboard for reading.* Retrieved December 12, 2010, from http://www.pcworld.com/article/211693/scribd_stats_new_social_dashboard_for_reading.html.

Lopez, R., & Kossack, S. (2007). Effects of recurring use of self-assessment in university courses. *The International Journal of Learning*, *14*(4), 203–216.

Lord, G. (2008). Podcasting communities and second language pronunciation. *Foreign Language Annals*, *41*(2), 364–380. doi:10.1111/j.1944-9720.2008.tb03297.x

Loureiro, A., & Bettencourt, T. (2010). Building knowledge in the virtual world–Influence of real life relationships. *Journal of Virtual Worlds Research*, *2*(5).

LSU Ag Center. (2010). *La House*. Retrieved September 28, 2010 from http://www.lsuagcenter.com/en/family_home/home/la_house/.

Lumana. (2006). *Metacognition and reflection*. Retrieved 30 September, 2010, from http://www.lumana.com/Education_Director_Website/Personal_Projects/Instructional_Design/research/Metacognition/Chapter2_Gama.pdf.

Lynch, K. (1960). *The image of the city*. Cambridge, MA: MIT Press.

Lynn, L. E. (1996). *What is the case method? A guide and casebook*. Japan: the Foundation for Advanced Studies on International Development.

Mackenzie, A. (2003). These things called systems: Collective imaginings and infrastructural software. *Social Studies of Science*, *33*(3), 365–387. doi:10.1177/03063127030333003

Maclellan, E. (2005). Conceptual learning: The priority for higher education. *British Journal of Educational Studies*, *53*(2), 129–147. doi:10.1111/j.1467-8527.2005.00287.x

Malhotra, Y., Galletta, D., & Kirsch, L. (2008). How endogenous motivations influence user intentions: Beyond the dichotomy of extrinsic and intrinsic user motivations. *Journal of Management Information Systems*, *25*(1), 267–299. doi:10.2753/MIS0742-1222250110

Malone, D. M. (2008). Inquiry-based early childhood teacher preparation: The personal learning plan method. *Early Childhood Education Journal*, *35*, 531–542.. doi:10.1007/s10643-008-0237-4

Maranto, G., & Barton, M. (2010). Paradox and promise: MySpace, Facebook, and the sociopolitics of social networking in the writing classroom. *Computers and Composition*, *27*, 36–47. doi:10.1016/j.compcom.2009.11.003

Marsh, T., Nitsche, M., Liu, W., Chung, P., Bolter, J. D., & Cheok, A. D. (2008). Film informing design for contemplative gameplay. In the *Proceedings of the Sandbox Symposium*, Los Angeles, California, (pp. 99–106).

Maslow, A. (1971). *The farther reaches of human nature*. New York, NY: The Viking Press.

Maslow, A. (1943). A theory of human motivation. *Psychological Review, 50,* 370-396. Retrieved September 15, 2010 from http://citeseerx.ist.psu.edu/viewdoc/download?doi=10.1.1.152.465&rep=rep1&type=pdf.

*Maslow's hierarchy of needs*. (2010, Oct. 16). Wikipedia. Retrieved on October 16, 2010, from http://en.wikipedia.org/wiki/Maslow%27s_hierarchy_of_needs.

Mason, R., & Rennie, F. (2008). *E-learning and social networking handbook: Resources for higher education*. New York, NY: Routledge.

Mason, R. (1998). Models of on-line courses. *ALN Magazine, 2*(2). Retrieved 24 March, 2011, from http://www.aln.org/publications/magazine/v2n2/mason.asp.

Matei, S. A., Miller, C. C., Arns, L., Rauh, N., Hartman, C., & Bruno, R. (2007). Visible past: Learning and discovering in real and virtual space and time. *First Monday, 12*(5).

Mayer, R. (2004). Should there be a three-strikes rule against pure discovery learning? *American Psychologist, 59*(1), 14–19. Retrieved February 12, 2011, from http://www.katharinenewman.com/Research/Desktop/amp-59-1-14.pdf.

Mayes, T. (2000). *Pedagogy, lifelong learning and ICT*. Retrieved on 16 December, 2010, from http://www.ipm.ucl.ac.be/ChaireIBM/Mayes.pdf.

McCarty, S. (2005). Spoken Internet to go: Popularization through podcasting. *JALT CALL Journal, 1*(2), 67–74.

McClean, P., Bernhardt, S. E., Donald, S., Slator, B., & White, A. (2001). Virtual worlds in large enrollment biology and geology classes significantly improve authentic learning. In J. A. Chambers (Ed.), *Selected Papers from the 12th International Conference on College Teaching and Learning (ICCTL-01),* (pp. 111-118). Jacksonville, FL: Center for the Advancement of Teaching and Learning, April 17-21.

McDonald, M., Dorn, B., & McDonald, G. (2004). A statistical analysis of student performance in online computer science courses. In *Proceedings of the 35th SIGCSE Technical Symposium on Computer Science Education* (pp. 71–74). New York, NY: ACM Press.

McHaney, R. (2009). *Understanding computer simulation.* Retrieved May 3, 2010, from http://bookboon.com/us/textbooks/it/understanding.

McHaney, R. (2009, March). Implementation of ELATEwiki. *EDUCAUSE Quarterly, 32*(4). Retrieved July 10, 2010, from http://www.educause.edu/EDUCAUSE+Quarterly/EDUCAUSEQuarterlyMagazineVolum/ImplementationofELATEwiki/192968.

McHugh, N. (1997). Teaching the domains of writing. In Olson, C. B. (Ed.), *Practical ideas for teaching writing as a process at the high school and college levels* (pp. 112–118). Sacramento, CA: California Department of Education.

McLellan, H. (1996). Virtual realities. In Jonassen, D. (Ed.), *Handbook of research for educational communications and technology*. New York, NY: Macmillan.

McLoughlin, C. (2002). Learner support in distance and networked learning environments: Ten dimensions for successful design. *Distance Education, 23*, 149–162. doi:10.1080/0158791022000009178

Means, B., Toyama, Y., Murphy, R., Bakia, M., & Jones, K. (2009). *Evaluation of evidence-based practices in online learning: A meta-analysis and review of online-learning studies*. Washington, DC: U.S. Department of Education.

Medina, E., Fruland, R., & Weghorst, S. (2008). VIRTUSPHERE: Walking in a human size VR hamster ball. In *Proceedings of the Human Factors and Ergonomics Society 52nd Annual Meeting* (pp. 2102-2106). New York, NY: HFES.

Merriam, S. B., & Caffarella, R. S. (1999). *Learning in adulthood: A comprehensive guide* (2nd ed., p. 289). San Francisco, CA: Jossey Bass Publishers.

Merrill, M. D. (2008). Why basic principles of instruction must be present in the learning landscape, whatever form it takes, for learning to be effective, efficient, and engaging. In J. Visser & M. Visser-Valfrey (Eds.), *Learners in a changing learning landscape* (pp. 267–275). Springer Science + Business Media B.V.

MetLife Mature Market Institute. (2010, September). *The MetLife report on aging in place 2.0: Rethinking solutions to the home care challenge*. Retrieved on September 22, 2010, from http://www.metlife.com/assets/cao/mmi/publications/studies/2010/mmi-aging-place.pdf.

Michaels, C. F., & Carello, C. (1981). *Direct perception* (pp. 1–200). Englewood Cliffs, NJ: Prentice-Hall, Inc.

Middleton, J., & Mather, R. (2008). Machinima interventions: Innovative approaches to immersive virtual world curriculum integration. *Research in Learning Technology*, *16*(3), 207–220. doi:10.1080/09687760802526723

Miles, M. B., & Huberman, A. M. (1994). *Qualitative data analysis: An expanded sourcebook*. Thousand Oaks, CA: Sage.

Miller, R. B., & Brickman, S. J. (2004). A model of future-oriented motivation and self-regulation. *Educational Psychology Review*, *16*(1), 9–33. doi:10.1023/B:EDPR.0000012343.96370.39

Mindomo. (2010, September). *Mindomo home page*. Retrieved September 10, 2010, from Mindomo.com: http://www.mindomo.com.

Mishra, S. (2002). A design framework for online learning environments. *British Journal of Educational Technology*, *33*(4), 493–496. doi:10.1111/1467-8535.00285

Mishra, S. (2001). *Designing online learning*. COL Knowledge Series. Vancouver, Canada: The Commonwealth of Learning. Retrieved on 19 November, 2010, from http://www.col.org/Knowledge/ks_online.pdf.

Mitra, S., Dangwal, R., Chatterjee, S., Jha, S., Bisht, R., & Kapur, P. (2005). Acquisition of computing literacy on shared public computers: Children and the "hole in the wall.". *Australasian Journal of Educational Technology*, *21*(3), 407–426.

Mitra, S., & Rana, V. (2001). Children and the Internet: Experiments with minimally invasive education in India. *British Journal of Educational Technology*, *32*(2), 221–232. doi:10.1111/1467-8535.00192

Mitra, S. (1999). Virtual institutions in the Indian subcontinent. in Farrell, G. (Ed.), *The development of virtual education: A global perspective* (pp. 125-134). Vancouver, Canada: The Commonwealth of Learning.

Mok, M. M. C., Lung, C. L., Cheng, D. P. W., Cheung, R. H. P., & Ng, M. L. (2006). Self-assessment in higher education: experience in using a metacognitive approach in five case studies. *Assessment & Evaluation in Higher Education*, *31*(4), 415–433. doi:10.1080/02602930600679100

Moore, M. (1993). Theory of transactional distance. In Keegan, D. (Ed.), *Theoretical principles of distance education* (pp. 22–38). London, UK: Routledge.

Naidu, S., Anderson, J., & Riddle, M. (2000). The virtual print exhibition: A case of learning by designing. In Sims, R., O'Reilly, M., & Sawkins, S. (Eds.), *Learning to choose: Choosing to learn (short papers and works in progress)* (pp. 109–114). Lismore, Australia: Southern Cross University Press.

NASA administrator. (2010a, Feb. 25). *RE: 1.STEM resources from discovery education* [web log comment]. Retrieved from http://www.nasatalk.com/index.php?option=com_resource&controller=article&article=725&category_id=99&Itemid=147.

NASA administrator. (2010b, Feb. 25). *RE: 4.seeing the moon* [Web log comment]. Retrieved from http://www.nasatalk.com/blog/article/bylines/99-nasa-stem-educators-conference/722-4-seeing-the-moon.html.

NASA administrator. (2010c, Feb. 25). *RE: 7.rocket science* [web log comment]. Retrieved from http://www.nasatalk.com/blog/article/bylines/99-nasa-stem-educators-conference/719-7-rocket-science.html.

NASA. *Talk*. (2010). *2nd Annual NASA STEM Educators Workshop Series* [web page]. Retrieved from http://www.nasatalk.com/collaboratives/nasa-stem-educators-workshop.html.

National Alliance for Caregiving & AARP. (2009). *Caregiving in the US*. Retrieved September 26, 2010, from www.caregiving.org/data/Caregiving_in_the_US_2009_full_report.pdf.

National Institute of Food and Agriculture. (2009). *About us*. Retrieved September 22, 2010, from http://www.csrees.usda.gov/about/background.html.

National Institute of Food and Agriculture. Family Science. (2010). *Family & consumer sciences*. Retrieved September 22, 2010, from http://www.csrees.usda.gov/familyscience.cfm.

National Resource Center on Supportive Housing and Home Modifications. (2003). *Home modification resource guide* (4th ed.). Los Angeles, CA: University of Southern California Andrus Gerontology Center.

Nedic, Z., Machotka, J., & Nafalski, A. (2003). Remote labs versus virtual and real labs. Paper published in the *Proceedings of the 33rd ASEE/IEEE Frontiers in Education Conference*, November 5-8, 2003.

Neuhauser, P. C. (1993). *Corporate legends and lore: The power of storytelling as a management tool*. New York, NY: McGraw-Hill.

Neviarouskaya, A., Prendinger, H., & Ishizuka, M. (2010). Recognition of affect, judgment, and appreciation in text. *23rd International Conference on Computational Linguistics (Coling, ed.)*, (pp. 806-814). Beijing.

NexLearn. (2010, August). *SimWriter*. Retrieved September 21, 2010, from http://www.nexlearn.com/?q=node/1.

Ngu, B. H., Mit, E., Shahbodin, F., & Tuovinen, J. (2009). Chemistry problem solving instruction: A comparison of three computer-based formats for learning from hierarchical network problem representations. *Instructional Science*, *37*, 21–24..doi:10.1007/s11251-008-9072-7

Noma, H., & Miyasato, T. (1999). A new approach for canceling turning motion in the locomotion interface. *ATLAS, ASME-DSC*, *67*, 405–407.

Noma, H., & Miyasato, T. (1998). *Design for locomotion interface in a large scale virtual environment. ATLAS: ATR Locomotion interface for active self motion*. 7th Annual Symposium on Haptic Interfaces for Virtual Environment and Teleoperator Systems. The Winter Annual Meeting of the ASME. Anaheim, USA.

Noma, H., Sugihara, T., & Miyasayo, T. (2000). Development of ground surface simulator for Tel-E-Merge System. *Proc. of IEEE-Virtual Reality 2000 Conference*, (pp. 217-224).

O'Bryan, A., & Hegelheimer, V. (2007). Integrating CALL into the classroom: The role of podcasting in an ESL listening strategies course. *ReCALL*, *19*(2), 162–180. doi:10.1017/S0958344007000523

O'Reilly, T. (2005). *What is Web 2.0*? O'Reilly Network. Retrieved October 1, 2010, from http://www.oreillynet.com/pub/a/oreilly/tim/news/2005/09/30/what-is-web-20.html.

Oblinger, D. G., & Oblinger, J. L. (Eds.). (2005). Educating the Net generation. Boulder, CO: Educause. Retrieved on 3 December, 2010, from http://www.educause.edu/educatingthenetgen.

Oehlmann, R. (2002). Metacognitive and computational aspects of chance discovery. *New Generation Computing*, *21*(2003), 3–12. Ohmaha, Ltd., Springer-Verlag.

Oliver, R. (1999). Exploring strategies for online teaching and learning. *Distance Education*, *20*(2), 240–254. doi:10.1080/0158791990200205

Olsen, R. V., Ehrenkrantz, E., & Hutchings, B. (1993). *Homes that help: Advice from caregivers for creating a supportive home*. Newark, NJ: New Jersey Institute of Technology.

Open Courseware Consortium. (2008). *Open Courseware Consortium homepage*. Retrieved October 16, 2008, from http://www.ocwconsortium.org/.

Oswald, F., & Wahl, H. (2004). Housing and health in later years. *Reviews on Environmental Health*, *19*(3-4), 223–252.

Owen, A. M., Hampshire, A., Grahn, J. A., Stenton, R., Dajani, S., & Burns, A. S. (2010). Putting brain training to the test. *Nature*, *465*, 775–778. doi:10.1038/nature09042

Pachler, N., & Daly, C. (2009). Narrative and learning with Web 2.0 technologies: Towards a research agenda. *Journal of Computer Assisted Learning*, *25*, 6–18. doi:10.1111/j.1365-2729.2008.00303.x

Pahl, C. (2003). Managing evolution and change in web-based teaching and learning environments. *Computers & Education*, *40*(2), 99–114. doi:10.1016/S0360-1315(02)00100-8

Pane, J. (2010, Feb. 19). *RE: 8.paper plate Astronomy* [web log comment]. Retrieved from http://www.nasatalk.com/index.php?option=com_resource&controller=article&article=718&category_id=99&Itemid=147.

Paris, S. G., & Paris, A. H. (2001). Classroom applications of research on self-regulated learning. *Educational Psychology*, *36*(2), 89–101. doi:10.1207/S15326985EP3602_4

Pavlov, I. (1927). *Physiological activity of the cerebral cortex – Lecture II*. Retrieved August 2, 2010, from http://psychclassics.yorku.ca/Pavlov/.

Penfold, P. (2010). A Second Life first year experience. *Journal of Virtual Worlds Research*, *2*(5).

Peterson, M. (2010). Learner participation patterns and strategy use in Second Life: An exploratory case study. *ReCALL*, *22*(3), 273–292. doi:10.1017/S0958344010000169

Petrakou, A. (2010). Interacting through avatars: Virtual worlds as a context for online education. *Computers & Education, 54*(4), 1020–1027. doi:10.1016/j.compedu.2009.10.007

Pew Research Center. (2010). *Millennials protrait of generation next: Confident. Connected. Open to change.* Pew Research Center. phpBB. (2010, September). *phpBB home page*. Retrieved September 20, 2010, from http://www.phpbb.com/.

Piaget, J. (1972). *To understand is to invent*. New York, NY: The Viking Press, Inc.

Pieschl, S., Stahl, E., & Bromme, R. (2008). Epistemological beliefs and self-regulated learning with hypertext. *Metacognition Learning, 3,* 17–37. Springer Science + Business Media, LLC. DOI 10.1007/s11409-007-9008-7

Pink, D. H. (2009). *Drive: The surprising truth about what motivates us* (pp. 79, 126–127). New York, NY: Riverhead Books.

Pinkman, K. (2005). Using blogs in the foreign language classroom: Encouraging learner independence. *The JALT CALL Journal, 1*(1), 12-24. Retrieved October 1, 2010, from http://jaltcall.org/journal/articles/1_1_Pinkman.pdf.

Porter, L. R. (1997). *Creating the virtual classroom distance learning with the Internet*. New York, NY: John Wiley & Sons.

President's Committee on Advisors on Science and Technology. (1997). *Report to the President on the use of technology to strengthen K-12 education in the United States*. Washington, DC: U.S. Government Printing Office.

Pressler, K. A., & Ferraro, K. F. (2010). Assistive device use as a dynamic acquisition process in later life. *The Gerontologist, 50*(3), 371–381. doi:10.1093/geront/gnp170

Protonmedia Protosphere. (2010). *About Protosphere*. Retrieved from http://protonmedia.com/resourcePage/10/about-protosphere.pdf.

Puls, J., & van den Munkhof, R. (2010). *Studentinzicht VII*. Heerlen, The Netherlands: Open Universiteit CELSTEC.

Purdie, N., & Hattie, J. (1996). Cultural differences in the use of strategies for self-regulated learning. *American Educational Research Journal, 33*(4), 845–871.

Quest 3D. (2010). *Home page.* Retrieved from http://quest3d.com/.

Questler. (2010). *Questler FAQs*. Retrieved September 23, 2010, from http://questler.com/faqs.

Ragan, L. C. (1999). Good teaching is good teaching: An emerging set of guiding principles and practices for the design and development of distance education. *Cause/Effect, 22*(1). Retrieved September 30, from http://net.educause.edu/ir/library/html/cem/cem99/cem9915.html.

Ranson, S., Martin, J., Nixon, J., & McKeown, P. (1996). Towards a theory of learning. *British Journal of Educational Studies, 44*(1), 9–26. doi:10.1080/00071005.1996.9974055

Raymond, E. S. (2003). The cathedral and the bazaar. *First Monday*. Retrieved from http://rfrost.people.si.umich.edu/courses/SI110/readings/IntellecProp/Cathedral-Bazaar.pdf.

Redfoot, D. L., & Houser, A. (2010, September). *More older people with disabilities living in the community: Trends from the National Long-Term Care Survey, 1984–2004.* Washington, DC: AARP Public Policy Institute. Retrieved October 13, 2010, from http://assets.aarp.org/rgcenter/ppi/ltc/2010-08-disability.pdf.

Reingold, R., & Rimor, R. (2008). Instructor's scaffolding in support of student's metacognition through a teacher education online course - A case study. *Journal of Online Interactive Learning, 7*(2), 139–151.

Renkl, A., Atkinson, R. K., & Maier, U. H. (2000). From studying examples to solving problems: Fading worked-out solution steps helps learning. In L. Gleitman & A. K. Joshi (Eds.), *Proceeding of the 22nd Annual Conference of the Cognitive Science Society* (pp. 393–398). Mahwah, NJ: Lawrence Erlbaum Associates, Inc.

Rice University. (2010, December 1). *FirstScience news*. Retrieved December 12, 2010, from http://www.firstscience.com/home/news/science-business/ieee-signal-processing-society-offers-free-educational-content-via-connexions_96496.html.

Riel, M., & Polin, L. (2004). Learning communities: Common ground and critical differences in designing technical support. In Barab, S. A., Kling, R., & Gray, J. (Eds.), *Designing for virtual communities in the service of learning* (pp. 15–52). Cambridge, MA: Cambridge University Press.

Rimor, R., Reingold, R., & Kalay, A. (2006, July). *The relationship between students' metacognition and instructor's scaffolding in online academic courses*. Paper presented at the 2nd Meeting of EARLI SIG 16 Metacognition, University of Cambridge, Faculty of Education, Cambridge, UK. Retrieved September 15, 2006, from http://www.educ.cam.ac.uk/download/MetacogAbstr.pdf.

Rittle-Johnson, B. (2006). Promoting transfer: Effects of self-explanation and direct instruction. *Child Development, 77*, 1–15. doi:10.1111/j.1467-8624.2006.00852.x

Roberts, T. S. (2006). The use of multiple choice tests for formative and summative assessment. *ACM International Conference Proceeding Series, 165*, 175–180.

Robin, B. R. (2008). Digital storytelling: A powerful technology tool for the 21st century classroom. *Theory into Practice, 47*, 220–228. doi:10.1080/00405840802153916

Rogers, E. M. (2003). *Roger's diffusion of innovations theory*. New York, NY: Free Press.

Rosen, L., & Kato, K. (2006). *Building community, improving oral proficiency: A Wiki case study*. Poster session, ACTFL 2006. Retrieved Retrieved October 1, 2010, from http://www.actfl.org/files/ACTFL06handouts/Session371.pdf.

Rossiter, M., & Garcia, P. A. (2010). Digital storytelling: A new player on the narrative field. *New Directions for Adult and Continuing Education, 126*, 37–48. doi:10.1002/ace.370

Roston, G. P., & Peurach, T. (1997). A whole body kinesthetic display device for virtual reality applications. *Proc. of IEEE Int'l Conf. on Robotics and Automation*, (pp. 3006-3011).

Roussos, M., Johnson, A., Moher, T., Leigh, J., Vasilakis, C., & Barnes, C. (1999). Learning and building together in an immersive virtual world. *Presence (Cambridge, Mass.), 8*(3), 247–263. doi:10.1162/105474699566215

Roussou, M. (2004). Learning by doing and learning through play: An exploration of interactivity in virtual environments for children. [CIE]. *Computers in Entertainment, 2*(1), 10. doi:10.1145/973801.973818

Roussou, M., & Efraimoglou, D. (1999). *High-end interactive media in the museum* (pp. 59–62). ACM SIGGRAPH Computer Graphics.

Roussou, M. (2001). *Immersive interactive virtual reality in the museum.* Intuition Network of Excellence. Retrieved from http://www.intuition-eunetwork.org/documents/papers/Culture%20History/mroussou_TiLE01_paper.pdf.

Rovai, A. P. (2001). Building classroom community at a distance: A case study. *Educational Technology Research and Development, 49*(4), 33–48. doi:10.1007/BF02504946

Rovai, A. (April, 2002). Building sense of community at a distance. *International Review of Research in Open and Distance Learning (IRRODL), 3*(1). Retrieved September 30, 2010, from http://www.irrodl.org/index.php/irrodl/article/viewArticle/79/152.

Rowe, G., Hirsh, J. B., & Anderson, A. K. (2007). Positive affect increases the breadth of attentional selection. *Proceedings of the National Academy of Sciences of the United States of America, 104*(1), 383–388. doi:10.1073/pnas.0605198104

Ruberg, L., Calinger, M., & Howard, B. (2009). Evaluating educational technologies: Historical milestones. In Tomei, L. A. (Ed.), *Designing instruction for the traditional, adult, and distance learner: A new engine for technology-based teaching* (pp. 285–297). Hershey, PA: IGI Global.

Ryan, M., & Woodward, L. (1997). *Impact of computer mediated communication (CMC) on distance tutoring*. In ED-MEDIA & ED-TELECOM World Conference June 1998, Freiburg, Germany. AACE.

Ryder, M. (2009). The cyborg and the noble savage: Ethics in the war on information poverty. In Luppicini, R., & Adell, R. (Eds.), *Handbook of Research on Technoethics* (pp. 232–249). Hershey, PA: IGI Global.

Saab, N., van Joolingen, W. R., & van Hout-Wolters, B. H. A. M. (2005). Communication in collaborative discovery learning. *The British Journal of Educational Psychology, 75*, 603–621. doi:10.1348/000709905X42905

Saab, N., & van Joolingen, W. (2005). Supporting collaborative discovery learning by presenting a tool. In the *Proceedings of the Computer Support for Collaborative Learning* (CSCL) (pp. 541–546). International Society of the Learning Sciences.

Sadler, D. R. (1989). Formative assessment and the design of instructional systems. *Instructional Science, 18*, 119–144. doi:10.1007/BF00117714

Sahin, S. (2006). Computer simulations in science education: Implications for distance education. *Turkish Online Journal of Distance Education, 7*(4).

Salmon, G. (2009). The future for (second) life and learning. *British Journal of Educational Technology, 40*(3), 526–538. doi:10.1111/j.1467-8535.2009.00967.x

Salmon, G. (2000). *E-moderating: The key to teaching and learning online*. London, UK: Kogan Page.

Sandi-Urena, S., Cooper, M. M., & Stevens, R. H. (2010). Enhancement of metacognition use and awareness by means of a collaborative intervention. *International Journal of Science Education, 33*(3).

Schank, R. (1997). *Virtual learning: A revolutionary approach to building a highly skilled workforce*. New York, NY: McGraw-Hill.

Schilling, M. A., Vidal, P., Ployhart, R. E., & Marangoni, A. (2003). Learning by doing something else: Variation, relatedness, and the learning curve. *Management Science, 49*(1), 39–56. doi:10.1287/mnsc.49.1.39.12750

Schmidt, H., Sorowka, D., Hesse, S., & Bernhardt, R. (2002). Design of a robotic walking simulator for neurological rehabilitation. *IEEE/RSJ Int. Conf. On Intelligent Robots and Systems*, (pp. 1487-1492).

Schön, D. A. (1983). *The reflective practitioner*. New York, NY: Basic Books.

Schraw, G., & Dennison, R. S. (1994). Assessing metacognitive awareness. *Contemporary Educational Psychology, 19*, 143–154. doi:10.1006/ceps.1994.1013

Schwartz, D. L., Lin, X., Brophy, S., & Bransford, J. D. (1999). Toward the development of flexible adaptive instructional designs. In Reigelut, C. M. (Ed.), *Instructional design theories and models* (*Vol. II*, pp. 183–213). Hillsdale, NJ: Erlbaum.

Schwartz, L., Clark, S., Cossarin, M., & Rudolph, J. (2004). Educational wikis: Features and selection criteria. *International Review of Research in Open and Distance Learning, 5*(1). Retrieved July 10, 2010, from http://www.irrodl.org/index.php/irrodl/article/view/163/692.

Segers, M., & Dochy, F. (2001). New assessment forms in problem-based learning: The value-added of the students' perspective. *Studies in Higher Education, 26*(3), 327–343. doi:10.1080/03075070120076291

Sellers, D. (2010, June). *Impact report for fashion an easier lifestyle with assistive technology (AT)*. Retrieved September 8, 2010, from http://www.aging.ksu.edu/DesktopDefault.aspx?tabid=86.

Sellers, D., Crocker, A., Nichols, A., Kirby, S., & Brintnall-Peterson, M. (2009). Creating the eXtension family caregiving community of practice. *Journal of Extension, 47*(5), Article 5FEA1. Retrieved from http://www.joe.org/joe/2009october/a1.php.

Senge, P. M. (1990). *The fifth discipline: The art and practice of the learning organization*. New York, NY: Doubleday Currency.

Shank, R. C., & Cleary, C. (1994). *Engines for education*. Hillsdale, NJ: Lawrence Erlbaum.

Shannon, S. (2008). Using metacognitive strategies and learning styles to create self-directed learners. *Wayne State College Institute for Learning Styles Journal, 1*, 14-28.

Sharma, R. C., & Mishra, S. (2007). *Cases on global e-learning practices: Successes and pitfalls*. Hershey, PA: Idea Group Publishing.

Sheridan, J. (1989). Rethinking andragogy: The case for collaborative learning in continuing higher education. *Journal of Continuing Higher Education, 37*(2), 2–6. doi:10.1080/07377366.1989.10401167

Sherman, W. S., & Craig, A. B. (2003). *Understanding virtual reality*. Morgan Kaufmann.

Shih, Y. C. (2010). Immersive language learning in collaborative virtual environments: The current status and possible trends. In Hai-Jew, S. (Ed.), *Virtual immersive and 3D learning spaces: Emerging technologies and trends*. Hershey, PA: IGI Global. doi:10.4018/978-1-61692-825-4.ch005

Shin, Y. S. (2003). Virtual experiment environments design for science education. *Proc. of IEEE International Conference on Cyberworlds* (CW03).

Shingledecker, C. A., & Foulke, E. (1978). A human factors approach to the assessment of mobility of blind pedestrians. *Human Factors*, *20*, 273–286.

Sibert, L., Templeman, J., Page, R., Barron, J., McCune, J., & Denbrook, P. (2004). *Initial assessment of human performance using the gaiter interaction technique to control locomotion in fully immersive virtual environments. (Technical Report)*. Washington, DC: Naval Research Laboratory.

Siemens, G. (2008). *Siemens' connectivism theory: Learning as network creation*. Elearnspace. Retrieved from http://www.elearnspace.org/Articles/networks.htm.

Siribaddana, P. (2010). *Limitations in using Second Life for adult learning*. Retrieved September 27, 2010, from http://www.helium.com/items/1928727-limitations-in-using-second-life-for-adult-learning.

Skinner, B. (1953). *Science and human behavior*. Pearson Education, Inc. Retrieved August 5, 2010 from http://www.terapia-conductual-cognitiva.cl/archivos/descargas/B%20F%20Skinner%20-%20Science%20And%20Human%20Behavior.pdf.

Slater, M. (1995). Taking steps: The influence of a walking metaphor on presence in virtual reality. *ACM Transactions on Computer-Human Interaction*, *2*(3), 201–219. doi:10.1145/210079.210084

Smith, D., & Hatton, N. (1993). Reflection in teacher education: A study in progress. *Education Research and Perspectives. The University of Western Australia*, *20*(1), 13–23.

Smith, M. S. (2009). Opening education. *Science*, *323*(5910), 89–101. doi:10.1126/science.1168018

Smith, J. L., Smith, R., Willis, H., Levine, A., & Haywood, K. (2011). *The 2011 Horizon Report*. Austin, TX: The New Media Consortium.

Smith, D. (2010a, Feb. 25). *9.starry night from Fisher Scientific* [web log comment]. Retrieved from http://www.nasatalk.com/index.php?option=com_resource&controller=article&article=717&category_id=99&Itemid=147.

Smith, D. (2010b, Feb. 25). *RE: 17.robot ecology* [web log comment]. Retrieved from http://www.nasatalk.com/index.php?option=com_resource&controller=article&article=707&category_id=99&Itemid=147.

Sobrero, P. M. (2008). Essential components for successful virtual learning communities. *Journal of Extension*, *46*(4), Article 4FEA1. Retrieved from http://www.joe.org/joe/2008august/a1.php.

Spitzer, D. R. (1998). Rediscovering the social context of distance learning. *Educational Technology*, (March/April): 52–56.

Stake, R. E. (2000). Case studies. In Denzin, N. K., & Lincoln, Y. S. (Eds.), *Handbook of qualitative research* (2nd ed., pp. 435–454). Thousand Oaks, CA: Sage.

Stanley, G. (2006). Podcasting: Audio on the Internet comes of age. *Teaching English as a Second or Foreign Language, 9*(4). Retrieved October 1, 2010, from http://www-writing.berkeley.edu/TESL-EJ/ej36/int.html.

StateUniversity.com. (2010). *Individualized instruction - Pace, method, content, examples of individualized instruction, final issues.* Retrieved September 30, 2010, from http://education.stateuniversity.com/pages/2085/Individualized-Instruction.html.

Steers, R. M., Porter, L. W., & Bigley, G. A. (1996). *Motivation and leadership at work* (6th ed., p. 558). Boston, MA: McGraw Hill.

Steffens, K. (2006). Self-regulated learning in technology-enhanced learning environments: Lessons of a European peer review. *European Journal of Education*, *41*(3/4), 353–379. doi:10.1111/j.1465-3435.2006.00271.x

Stories2Learn. (2010, September). *Stories2Learn home page*. Retrieved September 14, 2010, from http://www.stories2learn.com/alllist.php.

Strangman, N., & Hall, T. (2003). *Virtual reality/simulations.* Wakefield, MA: National Center on Accessing the General Curriculum. Retrieved March 2007 from http://www.cast.org/publications/ncac/ncac_vr.html.

Strauss, A., & Corbin, J. (1998). *Basics of qualitative research* (2nd ed.). Thousand Oaks, CA: Sage.

Strohecker, C., & Butler, D. (2004). The informal informing the formal to form new models of learning. In the *Proceedings of the IDC 2004*, (pp. 151–152). College Park, MD: ACM.

Sun Microsystems. (2009). *Project Wonderland*. Retrieved from http://www.sun.com/solutions/landing/industry/education/pdf/ed_project_wonderland.pdf?facet=-1.

Swaak, J., & De Jong, T. (2000). Learner vs. system control in using online support for simulation-based discovery learning. *Learning Environments Research*, *4*, 217–241. doi:10.1023/A:1014434804876

Swan, K. (2002). Building learning communities in online courses: The importance of interaction. *Education, Communication & Information, 2*(1). Retrieved February 28, 2011, from http://coe.nevada.edu/larchambault/CIG%20790/Lit.%20Review/Building%20Online%20Community.pdf.

Swiss-Projects. (2010, January 1). *Kitchen Fire - Fire simulation in Second Life*. Swiss. Retrieved August 20, 2010, from http://www.swiss-projects.ch/?q=de/node/243.

Sykes, J., Oskoz, A., & Thorne, S. L. (2008). Web 2.0, synthetic immersive environments, and mobile resources for language education. *CALICO Journal*. Retrieved October 1, 2010, from http://language.la.psu.edu/~thorne/SykesOskozThorne_CALICO_08.pdf.

Sze, P. (2006). Developing students' listening and speaking skills through ELT podcasts. *Education Journal*, *34*(2), 115–134.

Talk with Me Project. (n.d.). *About the project*. Retrieved October 1, 2010, from http://www.talk-with-me.eu/cms/index.php?id=203.

Taylor, R. N. (1975). Perception of problem constraints. *Management Science*, *22*(1), 22–29. doi:10.1287/mnsc.22.1.22

The Croquet Consortium. (2010). *Home page*. Retrieved from http://www.opencroquet.org/index.php/Main_Page.

The Morrill Act, 7 U.S.C. Sec.304. (1862).

Theories, L. (2008). *Communities of practice (Lave and Wenger)*. Retrieved July 28, 2010, from http://www.learning-theories.com/communities-of-practice-lave-and-wenger.html.

Thomas, M. (Ed.). (2009). *Handbook of research on Web 2.0 and second language learning*. Hershey, PA: IGI Global Publishing. doi:10.4018/978-1-60566-190-2

Thompson, G., Pilgrim, A., & Oliver, K. (2005). Self-assessment and reflective learning for first year university geography students: A simple guide or simply misguided? *Journal of Geography in Higher Education*, *29*, 403–420. doi:10.1080/03098260500290959

Tilly, J. (2010). The Administration on Aging's experiences with health, prevention, and wellness. *Generations (San Francisco, Calif.)*, *34*(1), 20–25.

Tompkins, G. E. (2005). *Language arts: Patterns of practice* (6th ed.). Upper Saddle River, NJ: Pearson.

Toth-Cohen, S., & Gallagher, T. (2009). Development and evaluation of health and wellness exhibits at the Jefferson Occupational Therapy Education Center in Second Life. *Journal of Virtual Worlds Research*, *2*(2), 3–13.

Trueman, M., & Hartley, J. (1996). A comparison between the time-management skills and academic performance of mature and traditional-entry university students. *Higher Education*, *32*(2), 199–215. doi:10.1007/BF00138396

Tuzun, H. (2004). *Motivating learners in educational computer games*. Unpublished dissertation, Indiana University, Bloomington, IN.

U.S. Congressional Research Service. (2009). *United States military casualty statistics: Operation Iraqi freedom and Operation Enduing Freedom* (7-5700; March 25, 2009), Congressional Research Digital Collection. Retrieved on September 27, 2010, from www.fas.org/sgp/crs/natsec/RS22452.pdf.

U.S. Department of Education. (2009). *Evaluation of evidence-based practices in online learning: A meta-analysis and review of online learning studies.* U.S. Department of Education Office of Planning, Evaluation, and Policy Development Policy and Program Studies Service. Retrieved September 30, 2010, from http://www.educause.edu/Resources/EvaluationofEvidence-BasedPract/174235.

Unity 3D. (2010). *Home page*. Retrieved from http://unity3d.com/.

Universal Design Education. (2009). *Learning universal design*. Retrieved September 13, 2010, from http://www.udeducation.org/learn.html.

Urdan, T., & Maehr, M. (1995). Beyond a two-goal theory of motivation and achievement: A case for social goals. *Review of Educational Research, 65*(3), 213-243. Retrieved September 30, 2010, from http://www.jstor.org/stable/pdfplus/1170683.pdf.

Utah State University. (2010). *Utah house*. Retrieved September 27, 2010 from http://theutahhouse.org/.

van der Veer, G. C. (1989). Individual differences and the user interface. *Ergonomics, 32*, 1431–1449. doi:10.1080/00140138908966916

Van Grove, J. (2010, December 10). *How Evernote turned note taking into a $10 million business*. Retrieved December 12, 2010, from http://mashable.com/2010/12/10/evernote-growth/.

Vesely, P., Bloom, L., & Sherlock, J. (2007). Key elements of building online community: Comparing faculty and student perceptions. *Journal of Online Learning and Teaching, 3*(3). Retrieved February 28, 2011, from http://jolt.merlot.org/vol3no3/vesely.htm.

Vickers, H. (2007a). *SurReal language quests*. AvatarLanguages.com/Blog. Retrieved October 1, 2010, from http://avatarlanguages.com/blog/?p=14.

Vickers, H. (2007b). SurReal quests: Enriched, purposeful language learning in Second Life. *The Knowledge Tree*. Retrieved October 1, 2010, from http://kt.flexiblelearning.net.au/tkt2007/edition-15/surreal-quests-enriched-purposeful-language-learning-in-second-life.

VoiceThread. (2010, July 28). *About VoiceThread*. Retrieved July 28, 2010, from http://voicethread.com/about/.

VoiceThread. (2010, September). *VoiceThread home page*. Retrieved September 3, 2010, from http://www.voicethread.com.

VRML International Standard. (1997). *VRML-97 functional specification*. International Standard ISO/IEC 14772- 1:1997. Retrieved from http://www.web3d.org/x3d/specifications/vrml/ISO_IEC_14772-All/index.html.

Vroom, V. (1964). *Work and motivation*. New York, NY: Jon Wiley & Sons.

Vygotsky, L. (1978). *Mind and society: The development of higher mental processes*. Cambridge, MA: Harvard University Press.

Vygotsky, L. S. (1986). *Thought and language: The development of higher psychological processes* (Kozulin, A., Ed.). Cambridge, MA: MIT Press.

Wang, J., & Li, F.-Z. (2007). Autonomic learning model and algorithm based on DFL. *2007 IEEE International Conference on Granular Computing*, (pp. 259–264). IEEE.

Wang, Z., Bauernfeind, K., & Sugar, T. (2003). Omnidirectional treadmill system. *Proc. of 11th Haptic Interfaces for Virtual Environment and Teleoperator Systems*, (pp. 367–373).

Warburton, S. (2009). Second Life in higher education: Assessing the potential for and the barriers to deploying virtual worlds in learning and teaching. *British Journal of Educational Technology, 40*(3), 414–426. doi:10.1111/j.1467-8535.2009.00952.x

Ward, B. (2010a, Feb. 27). *RE: 2nd Annual NASA STEM Educators Workshop Series* [web log comment]. Retrieved from www.nasatalk.com.

Warren, S. J., Dondlinger, M. J., & Barab, S. A. (2008). A MUVE towards PBL writing: Effects of a digital learning environment designed to improve elementary student writing. [JRTE]. *Journal of Research on Technology in Education, 41*(1), 113–140.

Warren, S. (2006). Researching a MUVE for teaching writing: The Anytown experience. In C. Crawford et al. (Eds.), *Proceedings of Society for Information Technology and Teacher Education International Conference 2006* (pp. 759-764). Chesapeake, VA: AACE.

Warren, S., Dondlinger, M. J., Stein, R., & Barab, S. (2009). Educational game as supplemental learning tool: Benefits, challenges, and tensions arising from use in an elementary school classroom. *Journal of Interactive Learning Research, 20*(4), 487-505. Chesapeake, VA: AACE. Retrieved October 1, 2010, from http://www.editlib.org/p/28349.

Warren, S., Stein, R. A., Dondlinger, M. J., & Barab, S. A. (2008). A look inside a MUVE design process: Blending instructional design and game principles to target writing skills. *Journal of Educational Computing Research, 40*(3). Baywood Publishing Company.

Watson, J., & Rayner, R. (1920). Conditioned emotional reactions. [from http://psychclassics.yorku.ca/Watson/emotion.htm.]. *Journal of Experimental Psychology, 3*(1), 1–14. Retrieved July 30, 2010. doi:10.1037/h0069608

Web Transitions. (2010). *FastTalk: Easy to use threaded discussion software.* Retrieved December 12, 2010, from http://www.webtransitions.com/components-discussion.asp.

Web, G. L. (2010). *Kronos Group*. Retrieved from http://www.khronos.org/webgl/.

Weick, K. E. (1984). Small wins: Redefining the scale of social problems. *The American Psychologist, 39*(1), 40–49. doi:10.1037/0003-066X.39.1.40

Weick, K. E. (1989). Theory construction as disciplined imagination. *Academy of Management Review, 14*(4), 516–531.

Weigel, V. (2000). E-learning and the tradeoff between richness and the reach in higher education. *Change, 33*(5), 10–15. doi:10.1080/00091380009605735

Weiner, B. (1996). Attribution, emotion, and action. In R. Sorrentino & E. Higgins (Eds.), *Handbook of motivation and cognition, volume 3: The interpersonal context* (pp. 281-311). Western Ontario, Canada: The Guilford Press.

Weir, L. (2008). *VoiceThreads: Extending the classroom with interactive multimedia albums.* Retrieved December 12, 2010, from http://www.edutopia.org/voicethread-interactive-multimedia-albums.

Wellman, H. M. (1985b). The origins of metacognition. In Forrest-Pressley, D. L., MacKinnon, G. E., & Waller, T. G. (Eds.), *Metacognition, cognition and human performance* (*Vol. 1*, pp. 1–31). Orlando, FL: Academic Press.

Wenger, E., McDermott, R. A., & Snyder, W. M. (2002). *Cultivating communities of practice: A guide to managing knowledge*. Boston, MA: Harvard Business School Press.

Wenger, E. (1996). Communities of practice: The social fabric of the learning organization. *The Healthcare Forum Journal, 39*(4), 20–26.

Whitney, L. (2010, December 8). *Google Groups gets a revamp.* Retrieved December 12, 2010, from http://news.cnet.com/8301-1023_3-20025009-93.html.

Whitton, N. (2010). *Learning with digital games: A practical guide to engaging students in higher education.* New York, NY: Routledge.

Wiley, D., & Henson, S. (2006). An initial characterization of engagement in informal social learning around MIT OCW. In the *Proceedings of the International Conference of the Learning Sciences* (ICLS 2006), Bloomington, Indiana, (pp. 832–837).

Williams, J. J., & Lombrozo, T. (2010). The role of explanation in discovery and generalization: Evidence from category learning. *Cognitive Science, 34*, 776–806.. doi:10.1111/j.1551-6709.2010.01113.x

Willis, B. (1992). *Strategies for teaching at a distance.* (ERIC Document Reproduction Service No. ED351008).

Winn, W. (2002). Current trends in educational technology research: The study of learning environments. *Educational Psychology Review, 14*(3), 331–351. doi:10.1023/A:1016068530070

Wood, P. (2010, Feb. 24). *RE: 17.robot ecology* [web log comment]. Retrieved from http://www.nasatalk.com/index.php?option=com_resource&controller=article&article=707&category_id=99&Itemid=147.

Woods, K. (2010). Engaging emerging populations of adults with interactive activities in a 3D virtual learning environment. *Journal of Extension, 48*(5), Article 5FEA3. Retrieved from http://www.joe.org/joe/2010october/a3.php.

World of Warcraft. (2010, July 10). *Info.* Retrieved July 10, 2010, from http://www.worldofwarcraft.com/info/basics/guide.html.

X3D International Standard. (2004). *X3D framework & SAI.* ISO/IEC FDIS (Final Draft International Standard) 19775:200x. Retrieved from http://www.web3d.org/x3d/specifications/ISO-IEC-19775-IS- X3DAbstract-Specification/.

Yakel, E., & Torres, D. A. (2003). AI: Archival intelligence and user expertise. *The American Archivist*, *66*(1), 51–78.

Yakimovicz, A. D., & Murphy, K. L. (1995). Constructivism and collaboration on the internet: Case study of a graduate class experience. *Computers & Education*, *24*(3), 203–209. doi:10.1016/0360-1315(95)00015-E

Yearns, M. H. (2004). *Universal design for better living*. Iowa State University, University Extension. Retrieved October 13, 2010, from http://www.extension.iastate.edu/UniversalDesign/Resources/

Zagorski, N. (2010). Virtual reality in science education. *ASBMB Today*. September 2010. Retrieved from http://www.asbmb.org/asbmbtoday/asbmbtoday_article.aspx?id=9178.

Zara, J. (2004). Virtual reality and cultural heritage on the Web. *Proc. of the 7th International Conference on Computer Graphics and Artificial Intelligence* (3IA 2004), Limoges, France, 2004, (pp. 101-112).

Zielke, M. A., Roome, T. C., & Krueger, A. B. (2009). A composite adult learning model for virtual world residents with disabilities: A case study of the Virtual Ability Second Life® Island. *Journal of Virtual Worlds Research*, *2*(1), 3–21.

Zietsman, A. I., & Hewson, P. W. (1986). Effect of instruction using microcomputer simulations and conceptual change strategies on science learning. *Journal of Research in Science Teaching*, *23*, 27–39. doi:10.1002/tea.3660230104

Zimmerman, F. J., Christakis, D. A., & Meltzoff, A. N. (2007). Associations between media viewing and language development in children under age 2 years. *The Journal of Pediatrics*, *151*, 364–368. doi:10.1016/j.jpeds.2007.04.071

Zumbach, J., Schmitt, S., Reimann, P., & Starkloff, P. (2006). Learning life sciences: Design and development of a virtual molecular biology learning lab. *Journal of Computers in Mathematics and Science Teaching*, *25*(3), 281.

# About the Contributors

**Shalin Hai-Jew** works as an Instructional Designer at Kansas State University, where part of her work involves the creation of self-discovery learning spaces on a range of projects. She has BAs in English and Psychology and an MA in English from the University of Washington; she earned a doctorate in Educational Leadership with a focus on Public Administration from Seattle University (2005), where she was a Morford Scholar. She was a tenured Professor at Shoreline Community College but left that to pursue a career change in instructional design. She has taught at universities in the PRC from 1988 – 1990 (with the United Nations Development Programme) and 1992 – 1994. She has written for and published with IGI-Global and other presses. She teaches for WashingtonOnline. She was born in Huntsville, Alabama, in the US.

***

**Nicoletta Adamo-Villani** is an Associate Professor of Computer Graphics Technology at Purdue University and a University Faculty Scholar. She received her MS in Architecture from University of Florence, Italy, and she is a certified 3D modeler/animator for Autodesk. Adamo-Villani is an award-winning animator and creator of 2D /3D films that aired on national television. Her research interests focus on the application of 3D animation to education, Human Computer Communication (HCC), and visualization.

**Brent A. Anders** is an Electronic Media Coordinator (educational media consultant) for the Office of Mediated Education at Kansas State University. He has worked in higher education as well as with military education for over 12 years. His Bachelor's degree is in Psychology with a human computer interaction focus, and his Master's degree is in Education with an instructional technology focus. Brent A. Anders also serves in the National Guard as a Master Sergeant (E-8). His main duty is as an instructional Branch Chief, teaching the Army Basic Instructors Course, which produces highly capable military instructors.

**Laura Benvenuti** studied Mathematics and Philosophy in the Netherlands and obtained her Master's degree in Italy with a thesis on Computer Science. She worked as a Software Engineer in Italy, Belgium and the Netherlands. At the Open Universiteit, the Dutch University for distance learning, she alternates her research with the development of Web-based courses, online classes, and face to face lectures.

**Kari L. Clase** is an Associate Professor at Purdue University with a joint appointment in the Departments of Technology, Leadership and Innovation and Computer and Information Technology. She also has a courtesy appointment in the Department of Agricultural and Biological Engineering and is the Lead Scientist for Learning with Bindley Bioscience Center. Her research interests include the use of emerging technologies for science education and the elucidation of signaling pathways that control stem cell fate. She is a recent member of the Howard Hughes Medical Institute's Science Education Alliance and the Genomics Education Partnership, which are both engaging students with authentic research in the classroom.

**Elicia Dynae Fullwood**, a native of Baton Rouge, Louisiana, was the valedictorian of the 1994 Capitol Senior High School Class. She received a Bachelor's of Science degree in Biology from the University of Houston main campus in Houston, Texas and a Master's of Education degree with specialties in Secondary Education and Education Administration from the University of St. Thomas in Houston, Texas. She has completed all requirements but a dissertation in the pursuit of a Doctoral degree in Instructional Technology and Distance Education from Nova Southeastern University in Miami, Florida. Fullwood currently serves as an Aerospace Education Specialist with Pennsylvania State University to represent the National Aeronautics and Space Administration in the education community. Prior to joining the Aerospace Education Services Project, Fullwood taught high school science in the Houston Independent School District of Houston, Texas at James Madison High School and the School for Meteorology and Space Science. With certifications in Early Childhood through Twelfth Grade Level Administration and Secondary Level Biology, she was inducted into the National Honor Society for Education, Kappa Delta Pi. She has been recognized for several Teacher of the Year, Assistant Coach of the Year, and Who's Who Among America's Teachers awards throughout her career in education. Fullwood completed the 2006 Honolulu Marathon and is a member of Alpha Kappa Alpha Sorority, Inc. She regards her personal hobbies and professional work as support for the organization's creed: Service to all mankind. Her future ambitions include learning to speak a foreign language and traveling to exotic destinations.

**Robin J. Heyden** is an Education Consultant, Developer and Writer. She works with education and training professionals to research, conceptualize, and produce print and online educational materials and experiences. Robin is a published author (Biology: Exploring Life) and community manager of an annual education conference (Biology Leadership Conference) of college biology faculty. Her work with new media tools has established Robin as a leader in the use of social media and virtual worlds in teaching and learning. Heyden develops and facilitates Continuing Medical Education events in the virtual world of Second Life.

**Paul Kawachi** is Professor of Instructional Design, and Senior Research Fellow at the Institute of Open and Distance Education Research at the Open University of China. He is a Fellow of the Royal Society of Arts, a Fellow of the British Institute of English Language Teaching, and a Fellow of the Asian Society of Open and Distance Education. He is Editor of the *Asian Journal of Distance Education*, and on the editorial boards of many others. His research interests are in third-generation instructional design, e-ID3, and how this facilitates lifelong learning, teacher professional development, cognitive learning theories, especially lifelong learning and adult learning theories, educational psychology, and learning technologies, especially when applied across cultures. He does international consultancy on curriculum design, applying learning technologies, and e-learning. He is widely published in books and leading international journals.

**Sarah D. Kirby** is an Associate Professor and Extension Housing Specialist in the Department of 4-H Youth Development and Family & Consumer Studies at North Carolina State University. Dr. Kirby's responsibilities involve developing, implementing, and evaluating quality housing educational programs in focus areas that include accessible housing and universal design, safe and healthy home environments, and energy efficiency and conservation. Dr. Kirby is a certified Healthy Homes Specialist and provides instruction for the North Carolina Healthy Homes Training Center. She serves as the state coordinator for the Healthy Homes Partnership focused on improving the health and safety of children in homes by reducing housing hazards that cause injury and disease. Dr. Kirby is a member of the Family Caregiving Community of Practice and the Home Energy Community of practice for eXtension. In 2010, she was inducted into the North Carolina State University Academy of Outstanding Faculty Engaged in Extension. Prior to her work in North Carolina, Dr. Kirby served as Extension Housing Specialist for the Oklahoma Cooperative Extension Service for nearly ten years. She received her Ph.D., M.S., and B.S. degrees from Oklahoma State University.

**Paul A. Kirschner** studied Psychology at the State University of New York at Stony Brook and the University of Amsterdam. In 1991 he obtained his PhD from the Open Universiteit. Paul has been designing and developing educational materials since 1979 and is currently Chair of the Learning and Cognition program of the Centre for Learning Sciences and Technologies (CELSTEC) and Chair Cognition and Education program at the Netherlands laboratory for Lifelong Learning (NeLLL) of the at the Open Universiteit.

**Roger W. McHaney**, Professor of Management Information Systems and university distinguished teaching scholar, studies business use of technology to promote organizational mission, and the integration of Web 2.0 technologies with teaching/learning in higher education and business training. He currently holds the Daniel D. Burke Chair for Exceptional Faculty in Kansas State University's College of Business Administration. His recent projects include co-developing ELATEwiki (E-Learning and Teaching Exchange) -- used for faculty enhancement -- which received the Sloan-C Effective Practice Award for 2009. His Distance Learning Video Gallery -- a year-long effort to collect successful instructional distance education techniques, ideas, and methodologies -- won the 2009 Creative Use of Technology Award from the Association for Continuing Higher Education. He earned degrees from Lake Superior State University, and a Doctorate in Computer Information Systems and Quantitative Analysis from the Sam M. Walton College of Business at the University of Arkansas.

**Maria Menendez** studied Computer Science at the Universidad Complutense of Madrid. She finished her MSc at the Technische Universiteit of Eindhoven where is currently working as a researcher in User System Interaction. During the last two years, she has been working in an international and heterogeneous research group where psychologists, industrial designers, and engineers collaborate to create User Centered Designs.

**Kanubhai K. Patel** is an Assistant Professor at the Schools of ICT of Ahmedabad University, Ahmedabad, India. He was previously a faculty member at GLS ICA, Gujarat University, Ahmedabad. He is pursuing a PhD degree from the Faculty of Technology at Dharmsinh Desai University, Nadiad. He received his MCA from Gujarat Vidyapith, Ahmedabad in June 1997. His research interests include assistive technology, spatial cognition, human-computer interaction, and virtual learning environments. He has authored over nine publications, including refereed journal paper and two book chapters. He has also authored a book – "Data Structures: Theory and Problems."

**Debra C. Burkey Piecka** is an Educational Researcher/Instructional Designer at the Center for Educational Technologies (CET) at Wheeling Jesuit University. She earned B.S. degrees in Industrial and Administration Management, Economics, and Mathematics from Carnegie Mellon University, a MBA from the University of Pittsburgh, and an Ed.D. and graduate certificate from Duquesne University's Instructional Technology program and Certificate in Interpretive and Qualitative Research. Dr. Piecka's research interests include students' meaning making while learning with interactive technologies, technology-supported collaborative learning, simulations, qualitative research methods, ethnography, and early childhood education. She works on the NASA*Talk* collaborative website where she blogs about using NASA educational resources and promotes STELLAR Awards, a program that recognizes teachers for their exemplary use of NASA resources. Dr. Piecka's responsibilities also include research and evaluation of other CET projects such as the live simulation project *CyberSurgeons* funded by the National Institutes of Health and the NASA-funded *Micronauts* program evaluation. Her recent publications and presentations focus on students' meaning making when learning with interactive technologies, data visualization for data analysis and meaning making, and applications of Vygotskian learning theory.

**Laurie Ruberg** received her Ph.D. in Curriculum and Instruction from Virginia Tech, and has been with the Center for Educational Technologies at Wheeling Jesuit University since 1995—first, as a Senior Instructional Designer and (since 2006) as the Associate Director. She serves as project manager for the NASA*Talk* web-based collaborative. She is the PI on Global Climate Change Education project. She recently completed program evaluations for NASA-funded *Micronauts* and NOAA-funded *STORM-E* simulation education projects. She has also served as the lead for the evaluation for NIOSH-funded health and safety training projects. Ruberg has received several awards for her design and evaluation work.

**Christopher Ruckman** is a Computer Programmer for the Center for Educational Technologies. A Wheeling Jesuit University alumnus with a Bachelor's degree in Computer Science, Ruckman has worked five years in professional desktop and web-based application development. He is currently developing the NASA*Talk* website and a teacher training website for WV Storm.

**Debra M. Sellers** is an Assistant Professor and Extension Specialist in Adult Development & Aging, School of Family Studies and Human Services, Kansas State University. Her primary area of focus is adaptive living for people with aging-related limitations or disabilities and their families and caregivers, with an emphasis on supporting functional abilities through access to services and technology. As an Extension Specialist, she is also interested in the transformative process of Cooperative Extension to increase capacity, relevancy, and impact for the 21st century. Dr. Sellers is the past national Chairperson and is a current steering committee member of the Family Caregiving Community of Practice for eXtension, an educational partnership of the land-grant university system. She is a volunteer puppy raiser for Canine Companions for Independence, and was voted one of her city's most admired people in 2001 (Manhattan, KS). Dr. Sellers has more than 15 years of experience serving older adults and their families in a variety of settings, including long-term care facilities, retirement communities, and government agencies. She received her doctorate from Kansas State University in lifespan human development with an emphasis in gerontology, and her Master of Science and undergraduate degrees from the University of Florida.

**Ramesh C. Sharma** holds a PhD in Education in the area of Educational Technology and is currently (since July 2009) working as Director (Distance Education), Institute of Distance and Continuing Education, Guyana (South America) under an assignment of the CFTC, London, United Kingdom. He has been a Regional Director in Indira Gandhi National Open University (IGNOU), India and has been instrumental in strengthening distance education in the states of Shillong, Rajasthan, Haryana, Maharastra, in addition to serving in New Delhi, HQs. He has been a teacher trainer and has taught Educational Technology, Educational Research and Statistics, Educational Measurement and Evaluation, Special Education, and Psychodynamics of Mental Health Courses to BEd and MEd students. He has supervised research dissertations at Master's and Doctoral levels. He is on the panel of external examiners of different universities in India, Pakistan, and Massey University, New Zealand. He has conducted many Human Development training programmes for the in- and pre-service teachers. He had established a Centre of ICT. He is a member of many committees on implementation of technology in the Open University. His areas of specialization include staff development, on-line learning, student support services in open and distance learning, and teacher education.

**Ya-Chun Shih** was born in Taiwan on November 16, 1971. She received her M.A. and Ph.D. degrees in Curriculum and Instruction (Bilingual Education emphasis) from Pennsylvania State University in 1997 and 2000, respectively. In 2001, Dr. Shih joined the faculty of National Hualien University of Education, located near the world-famous Taroko Gorge, as Assistant Professor of English Language Teaching. In 2009, the University was renamed as National Dong Hwa University. She is currently Assistant Professor in the Department of English at National Dong Hwa University, Hualien, Taiwan and one of the computer-assisted language learning (CALL) practitioners. She has pursued a wide range of technology supported language learning issues, including serving as an Instructor, Instructional Designer, Researcher, Journal Reviewer, Guest Speaker, Advisor, and Committee Member on related issues. Under Dr. Shih's leadership, the VEC3D (3D Virtual English Classroom), an interdisciplinary research team of instructional designers and computer science experts, designed and developed a variety of innovative language learning platforms. The VEC3D innovation started with an inspired idea for contextual language learning. Dr. Shih and her research team are expanding beyond the traditional language learning environments and methods by incorporating technology into daily lessons and communicative activities. Her current research focuses on integrating virtual reality technologies and language learning in education. She has investigated the effect of virtual reality assisted language learning on students' achievement of English as a foreign language. She has also explored issues related to the use of 3D collaborative virtual environments within a social and cultural context. The central research issues for the VEC3D project include research on (non)verbal communication, developing communicative competence, and cultural awareness.

**Gerrit van der Veer** developed computer supported learning approaches, and taught User Centered Design to students of Psychology, Ergonomics, and Information Sciences in the Netherlands, Rumania, and Spain. Currently he teaches Computer Science students in the Netherlands, and Architecture students in Italy.

**Sanjay Kumar Vij** received his PhD degree from IIT, Bombay, in 1974. He is currently a Director in the Department of CE-IT-MCA, Sardar Vallabhbhai Patel Institute of Technology (SVIT), Vasad. His research interests include text mining, knowledge management, and NLP. He has authored over twenty publications, including over seven refereed journal papers and two book chapters. He is a registered PhD guide with Dharmsinh Desai University, Nadiad. He is Member Board of Studies at MS University, Baroda and Dharmsinh Desai University, Nadiad. He had been a panel of experts/advisor in GSLET and GPSC. He is reviewer in a couple of peer reviewed journals. He has been Chairman of Computer Society of India, Vadodara Chapter.

**John Wiecha**, MD, MPH is the Director of Medical Student Education in the Department of Family Medicine and Assistant Dean of Academic Affairs at Boston University School of Medicine, and an Associate Professor. He received his M.D. from the State University of New York at Stony Brook and his M.P.H from the University of Massachusetts. He completed residencies in Family Medicine and in Preventive Medicine at the University of Massachusetts. Dr. Wiecha has published studies on patterns of preventive health care among disadvantaged populations, on tobacco abuse among vulnerable populations, and on methods and evaluation of distance medical education which have received national recognition. He has received funding for research and educational program development from numerous private foundations including The Commonwealth Fund, Robert Wood Johnson Foundation, The Physicians' Foundation, The World Health Organization, and U.S. government sources including the U.S. Public Health Service and the National Institutes of Health. He lives in Wellesley, Massachusetts, and is married with two children.

# Index

## A



## B



## C



## D

## E



## F



## G



## H



## I



## K



## L

## M



## N



## O



## P



## R



## S

## T



## U



## V



## W



## Y

CPSIA information can be obtained at www.ICGtesting.com
Printed in the USA
BVOW050748261111

276491BV00003B/9/P